GREAT EATS
PARIS

SANDRA GUSTAFSON

ELEVENTH EDITION

CHRONICLE BOOKS
SAN FRANCISCO

ELEVENTH EDITION
ISBN-10: 0-8118-5394-2
ISBN-13: 978-0-8118-5394-1
ISSN: 1074-5068

Manufactured in the United States of America.

Cover design by Jay Peter Salvas
Book design: Words & Deeds
Typesetting: Jack Lanning
Series editor: Jeff Campbell
Author photograph: Marv Summers

Distributed in Canada by
Raincoast Books
9050 Shaughnessy Street
Vancouver, British Columbia V6P 6E5

10 9 8 7 6 5 4 3 2 1

Chronicle Books LLC
680 Second Street
San Francisco, California 94107

www.chroniclebooks.com
www.greateatsandsleeps.com

For great friends Sue Randerson and Mary Harker, whose companionship added so much to the pleasurable research for the eleventh edition of Great Eats Paris.

Contents

To the Reader

Paris is a feast, but the banquet has become painfully expensive.

—*Anthony Dias Blue*

Eating is a serious venture, if not a patriotic duty, in France.

—*Patricia Roberts*

Paris is famous for its fashion, acclaimed for its art, and notorious for its nightlife, but to visit Paris and bypass the endless opportunities for sampling its wonderful cuisine is absolutely unthinkable. Thus, along with visits to the Louvre, the Eiffel Tower, and the Champs-Élysées, dining is almost always an integral part of any successful trip to Paris.

The French know how to eat; if there is something a Frenchperson would rather do, no one has yet discovered it. For the French, good food is not a casual pastime reserved only for dining out, but it's a way of life, a celebration of the bounty of foods available throughout the year. As a result, French cooking is an art form; chefs with great talent and skill are awarded the Legion of Honor and given the same media attention Americans reserve for rock stars. One of the most well-known statements by former French president Charles de Gaulle refers not to politics or war but cheese. The ritual of Sunday lunch has almost been canonized, and even *Le Monde,* the country's largest and most serious newspaper, runs front-page stories about *cornichons,* types of bread, and the wines and cheeses that go best with them. In Paris you will find this love of eating well reflected in more than twenty thousand cafés, bistros, brasseries, and restaurants, which cater to every taste and budget, from haute cuisine to hole-in-the-wall.

Because the French demand a higher quality of food and preparation, they are usually willing to pay for it. It is easy, if you have unlimited funds, to dine at one of the Parisian cathedrals of cuisine and have an exquisite meal for over $200 per person. For most visitors to Paris, this would be a one-time-only indulgence if it could be afforded at all. However, too often visitors determined to partake in Paris's ultimate culinary pleasures rush only to those restaurants with at least one Michelin star and, in so doing, overlook many up-and-coming restaurants that serve remarkable food at a fraction of the price. The ongoing demands for *bon rapport et qualité prix* (good value for money), along with the fluctuating French economy and shortened work week, have challenged the bloated tabs of the culinary all-stars, forcing many to either lower their prices and add affordable *prix-fixe* (set-price) lunch menus or go out of business altogether. At the same time, it has encouraged diners to experiment with less-expensive bistros and family-run restaurants further away from the usual tourist haunts. Hands-on newcomers, who learned their cooking craft from the masters, are redefining the Parisian dining palate by branching out on their own in low-end, off-the-beaten-track establishments. Most seat diners in bare, humdrum surroundings, but the high-quality food and fair prices more than compensate for the lack of elegance and sometimes less-than-central locations. Talented regional chefs have put sizzle into the Paris dining scene with their artfully inspired dishes, giving foreign diners a chance to acquaint themselves with France's many regional cuisines—and all for the price of a main course in the restaurants these chefs once cooked in.

As we all know, selecting a place to eat can be frustrating and time-consuming because it is also quite possible, especially in Paris, to pay too much and eat badly. Whether you're visiting for a day or for several weeks, you don't want to waste time and money on a mediocre meal when you could be eating magnificently and paying less just around the corner. Here is where *Great Eats Paris* comes to the rescue—it takes the uncertainty out of dining and puts you on the inside track to some of the best dining deals in Paris. *Great Eats Paris* will improve the quality of your Parisian dining experiences and save you money by leading you away from the tourist-packed, high-priced restaurants and toward the well-located, picturesque ones serving reasonably priced meals of good value to mostly French patrons. With *Great Eats Paris* in hand, you will discover a world of good taste and affordable food in a wide array of genuinely Parisian establishments: crowded, noisy cafés with a haze of pungent smoke and a coterie of colorful regulars; family-run bistros with red-and-white-checked tablecloths and sawdust on the floor; sophisticated wine bars; cozy tearooms; simple soup kitchens; big brasseries serving steaming platters of *choucroute;* and candlelit restaurants from which couples depart more in love than when they arrived. Some of these are classics everyone has heard about. Others, until now, have been virtually unknown to foreigners. A few are Big Splurges that have been selected for special occasions when you want to sample an abundance of the very best.

My research trip for this edition took me to parts of Paris I otherwise would not have visited and led me to many new and exciting dining discoveries. In an effort to help you save money and, as much as possible, keep you from making mistakes, I revisited every listing in the previous edition, and I tried countless other restaurants that for one reason or another did not make the final cut. I dined anonymously and paid my own way, which enabled me to objectively evaluate the good and the bad and to report the findings to you freely, fairly, and honestly. In the process, I walked hundreds of miles in all types of weather, ate out every day, and loved every minute of it. On occasion, I was seated in English-speaking Siberia near the kitchen, under the fan, or behind a post; suffered through nearly inedible meals; was overcharged by condescending waiters who thought I didn't know beans when the bag was open; sat on chairs that must have been used during the Inquisition; and received a cool shoulder from apéritif to *digestif,* all just so you can avoid suffering the same fate. On the other hand, I had some unforgettably wonderful meals and experiences, met fascinating people, and learned more about Paris than I ever thought possible. Many old favorites remain. Unfortunately, some entries from past editions have been dropped. Places that were once excellent are now sadly lacking; chefs and owners changed, quality dropped severely, and/or prices rose to a mind-numbing level. Cozy corner cafés fell victim to fast-food joints, and the age of concrete and modernization removed others. The result of my months of research is the eleventh edition of *Great Eats Paris,* filled with my hand-picked selections of more than two hundred cafés, bistros, brasseries, restaurants, tearooms, and wine bars offering good food quality and top value dining in a range of price categories.

I hope you are as enthusiastic about the restaurants you choose from *Great Eats Paris* as I was in selecting them. I also hope this book will inspire you to strike out on your own and make your own dining discoveries. If you find a place you think I should know about or want to report a change in a restaurant I've listed, please take a few moments to write me a note telling me about your experience (see Readers' Comments, page 320). I read every piece of correspondence and respond to as many as possible. I cannot emphasize enough how important your comments are in improving each edition.

Whether for business, sightseeing, or as a stop on the way to another destination, Paris has been beckoning travelers for centuries, and most visitors have treasured memories of their stay in the City of Light. One of the best souvenirs you can have of your trip to Paris is the memory of a good meal. I hope that by using *Great Eats Paris* you will have some very special memories of Paris to take home with you. If I have helped you do that, I consider my job well done. *Bon voyage,* and of course, *bon appétit!*

Tips for Great Eats in Paris

Animals feed themselves, men eat; but only wise men know the art of eating.
> —*Jean Anthelme Brillat-Savarin,*
> La Physiologie du Gout, *1826*

There is no love sincerer than the love of food.
> —*George Bernard Shaw,* Man and
> Superman, *1903*

1. Eat and drink a block or two away from the main boulevards and tourist attractions. The difference in price for even a coffee can be considerable.

2. In smaller restaurants and cafés, arrive early for the best selection of seats and food. Remember that the last order is usually taken no less than fifteen minutes before closing.

3. If you want to eat a meal outside the normal Parisian lunch or dinner times, go to a brasserie. These places serve continually throughout the day, often until midnight.

4. French law states that all restaurants must post a menu outside. *Always* read it before going in to make sure the menu has something you want at a price you can afford.

5. Eat where you see a crowd of French people. At mealtime, if a restaurant is either empty or full of tourists, or it posts a plasticized menu outside in five languages, you can assume the locals know something you do not, and move on.

6. Be prepared to rub elbows with your dining neighbor. All but the most elegant Paris dining establishments maximize space by squeezing tables as close together as possible.

7. Stay within and respect the limits of the kitchen. Don't expect gourmet fare from a corner café, and don't go to a fine restaurant and order only a salad.

8. The set-price menu, called a *prix fixe* or *formule,* will always be the best value. The next best bet is the *plat du jour* ordered à la carte. This is always fresh and usually garnished with potatoes and/or a vegetable.

9. It's an open secret. In most places, especially more expensive restaurants, the money-saving tactic is to go for lunch and order the *prix-fixe* menu. This usually costs a fraction of what it would for dinner and sometimes includes wine and coffee. But be aware

that there are no substitutions on these menus—what you see listed on the menu is what you get (for more on Big Splurge lunches, see "Gourmet Lunching for Less," page 37).

10. Order the house wine *(vin de la mason* or *vin ordinaire).* Ask for *une carafe de l'eau ordinaire* (tap water), which is free, rather than paying for a bottle of mineral water.

11. Don't sit down! Have your morning *café au lait* and croissant standing at the bar at the corner café. They will cost twice as much if they are served at a table and even more at your hotel.

12. Always double-check the math on your bill. Mistakes are frequent and are usually not in your favor. By law, restaurants must include the 15 percent service charge (which *is* the tip) in the price. No additional tip is necessary unless either the food or the service has been very special. If you are drinking at the bar, it is customary to leave small change.

13. Restaurants change their hours, days closed, and annual vacations to accommodate tourist demand, economics, and owner whims, so call ahead to make sure the place you have selected will be open, especially if you're making a special trip. All of the information given in *Great Eats Paris* was accurate at press time, but closings change frequently around holidays, on the weekends, and during July and August.

14. It is always better to arrive at a restaurant with reservations than to not have them and be turned away, especially if no backup choice is close by. If you are a solo diner, always make the reservation for two (see "Reservations," page 15).

15. For a really cheap meal, a street *marché* (or market; see "Food Shopping," page 39) is the perfect place to pick up fixings for a park *déjeuner sur l'herbe* (lunch under a tree). A piece of ripe Brie cheese, a fresh baguette, a juicy apple or pear, and a bottle of young Beaujolais wine . . . ah, that's Paris. Other very Parisian cheap eats are piping hot, made-to-order crêpes from one of the many corner crêpe stands and fresh baguette sandwiches from a bakery. Inexpensive restaurant options are listed in the index under Cheap Eats (see page 317).

16. The free maps you can pick up around town are worth what they cost: nothing. You will never get lost if you buy a copy of the *Plan de Paris par Arrondissement.* This invaluable and timeless map is available at all news kiosks and bookstores in Paris and at many travel bookstores in the United States.

If you have particularly enjoyed a place recommended by *Great Eats Paris,* be sure to tell the owner or manager where you found out about them. They are always very appreciative.

How to Use Great Eats Paris

Each listing in the book includes the following information: the name of the establishment, the address, the telephone number, the most convenient métro stop, the days and hours it is open and closed, whether reservations are necessary, which credit cards are accepted, the average price for a three-course à la carte meal without wine, the price for a prix-fixe meal (also without wine, unless it is included in the prix-fixe cost), and whether or not English is spoken and to what degree. If the restaurant is 100 percent nonsmoking, the listing notes it. Most include a map key number in parentheses to the right of the restaurant name; an entry without a number means it is located beyond the parameters of the map. A dollar sign ($) to the right of the name indicates the restaurant is a Big Splurge; a cent sign (¢) indicates a Cheap Eat.

At the end of the book there is a glossary of French dining phrases and menu terms; an index of all restaurants, plus indexes by category; and finally, a "Readers' Comments" page.

Big Splurges and Cheap Eats

When you have only two pennies left in the world, buy a loaf of bread with one and a lily with the other.
—*Chinese proverb*

Most of the restaurants in this guide are in the midrange price category. However, a few are more expensive and designated as "Big Splurges," and a few are bargain finds and designated as "Cheap Eats." It is not hard in Paris to spend considerable money for a fine meal, but they are not all worth the cost. Restaurants in the Big Splurge category offer exceptional dining experiences not only for the food but for the service and total ambience. Also, in almost every case, these restaurants offer a prix-fixe menu, especially at lunch, that is within the budget of most diners. They become Big Splurges when you order à la carte. The exception to this is the list of haute-cuisine establishments in "Gourmet Lunching for Less" (page 37): these are always Big Splurges, though they offer a prix-fixe lunch for much less than you would pay à la carte or for dinner. Big Splurges are excellent choices for special-occasion dining or to celebrate just being in Paris. In the text, Big Splurges are marked with a dollar sign ($). There is a complete listing of Big Splurges in the index.

Being labeled a Cheap Eat doesn't mean a restaurant lacks quality or value. On the contrary, these establishments offer exceptional value for money and constitute some of the great bargain eats to be found in Paris. In the text, a Cheap Eat is marked with a cent sign (¢), and they are listed in the index.

The Euro

The euro is now the sole official legal tender of the eleven-nation European Union, of which France is a part. However, it is clear that old habits die hard. Mainly as a courtesy to the many French who still think monetarily in francs, menu prices are often shown in both French francs and the euro. However, the euro is the only currency accepted.

All prices in *Great Eats Paris* are quoted in euros. At press time, 1 euro = 1.29 U.S. dollars. But please be aware that this rate fluctuates constantly.

Holidays

Very few Paris eating establishments are open every day of the year. Most close at least one day a week, and sometimes for either lunch or dinner on Saturday and all day Sunday. Many close for public holidays (listed below), as well as for one week at Christmas and Easter. Some smaller family-run operations also close for the school holidays in the fall and winter. The French consider their annual vacation time to be a God-given right. In fact, every working person in France is guaranteed a five-week vacation, no matter how long they have been employed in their present job. Despite government pleadings and tourist demands, many still have an annual closing (*fermeture annuelle*) for all or parts of July and August, when 75 percent of all Parisians leave the city. Closures also vary with the mood of the owner and to adjust to the changing patterns of tourism and inflation. More places are opting for a one- or two-week closure and allowing their employees to rotate their vacation times. It is impossible to guarantee that one year's policy will carry over to the next. To avoid arriving at a restaurant only to find it closed, always call ahead to check, especially on a holiday and in July and August.

The restaurant listings note all vacation and holiday closing dates. If a restaurant has no annual closing, this is indicated by the abbreviation NAC, for "no annual closing."

January 1	New Year's Day	*Jour de l'An*
	Easter Sunday and Monday	*Pâques et Lundi de Pâques*
	Ascension Day	*Ascension* (40 days after Easter)
Whit Monday	*Lundi de Pentacôte*	Second Monday after Ascension
May 1	Labor Day	*Fête du Travail*
May 8	VE Day	Armistice 1945
July 14	Bastille Day	*Quatorze Juillet/Fête Nationale*
August 15	Assumption Day	*Assomption*
November 1	All Saints' Day	*Toussaint*
November 11	Armistice Day	Armistice 1918
December 25	Christmas Day	*Noël*

Maps

Oh! To wander Paris! Such a lovely, delectable experience.
— *Honoré de Balzac,* La Physiologie
du Mariage, *1829*

Most of the Paris arrondissements covered in *Great Eats Paris* have an accompanying map and restaurant key, and in the text, these map key numbers appear in parentheses to the right of the restaurant's name. If a restaurant does not have a number, it is located beyond the boundaries of the map.

Please note that the maps in *Great Eats Paris* are designed to help readers locate the restaurant listings; they are not meant to replace fully detailed street maps. If you plan on being in Paris for more than a day or two, I strongly suggest you buy *Plan de Paris par Arrondissement.* It is available at all news kiosks and bookstores for somewhere between 10€ and 20€, and it contains a detailed map of every arrondissement, with a complete street index, métro and bus routes, tourist sites, and much more. It is pocket-size and every Parisian has one. It is a purchase that will never go out of style or change much.

Nonsmoking Restaurants

The reason the French drink so much is to help them forget what they are doing to themselves by smoking.
— *Art Buchwald,* Vive la Cigarette

Concerning this problem, there is a lack of political courage.
— *Nicolas Villain, codirector of the French
National Committee Against Tobacco*

Cigarette stubs make up three of the twenty tons of trash collected daily in the Paris métro, even though no smoking is allowed inside the trains or on the platforms! There has been a lukewarm attempt to cut down on smoking in public places, but there is no French surgeon general extolling the virtues of a smoke-free environment, and the 30 percent of Parisians who light up daily show no signs of quitting. One existing antismoking law stipulates that all places serving food designate separate smoking and nonsmoking sections. Cafés ignore this completely because the staff all smoke . . . and on the job. During the busiest times in cafés it is nearly impossible to escape from the Gauloise-induced haze. While most restaurants have a nonsmoking seating area, these are usually only a token table or two by the door, in a dreary back room, or worse yet, surrounded by those puffing throughout the entire meal. When a nonsmoker questions the designation of such a table, he or she will be told in no uncertain terms, "Yours *is* a nonsmoking table."

However, as of presstime, more far-reaching nonsmoking legislation was being proposed: a total ban on smoking in all public places. In typical French fashion, this will become the subject of lengthy debate and discussion . . . so don't hold your breath! In *Great Eats Paris,* those establishments where smoking is prohibited completely have been noted in the writeup and are listed in the index (see page 318). Otherwise, *bonne chance.*

Paying the Bill

> **What's money? A man is a success if he gets up in the morning,
> goes to bed at night, and in the middle does what he wants to do.**
> —*Bob Dylan*

After the mysteries of the French menu, no subject is more confusing to foreigners than French restaurant bills. Your bill will not automatically be brought to your table at the end of the meal; you usually must ask for it *(l'addition, s'il vous plaît).* If you are eating with a group and plan on paying individually, please don't expect your waiter to provide separate checks. Appoint a designated mathematician to keep track of everyone's order. Otherwise, you will develop indigestion trying to make sense of the lumped-together charges on *l'addition.*

Credit Cards

In Paris, it is almost always possible to pay for meals with a credit card. Policies often change, however, so when reserving, it is wise to double-check which cards the restaurant accepts. In smaller places, a 15€ minimum is often required before a credit card will be accepted. The most popular cards are Visa, known as Carte Bleu, and MasterCard, known as Eurocard. American Express and Diners Club, in particular, are much less popular because they charge high fees to merchants and are slow to pay.

The following abbreviations are used for the major credit cards:

American Express	AE
Diners Club	DC
MasterCard	MC
Visa	V

Prices

In most cases, the size of the bottom line on your restaurant bill will depend on your choice of wine and other beverages. All prices quoted in *Great Eats Paris* are for one person and specify whether or not drinks are included using the following abbreviations:

Boissons compris	Drinks included	BC
Boissons non-compris	Drinks *not* included	BNC

In determining price quotations, the cheapest menu items have been avoided. The à la carte prices that are quoted represent the median cost of an à la carte meal with a starter *(entrée)*, main course *(plat)*, and dessert, but without wine or coffee. The prix-fixe prices state how many courses you can expect and whether drinks are included or extra. Even though every attempt has been made to ensure the accuracy of the information given, there is a certain margin of error in pricing due to fluctuating exchange rates, inflation, escalating food costs, and the whims of restaurant owners.

Service Charge

In Paris, always remember that *the service charge is the tip*. By law, all restaurants in France must include a 12 to 15 percent service charge in the price of all food and beverages served. This will be stated on the menu by the words *service compris* or *prix nets*. No additional service charge may be added to your bill. Always check your bill very carefully because mistakes are too frequent.

Important! *Beware of the service charge/credit card scam.* This is a deliberate gouging of the customer that should not be tolerated. If you are paying by credit card, the total should be at the bottom. If the restaurant has left the space on your credit card slip for the "tip/gratuity" blank, they are hoping you will fill in an amount, thus paying the tip twice, since the service charge has already been included. To avoid this, draw a line from the top total to the bottom total and draw an additional line through the space marked "tip/gratuity."

Tipping

Americans seem to have a hard time with this concept, so it bears repeating: *The service charge is the tip.* You do not have to leave one euro more than the price of your meal. In France you are obliged to tip the butcher, the delivery boy, and the theater usher but not the waiter, even in the finest restaurants. However, if the waiter has performed some extraordinary service or if you were particularly pleased, then an additional tip may be in order. Depending on the size and type of place, anything from a few euros to 5 or 10 percent of the bill would be more than acceptable. In cafés, patrons standing at the bar usually leave some small change.

Reservations

To avoid disappointment, it is always better to arrive with reservations. While reservations are not necessary or accepted in a café, they are essential in most restaurants and in popular bistros and brasseries. If you arrive without a reservation, you might be told that the restaurant is *complet* (full) even when there are empty tables. The reason is that those empty tables have been reserved and are being held.

If you are a solo diner, always make the reservation for two people. When you arrive, tell the maître d' that your companion will arrive shortly. Soon the waiter will inquire about the empty chair. Look soulfully at your watch and say, "Oh, he/she must not be coming.

I will order now." Believe me, it works every time. You will not be relegated to a table behind a post (as many single diners are), the waitstaff will become very solicitous of your predicament, and the service will improve immediately.

When you have a reservation, don't be late. French restaurants honor their reservation times and do not relegate patrons to the bar to wait for the present occupants to gulp down the last drop of espresso before relinquishing the table. Many places have only one or two seatings for both lunch and dinner, so if you change your plans after booking, you should always call to cancel so that your table can be rebooked. Some places tend to seat all the English-speaking diners together. I find this very annoying, but if there is only one English-speaking waiter, it does make sense on the part of management.

All entries in *Great Eats Paris* state the reservation policy, so you will know exactly what to do and expect. If you do not feel comfortable making the reservation yourself, the hotel desk personnel can do it for you, possibly getting a better table than if you had tried yourself.

Transportation

In *Great Eats Paris,* the nearest Paris métro stop is given for each restaurant, and in central Paris the métro is so comprehensive there are often two or three stops that are equally convenient. The Paris métro is safe, efficient, and fast, and it is the best way to get around. While buses are not hard to figure out and are more interesting, since you can see the neighborhoods you are passing through, they often get stuck in traffic, and you could walk to your destination in the time the bus will take. The same can sometimes be said of taxis, though now and then I recommend using them late at night in some of the outer arrondissements. Please remember that taxis are not required to take more than four people, and perhaps only three if the driver's dog is occupying the front passenger seat.

General Information about French Dining

Like theater, offering food to people is a matter of showmanship, and no matter how simple the performance, you have to do it well, with love and originality.

—*James Beard*

Where to Eat

"Is this a café, a bistro, a brasserie, or a restaurant?" This is the first question many foreigners ask, with the second one usually being, "What's the difference?" In the pecking order of eateries, a bistro is a cut above a café and a notch below a restaurant, and brasseries can fall anywhere among them all. The following explanations should help to clear away some of the confusion while giving you the flavor of these various establishments.

Cafés

**The last time I saw Paris
Her heart was warm and gay.
I heard the laughter of her heart in
Ev'ry street café.**

—*Oscar Hammerstein II*

The French don't go to priests, doctors, or psychiatrists to talk over their problems; they sit in a café over a cup of coffee or a glass of wine and talk to each other.

—*Eric Sevareid,* "Town Meeting of the World," *CBS Television, March 1966*

For the visitor to Paris, the café is a living stage and the perfect place to feel the heartbeat of the city. The café experience lets anyone become a Parisian in the space of an hour or so, since by coming here, you are immediately cast into one of the best scenes in the city. For the French, it would be easier to change their religion than their favorite café. Depending on the area, it can be a café pouring a wake-up Calvados to workers at 4 A.M., the lunch spot for local merchants, a lively afternoon rendezvous for students and gossiping civil servants, or a meeting place to have "a few with the boys" on the way home from work. People who are lonely find company, foreigners find a place to write postcards, countesses rub elbows with cab drivers, and everyone finds *égalité*.

In a café, you can eat, drink, and sleep it off afterward, flirt, meet your lover, play pinball, hide from your boss, talk, listen, dream, read, write, order takeout sandwiches, tap into a WiFi network, make telephone calls, use the toilet, pet the lazy dog sprawled across the entrance, and sit at a table for as long as you like, engaging in prime people-watching. If the café is also a *tabac,* you can buy cigarettes, pipes, postcards, stamps, razor blades, cheap watches, lottery tickets, and *telecartes,* the wallet-size cards that take the place of coins in most public telephone booths in Paris. If the café has a PMU sign, you can place a bet on your favorite horse or political candidate. Talk about convenience! No wonder there are fifty thousand cafés in France and six thousand in Paris, which means you can find a café on almost every corner in the city.

Cafés don't try to be trendy. The management will never consult a decorator, and they don't listen to talk about *nouvelle cuisine,* lowering cholesterol, or controlling fat grams. You can expect cafés to be smoky. Even though the government is trying to curtail cigarette smoking, puffing away remains a solid fact of café life in Paris. At peak hours, the hectic, noisy, smoky ambience is part of the café's charm. The lunch hour is always lively, with service by acrobatic waiters who commit orders to memory, run with plates full of food, and never mix an order or spill a drop. The hearty *bonne maman* food is offered at prices that even struggling students can afford.

Parisians are masters of the art of the café. Almost any time of year, the most popular tables are those on the sidewalk. Even when the temperatures are in the single digits, you will find bundled Parisians huddled outside under heat lamps. Cafés offer a window on contemporary life in Paris and allow you to linger for hours over a single drink and perfect the Parisian art of doing nothing while watching the world pass by. Of course, if you stand at the bar, whatever you order will cost less, but by paying the premium and occupying a table, you acquire privileges bordering on squatter's rights. If the table has a cloth or paper placemat, that means that the table is only for patrons who want to eat. If it is bare, you are welcome to sit, have a drink, and stay as long as you like. No one will rush you or ask you to pay until you are ready to leave, unless the waiters are changing shifts and need to settle their daily take or if the café is about to close. Don't complain when the bill comes; you are not paying $4 for a tiny, strong cup of coffee—you are paying for the privilege of sitting in a constantly changing theater of activity and enjoyment for as long as your heart desires.

Bistros

After the fall of Napoléon, the Russian soldiers who occupied Paris would bang on the zinc bars and shout *bistrot!*—which means "hurry" in Russian. Many say that bistros served the world's first fast food. In the past, when bistros were all simple *maman et papa* places, fast food was the order of the day. Today, bistros still make up the heart and soul of Parisian dining. Some are small, unpretentious, and family run, with handwritten menus and a waitstaff and decor that have not changed in thirty years, which is just the way their equally dedicated and unchanging customers like it. Others are elegant, with starched linens, formally clad waiters, and prices to match. Culinary habits in Paris are changing, thanks to the new generation of chefs who, having trained with the culinary maestros, now offer a similar, more affordable cuisine in bistros located in lower-rent, out-of-the-way neighborhoods. In any bistro, the atmosphere is friendly, and the room is packed with loyalists who know every dish on the menu. When you are hungry enough to dig in to a steaming platter of rib-sticking fare, head for a bistro. Farm-kitchen renditions of *pot-au-feu, boeuf bourguignon,* Lyonnaise sausages, thick *cassoulets,* duck *confit,* salt cod, and the quintessential bistro dessert, *tarte Tatin,* are the once-lost and now-found dishes that salute the robust, nostalgic bistro cooking firmly rooted in the French past.

Brasseries

The earliest brasseries began in Alsace, along the eastern border between France and Germany. Open from early morning until past midnight, they are big, brightly lit, and perpetually packed with a noisy, high-energy crowd enjoying service in the best long-aproned tradition. As opposed to bistros and restaurants, you can order food at almost any time of the day, delving into platters of *choucroute,* fresh shellfish, steaks, and chicory salad loaded with bacon and topped with a poached egg. Everything is washed down with bottles of Alsatian wine and cold beer. While reservations are appreciated, you can usually get a table without them.

Restaurants

With more than twenty thousand places to eat, Paris can accommodate any dining mood. A restaurant serves only full two- or three-course meals at set times for lunch and/or dinner. It is not the place to go if you want a quick sandwich or a big salad on the go. Restaurants offer a complete menu with impressive wine lists, and diners are expected to order accordingly. They are more formal in service, food preparation, and presentation than cafés, bistros, and brasseries. Because eating is such a serious business in France, especially in Paris, most restaurants have only one seating to allow for leisurely dining. No waiter worth his or her white apron or black tie would ever rush a Frenchperson through a meal in order to free the table for other diners. You can count on spending almost two hours for a serious lunch and at least three for a nice dinner. Do as the French do: relax, take your time, enjoy each course and the wine, and above all, be happy you are in Paris.

Tearooms

Tearooms play an important part in the lives of most Parisians. In fact, there are more tearooms in Paris than there are in London! The French *salons de thé* are romantic, hospitable places where you are encouraged to get comfortable and stay awhile. Hidden away in all corners of Paris, they are a welcome stop for those looking for a relaxing lunch, a sightseeing or shopping break, or an afternoon of quiet, unhurried conversation with an old friend over a rich dessert and a pot of brewed tea. In addition, they are havens for single diners, and they are nice places to go for a light lunch, brunch, or late-afternoon snack if you know dinner will be very late. Almost every neighborhood has its *salon de thé,* and each is as different as its owner: some are elegant, some quaint, and others high-tech modern. They often have a friendly cat to pet, periodicals to glance through, and an air of intellectualism.

Wine Bars

Un bon repas favorise la conversation. Un bon vin lui donne de l'espirit. ("A good meal favors conversation. A good wine gives it spirit.")
—*Note found on the back of a napkin in a Parisian wine bar*

Average life of a drinker of water: 56 years
Average life of a drinker of wine: 77 years
Choose!
—*Sign in a French railroad station*

The popularity of *bars à vin* continues in the City of Light. Most wine bar owners have not only a passion for good wine but an interest in good food. The friendly rendezvous for Parisian pacesetters, wine bars are a smart solution for those looking for a place to relax over a glass or two of nice wine while enjoying a light meal from noon until late in the evening. Ranging from rustic to futuristic, they serve fine wines as well as little-known vintages by the glass or bottle, along with simple meals of salads, *tartines* (slices of baguette or country bread spread with pâté or cheese), cold meats, cheeses, and usually hot main dishes.

University Restaurants

A discussion of Paris dining establishments would be incomplete without a mention of the amazingly cheap if unremarkable fare that is available at university restaurants, commonly known as Restos-U. If you have an international student card, you will qualify for rock-bottom prices; nonstudent companions will pay twice that, but it's still a bargain. For more information on Restos-U, see "University Restaurants," page 291.

The French Menu

Paris is just like any other city, only the people eat better.
　　　　　—*Maurice Chevalier,* Love in the
　　　　　Afternoon

Dining in Paris is often anticipated as the most pleasurable aspect of any visit, but it can sometimes be a very disappointing and unsettling experience. Let's face it: whether it is neatly printed on an oversized menu in a fine restaurant, whitewashed on a bistro window, written in fading chalk on a blackboard, or handwritten on a sheet pinned to a café curtain, the French menu can be intimidating. This section will take the mystery out of the menu, so that you will feel confident to go anywhere and order with style and ease.

All French eating establishments must, by law, post a menu outside showing the prices of the food they serve. *Great Eats Paris* gives you enough information about each restaurant so that you will know generally what to expect before you get there. Still, when you arrive at your destination, read the posted menu *before* going in. This avoids unpleasant surprises and embarrassment in the event that what is offered that day does not appeal to your taste or budget.

Once inside and seated, do not ask for *le menu;* ask for *la carte.* That way you will get the complete listing of all the foods served, from appetizers to desserts on *both* the à la carte and prix-fixe menus. If you say, *le menu, s'il vous plaît* ("the menu, please"), you could get a strange look from the waiter, cause some confusion, and possibly end up with the prix-fixe meal, which is also referred to as *le menu.*

When reading a menu *(la carte),* look at the *menu prix fixe* (sometimes called a *formule* or *menu conseille*) as well as the à la carte menu. The prix-fixe menu usually consists of a combination of two or three courses—the *entrée* (first course), the *plat* (main course), and cheese and/or dessert—all for one price. The drinks (wine, beer, or mineral water, and sometimes coffee) may or may not be included. The prix fixe is often a terrific bargain, especially in higher-priced restaurants and during lunch, enabling those on a tighter budget to dine in luxury (see "Gourmet Lunching for Less," page 37). Very often the same dishes are offered at night at more than double what savvy diners paid at noon. The prix-fixe choices may be limited, but the value is always there. If you opt for this menu, you will be expected to take all of the courses offered and not make any substitutions. If you want only one or two courses, and three are offered, there will generally be no reduction in price, but don't think that a three- or even four-course meal will be too much to eat. A good French meal is balanced, and the portions are not large. Enjoy your meal the way the French do—slowly—and you will not feel overfed.

Most restaurants also offer à la carte choices, and for those with lighter appetites, this often makes good sense because you are not paying for courses you do not want. Another smart, money-saving tactic in a café, bar, or brasserie is to order just a *(plat)* main course, or the *plat du jour*. However, exercise caution when ordering à la carte: if you start to order more than one dish, remember that each course is priced separately—and that the sum of the parts may add up to a very expensive meal compared to the prix-fixe menu.

When ordering, keep in mind what is likely to be fresh and in season, and consider, too, the specialties of the chef. No matter what the size or scope of the eating establishment, always consider the *entrée* or *plat du jour* (the daily special starter and main course). They usually change every day, the ingredients are fresh and seasonal, and there is a rapid turnover because the dishes are proven winners with the regulars. They will not be dishes whose ingredients have been languishing in the refrigerator for several days or relegated to the freezer due to lack of interest. The specialties of the house are sometimes starred or underlined in red on the menu. You will also see the word *maison* (house) written by some choices, which means that it is made "in house" and therefore considered a specialty. If you want a green salad and don't see one on the menu, almost every kitchen will have the fixings to put together a *salade verte* or *salade mixe* if you ask. It won't test the skill of the chef, but sometimes a light starter is in order. The day of the week is also important. Fish can be a poor choice on Sunday, when the wholesale food market at Rungis is closed, and on Monday, when most outdoor markets are closed. Also keep in mind where you are. If you are in a corner café, complete with a *tabac,* don't expect the chef to perform magic with wild game or to dazzle you with high-rising soufflés.

Meals

Every good meal in Paris is like a *petite vacance.*
—Ray Lampard

Proper French meals usually consist of three courses—an *entrée* (starter), a *plat* (main course), and cheese or dessert—but they can also be just the *plat* with either the *entrée* or the dessert. A sandwich is never considered to be a meal. At more formal restaurants, you can expect to be served additional courses up to as many as seven. Bread, an essential part of any French meal, is served free, and it is usually freshly cut just before it is brought to your table; you are entitled to as much as you want. Place your bread on the table, not on your plate, unless you are given a separate bread plate. Butter is usually not served with the bread, but you can always ask for it.

Here is a list of the traditional French courses:

apéritif	before-dinner drink, generally a kir
amuse bouche or	
amuse gueule	a plate of little hors d'oeuvres served with your apéritif
entrée	appetizer or starter
fish course	
plat	main course
salad or cheese	
dessert	
petits fours	plate of cookies served with after-dinner coffee
coffee	always espresso

The best way to experience Parisian life (or, for that matter, the way people live in any place) is to dine the way the locals do, at the same times, and on the native dishes and specialties that constitute their culinary heritage. The French take dining very seriously. In most French restaurants, no matter how big or small, time is not of the essence. A meal is to be savored and enjoyed, not dispatched in a rush to some other destination. This especially applies to dinner, which is often an event lasting the entire evening.

There was a time when one could honestly say, "You can't get a bad meal in Paris." With the influx of golden arches, pizza parlors, ethnic restaurants, and *le fast food,* it is definitely possible to suffer a bad Paris meal. Despite this, there are few cities in the world where you can consistently eat as well as you can in Paris, and if you plan carefully, you can have the gastronomic experience of a lifetime for much less than you would spend in any other major city in the world.

Just as Paris fashions change, so do the demands of restaurant patrons. Not too long ago dining before 8 P.M. was almost unheard of. Now, more and more restaurants are opening at 7 or 7:30 P.M. for dinner and staying open much later on Friday and Saturday nights. Many, too, are now staying open part of August, which a few years ago was absolutely unthinkable. Unfortunately, many of the time-honored restaurant standards regarding the waitstaff dress code have been dramatically relaxed. Levi's, T-shirts, and jogging shoes have replaced black pants, bow ties, and long white aprons, especially in the cheaper places.

As a result of the desire for lighter meals, wine bars and tearooms continue to flourish. To keep the cost of meals down and still cope with rising inflation, more and more restaurants are adopting the use of paper napkins and paper table coverings, the corners of which are then used by the waiter to tally the bill. The Parisian love affair with American food shows no signs of diminishing. Weekend brunch, chocolate chip cookies, cheesecake, brownies, apple crumble, baby back ribs, and pizza delivered to the door win converts daily.

No matter what the recipe or the time of year, a good French chef insists on the freshest ingredients, ignores frozen or, heaven forbid, canned, and does not cut corners or use artificial flavorings or preservatives. French eating establishments, from humble cafés to the great temples of gastronomy, seldom have teenagers working part-time in the kitchen or waiting tables between classes. From the chef on down, the employees are dedicated personnel who consider their jobs permanent, not way stations on the road to somewhere else. This makes a difference in everything from the quality of food on your plate to the service at your table.

Breakfast *(Petite Déjeuner)*

Breakfast is served from 7 to 10 A.M. in most cafés.

Parisians do not have a good grasp of what constitutes a real American breakfast, so do yourself a favor and follow the French example: start the day at the corner café with a *café au lait, grande crème,* or a *chocolat chaud* and a flaky croissant. If you are willing to eat standing at the bar, you will save significantly, and of course, you will save money eating breakfast almost any place but your hotel, where the markup can be 100 percent. Another breakfast option is to go to a bakery *(boulangerie)* that also has a counter or a few tables where you can eat your treats and be served coffee or hot chocolate. This opens the door to many more wonderful options from *croissants au beurre,* made with pure butter as opposed to *croissants ordinaires,* made with margarine, *pain aux raisins, pain au chocolat,* or *chausson pomme,* which is similar to an apple turnover . . . the delicious list is endless. If your hotel has a buffet breakfast, *please* do not try to bag enough extra to sustain you through lunch. *Hôteliers* take a very dim view of this practice, and if you attempt it, you will label yourself a greedy tourist without a *soupçon* of manners. If you do insist on bacon and eggs or other staples of the American breakfast table, be prepared to pay dearly for them. Astute diners save their omelettes or ham and eggs for a café lunch.

Lunch *(Déjeuner)*

The midday meal is served from noon to 2:30 P.M., with the last order taken about fifteen to thirty minutes before closing.

If you face a deadline or do not want a full-blown meal at lunch, grab a sandwich from the nearest *boulangerie* or *pâtisserie;* go to a café, wine bar, or tearoom; or put together *le snack.* Do not try to rush through a meal at a restaurant, and please do not go into a restaurant and order just a salad or an appetizer. It just is not done, and you will not be regarded well by the staff, which can result in embarrassment on your part.

A surprising number of French eat their main meal at noon. Recognizing this, many places offer very good value prix-fixe menus at lunch *only*. If you are on a shoestring budget or are willing to eat a large lunch, you'll find bargains in all categories of eateries. Many places have their biggest crowds at lunch, so if you do not have a reservation, keep this in mind and try to arrive early to be assured a good seat. Remember, too, that the specials often run out, making yet another reason to arrive earlier rather than later.

Paris has many delightful parks—such as the Luxembourg Gardens, the Tuileries, Champ-de-Mars, Jardin des Plantes, and the Bois de Boulogne—not to mention the romantic banks along the Seine and the many pretty squares throughout the city. The street *marchés* and shopping streets are the perfect places to purchase a satisfying and inexpensive al fresco *pique-nique* lunch (see "Food Shopping," page 39). If you have your picnic on a warm day in the park, you will probably share your bench with a French person on his or her lunch hour having a *pique-nique sur l'herbe,* too.

Dinner (Dîner)

Dinner is served from 7 or 7:30 P.M. to 10 or 11 P.M., with the last order being taken about fifteen to thirty minutes before closing.

Dinner is a leisurely affair; the lunchtime frenzy is replaced by a quiet, more sedate mood. American tourists usually eat between 7 and 8 P.M., while 8:30 or 9 P.M. is still the most popular Parisian dinnertime. Few cafés serve dinner, so your best bet is a brasserie, bistro, or restaurant. If you want a light evening meal, try a wine bar.

Fast Food à la Française (Le Snack)

Not everyone wants to devote a large segment of the day to a long lunch. Sometimes we get hungry at odd hours or have children who plead starvation if they do not have something within minutes. This is where *le snack* comes in.

Fast food *à la française,* or *le snack,* means a crêpe from the corner stand, a sandwich consumed at the bar of a café, a quiche or small pizza to go (*pour emporter*) heated at the *boulangerie,* or something from the *charcuterie* or nearby *traiteur.* There are the café standards: a *croque-monsieur* or a *croque-madame.* A *monsieur* is a toasted ham sandwich with cheese on top, and a *madame* adds a fried egg over that. *Boulangeries* also sell delicious sandwiches, where the classic ham and cheese becomes a *jambon et gruyère* on a half of a baguette without mustard or mayo, or it is toasted between two slices of *pain de campagne.* Vegetarians can order a crudités sandwich, which includes lettuce, hard-boiled eggs, tomatoes, and sometimes mushrooms. *Charcuteries* and *traiteurs* specialize in prepared salads, pâtés, terrines, whole roasted chickens, a variety of cooked dishes, and usually one or two daily hot specials. All items are packed to go, and sometimes you can get a plastic fork or spoon. Most large grocery stores also have a *charcuterie* section where they sell individual slices of cold meat and portions of cheese. Add a fresh baguette, yogurt, a piece or two of fruit, and a cold drink or bottle of *vin ordinaire,* and you have a cheap and filling meal for little outlay of time and money. You can also assemble your feast from the stalls of one of the colorful street *marchés* or *rues commerçants* (see "Food Shopping," page 39). At these, the sky is the limit for tempting gourmet meals on the run.

So, How Do the French Stay So Slim?

The perennial question that is asked about the French is, with all the rich food they eat, how do they avoid being chronically over-weight? Most people add pounds just thinking about all the foie gras, pâtés, sausages, rich *cassoulets,* creamy sauces, *magret de canard,* calorie-laden desserts, bread with every meal, and flowing wine that constitute the average French diet. Most French would rather have a heart attack than spend their time jogging or sweating off calories in a gym, and yet, by American standards, their restaurant menus are an overload of fat, cholesterol, and other nutritionally incorrect no-nos waiting to be served *à table.*

After you have been in Paris for more than a few days, it is easy to see why the French are not all tipping the scales into the fat zone. First, they walk more: they climb endless stairs to reach fifth-floor walk-up apartments, almost never drive, and hike through long métro changes. Second, they eat slowly, savoring smaller portions of balanced meals, and they consume less processed food with fewer additives. Finally, they rarely eat in-between meals, and they drink more water and less sugar-laden soft drinks. Indeed, if you follow their example, you too may avoid having to reaquaint yourself with a stairmaster on your return home.

Types of Food

> Cooking is about sharing pleasure. Food is only half of what is on the plate. There is also love and truth.
>
> —*Yves Camdeborde, owner/chef of*
> *Le Comptoir*

Bourgeoise Cuisine

Nostalgia continues to be very "in," declare the culinary pundits in Paris. There is no doubt about it: *bourgeoise cuisine à la grand-mère* continues to enjoy tremendous popularity in Paris, ensuring that cholesterol remains alive and well throughout France. This reassuring, back-burner fare is the traditional cooking on which the French have subsisted for centuries. On thousands of menus, you can expect to see its mainstays: pâté, terrines, *oeufs dur mayonnaise,* duck, rabbit, *cassoulet, pot-au-feu, boeuf bourguignon, blanquette de veau, tarte Tatin,* and crème caramel.

Nouvelle Cuisine

Nouvelle cuisine was coined by food critics Henry Gault and Christian Millau in the 1970s and has probably been one of the most widely talked about developments in French cooking in the past fifty years. Nouvelle cuisine scorns the use of rich and heavy sauces. It emphasizes instead a lighter style of classic French cooking with a greater use of vegetables, an imaginative combination of ingredients, and a stylish and colorful presentation of very small servings . . . all undercooked just a little. Over time, most people have decided that many of the dishes are contrived and result in unsatisfying dining adventures. As a result, the popularity of nouvelle cuisine has waned and the concept has almost disappeared.

Regional Cuisine

Solid regional cooking from the provinces, once snubbed by food lovers as parochial and unsophisticated, has made a remarkable comeback as the French get closer to their roots and bring back old favorites. You can travel gastronomically throughout France and never leave the Paris city limits. The finest regional cooking is to be found in the capital, and it represents some of the best food you will ever eat.

The big brasseries feature German-influenced Alsatian specialties of steaming platters of sauerkraut, sausages, and bacon; German Riesling wines; and mugs of frosty beer. If a restaurant features food from the Savoy region near the Swiss-Alpine border, look for a bounty of cheeses, fondues, and *raclettes*. Food from the southwest Basque area is spicy, influenced by its Spanish neighbor. Superb seafood comes from Brittany in the north and from Nice in the south. Food from Provence is heavy with herbs, garlic, olive oil, and tomatoes. You can sample bouillabaisse, *pistou* (a pungent paste of fresh basil, cheese, garlic, and olive oil), *salade niçoise,* and ratatouille made from eggplant, zucchini, garlic, sweet peppers, and tomatoes. Veal and lamb are gifts from Normandy, and hearty *cassoulets* and huge helpings of *l'aligot*—a blend of puréed potatoes, garlic, and melted cheese—signify the robust cooking of the Auvergne. If the dish is *à la Lyonnaise,* it will be cooked with sautéed onions and wine, while the food from Burgundy reflects this wine-growing region in lusty stews flavored with mushrooms, bacon, and onions.

Bread

> **Bring bread to the table and your friends will bring their joy to share.**
>
> —*French proverb*

It has been said that France gives bakers the same social status as priests. Bread is definitely the staff of life in France, and it is served with every meal. To give you some idea of the French love affair with bread: ten billion baguettes are consumed annually. There is also a highly prized city-wide competition to select the Best Baguette of the year. The winner is crowned with the responsibility of providing the baguettes served at the Élysée Palace for the next year. Because a baguette contains no fat, it gets stale quickly. That is why no French person would ever consider buying bread in the morning to eat with dinner. As a result, statistics show that the average Parisian makes at least three trips to the *boulangerie* per day and is willing to go the extra mile for the perfect loaf. In the morning, a baguette is split, spread with sweet butter and perhaps jam, and eaten with, or dunked in, a big cup of *café crème*. For lunch and dinner, it is served freshly cut, without butter, and is nibbled on throughout the meal and used at the end to wipe up the last few drops of juice on the plate. A fresh basket of bread is also usually served with the cheese course. French bread etiquette holds that you do not put your bread on your plate. It stays on the table next to your plate until you have finished it and are ready for the next piece.

In January 1997, the French government took drastic steps to protect the baguette from mass production and cost-cutting methods, such as using frozen dough. Aimed at safeguarding baker-artisans, a new law is in force that now restricts the name "bakery" *(boulangerie)* only to those shops where the bakers bake their own bread on the premises. This has required an estimated five thousand shops selling bread from factory-frozen dough to remove their *boulangerie* signs.

When looking for a *boulangerie,* watch for those with long lines (see "*Boulangeries* and *Pâtisseries*" in the index, page 317, for a few good bets). You can be sure the neighborhood knows where to go for the best bread and patronizes those bakers who make their own dough and bake it on the premises. There are hundreds of types of bread available. The following list just hits the high spots.

baguette	a loaf legally weighing eight ounces, this is the long, crisp bread served most often in restaurants; it contains no fat
baguette *tradition*	caramelized, crispy crusted baguettes with sweet, buttery flavor and chewy inside
bâtard	similar to a baguette but with a softer crust
ficelle	a very thin, crusty baguette
pain complet	a whole-grain loaf that comes in various shapes and sizes
pain de campagne	a blend made with whole wheat, rye, and bran that is heavier in texture and comes in all sizes and shapes; it can also be a large white loaf dusted with flour
pain grillé	toasted bread
pain au noix	rye or wheat bread with nuts

pain au son	with bran
pain d'épices	gingerbread
pain de seigle	rye bread
pain Poilâne	Poilâne is the most famous bakery in Paris, with outlets in Japan and London and mail orders sent to the United States. It is famous for its dark sourdough blend baked in a wood-burning oven. Though *pain Poilâne* can be found elsewhere and is served in many restaurants, the main source is at the Poilâne bakery in the sixth arrondissement (see page 156 for details).

Cheese

The French will only be united under the threat of danger. No one can simply bring together a country that has over 265 kinds of cheese.
     —*Charles de Gaulle*

Actually, France produces more than four hundred varieties of cheese, and the average Frenchperson consumes between forty and fifty pounds of it per year. When dining in France, you will quickly recognize that cheese is a vital ingredient in any meal. Cheese is served after the main course, never before dinner with cocktails or a glass of wine as it is in the United States. When you are presented the cheese tray, don't be afraid to branch out and select a variety you have never tasted. If you are helping yourself, remember it is considered very bad manners to cut the point off any wedge of cheese. Cut as you would a piece of pie. What about the rind . . . is it edible? Yes, except for hard rinds like with Emmenthal. And don't worry if you see some mold around the edges. For the French, runny, moldy, smelly cheeses are the best. If a cheese does not mold a little, it is too pasteurized to be worth anything. "Cheese is one of the only things in life that you can judge by its cover. In general, the rougher a rind looks, the more interesting the cheese," says Steven Jenkins, author of *Cheese Primer*.

After you return home, you may wonder why the chèvre in your market does not compare to that in your favorite Parisian bistro. The answer is simple: exported cheese must be sterilized, which kills the bacteria that add flavor. When shopping for cheese, look for the sign *maître fromager affineur*, which means that the shop owner ages the cheese himself. *Fromage fermier* means the cheese is produced on the farm, and *fromage au lait cru* means raw milk cheese. The following list of cheese types should help you when the cheese tray appears after a meal, or when you are trying to decide which cheese to buy at the *marché*.

mild	*beaufort, beaumont, belle étoile, boursin, brie, cantal, comté, petit-suisse, port-salut, reblochon, saint-paulin, tomme*
sharp	*bleu de Bresse, brousse, camembert, livarot, maroilles, muenster, pont-l'évêque, Roquefort, vacherin*
goat's milk	*bûcheron, cabécou, chèvre, crottin de Chavignol, rocamadour, st-marcellin*
Swiss cheese	*emmental, gruyère*

Meat

The French cook their meat much less than Americans do. Witness the popularity of steak tartare, a reoccurring specialty in many of the best restaurants in Paris. Pink chicken is the norm, and *bleu* beef (blue, or blood raw to most Americans) is considered the height of good eating. *Saignant* (rare) is only slightly better done, but *à point* (medium rare) approaches the edible. *Bien cuit* (well done) may still be dripping blood, but it is at least hot and most of it will be cooked. Some meats simply do not taste good when they are well cooked, and the waiter will tell you, "It cannot be done." Trust him or her and order something else.

To help you answer the inevitable question, *Quelle cuisson?* ("How do you want that cooked?"), here is a list of responses:

cru	raw
bleu	almost raw
saignant	rare, still bleeding
rosé	pink
à point	medium rare
bien cuit	well done
très bien cuit	very well done

French beef tends to have less fat than most Americans are used to, and as a result, many beef cuts are tough by our standards. The cuts also have different names, so you won't find prime rib or T-bone steaks by name, but you will find the following:

bavette	skirt steak
chateaubriand	a tender filet
entrecôte	rib steak
pavé	thick cut of boneless beef
steack	catch-all term that can mean almost any cut, and seldom a tender one
steack hachis	chopped steak

In addition, Parisians eagerly await the arrival of the autumn game season each year, which coincides with their love affair of fungi, including *cèpes, morilles, bolets,* and the truffle. From September through November, wild game you can expect to see on menus include *perdrix* (partridge) and *lièvre* (wild hare), followed by *faisans* (pheasants) and *canard* (duck). Larger game, *sanglier* (wild boar), *cerf* (male deer), and *chevreuil* (venison) are available until February.

Pâtisseries

French pastries, like French women, are put together with precision.
—*Anonymous*

The Gallic passion for *pâtisserie* is a national obsession, arousing cravings unknown to most foreigners. Paris pastry lovers think nothing of traveling across the city in search of the perfect *éclair au café, charlotte au chocolat, forêt-noire* (a rich fudge cake with a cherry topping), or a *mille-feuille* (layers of thin, buttery, flaky pastry holding cream, custard, and/or fruit). Fine *pâtisserie* is a creation using the best ingredients, made fresh each day, and meant to be eaten immediately, if not sooner. There are *pâtisseries* all over Paris, all offering an Ali Baba's cave of tempting treats. Your waistline is the only barometer of how much you will consume and enjoy. In this book, I have included a few Parisian *pâtisseries* that I particularly like, but there are literally hundreds more. Those mentioned in this guide should at least get you started in the limitless world of Parisian pastries (see *"Boulangeries* and *Pâtisseries"* in the index, page 317).

Unusual Foods

There is nothing discreet about French food. Remnants that are discarded in the United States, or animals not normally eaten, are here transformed into gastronomical delicacies. You will encounter *rognons* (kidneys), *cervelles* (brains), *ris de veau* (veal sweetbreads), *mouton* (mutton), *lapin* (rabbit), *langue de boeuf* or *agneau* (beef or lamb tongue), and the head, ears, toes, lips, cheeks, and tails of many other animals. There are butchers selling only horse meat—you can recognize them by the golden horse head hanging over their shops. Depending on the season, you will also find *pintade* (guinea fowl), *sanglier* (wild boar), *chevreuil* (young deer), and *civet de lièvre* (wild hare stew). Blood is often used to thicken sauces, especially in *civet de lièvre*. Blood is also used to make sausage, as in the *boudin noir* (pork blood sausages). When ordering *andouillettes* (chitterling sausages, or the intestines of hogs), be sure they are rated "A.A.A.A.A.," which stands for Association Amicale des Authentiques Amateurs d'Andouillettes, or the Amiable Association of Amateurs of the Authentic Andouillette. This presumably voluntary organization makes sure members follow certain preparation guidelines, and the notification confirms that these are the Rolls-Royce of French chitterlings. All of these dishes can be delicious, and the French excel in their preparation. They represent dining experiences you must try—at least once.

Vegetarian

A *végétarien(ne)* in Paris need not starve. Gone are the days when one had to settle for boring meals or a plate of crudités and a cup of lukewarm tea at the corner café. While vegetarianism in France is not what it is in the United States, it is gaining ground in Paris. Those who eat some cheese and fish will have the easiest time, but there are also havens for those who eat no animal or dairy products. Most vegetarian restaurants serve a wide range of dishes that are guaranteed to please every dedicated veggie lover as well as carnivores who don't mind hitching a ride on the green bandwagon, if only for one or two meals. I have noted a number of my favorites in this book (see the index, page 319).

Very often, if you call ahead to better restaurants and ask if the chef can prepare something for a vegetarian, your request will be met with pleasure. This is the best way to handle the situation, rather than arriving and not giving the chef any advance notice. If the kitchen is busy, your dish may not be very inspired, or you may have to make do with a large order of the vegetable of the day and a side of rich potatoes.

Drinks

Apéritifs, Between-Meal Drinks, and *Digestifs*

The cocktail hour *(l'heure de l'apéritif)* in Paris usually lasts from around 6 to 8 P.M. The French prefer not to anesthetize their taste buds with American-style cocktails before a meal. If you usually order a dry martini or double scotch on the rocks before dinner, try instead one of the mildly alcoholic wine apéritifs such as a kir or kir royale. A kir is made from crème de cassis and chilled white wine. A kir royale substitutes champagne for the wine. The slightly bitter Campari and soda or a Pernod, an anise-flavored drink, are two other good choices.

If you are hot and thirsty in the afternoon, order a Vittel menthe: a shot of crème de menthe diluted with Vittel mineral water and served icy cold. It is one of the cheapest and most refreshing between-meal drinks. For a nonalcoholic beverage, a good choice is *l'orange pressé* (fresh orange juice) or *le citron pressé* (lemonade). Coca-Cola (Coka) and Orangina, a carbonated orange drink, are popular soft drinks, as are any of the mineral waters served with a twist of lemon or lime. An important tip for Coke lovers . . . don't order a Coke with your meal. The French consider this absolutely unacceptable.

France is not known for beer, but if you do want a beer, don't say so. There is a French product, *Byrrh,* that sounds the same but is a bitter quinine-based wine apéritif, and this is what you are likely to get if you order "a beer." If you want a draft beer, ask for *un demi* or *une bière à la pression*. They come in three sizes: *demi* (eight ounces), *sérieux* (sixteen ounces), and *formidable* (one quart). Remember, it is pronounced "be-air," not "beer." If you ask simply for *une bière,* you will be asked what kind because you will have ordered a bottle of beer. The best, and usually the cheapest, bottled beer in France is Kronenbourg.

After-dinner drinks *(digestifs)* are popular in Paris. The most common are cognac and various distilled fruit brandies: Calvados (apple), *kirsch* (cherry), *marc* (grape), and *quetsch* (plum). These are not intended to aid digestion, but because of their high alcoholic content (more than 30 percent), they can be tolerated after a full meal. Measures are generous, but they are generally not bargains.

Coffee

> **Good coffee should be black like the devil, hot like hell, and sweet like a kiss.**
>
> —*Hungarian proverb*

If you order *un café, s'il vous plaît* ("a coffee, please"), you will be served a small cup of very strong espresso with lumps or packets of sugar on the side. The French consider it barbaric to drink coffee with a meal. Coffee is drunk after a meal or by itself in a café, but never *with* the meal and, after dinner, certainly not with milk or cream. You may order an espresso with dessert, but you will receive an arched eyebrow from the waiter and be considered a rank tourist if you insist on it. Your after-dinner coffee is meant to arrive after dessert, not with it.

French coffee is wonderful. It comes in various bewildering forms, all of which are stronger and more flavorful than American coffee. All coffee is served by the cup, and there are no free refills. The following glossary of coffees should help you get what you want.

Café arrosé is an espresso with a shot of Calvados or *eau-de-vie*. If you order a *Calva* or an *eau-de-vie* without the espresso, you will be taking part in an old folk remedy known as *tuer le ver* (killing the worm).

Café express, or *café noir,* is espresso made by forcing hot steam through freshly ground beans. If you prefer it weaker, ask for *café allongé,* and you will be given a small pitcher of hot water to dilute it. If you want double the kick, ask for a *café grand.*

Café crème is espresso made with steamed milk, and *café au lait* is espresso with warmed milk. Neither of these is ordered after lunch or dinner. They are strictly breakfast or between-meal *boissons.*

Café filtre is filtered coffee that is the closest to American in taste, but it is often available only in more expensive restaurants and very seldom in a basic café.

Cafe serré is a concentrated espresso.

Café noisette is an espresso with a drop of foamy milk on top.

Déca or *café décaféiné* is decaffeinated espresso and bears no resemblance to the tasteless U.S. version.

Double and *grand* are terms used to request a double-size cup of any of the above; *petit* means small.

Tea

Tea is considered a breakfast or between-meal beverage, not a drink to have with a meal or immediately after it. Outside a fancy tearoom, you will usually be served the tea-bag variety, and the water will often be tepid. *Tisanes* or *infusions* are the terms used for herb teas. Every café serves them. They are very nice to order when you have overeaten or feel stressed. The most common infusions are *verveine* (verbena), *menthe* (mint), chamomile, and *tileul* (linden). Iced tea is not really popular.

Water

You could almost die of thirst before getting a simple glass of water in Paris, let alone a glass of ice water. You will not automatically be served water the minute you sit down. If you want water, you must ask for it. If you are a purist, order bottled water, which is very popular and available everywhere. You will, however, be just as well off and money ahead by ordering tap water (*une carafe d'eau* or *l'eau ordinaire*), which is one of the few free things you will get in Paris. Favorite bottled mineral waters are Evian and Vittel, which are noncarbonated (*plat* or *non-gazeuse*), and Badoit, Chateaudun, and Perrier, which are sparkling (*gazeuse*). Perrier is always a between-meal drink because the French consider it too gaseous to be drunk with meals. If you want ice cubes, ask for *glaçons,* but don't always expect to get them.

Wine

Ask any well-fed Frenchperson and he or she will tell you that a meal without wine is like a kiss without the squeeze. Wine (*vin*) is drunk at almost every meal, including before breakfast for some. Red is *rouge,* white is *blanc,* and rose is *rosé.* In a bar, you will get the cheapest glass if you ask for *un verre de rouge* or *un ballon de vin rouge* (a glass of red wine) or *un verre de blanc* or *un blanc sec* (a glass of white or dry white wine). The basic wine terms are *brut,* very dry; *sec,* dry; *demi-sec,* semisweet; *doux,* very sweet; and *champagne* is champagne. There are many grape varieties, and the endless complexities of that subject could fill a library's-worth of books. It is beyond the scope of *Great Eats Paris* to attempt a thorough discussion of French wines or to provide a formula for selecting the perfect wine for every meal. However, one change has made it easier: The old rule that red was drunk only with red meat and white with chicken or fish is out—order what you want, and no one will look twice.

If you are interested in saving money, order the house wine (*vin de la maison*) or a pitcher of table wine (*un pichet du vin ordinaire*) or a bottle from the patron's own cave *(cuvée du patron)*. Many restaurateurs seek out small producers of wines that work well with the house specialties. Any of these will be perfectly drinkable and usually quite reasonably priced. The wine *carte* can be a budget killer, as most bottled vintages tend to drive up the cost of the meal inordinately. Unless you are a true wine connoisseur, it seems foolish to spend twice as much on the wine as on the food. You can bet that the Frenchperson sitting next to you won't be doing it. If you do decide to branch out and yet find the wine list perplexing, don't be afraid to ask questions, state your budget, or take advice.

The following should take some of the confusion out of reading a French wine label.

AOC appelation d'origine contrôlée	highest quality, most expensive wine
cépage	grape variety
cru	superior
mis en bouteilles à la château	made at the wine-producing estate
mis en bouteilles par	bottled by
mousseux	sparkling
vin de pays	local wine, less quality control than AOC wines
vin de table	varying quality, usually acceptable
vin ordinaire	means the same as *vin de table,* usually acceptable

French Dining Manners

This is the latest trend. Waiters are becoming *nice!*
—An alarmed French friend in Paris

Crowding

When judging a restaurant, don't be put off by location, appearance, or decor. A better gauge is how crowded it is with local French, since as everyone knows, a full house is always a good sign. Crowded restaurants are an accepted fact of dining life in Paris, with the distance between tables often only one thin person wide, if that. You can't fight this phenomenon, and besides, being comfortably wedged in along a banquette leads to some mighty interesting benchmates and conversations, both shared and overheard.

Doggie Bags + Splitting an Order = Two No-Nos

The French have more dogs per capita than any other people on earth. Short of being given the vote, dogs have many rights in Paris, not the least of which is dining out with their owners. While you will seldom see anyone under eighteen in a restaurant, you will always see well-behaved dogs, especially in cafés, sitting on the seat next to their master or quietly lying at his or her feet. You would think this enormous dog population would create a demand for doggie bags, at least for the stay-at-home canines. Wrong. Half of France is on some kind of *régime* (diet), and leaving food on your plate is acceptable. Asking for a doggie bag, whether for Fido or yourself, is not.

Considered just as gauche and unacceptable as the doggie bag is asking to split dishes. Despite the number of courses in a typical French meal, portions are smaller than most Americans are used to, thus diners are expected to order accordingly and do the best they can.

Mind Your Manners and Dress for Success

Good manners don't show, bad ones always do.
—*Neva C. Abernethy*

Wear black, make it tight, accessorize . . . you'll look Parisian.
—*Sandra Busby*

Good manners are international, and *la politesse* is central to all transactions in France. The French are also more formal than we are. They don't call people by their first names, and they preface statements with *Pardon, Monsieur, S'il vous plaît, Madame,* or *Excusez-moi, Mademoiselle.* They will consider you to be rude if you do not do the same, or if you omit the words *monsieur, madame,* or *mademoiselle* when you speak to someone. If you want good service, a *Bonjour, Monsieur,* or *Merci, Mademoiselle,* along with lots of *s'il vous plaîts* and *merci beaucoups* thrown in, will go a long way toward making your dining experience better.

To get the waiter's attention, don't shout *Garçon!* Contrary to most Americans, the French consider all restaurant work to be a profession, not a filler-job while waiting for something better to come along. For best results, always refer to the waiter as *monsieur* and the waitress as *mademoiselle,* regardless of age or marital status.

It is considered very rude to eat your *frites* (french fries), chicken, or any other food, for that matter, with your fingers. It is not uncommon to see diners peeling a pear or other piece of fruit with a knife and fork, and eating it with a fork.

The French can spot Americans in any dining establishment without looking: they are the ones with the loud, booming voices that seem to carry out into the street. If you want to blend in and not look like a green tourist, keep your voice down.

Dressing well is part of a Frenchperson's makeup, especially in Paris. While men do not always need to wear a coat and tie and women are not always required to dress to the nines, a little conservative good judgment is in order. The French have limited tolerance for the concept of sacrificing fashion for comfort. This is especially true when it comes to footwear. But while Parisian women can squeeze their feet into dragon-toed, four-inch-high heels, female visitors are not expected to negotiate the tourist trails in such shoes. However, white athletic shoes are definitely *out* for all adults . . . both men and women. Yes, wear a good pair of walking shoes, but be sure they are a dark color. In addition, short shorts, halter or tank tops, T-shirts with insignias, and baseball caps in restaurants are frowned on.

French etiquette demands that both hands be kept above the table while eating, not in the lap. And, finally, if you are full, don't look up "full" in your French dictionary and say, *Je suis plein*. This is a phrase used for cows, meaning they are pregnant. If you do not want anymore to eat, say, *Je n'ai plus faim* ("I am not hungry any longer").

Gourmet Lunching for Less

All savvy great eaters know that the best meal deals are dished out for lunch. Listed below are noted Parisian restaurants where the extraordinary experience is not only about the glorious food created by these talented *chefs de cuisine,* but in the overall experience, which is guaranteed to be a dining memory that lasts a lifetime. These luxurious lunches for less are generally not offered on weekends or holidays, your selections will be limited, and wine will be extra. Note, too, that these specials don't come cheap; each of these lunches qualifies as a Big Splurge. Still, you will be dining in magnificent style for at least half the price you would expect to pay for the same food preparations at dinner. All prices quoted here are per person, without wine, and are subject to change without notice. It is a good idea to verify the price when calling for reservations, and to reconfirm your reservation the day before or risk losing it. These restaurants all take MasterCard and Visa, and they are noted on the arrondissement maps in this guide.

Jamin ($)
32, rue de Longchamp, 16th
MÉTRO Trocadéro **TEL** 01-45-53-00-07
LUNCH MENU 50€; average dinner price: 110€

La Tour d'Argent ($)
15-17, quai de la Tournelle, 5th
MÉTRO Cardinal Lemoine **TEL** 01-43-54-23-31
LUNCH MENU 70€; average dinner price: 180€

Laurent ($)
41, avenue Gabriel, 8th
MÉTRO Champs-Elysées-Clemenceau **TEL** 01-42-25-00-39
LUNCH MENU 70€; average dinner price 150€

Le Bristol ($)
Hôtel Bristol, 112, rue du Faubourg-St-Honoré, 8th
MÉTRO Miromesnil **TEL** 01-53-43-43-00
LUNCH MENU 70€; average dinner price: 100€

Le Carrè des Feuillants ($) 14, rue Castiglione, 1st
MÉTRO Tuilleries **TEL** 01-42-86-82-82
LUNCH MENU 65€; average dinner price: 130€

Ledoyen ($)
1, avenue Dutuit, 8th
MÉTRO Champs Élysées-Clémenceau **TEL** 01-53-05-10-01
LUNCH MENU 73€; average dinner price: 180€

Le Grand Vefour ($)
17, rue de Beaujolais, in the Palais Royal, 1st
MÉTRO Palais Royal **TEL** 01-42-96-56-27
LUNCH MENU 78€; average dinner price 200–250€

Le Jules Verne ($)
Second level of the Eiffel Tower, 7th
MÉTRO Champ-de-Mars Tour Eiffel **TEL** 01-45-55-61-44
LUNCH MENU 58€; average dinner price:160€

Le Meurice ($)
Hôtel Meurice, 228, rue de Rivoli, 1st
MÉTRO Tuileries **TEL** 01-44-58-10-10
LUNCH MENU 68€; average dinner price 110€

Le Prè Catelan ($)
Route de Suresnes, Bois de Boulogne, 16th
MÉTRO Porte Maillot **TEL** 01-44-14-41-14
LUNCH MENU 60€, average dinner price 150€

Les Ambassadeurs ($)
Hôtel de Crillon, 10, place de la Concorde, 8th
MÉTRO Concorde **TEL** 01-44-71-16-16
LUNCH MENU 70€; average dinner price: 185€

L'Espadon ($)
Hôtel Ritz; 15, place Vendôme, 1st
MÉTRO Concorde **TEL** 01-43-16-30-80
LUNCH MENU 70€; average dinner price: 180€

Le V ($)
Hôtel Four Seasons George V, 31, avenue George V, 8th
MÉTRO George V **TEL** 01-49-52-70-00
LUNCH MENU 75€; average dinner price 250€

Michael Rostang ($)
20, rue Rennequin, 17th
MÉTRO Ternes, Péreire **TEL** 01-47-63-40-77
LUNCH MENU 70€; average dinner price: 120€

Food Shopping

**Paris in the early morning has a cheerful, bustling aspect—
a promise of things to come.**

—*Nancy Mitford,* The Pursuit of Love

Markets *(Marchés)*

The French shop for the meal, not for the week, and they measure the freshness of their food in minutes, not days. If you ask the fruit merchant if the pears are ripe, he or she will ask you when that day you will eat them, and often at what time, and then select just the right ones. It's customary at the smaller corner markets for the clerk to serve you; at larger *marchés,* they may or may not pick your fruits and vegetables for you, and if not, they will hand you a metal pan or basket to put your selections in. Even though indoor *supermarchés* are all over Paris, every neighborhood *quartier* has its own *rue commerçante* (shopping street) or *marché volant* (roving market), each with its own special character and offering an inspiring selection of food. These *marchés* offer an endless source of interest and insight into the hearts and minds of ordinary Parisians, and visiting one of them is a cultural experience you should not miss. Go in the morning and gather the ingredients for a picnic lunch or supper; admire the rows of produce arranged with the same care and precision as fine jewelry displays. In seeking out the best stalls, look for the sign *producteur,* which means these merchants are selling food they grow or produce themselves. Take your camera and a string bag, don't mind the crowds, watch your wallet, and enjoy these lively alternatives to galleries, monuments, churches, and other must-see stops on every visitor's list. When dining out, order the food you have seen in the market. You can bet the chef was there long before you were to select perfectly ripe strawberries, fat spears of asparagus, the freshest fish, and the ripest cheeses, all for that day's menu. (For a list of food shops, see the index, page 318.)

Roving Markets *(Marchés Volantes)*

Roving markets move from one neighborhood to another on specific days. They are open only on the days listed, and usually only from 8 A.M. to 1 P.M. (unless otherwise noted).

ST-HONORÉ, 1st, place du Marché St-Honore; Métro: Tuileries; Wed 3–7:30 P.M. and Sat morning. A classy *marché* in keeping with the neighborhood.

MONTMARTRE/ST-EUSTACHE, 1st, rue Montmartre, south of rue Etienne Marcel; Métro: Les Halles, Etienne-Marcel; Thur 3–7:30 P.M. and Sun morning. Large stand selling organic fruit and veggies, others hawking flowers, wines from small producers, chèvre cheese, roast chickens; various nonfood stands seem to show up on whim.

PLACE BAUDOYER, 4th, place Baudoyer, off rue de Rivoli; Métro: Hôtel de Ville; Wed 3–8 P.M. and Sat morning. Small, centrally located. Check out the paella being made on the spot.

CARMES, 5th, place Maubert; Métro: Maubert-Mutualité; Tues, Thur, and Sat. A small market with above-average food stalls. Popular with tourists who come for the Provençal table linens and oriental carpets.

MONGE, 5th, place Monge; Métro: Place Monge; Wed, Fri, and Sun. Small and easy to peruse, and then go back and buy.

PORT-ROYAL, 5th, in front of l'hôpital du val de Grâce at rue St-Jacques; Métro: Port-Royal; Tues, Thur, and Sat. Big, loud, fun.

RASPAIL, 6th, boulevard Raspail between rue de Cherche-Midi and rue de Rennes; Métro: Rennes or Sèvres-Babylone; Tues and Fri. On Sunday this is a *marché biologique* (organic market; see "Organic Markets" below).

SAXE-BRETEUIL, 7th, avenue de Saxe from avenue de Ségur to place de Breteuil; Métro: Ségur; Thur and Sat. This is one of the most beautiful markets, where you can see the Eiffel Tower in the distance between the rows of food and flower stalls.

BASTILLE, 11th, boulevard Richard-Lenoir at rue Amelot; Métro: Bastille or Bréquet Sabin; Thur and Sun. Huge, very popular, and the prices reflect the volume of sales.

BOULEVARD DE BELLEVILLE, 11th/20th; Métro: Belleville, Couronnes; Tues and Fri. Low prices, ethnic foods.

COURS DE VINCENNES, 12th; Métro: Nation; Wed and Sat. Blue-collar area.

BOULEVARD DE GRENELLE, 15th, between rue Lourmel and rue du Commerce; Métro: Dupleix or La Motte-Picquet-Grenelle; Wed and Sun. Another very popular market under the métro tracks along boulevard de Grenelle and close to the Eiffel Tower.

COURS DE LA REINE–MARCHÉ PRÉSIDENT WILSON, 16th, between rue Debrousse and Place Iéna; Métro: Alma-Marceau or Iéna; Wed and Sat. Very upscale, and so are the shoppers.

Organic Markets *(Marchés Bio or Biologique)*

RASPAIL, 6th, boulevard Raspail between rue de Cherche-Midi and rue de Rennes; Métro: Rennes or Sèvres-Babylone; Sun 8:30 A.M.– 1 P.M. In addition to organic food and drink, there are stalls selling lotions, potions and creams, pure woven cotton shirts, and a guy selling muffins and brownies from the oven in the back of his truck.

BATIGNOLLES, 17th, boulevard de Batignolles between rue de Rome and place de Clichy; Métro: Place de Clichy; Sat 9 A.M.–1:30 P.M. Not as big as the Marché Bio Raspail, but still worth the trip for those dedicated to organic products.

Shopping Streets (*Rue Commerçants*)

These permanent shopping streets are usually open from 8:30 or 9 A.M. to 1 P.M. and from 4 to 7 P.M. Tuesday through Saturday. Sunday they are open only in the morning. During holidays and in July and August, not all merchants are open.

RUE MONTORGUEIL, 2nd; Métro: Sentier or Étienne Marcel. One of the most authentic.

RUE DE BRETAGNE, 3rd; Métro: St-Sébastein Froissart. Trendy area.

RUE MOUFFETARD, 5th; Métro: Monge. Higher prices, very colorful and widely photographed.

RUE CLER, 7th; Métro: École-Militaire. Losing some of its panache.

RUE DES MARTYRES, 9th; Métro: Notre Dame-de-Lorette. Uphill on the way to Montmartre, and like the neighborhood, it's improving.

PLACE D'ALIGRÉ, 12th, place d'Aligré; Métro: Ledru-Rollin; Tues through Sun, mornings only. An ethnic market like no other in central Paris; it's best on Sunday.

RUE DAGUERRE, 14th; Métro: Denfert-Rochereau. The market begins at the southern end of the street near the Monoprix.

RUE DU COMMERCE, 15th; Métro: Commerce. Loads of shops that reflect the taste and budget of the bourgeoise neighborhood.

RUE DE L'ANNONCIATION, 16th; Métro: La Muette. The market begins at place de Passy and rue de l'Annonciation and reflects the blue-blood neighborhood.

RUE DE LEVIS, 17th; Métro: Villiers. The market begins at boulevard des Batignolles and is one of the best.

RUE PONCELET, 17th; Métro: Ternes. Another great, colorful market street with wealthy shoppers.

RUE LEPIC, 18th; Métro: Abbesses. I have never thought much of the quality here.

Supermarkets (*Supermarchés*)

In Paris you won't find huge supermarket chains offering double coupons and selling everything from apples and oranges to furniture and clothing. Parisian food shopping requires a different line of attack. Paris department stores are home to some of the most magnificently stocked supermarkets you will ever see. Fauchon, on place de la Madeleine (see page 186), once was the standard-bearer for gourmet grocery shopping. After being sold to an Asian conglomerate, it is sadly not what it was. Now real foodies go across the place de la Madeleine to Hediard (see page 188), to Lafayette Gourmet in Galeries Lafayette (see page 203), or La Grande Épicerie de Paris at Bon Marché (see page 170), three of the most luxurious gourmet hunting grounds. Most Monoprix stores have a basement grocery selling everything from bread and cheese to wine, beer, and frozen products. One of the best Monoprix locations is in the sixth arrondissement on rue de Rennes

(Métro: St-Germain-des-Prés). Grocery chains such as Shopi, Codec, Marché U, and le Marché Franprix sell all the canned, bottled, and packaged basics. Then there are the little stores, open every day and until late at night, selling wilted veggies and bruised fruit in front, but they are useful if you only need a bottle of mineral water or a box of tissues when everything else is closed.

Classes

PROMENADES GOURMANDES
187, rue du Temple, 75003
Métro: Temple, Arts et Mètiers

> **Not only did I learn a lot about cooking, but I had the opportunity to meet a wonderful person!**
> —*George Brooks, attorney-at-law*

It doesn't matter who you are—everyone from gourmet chefs to fledging novices will learn something from the dynamic Parisian chef Paule Caillat, whose love of cooking and culinary heritage transform everything she touches. Paule, who was born and raised in Paris and college-educated in the States, gives private and group cooking lessons for lunch or dinner, and I can assure you they are a quantum leap from the ordinary, stilted classes I have often attended. Menus are selected according to the season, student preferences, and a careful eye for product availability in your home country. Cooking with Paule means getting hands-on, from shopping at the market right through enjoying what you have prepared. On the trip to the market, you will learn how to recognize the best ingredients, discern the different types of bread and cheese, distinguish a French apricot from one imported from Israel and know which one to buy, select the perfect meats and fish, and avoid anything that is not absolutely fresh. Through her knowledge of food, you will also be able to place the products you buy into their historical and geographical context in France. After lunch (if you have signed up for a full-day session), Paule will take you on a *Promenade Gourmande* (gourmet walking tour) to visit famous bakeries, an exclusive wine store, landmark kitchen equipment emporiums, saffron producers, and much more. If you are not a serious chef but appreciate gourmet foods, join one of her three-hour gourmet walking tours in Paris, which are as much fun as they are interesting and informative.

Cooking lessons and gourmet tours in Paris are not the half of Paule and her enthusiasm about food. She can organize special events such as birthdays, anniversaries, or other celebrations. In addition, she leads small groups on excursions to areas in France that are specifically known for their exceptional food products. The trips include train travel, all meals and accommodations, and visits to points of interest. Three month advance reservation is required.

Paule is a delightful, dynamic, knowledgeable woman. If you love food and cooking, please treat yourself to one of her cooking lessons, gourmet walks, or trips. You won't regret it for a minute. As one very happy participant said, "This was the best day I have ever spent in Paris, and the highlight of my entire trip!" I agree, and so does everyone lucky enough to spend time with Paule.

NOTE: Paule takes off most of August, but during the rest of the year, to avoid disappointment, please make your reservation with her as far in advance as possible. The lunch classes are held from 9 A.M. to 3 P.M.; dinner classes from 4 to 10:30 P.M.

TEL 01-48-04-56-84, (cell) 06-16-72-79-00 **EMAIL** info@promenades gourmandes.com **INTERNET** www.promenadesgourmandes.com

RATES Half-day lunch or dinner class: 1 person 250€; 2–3 people 235€ per person; full day: 350€ per person. Three-hour Gourmet Walking Tour (without cooking class), 100€ per person. Discounts for groups of 4–6. Check her Website for special rates and new programs and classes.
CREDIT CARDS V

Ô CHATEAU
100, rue de la Folie Méricourt, 75011
Métro: République, Oberkampf

For a friendly, informal introduction to wines, Olivier Magny's Ô Chateau is a fun way to spend an hour or two picking up tips on basic wine appreciation. The classes are conducted by Olivier in his fourth-floor walk-up loft apartment near République. Guests sit around tables and taste as Olivier explains wine appreciation techniques, French wine regions, white versus red, and more. There are several tasting options: Wine Two Three is a one-hour introductory tasting of three wines; Cheese & Wine Lunch includes one champagne and three wines, cheese and *charcuterie* platters, French bread and fresh fruit; and the Grand 7 is a two-hour session with seven different wines.

TEL 01-44-73-97-80, (cell) 06-24-31-20-18, toll-free in U.S. 1-847-305-1615, toll-free in France 0 800 801 148 **EMAIL** olivier@o-chateau.com **INTERNET** www.o-chateau.com

RATES Wine Two Three (conducted daily), 20€ per person; Cheese & Wine Lunch (Mon, Wed, Fri, Sat), 65€ per person; Grand 7 (daily), 50€ per person **CREDIT CARDS** V

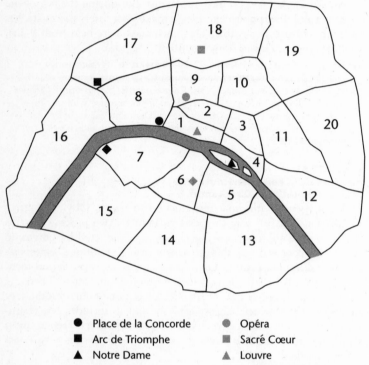

● Place de la Concorde	● Opéra
■ Arc de Triomphe	■ Sacré Cœur
▲ Notre Dame	▲ Louvre
◆ Tour Eiffel	◆ Jardin du Luxembourg

RESTAURANTS IN PARIS BY ARRONDISSEMENT

Paris is divided into twenty districts, or zones, known as *arrondissements*. Knowing which arrondissement is which is the key to understanding Paris and quickly finding your way around. Starting with the first arrondissement, which is the district around the Louvre, the numbering goes clockwise in a snail-like spiral. The postal code, or zip code, for Paris is 750, followed by the number of the arrondissement. Thus, 75001 refers to the first arrondissement, 75004 to the fourth, and 75016 means the location is in the expensive sixteenth. If you are going to be in Paris for more than one or two days, I highly recommend you purchase a copy of the *Plan de Paris par Arrondissement* (see "Maps," page 13).

An arrondissement has its own special character and feeling, so that Paris, when you get to know it, is a city of twenty neighborhood villages. Each has its own mayor, central post office, police station, and town hall, where marriages can be performed and deaths recorded. It takes a few afternoons of what the French call *flânerie*—unhurried, aimless wandering—to truly appreciate some of the more intriguing neighborhoods. When you go out, prepare to be sidetracked, diverted, and happily lost discovering all sorts of wonderful places and things.

In addition, each arrondissement has a name as well as a number (and in some cases, two names). For instance, the first arrondissement is commonly referred to as Louvre, and the second as Bourse. You may hear Parisians say, "I live in the eleventh, République," or "I live in the sixth, Luxembourg." The following is a list of all the names.

First	Louvre
Second	Bourse
Third	Marais
Fourth	Hôtel de Ville
Fifth	Panthéon
Sixth	Luxembourg
Seventh	Invalides
Eighth	Elysée
Ninth	Opéra
Tenth	Magenta
Eleventh	République (northern section), Voltaire (southern section)
Twelfth	Bercy (eastern section), Reuilly (western section)

Thirteenth	Bibliothèque Nationale de France (eastern section), Italie (western section)
Fourteenth	Observatoire (eastern section), Montparnasse (western section)
Fifteenth	Vaugirard (eastern section), Grenelle (western section)
Sixteenth	Passy
Seventeenth	Ternes (western section), Batignoles (eastern section)
Eighteenth	Butte Montmartre (western section), La Chapelle (eastern section)
Nineteenth	La Villette (northern section), Buttes Chaumont (southern section)
Twentieth	Ménilmontant (northern section), Père Lachaise (southern section)

First Arrondissement

The Île de la Cité is the historic heart of Paris. It was on this island in the middle of the Seine that a Celtic tribe of fishermen called the Parisii settled in the third century B.C. and where the Gallo-Romans later built the city they called Lutetia in the first century A.D.

The Jardin des Tuileries lies in the very center of Paris, extending from the Louvre to Place de la Concorde as part of the Grand Axis of Paris. The gardens were first developed in 1564 but were transformed in 1666 by Le Nôtre.

The history of Les Halles parallels the growth of Paris itself. For eight hundred years Les Halles was the central wholesale food market in Paris. Nicknamed "the belly of Paris," it was an early-morning place of meat markets, fishmongers, fruit and vegetable sellers, and cheese merchants. In 1969, the market was moved to Rungis on the outskirts of Paris, and in its place was built the Forum des Halles, a tremendous, multilevel indoor shopping complex housing shops and the biggest métro station in the world. It is claimed you can walk here for hours and never see daylight. The area around the Forum des Halles now teems night and day with an inexhaustible supply of people of every size, shape, and style, providing the observer with an eye-opening look at the fashion crazes and hip-hop teens of the moment. While here, you can watch a fire-eating act, a sword swallower, and an ascetic lying on a bed of nails, listen to all sorts of street-corner music, buy far-out fashions, get your hair colored, braided or spiked, get a tattoo, have body studs put in, see an X-rated film, fill up on fast food, or sit in a café and almost literally watch the world parade by.

RIGHT BANK

Comédie Française
Conciergerie (where Marie Antoinette was beheaded)
Île de la Cité
Jardin des Tuileries
Les Halles
Louvre
Palais de Justice
Palais Royal
place Vendôme
Pont Neuf (the oldest bridge in Paris)
Quai de la Mégisserie (bird and animal market)
Ste-Chapelle

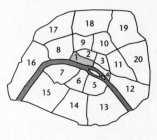

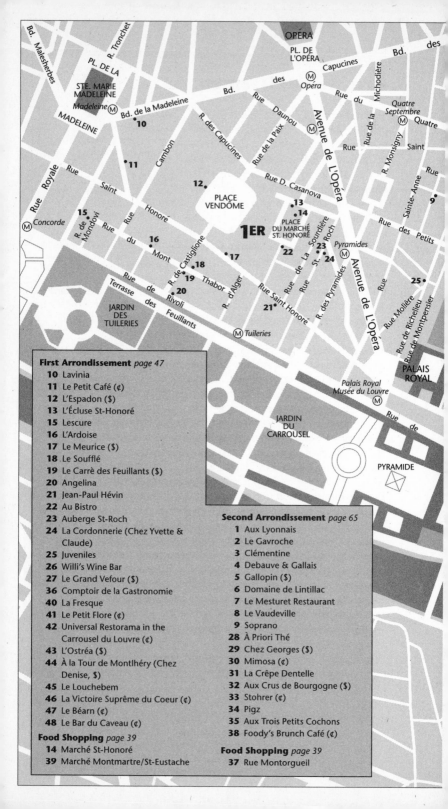

FIRST ARRONDISSEMENT RESTAURANTS

($) indicates a Big Splurge; (¢) indicates a Cheap Eat

À LA TOUR DE MONTLHÉRY (CHEZ DENISE; $, 44)
5, rue des Prouvaires
Métro: Châtelet, Les Halles, Louvre-Rivoli

"It's not good, it's wonderful!" That is what the man seated one elbow away told me the first time I ate here. He knew what he was talking about: he had eaten here every day for years, as have scores of other robust French. If you are looking for a colorful and authentic Les Halles bistro that has not changed in a hundred years, À la Tour de Montlhéry, or Chez Denise to the regulars, is a must if you are willing to spend a little more. The classic spot is busy almost twenty-four hours a day with a colorful mixture of artists, businesspeople, and writers, all served by sure-footed career waiters who keep running, flirting, and smiling despite the crunch. The small tables are always jam-packed, and the din of happy diners creating a blue haze of Gauloise smoke is typically French.

Eternity stands behind the chalkboard menu, and no dieters need apply. Instead be prepared for hearty food, served in portions that some might consider lethal. To start, order the snails in garlic butter or the *salade frisée* with crisp homemade croutons. Follow this with *tripes au Calvados, haricot de mouton* (mutton and beans), tender rabbit in grainy mustard sauce, or the wonderful stuffed cabbage. Complement your meal with a bottle of Brouilly, the house wine. The desserts can be ignored if you insist, but I always try to save room to sample the generous cheese tray, the *île flotante* (meringue floating on liquid custard, drizzled with caramel), or a slice of the fresh fruit tart.

TEL 01-42-36-21-82
OPEN Mon–Fri: lunch noon–4 P.M., dinner 7:30 P.M.–6 A.M., continuous service
CLOSED Sat (after 6 A.M.)–Sun; holidays, July 14–Aug 15
À LA CARTE 45–55€, BC **PRIX FIXE** None **CREDIT CARDS** MC, V
RESERVATIONS Essential **ENGLISH SPOKEN** Yes

ANGELINA (20)
226, rue de Rivoli
Métro: Tuileries

Chocoholics agree: The best cup of hot chocolate in Paris is found at Angelina, a Belle Epoque tearoom founded a century ago by the Austrian Antoine Rumplemayer and named for his daughter-in-law. Guests are seated at tiny round tables and served by waitresses with serious attitudes. Never mind, just be glad you are not in their too tight shoes. History and/or fashion buffs will be interested to know that later in her life Coco Chanel came daily and always sat at table number 11, which was the third from the back in the main room. No matter who you are, the order of the day is always the same: a pot of the *Chocolate African* made with 75 percent pure cocoa. As an accompaniment, ask for a *mont-blanc,* a delicious soft meringue served with chestnut cream and whipped cream. Of course, these two divinely decadent treats will send calorie counts soaring, but I guarantee it is absolutely worth the splurge. If you can manage lunch as well, they do a nice job with salads, quiches, club sandwiches, and hot dishes. Their hot chocolate mix is for sale in the boutique, as are complete chocolate serving sets.

TEL 01-42-60-82-00 **INTERNET** www.angelina.fr
OPEN Daily: Mon–Fri 8 A.M.–7 P.M., Sat–Sun 9 A.M.–7 P.M., continuous service
CLOSED Tues in July & Aug, NAC
À LA CARTE 15–30€ **PRIX FIXE** None **CREDIT CARDS** AE, MC, V
RESERVATIONS Preferred **ENGLISH SPOKEN** Enough to order

AUBERGE ST-ROCH (23)
33, rue St-Roch
Métro: Tuileries

Destination dining? No. A casual neighborhood favorite for lunch and dinner? Absolutely. It is the sort of regular place the nearby locals rely on when no one wants to cook. The rustic stone-walled interior is filled with a collection of black-and-white vintage photos of French film stars. Seating is at the usual bare bistro tables and hard chairs, and service is by jean-clad waiters. The basic food, which does not try to put on airs, is predictable, nourishing, and good. Starters might include a crayfish salad or the time-honored *chèvre chaud* on a bed of mixed greens. The duck with honey and lemon or the medallions of veal with mushrooms are reliable mains. Dessert can safely be skipped, especially the *fondant au chocolate* and the prunes marinated in armagnac. Add a *pichet* of the house red or white, and you will have had a modest Great Eat in Paris that won't blow the budget.

TEL 01-42-61-40-83 **INTERNET** www.auberge-saint-roch.com
OPEN Mon–Fri: lunch noon–2:30 P.M., dinner 8–11 P.M. **CLOSED** Sat–Sun, holidays, Aug, 1 week at Christmas
À LA CARTE None **PRIX FIXE** Lunch: 17€, 2 courses, 24€, 3 courses; dinner: 21€, 2 courses, 28€, 3 courses; all BNC **CREDIT CARDS** MC, V
RESERVATIONS Preferred **ENGLISH SPOKEN** Yes

AU BISTRO (22)
8, rue du Marché Saint-Honoré, corner of rue Saint-Hyacinthe
Métro: Tuileries

Book ahead . . . because you aren't the only one eager to have lunch in this haven of Paris nostalgia in the center of the spiffy Marché Saint-Honoré neighborhood. It is run by two formidable *mesdames* who came with the building. One works the bar and serves the seven or so diners perched on stools; the other hustles the dozen tables squeezed into this corner location. As the meal service wears on, the two "girls" become a bit more friendly, perhaps due to the "nips" taken with increasing frequency. Regulars know to forget the printed menu and to order either from the blackboard suggestions or the dish of the day: Monday, *hachis parmentier*; Tuesday, *blanquette de veau*; Wednesday, *choucroute*; Thursday, *pot-au-feu*; and Friday, *andouillette*. If these don't appeal, there is always an omelette or steak tartare. Desserts are all *faites maison* (made here) and usually include *tarte Tatin*, *mousse au chocolate* or crème caramel. Wines? Order a *pichet* of whatever the "girls" are drinking.

TEL 01-42-61-02-45
OPEN Mon–Sat: lunch 12:30–3:30 P.M.; bar 8 A.M.–8:30 P.M. **CLOSED** Sun; holidays, Aug (dates vary, call to check)
À LA CARTE 20–24€, BNC **PRIX FIXE** None **CREDIT CARDS** V
RESERVATIONS Suggested **ENGLISH SPOKEN** Very limited

COMPTOIR DE LA GASTRONOMIE (36)
34, rue Montmartre
Métro: Étienne-Marcel

Whether you are here to buy takeout from the Épicerie Fine or to sit down in the adjoining restaurant, you are in for a Great Eat in Paris. The only requirement is that you must love foie gras, *confit de canard* (preserved duck), terrines, *charcuterie,* Iberian ham, and smoked salmon.

When you walk into this wonderful 1894 Les Halles landmark building, you will be surrounded by hanging hams and walls lined with wines, champagnes, spirits, and their famous canned products; a refrigerated case in the window displays more of the house specialties. Next to this is the restaurant, where you can indulge anytime in *foie gras de canard* (duck liver) with onion chutney and sautéed potatoes or poached duck foie gras served with an herb salad and house chutney. If there are two of you and you want a light meal to share, order a platter of *charcuterie* and another with four cheeses, both garnished with green salad. Otherwise there are four smoked salmon plates, three beautiful main course salads featuring foie gras, raw ham, smoked quail, duck, or grilled chicken. If none of this appeals, there is always the toasted club sandwich piled high with grilled bacon, chicken, fresh tomatoes, and a side of cole slaw. At lunch there is also a two- or three-course menu, which might offer such mouthwatering temptations as the *salade gourmande* (with duck liver and smoked quail and duck), slow-cooked lamb with herb risotto, and duck with *aubergine* (eggplant) confit. For dessert, there is an irresistible lightly cooked chocolate cake with a cocoa custard sauce. An advantage for many is that meal service is continuous all day.

TEL 01-42-33-31-32 **INTERNET** www.comptoir-gastronomie.com
OPEN Mon–Sat: Épicerie Fine 6 A.M.–11 P.M.; restaurant noon–11 P.M., continuous service **CLOSED** Sun; holidays, NAC
À LA CARTE 15–25€ **PRIX FIXE** Lunch only: 17.50€, 2 courses, 21€, 3 courses, both BNC **CREDIT CARDS** AE, MC, V
RESERVATIONS Not necessary, but preferred **ENGLISH SPOKEN** Yes

JEAN-PAUL HÉVIN (21)
231, rue Saint-Honoré
Métro: Tuileries

If chocolate is your passion, a visit to Jean-Paul Hévin's chocolate boutique and tearoom is required anytime you are in Paris. The shop window seduces the chocolate lover with a precise, almost museum-like display of chocolates and chocolate fantasies. Up the steep steps is the tearoom done in chocolate brown (of course!) with white cotton coverlets on the chairs. Around the walls are photos of his famous chocolates. The menu is a delight in itself, with every illegally rich dessert pictured in its perfect entirety. Oh, decisions, decisions. Frankly, I think it is best to come with two or three friends, each order separately, and then share. Yes, you can have salmon blinis, chicken curry, or a veggie tarte, but what for? Why waste those calories and fill up on something nutritionally correct? Save everything for one of the forty types of chocolate or for a slice of cake or a pastry dessert, a pot of steaming aromatic tea, and a good chat with friends. If you can't wait until you arrive in Paris for your Hévin chocolates, order online.

NOTE: There are two other boutique locations in Paris in the sixth and seventh arrondissements, but they do not have tearooms (see pages 140 and 168). In Japan you can visit his chocolate boutiques in Tokyo, Hiroshima, Kokura, and Hakata.

TEL 01-55-35-35-96 **INTERNET** www.jphevin.com
OPEN Mon–Sat: chocolate boutique 10 A.M.–7:30 P.M.; tearoom for lunch
noon–3 P.M., for tea 3–7 P.M. **CLOSED** Sun; holidays, Aug
À LA CARTE Lunch 10–20€; pastries from 4€ **PRIX FIXE** None
   CREDIT CARDS AE, DC, MC, V
RESERVATIONS Preferred for lunch **ENGLISH SPOKEN** Yes

JUVENILES (25)
47, rue de Richelieu
Métro: Pyramides, Palais-Royal

Juveniles is a smart address to remember if you want a light meal at any time of the afternoon or evening, accompanied by a glass or two of a little-known but superb Spanish, French, or Australian wine. It is also a good place for those who enjoy malt whiskey or sour mash straight bourbon.

Tim Johnston opened Juveniles almost twenty years ago. The restaurant was an instant hit: it was voted one of the best places to drink wine in Paris and is especially popular with readers of *Great Eats Paris*. In addition to wines and spirits, sold by the glass, bottle, or case, Juveniles excels in serving tapas—small plates of food that can be ordered individually or in multiples. Your meal might include a warm basil-spiked ratatouille, an eggplant tapenade, or a potato gratin followed by marinated quail served on a bed of greens, a simply grilled piece of fresh seasonal fish, and the famous Donald's chocolate cake for dessert. Cheese lovers will revel in a chunk of English cheddar or Stilton blue cheese accompanied by a glass of East India sherry.

While you are here, be sure to notice the children's drawings hanging prominently. They are all by Tim's daughters.

TEL 01-42-97-46-49
OPEN Mon–Sat: noon–11 P.M., continuous service **CLOSED** Sun; NAC
À LA CARTE 25–30€, BNC **PRIX FIXE** Lunch: 14.50€, *plat du jour,* wine &
   coffee; dinner: 17€, 2 courses, 23€, 3 courses, both BNC
   CREDIT CARDS AE, MC, V
RESERVATIONS Suggested for Fri & Sat **ENGLISH SPOKEN** Yes

LA CORDONNERIE (CHEZ YVETTE & CLAUDE, 24)
20, rue St-Roch
Métro: Pyramides

La Cordonnerie is a little restaurant with two dining rooms that together seat just twenty-four people. One room is dominated by an open kitchen with an enviable collection of copper pots, pans, and molds; the other has a tiny bar, an antique icebox, a vintage cash register, and five tables with fresh flowers and matching red tablecloths and napkins. The restaurant was opened over thirty years ago by Claude and Yvette, with Claude in the kitchen turning out his renditions of soothing, old-fashioned French food, and Yvette acting as charming hostess and helper. The cooking is now done by their son, Hugo, and the hostess duties are shared by his wife, Valerie, during the evening and by Yvette during lunch. Hugo does the shopping at Rungis, the huge wholesale food market outside Paris, and he prepares everything here, including the ice creams and sorbets.

I like to start my meal with endive salad topped with chèvre and smoked bacon, or the *terrine de foie de volaille maison,* a creamy chicken liver pâté. For my main course I always pay attention to the *plat du jour* and the daily fresh fish. For dessert, there is sometimes a *tarte au citron* with a meringue topping, one of his father's specialties, but always you can count on Hugo's *fondant au chocolate.* Made with whipped cream and dark chocolate, it is warm on the outside, cool inside, and decadently wonderful to the last bite. The house wine is good quality, but if you want to try something more interesting, consider Hugo's recommendation from his *cave* of little-known, well-priced vintages.

TEL 01-42-60-17-42
OPEN Mon–Fri: lunch noon–2:30 P.M., dinner 7:30–10 P.M. **CLOSED** Sat–Sun; holidays, 1 week between Christmas and New Year's and sometimes at Easter, Aug
À LA CARTE 35–40€, BC **PRIX FIXE** None **CREDIT CARDS** AE, MC, V
RESERVATIONS Advised **ENGLISH SPOKEN** Yes

LA FRESQUE (40)
100, rue Rambuteau
Métro: Étienne-Marcel, Les Halles

La Fresque is a good budget bet in an area around the Forum des Halles otherwise dominated by fast-food joints and slick tourist traps. It is just far enough from the main tourist artery to be authentic. The food is traditional French, and so are the patrons, who pack the banquettes and heated terrace tables, eagerly lapping up the amazing bargain lunch *formule* that includes two courses and wine. There are always four choices for both the starter and main course. You could begin with a simple tomato and fresh mint salad or a bowl of soup, and follow with *magret de canard,* the daily special, a chèvre and spinach tart, or the vegetable plate. In the evening the prices increase, and so do the choices, but for around 25€, you can still eat well and enjoy a pitcher of one of their featured wines. The *salade landaise* with foie gras and slices of duck is a rich beginning, and so is the *salade mega Roma,* which comes with mozzarella cheese, zucchini, and marinated artichoke hearts. Grilled swordfish or the roast pork with figs are both done well, as are the apple crumble and ever-popular crème brûlée.

TEL 01-42-33-17-56
OPEN Mon–Sat: lunch noon–3 P.M., dinner 7 P.M.–midnight **CLOSED** Sun; 1 week around mid-Aug
À LA CARTE 25€, BNC **PRIX FIXE** Lunch: 14€, 2 courses & wine
  CREDIT CARDS MC, V
RESERVATIONS Preferred **ENGLISH SPOKEN** Usually

L'ARDOISE (16)
28, rue du Mont-Thabor
Métro: Concorde, Tuileries

Small, tightly packed, brightly lit bistros offering a set menu for two or three courses now dot the Parisian dining landscape. At L'Ardoise, chef Pierre Jay—who honed his skills at several top Parisian dining cathedrals, including La Tour d'Argent—has energized the already flourishing dining scene in the first arrondissement. The frenetic lunch service, somehow carried out by two racing servers, is enjoyed mostly by businessfolk. Dinner, which is almost as rushed, draws a stylish crowd in dark suits or fashionable casual attire who are served with dispatch in order to turn the tables at least twice, hopefully more. Black-and-white vintage Paris photos dot the walls in the small room, where the bare tables are dressed with linen napkins and tumblers for the wine.

As soon as you are seated, a basket of dark bread and a dish of *fromage frais* laced with fresh herbs arrives. The blackboard *(ardoise)* lists a selection of a dozen *entrées* and *plats,* plus a final cheese course or one of six desserts, all featuring market-fresh ingredients simply prepared. Depending on the season and the mood of the chef, you might start with a plate of fresh oysters, a foie gras terrine, tomato *tarte* dressed with an eggplant confit, spinach and mussel ravioli, or a salad with two warm hearts of artichoke filled with potato purée sitting on a bed of warm endives and *pissenlits* (dandelion greens). Follow this with lamb tournedos, *coquilles St-Jacques,* fresh fish, or a perfectly roasted pigeon—all nicely garnished with at least one vegetable or potatoes. End the meal with a light *feuillantine au citron*—a flaky pastry layered with tangy lemon cream and dusted with sugar—or the hot apple tart. Despite the hustle of the service, the food is wonderful, the price is right, and the experience very Parisian.

TEL 01-42-96-28-18
OPEN Tues–Sat: lunch noon–2 P.M., dinner 6:30–11 P.M.; Sun: dinner
    6:30–11 P.M. **CLOSED** Sun lunch, Mon; Aug (call to check)
À LA CARTE None **PRIX FIXE** Lunch & dinner: 32€, 3 courses, BNC
    CREDIT CARDS MC, V
RESERVATIONS Essential **ENGLISH SPOKEN** Yes

LA VICTOIRE SUPRÊME DU COEUR (¢, 46)
41, rue des Bourdonnais
Métro: Châtelet

This is a serious vegetarian restaurant that focuses the mind on what's on the plate—simple food that's nicely presented and, above all, good for you. The busiest time is at lunch, when health-conscious office workers in the neighborhood (around what was once La Samaritaine department store) fill every seat. The set-price lunch menus, as well as the à la carte offerings, parade a list of vegetarian standbys with a few modern twists. Of course, tofu is presented every way imaginable, from fresh to smoked and sautéed. Then there are grains, veggies (both cooked and raw and served in terrines and quiches), salads, soups, daily pastries, and simple fruit desserts, along with ciders and assorted *cocktails maison,* such as the simple one made with apple, carrot, and soy milk or perhaps one featuring a mélange of passion fruit, mango, orange, and banana spiked with vanilla. Either way, you are guaranteed to have a clear head for the afternoon and no hangover tomorrow: even if you wanted a beer or glass of wine with your meal, you can't, as liquor is not served.

If you plan to be a regular and eat here seven times within thirty days, ask for a *Carte de Fidélité,* which will entitle you to a free *plat du jour* after the seventh meal. Afternoon tea is served from 3 to 6 P.M. and offers assorted teas, fresh fruit and veggie drinks, and desserts.

NOTE: The restaurant is nonsmoking inside, with smoking allowed on the outside terrace.

TEL 01-40-41-93-95
OPEN Mon–Sat: 11:45 A.M.–10 P.M., continuous service **CLOSED** Sun; major holidays, NAC
À LA CARTE Lunch 10–16€, dinner 14–20€, both BNC **PRIX FIXE** Lunch (until 6 P.M.): Assiettes Victoire Suprême: 10€, crudités, potatoes, and 2 other ingredients; 14€ for 3 other ingredients; both BNC
CREDIT CARDS MC, V
RESERVATIONS Not necessary **ENGLISH SPOKEN** Yes, and English menu

LAVINIA (10)
3, boulevard de la Madeleine
Métro: Madeleine

Welcome to one of the world's biggest wine shops, where over 6,000 bottles of wines and spirits are sold by the glass, bottle, or case in this multilevel, 16,000-square-foot *supermarché* of wines. Not only that, there is an eighty-seat restaurant (reservations essential), a tasting bar, wine accessory boutique, and a friendly multilingual staff to help you spend money on interesting wines from around the world (statistical average spent per customer is 100€). To encourage as much tasting and ultimately buying as possible, wine served at the bar or at the table is the same price as on the store shelf. Special wine tastings and theme events (conducted in French) are scheduled throughout the year.

TEL 01-42-97-20-20 **EMAIL** laviniafrance@lavinia.fr **INTERNET** www.lavinia.fr
OPEN Wine store: Mon–Fri 10 A.M.–8 P.M., Sat 9 A.M.–8 P.M.; restaurant: Mon–Sat noon–3 P.M.; tasting bar: Mon–Sat 3–8 P.M. **CLOSED** Sun; holidays, NAC
À LA CARTE 40–45€, BNC **PRIX FIXE** *Table du Chef:* 4 courses, 68€ per person, must be ordered by entire table **CREDIT CARDS** AE, DC, MC, V
RESERVATIONS Essential for lunch **ENGLISH SPOKEN** Yes

LE BAR DU CAVEAU (¢, 48)
17, place Dauphine
Métro: Pont-Neuf

Le Bar du Caveau occupies a prime spot on the charming place Dauphine, which is at the tip of Île de la Cité, just after you cross the Pont-Neuf bridge. Relatively undiscovered by tourists, this lovely little square was home to Yves Montand and Simone Signoret, and it boasts a half dozen or so restaurants and a famous bargain hotel, the Hotel Henri IV (see *Great Sleeps Paris*). Featuring sandwiches on *pain Poilâne, croques-monsieur* or *-madame,* salads, egg dishes, cheese and *charcuterie* plates, and a mix of Bordeaux and other wines by the glass, *pot* (refillable bottle), and bottle, Le Bar du Caveau appeals to upscale regulars who arrive early and stay late, idling away a lazy Paris afternoon in a cozy atmosphere over wine and fellowship.

NOTE: Be sure you go to the bar, not to either of its sister restaurants next door, which are not designed for the budgets of most value-conscious diners in Paris.

TEL 01-43-54-45-95
OPEN Mon–Fri: 8 A.M.–7 P.M., continuous service; Sat in summer only: 9 A.M.–7 P.M. **CLOSED** Sat in winter, Sun; NAC
À LA CARTE 8–12€, BNC **PRIX FIXE** None **CREDIT CARDS** None
RESERVATIONS Not accepted **ENGLISH SPOKEN** Limited

LE BÉARN (¢, 47)
2, place Ste-Opportune
Métro: Châtelet (exit place Ste-Opportune)

In addition to being a good food deal, Le Béarn is a great place to hone your people-watching skills. In the morning, you are likely to find red-cheeked workers standing at the bar, lingering over what is obviously not their first glass of *vin rouge* of the day. A predominantly young crowd of every conceivable orientation and dress pours in at lunchtime to take advantage of the low-priced *plats du jour,* which come in pre-nouvelle-size portions. These are usually overflowing plates of no-nonsense meats, accompanied by equally serious portions of homemade *frites.* From October to March, the *huître* (oyster) stand in front is one of the cheapest and best in the *quartier.* Unless it is raining or freezing cold, the outside tables on the place Ste-Opportune are the places to sit, serving as front-row vantage points for watching Les Halles fashion victims preen and prance and the surging crowds emerging from the métro stop next to it.

TEL 01-42-36-93-35
OPEN Mon–Sat: bar 8 A.M.–11 P.M., lunch noon–3:30 P.M., dinner 7–9 P.M.
CLOSED Sun; holidays, NAC
À LA CARTE 15–20€, BC **PRIX FIXE** None **CREDIT CARDS** MC, V
RESERVATIONS Not accepted **ENGLISH SPOKEN** Limited

L'ÉCLUSE ST-HONORÉ (13)
34, place du Marché St-Honoré
Métro: Pyramides, Tuileries

L'Écluse was a trailblazer in popularizing wine bars in Paris, and it is still one of the best and most popular. Offering wines by the glass or the bottle, these trendy spots cater to those seeking food, wine, and uncomplicated meals served in agreeable surroundings by a low-key waitstaff. The final bill ultimately depends on the modesty or the majesty of the vintages you consume—as well as, of course, how much food you order.

Specializing in Bordeaux wines, all L'Écluse locations have the same menu right down to an identical *plat du jour,* but each wine bar features a different type of Bordeaux wine. The upmarket clientele drops by for a quick breakfast from 8:30 to 10:30 A.M., and then from noon until the wee hours to sample wines ranging from 5€ for a simple glass to over 60€ for a bottle of a *grand cru.* The seasonal food is selected to go well with the varieties of Bordeaux served. Featured are house terrines, foie gras, platters of *charcuterie,* beef tartare, grilled meats, assorted cheeses, a hot plate of the day, and their famous diet-destroying chocolate cake.

NOTE: The other locations are in the sixth, eighth, eleventh, and seventeenth arrondissements (see pages 147, 193, 218, and 269).

TEL 01-42-96-10-18 **INTERNET** www.leclusebaravin.com
OPEN Daily: 8:30 A.M.–1 A.M., continuous service **CLOSED** Dec 24 evening, Christmas, Dec 31 evening, New Year's Day, NAC
À LA CARTE 28–38€, BNC **PRIX FIXE** Breakfast: 3.30€, Le Parisien (hot drink, orange juice, croissant); 4.85€, L'Énergétique (add toast, butter, and jam); 14€, Le Préférénce de Grand-Père (hot drink, orange juice, Evian, wine, toast, scrambled eggs with smoked salmon or cold meats and cheese)
CREDIT CARDS AE, DC, MC, V
RESERVATIONS Not accepted **ENGLISH SPOKEN** Yes, and English menu

LE LOUCHEBEM (45)
31, rue Berger, angle rue des Prouvaires
Métro: Les Halles, Châtelet-Les Halles

The red interior goes well with your beef and so do the many pictures of animals that line the walls at Le Louchebem, a temple of tradition in Les Halles. Despite its tourist-trap location near the Forum des Halles, it is largely unknown to outsiders. Featuring red meat in huge and satisfying portions, it has outlived dining and dietary crazes and continues to please a largely French audience that is serious about eating and drinking well.

If you go early and sit upstairs by a picture window overlooking the ornate Église St-Eustache, you will be captivated even before your waiter appears with bowls of olives and pieces of ham and beef to dip into a caper sauce. When ordering your meal, throw caution, calories, and cholesterol to the wind and dig into he-man servings of steak tartare, leg of lamb, *côte de boeuf,* roasted chicken and duck, or the daunting all-you-can-eat *assiette du rotisseur*—a mixed grill of beef, leg of lamb, and roast ham accompanied by three sauces. The standard dishes that regulars can depend on are as follows: Monday, lamb shoulder; Tuesday, *pot-au-feu;* Wednesday, baby pig; Thursday, *tête de veau* (calf's head); Friday, fresh fish; and Saturday, a beef dish. The salads are best forgotten, but not the desserts. If you can manage it by the end, go for the warm *tarte Tatin* or one of the ice cream or sorbet creations, such as the *Coupe de Lochebem* (apple sorbet topped with Calvados) or the *Coupe General,* a dish of pistachio ice cream covered with whiskey. The wine list is well priced. If you are dining with a friend, separate checks are possible without the waiter scowling, and if they forget to give you the prix-fixe menu, ask for it!

TEL 01-42-33-12-99 **INTERNET** www.le-louchebem.fr
OPEN Mon–Sat: lunch noon–2:30 P.M., dinner 7–11:30 P.M. **CLOSED** Sun; NAC
À LA CARTE 35–45€, BNC **PRIX FIXE** Lunch & dinner (until 9 P.M.): 13.90€,
   2 courses, BNC **CREDIT CARDS** AE, DC, MC, V
RESERVATIONS Advised, especially Fri & Sat **ENGLISH SPOKEN** Yes, and English
   menu

LE PETIT CAFÉ (¢, 11)
6, rue Duphot
Métro: Madeleine, Concorde

The Petit Café is a word-of-mouth choice for in-the-know foodies who work around this tiny street that connects the boulevard de la Madeleine with the chic rue St-Honoré. It is open for breakfast and lunch Monday to Friday, and for bar service until closing at 8 P.M. No hot meals are served after 2 P.M. Seating is at one of the five bar stools or at the half dozen booths that line a mirrored wall. The short, traditional menu is made up of fresh seasonal food . . . *jamais surgelé* (never frozen). The breakfast of scrambled eggs, sausage, toast, and a hot drink is one of the best in the *quartier,* and a definite steal at 4.50–5€. Lunch is not far behind, especially the creamy quiches and the wonderful composed salads that feature fruit, seafood, or foie gras. For a substantial repast, I like to start with the warm leeks vinaigrette or maybe a slice of the homemade chicken liver terrine. I always hope the tender *blanquette de veau* will be on the menu, or the *confit de Canard maison.* For dessert, the hands-down choices are the *tarte Tatin* or the *mousse au chocolate* . . . both made right here, of course.

TEL 01-42-60-01-25
OPEN Mon–Fri: 8 A.M.–8 P.M., breakfast 8 A.M.–11 A.M., lunch noon–2 P.M., bar
   service until 8 P.M. **CLOSED** Sat–Sun; holidays, Aug (dates vary)
À LA CARTE 15–18€ **PRIX FIXE** Breakfast: 4.50–5€; lunch: 14€, 2 courses
   CREDIT CARDS MC, V
RESERVATIONS Not necessary **ENGLISH SPOKEN** Limited

LE PETIT FLORE (¢, 41)
6, rue Croix des Petits Champs
Métro: Palais Royal, Musée du Louvre

From the outside, it looks like scores of other cafés, but what sets it apart is the quality of ingredients used in the kitchen. After sampling the food, I made Guy and Annie Dellac's welcoming bistro one of my neighborhood midday haunts. I only wish they would stay open for dinner as well. The appreciative lunch crowd knows to come early for the best selection of the hearty food, which is served at wallet-friendly prices. The traditional menu pleases with such longtime favorites as *oeufs dur mayonnaise* (hard-boiled eggs in a creamy sauce), herring with warm potato salad, grilled lamb chops, *confit de canard,* various omelettes, and fresh fish every Friday. The chocolate mousse, *île flottante,* and *tarte au citron* are made here and sell out on a daily basis. For visitors, it is close to the Louvre, the Palais Royal, and Le Louvre des Antiquaires, the magnificent museum-quality antique galleries along rue de Rivoli.

TEL 01-42-60-25-53
OPEN Mon–Sat: lunch noon–2:30 P.M. **CLOSED** Sun, holidays, Aug
À LA CARTE *Entrées* 4–6.50€, *plat du jour* 9.50€, other *plats* 12€, dessert 6€ **PRIX FIXE** Lunch: 14€, 2 courses, BC (coffee) **CREDIT CARDS** V (15€ minimum)
RESERVATIONS Not necessary **ENGLISH SPOKEN** Limited, and English menu

LESCURE (15)
7, rue de Mondovi
Métro: Concorde

Located at the end of a short street just around the corner from place de la Concorde, the restaurant was founded in 1919 by Lèon Lescure. Today it is still owned and operated by his family, who serve simple French *bourgeoise* cooking at very reasonable prices. For both lunch and dinner, diners vie for one of the sidewalk tables or else sit elbow-to-elbow inside beneath ropes of garlic and country sausages dangling from the rafters. The service is friendly and perhaps the fastest in Paris.

If you select a dish that must be prepared that day, or better yet, cooked to order, you will be happy. Otherwise, you may run into some ingredients that are past their prime or have been reheated too much. The poached haddock is always a safe bet, and so is *la poule au riz sauce basquaise*—chicken and rice with a tangy tomato and green pepper sauce (order it on the side). The most popular dessert is the special fruit tarte.

TEL 01-42-60-18-91
OPEN Mon–Fri: lunch noon–2:15 P.M., dinner 7–10:15 P.M. **CLOSED** Sat–Sun; holidays, Dec 22–Jan 1, Aug
À LA CARTE 25–27€, BNC **PRIX FIXE** Lunch & dinner: 23€, 3 courses, BC **CREDIT CARDS** MC, V (20€ minimum)
RESERVATIONS Not necessary **ENGLISH SPOKEN** Yes

LE SOUFFLÉ (18)
36, rue du Mont-Thabor
Métro: Tuileries, Concorde (exit rue Cambon)

It is unanimous: Everyone loves Le Soufflé.

Many Parisians as well as a host of international visitors know that in this uncertain world Le Soufflé is one restaurant you can always count on for a wonderful meal. It has been owned for thirty-three years by Claude Rigaud, and he is now helped by his son. After dining here, you will feel like you are in heaven—and know that you are in Paris. The interior glows with soft lighting, pale yellow walls, and fresh flowers in miniature pots. The tables are laid with starched linens, heavy cutlery, beautiful china, and sparkling crystal. The second dining room evokes the spirit of Paris with its fleur-de-lys wall treatment, murals of Parisian gardens, and royal red carpeting. Along with polite service and discreet waiters, Le Soufflé maintains its reputation for memorable dining in Paris. After all, what could be more Parisian than a soufflé? Whether you order a fluffy cheese or spinach soufflé, a delicate smoked salmon soufflé, or a rich chocolate or a classic Grand Marnier soufflé—or any of the other imaginative offerings—you will enjoy dramatic dining guaranteed to please even the most jaded palate. If you want to avoid the most tourists, however, book your dinner table for after 8:30 P.M.

In addition to the fantasia of soufflés, there are many appealing seasonal appetizers, hearty main courses, and luscious desserts. At the height of the spring season, the fat white asparagus vinaigrette is a definite must. The fresh artichoke heart and mushrooms dressed in a tangy lemon cream sauce is another popular *entrée*, as is the home-made terrine or the duck with green pepper and pistachios. For apple lovers, the *tarte fine aux pommes chaudes* is a dreamy dessert raising this standard French menu item to new heights. Another cloudlike choice is the *soufflé Rothschild*—a puffed *crêpe* doused in kirsch. When it arrives, covering the entire plate, you will think you can't finish it, but let me assure you that you will eat every bite and wish for more. Whatever you have at Le Soufflé will be divine and well worth the extra euros.

NOTE: There is no smoking in the second dining room.

TEL 01-42-60-27-19
OPEN Mon–Sat: lunch noon–2:30 P.M., dinner 7–10:30 P.M. **CLOSED** Sun; holidays, 2 weeks in mid-Feb, first 3 weeks of Aug (dates vary)
À LA CARTE 35–45€, BNC **PRIX FIXE** Lunch: 29€, 3 courses (all soufflés) and a green salad; dinner: 32€, 3 courses (some soufflés); both BNC
CREDIT CARDS AE, MC, V
RESERVATIONS Essential, several days in advance **ENGLISH SPOKEN** Yes

L'OSTRÉA ($, 43)
4, rue Sauval
Métro: Louvre-Rivoli

Diners seeking fresh fish expertly prepared by a master of the art need look no further than L'Ostréa.

The entrance to the stone-walled restaurant is near the aquarium, where your meal may be swimming, and the tiny corner kitchen, where you can see the chef/owner, M. Devaux, preparing the dishes. Inside there is a small wooden bar, the usual assortment of paintings and posters the owners have accumulated over the years, and their extensive collection of anything to do with the sea. Performing the hostess duties with charm is Madame. All dining choices include fish. The Big Splurge prices are well worth it for the tender *coquille St-Jacques,* the beautiful platter of seafood, a bowl of steaming mussels, or the *bouillabaisse,* which is so special it feeds four (minimum order) and must be ordered at least one day in advance.

TEL 01-40-26-08-07
OPEN Mon–Fri: lunch noon–2:30 P.M., dinner 8–11 P.M.; Sat: dinner
8–11 P.M. **CLOSED** Sat lunch, Sun; holidays, 1 week at Christmas and at
Easter; first 3 weeks of Aug
À LA CARTE 40–50€, BNC **PRIX FIXE** None **CREDIT CARDS** MC, V
RESERVATIONS Preferred **ENGLISH SPOKEN** Yes

UNIVERSAL RESTORAMA IN THE CARROUSEL DU LOUVRE (¢, 42)
Passage du Carrousel, under the Louvre (entrance
through 99, rue de Rivoli)
Métro: Palais-Royal

When the Carrousel du Louvre underground shopping mall opened in November 1993, the first North American–style food court opened on the top floor, serving fast food *à la française.* The self-service food stands are set on the mezzanine of the mall, just off I. M. Pei's majestic pyramid. (Avoid the Café du Louvre, which is near the food court and serves premade wrapped sandwiches.) The food certainly is not three-star gourmet, but it is filling, fresh, and inexpensive, especially when you consider the million-dollar surroundings. Judging by the crowds during lunch, the self-service concept is an unqualified hit. The best battle plan is to walk around, survey the stands, and then decide what looks best. The food stands come and go, so it is impossible to guarantee that your favorite stall will be in business the next time around. However, the round-the-world choices available during my last visit included Asian, Libyan, North African, Tex-Mex, Italian pizza and pasta, French crêpes, a health bar (with fresh fruits, veggie plates, and juices), hamburgers and fries, Hector le Poulet (serving rotisserie chicken), Spanish tapas, Boulangerie Paul (serving quiches, salads, sandwiches, and irresistible pastries), and a coffee stand dispensing muffins and cookies to munch with your *café au lait* or to buy for later indulging. The prime seating is at the tables along the edge of the food court, where you can sit and watch the throngs surging below.

NOTE: While you are here, stop by the information center under the pyramid and ask for the floor plan of each level of the Louvre, with small photos of the most important art available for viewing.

TEL 01-40-20-53-17
OPEN Daily: 11 A.M.–9 P.M., continuous service **CLOSED** Major holidays, NAC
À LA CARTE 5–18€, BC **PRIX FIXE** None **CREDIT CARDS** Depends on stand, but generally MC, V
RESERVATIONS Not accepted **ENGLISH SPOKEN** Depends on stand

WILLI'S WINE BAR (26)
13, rue des Petits-Champs
Métro: Pyramides

Willi's, a pioneer in chic Parisian wine bars, has been a success since the day it opened in 1980. Everyone loves it, and with good reason. The food is good, the welcome genuine, the wines well-selected, and the prices within most budgets. Reserve a table, or take your chances and hope for a spot at the bar. Actually, when I am alone, I like to eat at the long oak bar, because it is fun to shmooze with the barserver and my fellow diners perched on the stools. At noon, a quick lunch consisting of two courses is served to the coat-and-tie set who work in this banking and Bourse (former stock market) neighborhood. At night, the pace slows and it is filled with a good-looking, almost all-French crowd.

The menu changes every two or three months. In late spring look for asparagus to be highlighted in hot and cold soups, served warm with wild mushrooms and a poached egg on top, or in salads dusted with Parmesan shavings. Quickly grilled tuna, roast lamb, or a grilled steak with shallots are three of the seven or eight *plats*. The desserts provide a good grip on all sweet tooths with a flaky *tartelette aux poires* served with a caramel glaze and *crème anglaise* sprinkled with pistachios, or the famous *terrine au chocolate–Ancestral du Willi's*. That's it . . . the food, the scene, the bottom line. Don't miss it.

NOTE: Per Willi's request: "Smokers are cordially invited to pursue their habit on the pavement," i.e., no smoking is allowed.

TEL 01-42-61-05-09 **INTERNET** www.williswinebar.com
OPEN Mon–Sat: lunch 12:30–2:30 P.M., dinner 7–11 P.M. **CLOSED** Sun; holidays, 2 weeks in Aug (dates vary)
À LA CARTE 35–40€, BNC **PRIX FIXE** Lunch: 19.50€, 2 courses, 25€, 3 courses, both BNC; dinner: 34€, 3 courses, BNC **CREDIT CARDS** MC, V
RESERVATIONS Recommended **ENGLISH SPOKEN** Yes

Second Arrondissement

The second arrondissement can hardly be called a tourist hub in comparison to some others. It is the home of the stock market (Bourse), some big banks, and the lovely place des Victoires centered by a statue of Louis XIV and ringed with trendy, well-known, and up-and-coming designer boutiques. It is also dotted with *passages:* those shopping malls of the early 1900s, relics of the time before department stores. (See *Great Sleeps Paris,* "Shopping," for a listing of the most interesting *passages.*)

RIGHT BANK
Bibliothèque Nationale
Bourse
Cognacq-Jay Museum
passages
place des Victoires
rue Montorgueil shopping
    street

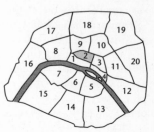

SECOND ARRONDISSEMENT RESTAURANTS
(see map page 48)

($) indicates a Big Splurge; (¢) indicates a Cheap Eat

À PRIORI THÉ (28)
4, rue des Petits-Champs, Galeri Vivienne, Nos. 35–36
Métro: Bourse

Galerie Vivienne is considered by many to be the most beautiful *passage* in Paris. It opened in 1823, and today reflects its beautiful surroundings in its magnificent boutiques. Adding to the allure is À Priori Thé, an inviting space with well-set tables and padded wicker armchairs arranged both inside and along the passageway. I think it is the perfect place to enjoy a leisurely lunch, afternoon tea, or a lazy Sunday brunch. The food tastes as good as the stylish menu reads. The variety of charms on offer include homemade scones, double chocolate brownies, a classic fruit crumble, big salads, and simple bowls of soul-warming soups. Brunch is served on Saturday and Sunday from noon to 4 P.M. and includes five prix-fixe menus all built around eggs with a variety of salads. Portions are so generous you won't be able to think about your next meal for the rest of the day.

TEL 01-42-97-48-75
OPEN Mon–Fri 9 A.M.–6 P.M., Sat 9 A.M.–6:30 P.M., Sun noon–6:30 P.M.;
   breakfast Mon–Fri 9–11:30 A.M.; lunch Mon–Fri noon–3 P.M.; teatime
   Mon–Fri 3–6 P.M., Sat–Sun 4–6:30 P.M.; brunch Sat–Sun noon–4 P.M.
   CLOSED Christmas Day & New Year's Day, NAC
À LA CARTE 10–25€, BNC **PRIX FIXE** 15–18€, BNC **CREDIT CARDS** MC, V
RESERVATIONS Sat & Sun brunch; preferred otherwise **ENGLISH SPOKEN** Yes

AUX CRUS DE BOURGOGNE ($, 32)
3, rue Bachaumont
Métro: Sentier, Étienne-Marcel

Plus ça change in this well-loved dining institution ever since M. Bouvier's grandmother arrived in Paris from Corsica in 1932 and bought the restaurant. Still in place are the brass-railed banquettes framing the two large rooms, the mosaic-tile floor, bentwood coat racks, bright lights, and career waiters in black rushing to serve the businesspeople at lunch and the neighbors sitting at candlelit tables in the evening. Fresh lobster, the specialty dish, is served for both lunch and dinner in various guises. The rest of the time-honored menu is a collection of solid standards that hardly chart new territory, but the locals wouldn't have it any other way. The prix fixe, available only at dinner, lists four *entrées* and five mains. *Entrées* include a platter of Corsican *charcuterie* and two salads: one loaded with fresh herbs, and the other, bitter *roquette* showered with fresh *bruccio* cheese. These are followed by main courses of *boeuf bourguignon,* tripe cooked in Calvados, a slab of fresh foie gras accompanied by a salad, and duck in a black currant sauce. On the à la carte side, if you don't start with one of the lobster salads, try the six garlicky Burgundy snails or parsley marbled ham. Main courses include fillet of sole sautéed in butter; a huge lobster-and-fresh-vegetable salad; chicken simmered in Brouilly wine and mushroom sauce, served on a bed of pasta; or a slab of rib steak. The strawberry tart, if it's on the menu, is fabulous, and so is the chocolate cake.

TEL 01-42-33-48-24
OPEN Mon–Fri: lunch noon–3 P.M., dinner 7:45–11 P.M. **CLOSED** Sat–Sun; holidays, NAC
À LA CARTE 45–50€, BNC **PRIX FIXE** Dinner: 27€, 2 courses, BNC
   CREDIT CARDS AE, MC, V
RESERVATIONS Essential **ENGLISH SPOKEN** Yes, and English menu

AUX LYONNAIS (1)
32, rue St-Marc
Métro: Bourse, Richelieu-Drouot

What more can anyone ask of a bistro? Pretty surroundings, interesting people, reliable food, pleasant staff, honest prices—Aux Lyonnais, under the helm of Alain Ducasse and Thierry de la Brosse, has them all. At lunch it hums with the voices of office workers and stockbrokers from the Bourse. In the evening, the pace slows and the service and mood become more relaxed and refined.

The menu offers dishes that have been served here and in bistros like it for generations. The first-rate fare is well prepared and all made here, including the pâtés, and there are no unpleasant surprises. You start with a basket of crispy baguettes to be spread with sweet butter. *Entrées* include eggs baked with crayfish, a lusty lentil terrine, or a salad of *frisée* with herring and pieces of lamb. Tripe, the Lyonnaise specialty, is a popular French choice. Others will be happy with the steak served with shallots and garlic mashed potatoes. The desserts not to be missed are the *île flottante,* a floating island topped with caramel glaze, or the Ambassadeur, a light sponge cake dotted with candied fruit and flavored with kirsch.

TEL 01-42-96-65-04
OPEN Tues–Fri: lunch 12:15–2 P.M., dinner 7:30–11 P.M.; Sat: dinner 7:30–11 P.M. **CLOSED** Sat lunch, Sun–Mon; holidays, Aug (dates vary)
À LA CARTE 45€, BNC **PRIX FIXE** Lunch & dinner: 30€, 3 courses, BNC
   CREDIT CARDS MC, V
RESERVATIONS Advised **ENGLISH SPOKEN** Yes

AUX TROIS PETITS COCHONS (35)
31, rue Tiquetonne
Métro: Étienne Marcel

Aux Trois Petits Cochons ("the three little pigs") stands for the original three very slim and slight friends who joined together to open this restaurant. Open only for dinner, the place comes into its own around 9:30 or 10 P.M. when it fills with a glossy mix of decidedly gay patrons.

These dedicated returnees know to book at least two or three days ahead to be assured a table. The seasonal prix-fixe menu offers a choice of two or three courses of up-to-date food that is imaginatively prepared and artistically presented. The service is always polite, the linen and crystal table settings correct, the flowers perfect, the art exhibits varying, and the candles glowing. Depending on the time of year, your dining might include a salad of warm white asparagus from Landes topped with truffle and herb vinaigrette; *lentilles du Puy* served with Lyonnaise sausage, shallots, and herbs; or pig's foot croquettes in a mustard sauce. Recent winter and springtime *plats* were an oven-roasted saddle of lamb with sautéed mushrooms and potatoes; baked scorpion fish fillet topped with a spicy crab sauce (*racasse*) and garnished with preserved tomatoes and sweet red peppers; or honey caramelized spareribs with sautéed apples and pears spiked with Szechuan pepper. Desserts keep up the pace with a soft, warm, bourbon-flavored chocolate cake served with a scoop of coffee ice cream and light custard sauce, strawberry and rhubarb sorbet on a bed of meringue, and the fresh strawberry tart.

NOTE: The owners of Aux Trois Petits Cochons also run Pigz (see page 74).

TEL 01-42-33-39-69 **INTERNET** www.auxtroispetitscochons.fr
OPEN Daily: dinner 8 P.M.–midnight **CLOSED** December 24–25, 31,
   first 3 weeks of Aug
À LA CARTE None **PRIX FIXE** Dinner: 26€, 2 courses; 31€, 3 courses; both
   BNC **CREDIT CARDS** AE, DC, MC, V
RESERVATIONS Essential, as far in advance as possible **ENGLISH SPOKEN** Yes,
   and English menu

CHEZ GEORGES ($, 29)
1, rue du Mail
Métro: Sentier, Etienne-Marcel

For a trip down memory lane, it doesn't get any better than Chez Georges. The restaurant, just off the fashionable place des Victoires, was opened in 1964 by Georges Constant and is now under the helm of his grandson, Arnaud Brouillet. Determined to honor the past, the restaurant displays a refreshing lack of concern for food fashions; its menu is a hit parade of French classics. Seated elbow-to-elbow along two rows of banquettes, eager diners select from the purple-and red-inked, hand-stenciled menu. While sipping a glass or two of Sancerre or Chînon wine, try a perfect salad of *frisée,* studded with bacon chunks and topped with a poached egg; *céleri rémoulade;* meaty terrines; smoked salmon; or a dozen garlic-infused escargots. Grilled turbot with béarnaise, tender chicken on a bed of wild mushrooms and pasta, pink lamb chops garnished with baby green beans, steak served several ways, and the usual French favorites of kidneys, liver, and *andouillette* are only a few of the dozen-plus main courses. Don't forget dessert, especially the profiteroles slathered in hot chocolate, the warm chocolate cake with an orange sauce, or the rich *tarte Tatin.*

TEL 01-42-60-07-11
OPEN Mon–Fri: lunch 12:15–2 P.M., dinner 7:30–10 P.M. **CLOSED** Sat–Sun;
   holidays, first 3 weeks of Aug
À LA CARTE 42–50€, BNC **PRIX FIXE** None **CREDIT CARDS** AE, MC, V
RESERVATIONS Essential **ENGLISH SPOKEN** Yes

CLÉMENTINE (3)
5, rue Saint-Marc
Métro: Bourse

Clémentine is a pretty little place that's outfitted in rose velvet banquettes, mirrored walls, and an original tiled floor. The prices at this 1905 bistrot near the Bourse keeps the regulars happy and in high spirits, and the traditional Southern-style cooking of chef/patron Franck Langrenne insures many repeat visits. The reliable menu, which is influenced by the seasons, does not wander too far from center. Look for escargots, chicken liver pâté with mushrooms, and everyone's favorite—leeks in a vinaigrette sauce. *Cassoulet* is a robust winter favorite, as is the rabbit in a lemon-mustard sauce. The warm, runny hot chocolate cake is a dieter's dilemma, but not the refreshing blood orange slices topped with a light orange sorbet. Wines from small producers are fairly priced and complement the food well. No smoking is allowed on the first floor.

TEL 01-40-41-05-65 **INTERNET** www.restaurantclementine.com
OPEN Mon–Fri: lunch noon–2:30 P.M., dinner 7:30–10:15 P.M.
    CLOSED Sat–Sun; holidays, NAC
À LA CARTE *Entrées* and desserts 7.50€, *plats* 15€ **PRIX FIXE** Lunch & dinner:
    26.50€, 3 courses, BNC **CREDIT CARDS** AE, MC, V
RESERVATIONS Preferred **ENGLISH SPOKEN** Yes, and English menu

DEBAUVE & GALLAIS (4)
33, Rue Vivienne
Métro: Bourse

This is the second location of the oldest chocolate maker is Paris. For a full description of the delights that await, see Debauve & Gallais in the seventh arrondissement (see page 168).

TEL 01-40-39-05-50
OPEN Mon–Sat: 9 A.M.–6:30 P.M.

DOMAINE DE LINTILLAC (6)
10, rue Saint-Augustin
Métro: Quatre-Septembre

Known fondly by its legions of regulars as "duck and more duck," Domaine de Lintillac serves only duck in every way imaginable. You can't miss the bright red exterior, and the red theme continues in the cozy interior, brightened by red-and-white cloths. Naturally, you are going to follow the regulars and start with a silky foie gras or pâté, which you spread on warm toast that you prepare in the toaster on your table. For the next course, there are four salads, ranging in size and complexity from a simple one featuring *gésiers* (gizzards) to *La Périgourdine Gourmande du Domain,* which is piled with nuts, potatoes, and slices of duck meat. *Confit* and *magret de canard,* duck sausage, and a duck *cassoulet* are the other main courses. Dessert? Though you may not be able to tackle *La Coupe Corrézienne de la Truffe Noir* (a combination of praline ice cream, chestnut cream, and a special nut liqueur, all covered in a mound of whipped cream), you might have room for a bolstering *digestif.* Should you wish to continue your duck feasting after leaving Paris, no problem: there is a huge selection of their products for sale in the restaurant's boutique or on their Website.

TEL 01-40-20-96-27 **INTERNET** www.domainedelintillac-paris.com
OPEN Mon–Fri: lunch noon–2:15 P.M., dinner 7–10:15 P.M. (Thur–Fri till
    11 P.M.); Sat: dinner 7–11 P.M. **CLOSED** Sat lunch, Sun; holidays, 2 weeks
    in Aug (dates vary)
À LA CARTE 30–45€, BNC **PRIX FIXE** Lunch: 9€, 2 courses & cheese, BNC
    CREDIT CARDS MC, V
RESERVATIONS Essential **ENGLISH SPOKEN** Yes

FOODY'S BRUNCH CAFÉ (¢, 38)
26, rue Montorgueil
Métro: Etienne Marcel, Les Halles

À votre santé! Good, healthy food that is value priced awaits the diners who fill this self-serve vegetarian hot spot on the rue Montorgueil, one of the liveliest market streets on the Right Bank. The menu spotlights three soups that change daily, fourteen salads, one or two pastas *du jour,* fresh pressed fruit juices, and American-style muffins and brownies. Seating in the summer expands to the sidewalk terrace, which affords some of the best people-watching in town.

TEL 01-40-13-02-53
OPEN Mon–Sat: lunch 11:30 A.M.–5 P.M., continuous service **CLOSED** Sun;
    holidays, 1 week in Feb, 2 weeks in Aug (dates vary)
À LA CARTE 6–14€, BNC **PRIX FIXE** Lunch: 9.50€, 11€, 13€, 3 courses, all
    BC **CREDIT CARDS** MC, V
RESERVATIONS Not accepted **ENGLISH SPOKEN** Yes

GALLOPIN ($, 5)
40, rue Notre-Dame-des-Victoires
Métro: Bourse

Since opening its doors in 1876, Gallopin has continually been one of the most popular brasseries around the Bourse (stock market). The interior showcases magnificent Art Nouveau painted windows, Delft tiles, massive mirrors, and brass hat and coat racks behind long banquette seating. Waiters are clad in traditional black with long aprons dusting the tops of their shoes.

The three menu choices, for both lunch and dinner, offer great value, and the variety allows most diners to ignore the more expensive à la carte suggestions altogether. The food consists of well-executed brasserie classics: platters of fresh seafood, bricks of foie gras, terrines, the venerable *oeufs dur mayonnaise,* and a mound of crisply tender baby green beans in vinaigrette, served with fresh mushrooms and bits of cashews. *Plats* run the gamut from a delicate sole *meunière* surrounded by parsleyed potatoes to grills and *andouillette,* certified "A.A.A.A.A." (see "Unusual Foods," page 31, for more on this designation). If you have never tried these soul-food sausages (made from hog intestines), now may be the time. The famous *crêpes Alexandre,* served only for dinner, is a classic dessert made with butter, caramelized sugar, and fresh orange and lemon juice, which is flambéed with a mixture of Cointreau, Grand Marnier, and fruit. The *baba au rhum* is not fancy, but it is rich, as are their profiteroles, filled with vanilla, coffee, and pistachio ice cream, and blanketed in hot chocolate.

TEL 01-42-36-45-38
OPEN Daily: noon–midnight, continuous service **CLOSED** Never, NAC
À LA CARTE 40–50€, BNC **PRIX FIXE** Lunch & dinner: 20€, 2 courses (limited choice), BC (wine & coffee); 24€, 2 courses, BNC; 30€, 3 courses, BNC; 35€, 3 courses & wine **CREDIT CARDS** AE, DC, MC, V
RESERVATIONS Suggested for lunch and weekend dinner **ENGLISH SPOKEN** Yes

LA CRÊPE DENTELLE (31)
10, rue Léopold-Bellan
Métro: Sentier, Étienne Marcel

Owner/chef Thierry Houel displays his Bretagne roots in his family-run *crêperie,* which is tucked away on a side street off rue Montorgueil. The stone-walled interior showcases his Brittany paintings and a lovely carved serving buffet next to the open kitchen. Service with a smile is provided by his wife, Katy, and daughter, Leticia. The menu lists twenty-seven main-course crêpes, four omelettes, nine salads, and thirty-six dessert crêpes in addition to ten ice-cream creations. All can be washed down with the trademark apple cider. Where do you start with a menu like this? First, select your ingredients, keeping in mind that a crêpe filled with mixtures of ham, egg, tomato, and cheese, plus one or two more ingredients, will probably be the most successful. For dessert, the sky's the limit, starting with a plain butter-and-sugar crêpe and finishing with one filled with apples and flambéed with Calvados. At lunch, the reasonable two-course menu, which includes a kir, a bowl of cider, and dessert or coffee, draws a hungry crowd from the nearby offices; if you are not here by 12:15 P.M., you will have to wait for a table, and no wonder. La Crêpe Dentelle has been named the *meilleure Crêperie Bretonne de Paris* (best Brittany crêpes in Paris) for three years running. When you consider the number of *crêperies* in Paris, this is a great honor and achievement.

TEL 01-40-41-04-23
OPEN Mon–Fri: lunch noon–3:30 P.M., dinner 8–11 P.M. **CLOSED** Sat–Sun; holidays, Aug
À LA CARTE 18–22€, BC **PRIX FIXE** Lunch: 12€, 2 courses, dessert or coffee, kir, cider **CREDIT CARDS** V
RESERVATIONS Recommended **ENGLISH SPOKEN** Yes

LE GAVROCHE (2)
19, rue St-Marc
Métro: Bourse, Richelieu-Drouot

Lovers of red meat, red wine, and plenty of both must head straight to Le Gavroche, where the fascinating cast of characters are like a theatrical vignette of Parisian life. The faded interior with its tightly packed tables and net curtains draws wall-to-wall diners. In the morning, regulars stroll in to jump-start their day with a coffee or something much stronger. At lunch, the clientele is mostly businesspeople, who loosen their ties, roll up their sleeves, and dive into plates overflowing with servings of barely cooked beef steaks, rabbit in mustard sauce, *tartare de boeuf,* tripe, sausages, and the blue-plate specials, all washed down with bottles of Beaujolais and topped off with *baba au rhum* or a *millefeuille* for dessert. The pace and the patrons mellow out in the evening with representatives of various ages in assorted garbs and guises, all eager to enjoy this type of old-fashioned Parisian-style comfort food.

TEL 01-42-96-89-70
OPEN Mon–Sat: 7 A.M.–2 A.M., continuous service from noon **CLOSED** Sun; major holidays, Aug
À LA CARTE 30–35€, BC **PRIX FIXE** None **CREDIT CARDS** MC, V
RESERVATIONS Recommended for lunch **ENGLISH SPOKEN** Usually

LE MESTURET RESTAURANT (7)
77, rue de Richelieu, corner rue St-Augustin
Métro: Bourse, Quatre-Septembre

Le Mesturet, which means "bad boy" in Southwestern French dialect, has all the food and beverage bases covered from 8 A.M. until midnight, when the last guest is served. This is the dream-come-true restaurant of Alain Fontain (formerly of Baracane—Bistrot de l'Oulette, page 91). The brightly lit setting is casual, with upside-down wine bottles hanging from the ceiling and friendly service, even during the lunch rush. You can sit at the bar anytime and be served from *Le Zinc du Mesturet* menu, which consists of such simple pleasures as sandwiches, *tartines,* salads, and soups. The lunch and dinner menu offers a battery of traditional dishes based on seasonal fish, game, meats, and produce. Fall starters may include grilled eggplant topped with a layer of fresh tomatoes and fresh chèvre cheese, fresh pea soup scattered with crisp bacon, or blood sausage served with a mound of lentils. Regulars know their *tartare de boeuf* served with perfect *frites* is a winner, and so is the *blanquette de veau* served with rice pilaf and baby onions. For dessert, you could not possibly go wrong with the warm chocolate cake with a cocoa sauce or the ever-popular crème brûlée. Wine choices are excellent and come in all sizes: glass, *pichet,* and bottle. Once a month, a small vintner is invited to visit the restaurant and offer his wines for tasting.

TEL 01-42-97-40-68
OPEN Mon–Fri: bar 8 A.M.–midnight, breakfast 8–11 A.M., lunch noon–4 P.M., dinner 7–10:30 P.M.; Sat: dinner 7–10:30 P.M. **CLOSED** Sat breakfast & lunch, Sun, week between Christmas and New Year's, NAC
À LA CARTE Bar: 5–12€; lunch or dinner: 30€, BNC **PRIX FIXE** Lunch & dinner: 19€, 2 courses, 25€, 3 courses, both BNC **CREDIT CARDS** MC, V
RESERVATIONS Recommended **ENGLISH SPOKEN** Yes

LE VAUDEVILLE (8)
29, rue Vivienne
Métro: Bourse

Le Vaudeville is a dining destination that aims to please and never fails. A polished crowd of locals and out-of-towners drifts into this classic 1920s-style brasserie for the pleasure of meeting and eating. At lunch, you will share your meal with stockbrokers and commodity traders from the Bourse across the street. Late in the evening, the sophisticated set arrives in anything from black tie and satin to pastel pullovers and athletic shoes. Formally clad waiters serve during the peak hours without appearing overworked or keeping anyone waiting too long.

On a warm day, the coveted terrace tables are a great place to sit and soak up the street scene as you delve into familiar dishes from the vast daily-changing menu. A good-value, two-course prix-fixe lunch option includes foie gras or oysters to start and a grilled fish or *tartare de boeuf* for the main course. The three-course menu again highlights oysters, fois gras, plus *côtes de boeuf* and their wonderful Alsatian apple-and-raisin tart. Children generally do not fare well in French restaurants, but here, those between four and twelve years have their own two-course menu accompanied by fruit juice or soda.

TEL 01-40-20-04-62 **INTERNET** www.vaudevilleparis.com, www.flobrasseries.com
OPEN Daily: bar 7 A.M.–closing, breakfast 7–11 A.M., lunch noon–3 P.M., dinner 7 P.M.–1 A.M. **CLOSED** Never
À LA CARTE 40–48€, BNC **PRIX FIXE** Lunch & dinner: 20€, 2 courses, 30€, 3 courses, both BNC; children's menu: 14€, 2 courses, BC; Faim de Nuit (after 10:30 P.M.): 20€, 2 courses, BNC **CREDIT CARDS** AE, DC, MC, V
RESERVATIONS Essential for dinner, weekends, and holidays
ENGLISH SPOKEN Yes

MIMOSA (¢, 30)
44, rue d'Argout
Métro: Sentier, Étienne Marcel

You can go with a slim wallet and a big appetite to Mimosa, a cheery yellow-and-green, pocket-size, budget Cheap Eat located on a side street near the main post office on rue du Louvre. This is a place where it pays to arrive early because once the homespun daily changing soups, salads, and *plats du jour* sell out, that's it. Desserts go just as fast, especially the hot chocolate cake and the fresh fruit tarts. Seating inside is at wooden tables; on sunny days, eight pavement tables are added outside.

TEL 01-40-28-15-75
OPEN Mon–Fri: lunch noon–3 P.M. **CLOSED** Sat–Sun; holidays, 3 weeks in mid-Aug
À LA CARTE 8–12€, BNC **PRIX FIXE** Lunch: 12€, 2 courses; 10€, *plat du jour;* both BNC **CREDIT CARDS** AE, MC, V
RESERVATIONS Not necessary **ENGLISH SPOKEN** Yes

PIGZ (34)
5, rue Marie Stuart
Métro: Étienne-Marcel, Sentier

Good things often come in small packages, and this is certainly true at Pigz, the latest culinary success story of the trio who own Aux Trois Petits Cochons around the corner (see page 67). At both venues, the diners are a mixed group of artists and neighbors. Both restaurants are incredibly popular, so don't even think of arriving without advance reservations; two or three days ahead wouldn't hurt. The mood at Pigz is informal; the small, simply decorated dining room is ringed with cushy banquettes and bare wooden tables so tightly packed that you need a shoehorn to wedge yourself in—and out. The menu keeps it short and on target, offering four seasonally correct selections for each course. The white mushroom and leek ravioli with a truffle broth and the red Belgian endive salad studded with *fourme d'ambert* cheese and bacon are two early spring *entrées*. Later on look for white asparagus with a foie gras and wild mushroom sauce. Main courses feature grills of lamb, steak, chicken, duck, and fish, all liberally garnished. Appealing desserts on my last visit were a divine white chocolate mousse accented with dark chocolate ice cream and a light meringue served with grapefruit sorbet and slices of fresh mango.

TEL 01-42-33-05-89 **INTERNET** www.pigz.fr
OPEN Winter: Tues–Sat dinner 8–11 P.M.; summer: Tues–Sun dinner
   8–11 P.M. **CLOSED** Winter: Mon, Sun; summer: Mon; Aug (dates vary)
À LA CARTE 23–25€, BNC **PRIX FIXE** None **CREDIT CARDS** AE, MC, V
RESERVATIONS Essential **ENGLISH SPOKEN** Yes, and English menu

SOPRANO (9)
5, rue Rameau
Métro: Bourse, Pyramide

It's popular, the food is great, the two owners (who once worked *chez* Cipriani and Regine) are *simpa,* and the chef, Giulia, is a creative cook. The décor is simple yet elegant, and the lunch and dinner menus are enticing renditions of Italian classics. I like to start with the grilled zucchini covered in melted smoked *scamorza* cheese, or for a lighter beginning, a salad tossed with artichokes, avocado, and showered with Parmesan cheese. The linguini with clams or sauced with wild mushrooms are both tempting, but so is the tender herb-roasted veal chop and the just-done fillet of beef. For dessert, *semifreddo della casa* or Giulia's chocolate cake floating in a *sabayon* sauce winds up this great taste of Italy in Paris. *Buon appetito!*

TEL 01-42-96-01-76
OPEN Mon–Fri: lunch noon–2 P.M., dinner 8–11 P.M.; Sat: brunch 11 A.M.–
   5 P.M., dinner 8–11 P.M.; Sun: dinner 8–11 P.M. **CLOSED** Dinner Sun &
   Mon in winter, NAC
À LA CARTE 35–38€ **PRIX FIXE** Lunch: 15€, any pasta & espresso; 19€,
   2 courses, BNC **CREDIT CARDS** AE, DC, MC, V
RESERVATIONS Essential **ENGLISH SPOKEN** Yes, and Italian

STOHRER (¢, 33)
51, rue Montorgueil
Métro: Étienne Marcel, Sentier

Parisian pastry lovers think nothing of crossing the city in search of the perfect croissant, the richest chocolate mousse cake, or the best lemon tart. At Stohrer's they come for the *puits d'amour* (wells of love)—individual, cream-filled, flaky puff pastries lightly caramelized with a hot iron. Others come for the famous seven-fruit tart made up of picture-perfect raspberries, strawberries, tangerines, peaches, kiwi fruit, rose figs, and white pears set in almond paste in a *sablé* crust. I like to go when the doors open and buy a bag of their buttery croissants, or at lunchtime and take out a picnic extraordinaire made up of quiche, pâtés, fresh salads, and of course, several divine desserts. In the afternoon, schoolchildren line up outside by the cart selling homemade ice cream and sorbet. During holiday periods, the cart is replaced by one selling Christmas and Easter treats to behold.

The shop has a long and interesting history. It was opened in 1730 by N. Stohrer, who was the pastry chef for Stanislas Leszczynski—the exiled king of Poland and later chief *pâtissier* to Louis XV and Marie Antoinette. Stohrer is also credited with inventing the *rum baba* (sponge cake soaked in rum), the *ali baba* (filled with confectioner's sugar), and the *baba avec chantilly* (whipped cream). This is the only place in Paris that still sells all three versions. In addition, it is the oldest *pâtisserie* in Paris and is now classified as a historic monument. Inside, the beautiful painted walls and ceiling depicting nymphs holding trays of pastries were done in 1864 by Paul Baudry, who is famous for his paintings in the foyer at the Opéra Garnier. It is interesting to note that the glass ceiling has not been painted, but rather it was placed on the canvas by the artist while the paint was still wet.

One final note of interest. This was the *pâtisserie* Queen Elizabeth II visited on her 2005 trip to Paris commemorating the sixtieth anniversary of D-Day. Inside the shop is a photograph of the owner presenting the Queen with an enormous Easter egg.

TEL 01-42-33-38-20 **INTERNET** www.stohrer.fr
OPEN Daily: 7:30 A.M.–8:30 P.M., continuous service **CLOSED** Never
À LA CARTE 2.50–15€, BNC **PRIX FIXE** None **CREDIT CARDS** MC, V (10€ minimum)
RESERVATIONS Not taken **ENGLISH SPOKEN** Some

Third Arrondissement

RIGHT BANK
Carnavalet Museum (the
   museum of the city of
   Paris)
French National Archives
Musée des Arts et Métiers
   (in the medieval abbey of
   St-Martin-les-Champs)
Part of the Marais
Picasso Museum
Wholesale garment district

Marais means "swamp" in French, and this area was just that until the fourteenth century, when it became a royal park. Today, a walk through this area is a lesson in the history of French domestic architecture. The area has been redeveloped with panache, and many of the seventeenth- and eighteenth-century buildings have been made into museums or returned to their former glory as sumptuous apartments. This heaven for walkers and wanderers of all types is full of shops, boutiques, appealing restaurants, and fascinating history.

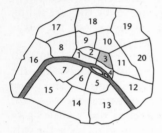

AU BASCOU (3)
38, rue de Réaumur
Métro: Arts et Métiers

If you can't go to the Basque region of France, Jean-Guy Loustau's Au Bascou will at least put you in a southwestern frame of mind with its modern Basque food and sensibly priced wines. The 1930s bistro, which won the 1995 Bistro of the Year award, is not near the usual tourist track. The area is full of wholesale clothing merchants and cheap Chinese restaurants, and it's largely inhabited by older Parisians carrying little dogs and feeding the ravenous pigeons. Don't let this slice of local color discourage you. The restaurant is less than a two-minute walk from the métro, and remember, you are here for the food, which is both rich and full-flavored.

The menu is seasonally based, but there are some standards that always appear. Count on starters of duck terrine, *piperade basquaise* (sweet peppers and tomatoes flavored with onion and garlic and served with scrambled eggs and cured ham), and their own foie gras. *Morue* (salted codfish) is the steady fish staple, but if you love abundance, order the roast leg of milk-fed lamb from the Pyrenees, which is served with fresh vegetables. I would skip the small and dry cheese offerings and order instead the different *baba du patxaran* (sponge cake with coffee ice cream, drizzled with prune, anise, and licorice) or the more traditional *béret basque,* a rich dark chocolate cake.

TEL 01-42-72-69-25
OPEN Mon–Fri: lunch noon–2 P.M., dinner 8–10:30 P.M. **CLOSED** Sat–Sun; holidays, week between Christmas and New Year's, Aug
À LA CARTE *Entrée* 9€, fish & meat 16€, cheese 7€, dessert 8€
   PRIX FIXE Lunch: 16€, 2 courses, BNC **CREDIT CARDS** AE, MC, V
RESERVATIONS Essential **ENGLISH SPOKEN** Yes

CAFÉ DES MUSÉES (17)
49, rue de Turenne
Métro: Chemin Vert

Café des Musées is a well-worn corner café that plays to a full house of contented regulars. For lunch, it is best to go early to nab one of the prized tables on the sidewalk; otherwise, you will be crowded inside, where it can get hot and smoky, not to mention very noisy with the din of the happy crowd. Don't come here for fancy garnishes or the latest food fad. Instead, bring your appetite and expect a satisfying meal quickly served by hardworking waitresses. Check the blackboard specials, and if the *moules* (mussels), creamy mushroom soup, or house *terrine de campagne au Calvados* don't speak to you, perhaps a *salade niçoise,* a juicy roast chicken with mushrooms, or smoked salmon quiche will. Desserts? Nothing stands out except the apple tart, which is made here.

TEL 01-42-72-96-17
OPEN Daily: bar 7 A.M.–2 A.M., continuous food service noon–11 P.M. **CLOSED** Christmas, NAC
À LA CARTE 25–30€, BNC **PRIX FIXE** Lunch: 12.50€, 2 courses; dinner: 19€, 3 courses; both BNC **CREDIT CARDS** V
RESERVATIONS Not accepted **ENGLISH SPOKEN** Yes

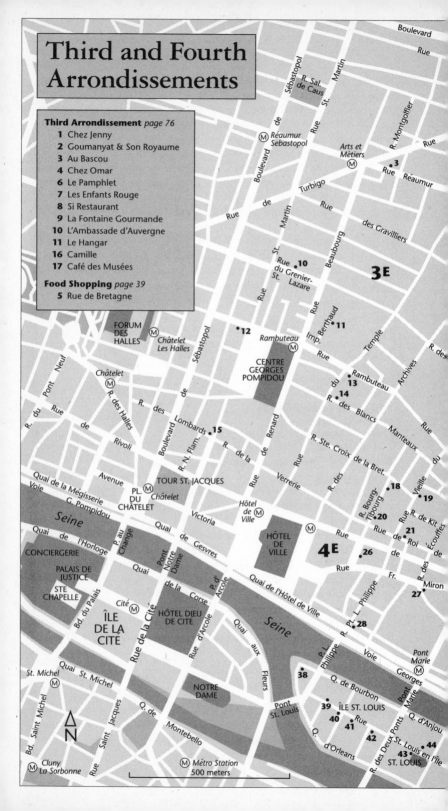

Third and Fourth Arrondissements

3E

4E

Boulevard
Rue
R. Sal de Caus
Sébastopol
St. Martin
de
Rue
Réaumur Sebastopol
Arts et Métiers
R. Montgolfier
Rue
Rue
3
Rue Réaumur
Boulevard
Turbigo
Rue
des Gravilliers
Rue
de
St. Martin
Beaubourg
Temple
R. des
Rue du Grenier-St.-Lazare
10
Imp. Berthaud
11
Archives
FORUM DES HALLES
Châtelet Les Halles
12
Rambuteau
Rue
CENTRE GEORGES POMPIDOU
Rambuteau
13
R. du
14
R. des Blancs Manteaux
Rue
Châtelet
Pont Neuf
R. des Halles
Lombards
15
R. N. Flam.
R. de la
R. de Renard
Rue Verrerie
R. Ste. Croix de la Bret.
Rue du
R. des
18
Vieille
19
Avenue
Rivoli
TOUR ST. JACQUES
R. Bourg-Tibourg
20
Rue de Kit
Quai de la Mégisserie
Voie G. Pompidou
PL. DU CHÂTELET
Châtelet
Victoria
Hôtel de Ville
R. de Roi
21
R. des Écouffes
Seine
Quai de l'Horloge
Quai de Gesvres
HÔTEL DE VILLE
26
de
Rue
Fr.
R. des
Miron
CONCIERGERIE
PALAIS DE JUSTICE
STE CHAPELLE
P. au Change
Pont Notre Dame
Quai de la Corse
P. d'Arcole
Quai de l'Hôtel de Ville
R. Pt. L. Philippe
27
ÎLE DE LA CITÉ
Cité
HÔTEL DIEU DE CITÉ
Rue de la Cité
Rue d'Arcole
Seine
28
St. Michel
Quai St. Michel
Q. de
NOTRE DAME
Quai aux Fleurs
Pont St. Louis
38
P. L. Philippe
Voie
Pont Marie
Bd. Saint Michel
Saint Jacques
Montebello
Q. de Bourbon
39
ÎLE ST. LOUIS
40
41 Rue
Pont Marie
Q. d'Anjou
Cluny La Sorbonne
Rue
Q. d'Orleans
Pont St. Louis
42
Q. des Deux Ponts
St. Louis en l'Île
44
43
ST. LOUIS

Ⓜ Métro Station
500 meters

N

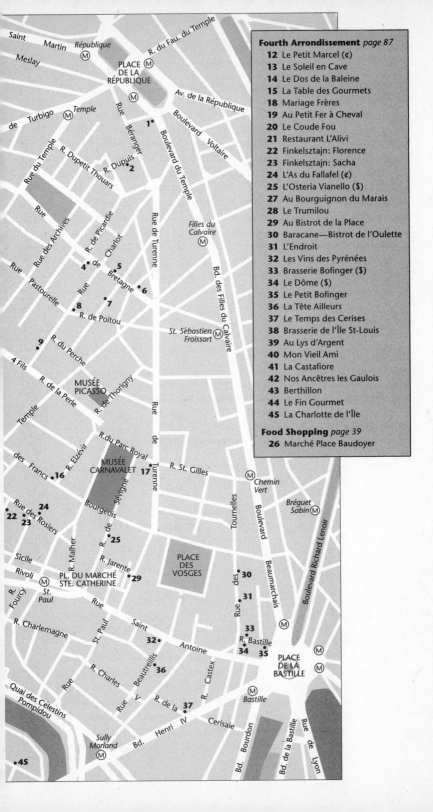

CAMILLE (16)
24, rue des Francs-Bourgeois
Métro: St-Paul

Camille is a useful spot to remember if you are looking for a place that is child-friendly or if you want to eat an early dinner. The corner location on one of the most interesting shopping streets in the Marais draws a diverse crowd. Tourists squeeze in for lunch and early dinners, and the French arrive for lazy weekend lunches and for dinner after 9 P.M. The kitchen turns out all the seasonal bistro classics, with only a few misses. In the winter, look for *entrées* of sausage with warm potato salad, leeks vinaigrette, green beans dotted with bits of foie gras, and just-cooked scrambled eggs with smoked salmon. *Salade niçoise* is added to the list in the summer; a plate of Auvergne *charcuterie* is always available. The filling *plats* include *blanquette de veau, confit de canard* or roast chicken (both with crispy sautéed potatoes), *petit sale aux lentilles, entrecôte,* veal kidneys, and liver. Desserts are not made here, but the *tarte au chocolat* is certainly far better than the runny *tarte aux pommes*.

TEL 01-42-72-20-50
OPEN Daily: bar 8 A.M.–midnight, continuous food service noon–11:30 P.M.
  CLOSED Dec 24 & 31 for dinner, NAC
À LA CARTE 30–35€, BNC **PRIX FIXE** Lunch: 20€, 2 courses, BNC (add 1€
  Sat–Sun) **CREDIT CARDS** AE, DC, MC, V
RESERVATIONS Recommended **ENGLISH SPOKEN** Yes, and English menu

CHEZ JENNY (1)
Place de la République, 39, boulevard du Temple
Métro: République

Chez Jenny celebrates the food and wine of Alsace, which is served in a magnificent old brasserie full of fabulous regional artwork. The cavernous interior is as impressive as the food: it's decorated with carved wall plaques, life-size wooden figures in native Alsatian dress, and lovely murals depicting life in this colorful region of France along the German border. For the best overall atmosphere, reserve a table on the ground floor.

Rosy-cheeked waitresses in red skirts, white blouses, and black vests serve the brimming plates with speed and good cheer. If you are looking for some of the best *choucroute* in Paris, you will find it at Chez Jenny. For the uninitiated, *choucroute* is a steaming platter or copper pot of smoked slab bacon, bratwurst, several plump sausages (including white veal), lean smoked pork loin, and savory sauerkraut and potatoes cooked with wine or champagne (which is called *choucroute royale*); a stein of golden beer is the perfect accompaniment. For a lighter supper, order the assorted *charcuterie* of mild Alsatian sausages or a *plat* of iced oysters and shellfish with a glass of chilled Riesling wine. Warning: The fish *choucroute* makes for a strange combination.

TEL 01-44-54-39-00 **INTERNET** www.chez-jenny.com
OPEN Daily: 11:30 A.M.–1 A.M., continuous service; happy hour 5–8 P.M.
  CLOSED Never

À **LA CARTE** 35–45€, BNC **PRIX FIXE** Lunch & dinner: L'Esprit du Boulevard, 21€, either main course & BC or 2 courses, BNC; 26.50€, either 2 courses & BC or 3 courses, BNC; 31€, 3 courses, BC (at lunch a kir is offered) **CREDIT CARDS** AE, DC, MC, V
RESERVATIONS Advised **ENGLISH SPOKEN** Yes

CHEZ OMAR (4)
47, rue de Bretagne
Métro: Arts et Métiers, St-Sébastien Froissart

Diners at Chez Omar arrive in droves to tackle monumental portions of some of the best couscous in Paris. This traditional Parisian café, which has not changed in fifty years, buzzes for both lunch and dinner with a trendy-by-association crowd that swears by Omar's six or more varieties of couscous. There are other choices on the menu, ranging from grilled fish to brochettes and plates of red meat, but when you are at Chez Omar, think only lamb, beef, *merguez* (spicy lamb sausage), chicken, or vegetable couscous. Warning: Portions are enormous. No one has room for any of the pastries, but everyone manages mint tea, which aids digestion. Here is one place you want to arrive early for dinner. Omar doesn't take reservations and after 8:30 or 9 P.M., especially on weekends, the line is out the door.

TEL 01-42-72-36-26
OPEN Mon–Sat: lunch noon–2:30 P.M., dinner 7 P.M.–midnight; Sun: dinner 7 P.M.–midnight **CLOSED** Sun lunch, NAC
À **LA CARTE** 25–35€, BNC **PRIX FIXE** None **CREDIT CARDS** None
RESERVATIONS Not acccepted **ENGLISH SPOKEN** Yes

GOUMANYAT & SON ROYAUME (2)
3, rue Charles-François Dupuis, corner of rue de la Corderie
Métro: Temple, République

The catalog says it all: "Goumanyat is a rediscovery of the pleasures of taste and the taste of pleasures . . . a rich and thrilling adventure for you and your guests."

For seven generations the Thiercelin family has searched the globe for the finest spices, essential oils, exotic herbs, and food products. It all began in 1809, when their forebearers began specializing in buying natural saffron, which the shop still sells in its purest form. Today the store is also a mecca for serious chefs who want the best in unusual herbs and spices, jam, honey, mustard, natural vinegar, or flavored salt and sugar. Sniffing, tasting, and enjoying are all encouraged by the friendly family members who graciously wait on their guests. Three-hour cooking classes are held using many of the ingredients available here.

TEL 01-44-78-96-74 **INTERNET** www.goumanyat.com
OPEN Tues–Fri: 2–7 P.M., Sat 11–7 P.M. **CLOSED** Mon, Sun; holidays, middle 2 weeks in Aug
PRICES From 5€ and up **CREDIT CARDS** AE, DC, MC, V
ENGLISH SPOKEN Yes

LA FONTAINE GOURMANDE (9)
11, rue Charlot
Métro: Filles du Calvaire

For a Great Eat in the Marais near the Musée Picasso, book a table at Valerie and Marie's charming La Fontaine Gourmande. A small place with only ten tables, it has a homey atmosphere achieved by the orange stone-walled interior decorated with food posters and an impressive collection of kitsch. Valerie, who learned her cooking techniques from her father, a Lyonnaise baker, presents a classically seasonal menu with modern light touches. The portions are plentiful and presentations attractive. At lunch, in addition to her *plat du jour* and three or four other hot dishes, she offers three *tartines* (open-faced sandwiches): the *Savoyarde,* piled with potatoes and bacon, and topped with melted cheese; *the végétarienne,* potatoes, tomatoes, mushrooms, and cheese; and the *fromagère,* a hefty mix of chèvre, Gruyère, Reblochon, and Camembert. Finally, there are four omelettes ranging from a no-frills plain version to ones filled with mushrooms, bacon, or cheese. Both the *tartines* and omelettes come with a salad.

Depending on the time of year, the pleasing dinner *entrées* might include Valerie's silky foie gras, highlighted by a compote of onions; a copious *salade landaise,* scattered with sliced duck breast and gizzards; or chèvre wrapped in slices of eggplant and zucchini and roasted. It only gets better as you move to the main course, especially if you are lucky enough to find on the menu her roast pork flavored with plums and bacon, filets of sole *meunière,* or on Saturday night, the tender *côte de boeuf* served with potatoes and a salad. For dessert Valerie always has a soufflé, perhaps a Grand Marnier or *à la poire William;* a fruit tart, such as a Calvados-flavored apple version gilded with vanilla ice cream and crème fraîche; and something chocolate, perhaps a warm cake with a fudgy inside and a scoop of ice cream melting on top. Coffee and the bill come with a chocolate.

NOTE: You may want to avoid the bathroom, which is in a coffin-like space reached by walking through the restaurant and outside into a small back courtyard.

TEL 01-42-78-72-40
OPEN Tues–Sat: lunch noon–2:30 P.M., dinner 7:30–10:30 P.M. **CLOSED** Mon, Sun; holidays, 1st week of Jan, Aug
À LA CARTE Lunch 9–18€, dinner 30–35€, both BNC **PRIX FIXE** Dinner (Tues–Thur): 20€, 3 courses, BNC **CREDIT CARDS** MC, V
RESERVATIONS Recommended **ENGLISH SPOKEN** Yes

L'AMBASSADE D'AUVERGNE (10)
22, rue du Grenier–St-Lazare
Métro: Rambuteau (rue du Grenier–St-Lazare exit)

The long-standing owners of L'Ambassade d'Auvergne regard themselves as culinary representatives of their native region. Throughout the years, their restaurant has remained true to its heritage, and today it is one of the finest regional restaurants in Paris. I have eaten here many times, and I always find all of the restaurant's elements working together to create a satisfying dining experience. Its several dining rooms are always filled, and its clientele includes prominent political figures. For the most authentic and beautiful atmosphere, reserve a table downstairs, which has massive beams from which hang hundreds of Auvergne hams. The nonsmoking section is upstairs. If you are eating alone, ask for a place at the *table d'hôte,* where you will be seated with other solo diners who probably won't be strangers by the end of the meal.

Country abundance is evident in every delicious dish, from the house specialties that remain the same each day of the week to the monthly and seasonal offerings. A variety of excellent, little-known regional wines are available to accompany your feast. Wonderful *entrées* anytime are the cabbage soup—with white beans, ham chunks, potatoes, carrots, and Roquefort cheese—and the warm *lentilles du puy* salad. Tempting main dishes include the spicy blood sausage with chestnuts, rosemary-roasted leg of lamb, and *porc confite.* An absolute must with whatever you order is *l'aligot,* a masterful blend of garlic-infused puréed potatoes and *tomme* cheese whipped at your table and served from copper pans. Trying to save room for dessert is next to impossible, but if you can, the creamy chocolate mousse served nonstop from a crystal bowl is worth the overload. If you can't do dessert, consider ordering one of their fruit *digestifs* as a grand finale.

TEL 01-42-72-31-22 **INTERNET** www.ambassade-auvergne.com
OPEN Daily: lunch noon–2 P.M., dinner 7:30–11 P.M. **CLOSED** Dec 24 & 31 for dinner, NAC
À LA CARTE 30–40€, BNC **PRIX FIXE** Lunch & dinner: 28€, 3 courses, BNC
CREDIT CARDS AE, DC, MC, V
RESERVATIONS Essential **ENGLISH SPOKEN** Yes

LE HANGAR (11)
12, impasse Berthaud
Métro: Rambuteau

Le Hangar is buried on a hidden *impasse* off the intersection of rue Rambuteau and rue Beaubourg, just steps from the Centre Pompidou and the little-known Musée de la Poupée (doll museum). This perennial favorite attracts a knowing clientele who value the chef's interpretations of familiar favorites and the smiling welcome extended by the owners. On a warm day, it is very pleasant to sit on the covered terrace, which is free from dust, birds, dirt, and automobile fumes. The mood inside is rather stark, with linens, crystal, green plants, and an efficient waitstaff changing the silver and crumbing the tables between courses. The prices are as attractive as the setting, with imaginative choices for each course and appropriate wines from small producers that enhance the dishes.

As you decide your order, you are served a rich olive tapenade and toast. Depending on the season, cold *entrées* may feature a salmon *tartare,* barely cooked green beans drizzled with olive oil, artichokes served in a balsamic vinaigrette, or a lusty lentil soup flavored with pieces of duck liver. Another delicious hot *entrée* is the ravioli in an eggplant cream sauce. Carnivores will love the meaty servings of *blanquette de veau,* the beef fillet with *morille* sauce, and the mouthwatering pan-fried foie gras served with the house specialty—creamy, olive oil–flavored mashed potatoes. Depending on the season, fish fanciers can look for *bar* (sea bass) or *morue* (salt cod) with steamed potatoes or scallops in a parsley cream sauce. Save room for dessert, especially the molten chocolate soufflé, orange *crêpes* with Grand Marnier sauce, the warm lemon *gateau* (cake), or the fresh fruit *clafoutis* cooked to order. A plate of their own cookies and an espresso is an ideal end to this truly wonderful meal.

TEL 01-42-74-55-44
OPEN Tues–Sat: lunch noon–2:30 P.M., dinner 7 P.M.–midnight **CLOSED** Mon, Sun; holidays, Aug
À LA CARTE 30–35€, BNC **PRIX FIXE** None **CREDIT CARDS** None
RESERVATIONS Recommended **ENGLISH SPOKEN** Yes

LE PAMPHLET (6)
38, rue Debelleyme
Métro: St-Sébastien Froissart

Le Pamphlet has everything a wonderful restaurant in Paris should: imaginative food, beautiful execution, comfortable surroundings, and a loyal French clientele who appreciate the excellent *rapport qualité-prix* (value for money). The two dining areas are decorated in Provençal reds and yellows, and the well-spaced tables are set with starched linens and contemporary china. Throughout the meal, the owner makes the rounds, checking whether you are satisfied and urging you to enjoy all three courses of your meal. Let me assure you, this is not difficult despite the generous portions.

When seated, you will be offered a basket of assorted breads and a silver container of butter, a plate of spicy *charcuterie,* and an *amuse bouche* (tiny appetizer) to whet your appetite for the good things ahead. And good things indeed are on Chef Alain Carrère's two-price seasonal menus, which he bases on fresh market availability. In late autumn, starters could include a warm green bean salad topped with grilled shrimp and sauced with crab, or *coquilles St-Jacques,* lightly cooked in butter, sitting atop a bed of fresh greens, and dusted with Parmesan cheese. There are always several choices of fish and meat for the main course. The rack of lamb garnished with baby vegetables, and the cod with a calamari-parsley sauce, accompanied by baby potatoes and red peppers, are two popular fall dishes. For dessert, lightly warmed fresh pineapple showered with spices and served with cinnamon ice cream receives very high marks, and so does the poached banana sprinkled with rum-soaked raisins and topped with chocolate sauce and vanilla ice cream. Coffee is served with an assortment of chocolates and *madeleines.* The wine list is not overwhelming, either in price or length.

TEL 01-42-72-39-24
OPEN Tues–Fri: lunch noon–2:30 P.M., dinner 7:30–11 P.M.; Mon, Sat: dinner 7:30–11 P.M. **CLOSED** Mon & Sat lunch, Sun; holidays, Jan 1–15, Aug 8–26
À LA CARTE None **PRIX FIXE** Lunch & dinner: 30€, 3 courses, BNC; *menu dégustation:* 50€, 2 *entrées,* a fish and meat dish, 2 desserts, BNC
CREDIT CARDS MC, V
RESERVATIONS Essential **ENGLISH SPOKEN** Yes

LES ENFANTS ROUGE (7)
9, rue de Beauce & 90, rue des Archives
Métro: Temple

Queen Margot, wife of Henri IV, established an orphanage on this site. The abandoned children who lived here wore red jackets, thus the name *les enfants rouge.* After the orphanage closed, the building became a convent and was ultimately destroyed in the French Revolution. Today it is an integral cornerstone of the revamped Marché des Enfants Rouge on rue de Bretagne. Owned by Dany Bertin-Denis and her husband, it is a lively wine bar serving wines from around France, with emphasis on vintages from the Loire and Rhône Valleys. The tiny entrance/bar area is continually packed three deep with a friendly crowd that shmoozes with the owners and happily meets and greets those coming to dine in the crowded adjoining dining room. Barflys can order cold meat and cheese plates or fat sausages, which they have to eat standing up. The little dining room is especially animated on the weekends, when families come for lunch, and on Thursday and Friday nights, when the night owls are out in force. The menu is unfussy but flavorful, and always includes a velvety winter soup, a summer salad, fresh fish, steak with great *frites,* and the usual sausages (blood and otherwise). Desserts—with the excetion of Dany's grandmother's recipe for *pain perdu*—are not a factor, but the excellent wines definitely are, especially the weekly specials, which can be ordered by the glass.

TEL 01-48-87-80-61
OPEN Tues–Sat: lunch noon–3 P.M., also Thur–Fri dinner 7 P.M.–midnight
CLOSED Mon, Sun; dinner Tues–Wed & Sat; 1 week at Christmas; Aug
À LA CARTE None **PRIX FIXE** Lunch: 16€, 2 courses, BNC; lunch & dinner: 28€, 3 courses, BNC **CREDIT CARDS** V
RESERVATIONS Essential **ENGLISH SPOKEN** Yes

SI RESTAURANT (8)
14, rue Charlot
Métro: St-Sébastien Foissart

Le nouveau buzz is all about Si, a laid-back, minimalist choice that has rapidly become the gathering place for the artistic, black-clad crowd who live in this corner of the Marais. The menu is short and to the point, and no wonder: it is presented to you inside a CD holder. Seating is along light tan banquettes in a ground-floor room and at round tables for six on the mezzanine. At night, the candles on the glass-topped tables add a soft touch. Whenever you go, it will always be possible to order a reasonably priced, satisfying meal of any size from either the lunch or dinner menus, where all choices within each course—*entrée, plat,* and dessert—are the same price. On a recent lunch visit, I started with a salad of fresh figs and mozzarella cheese dressed in a raspberry vinaigrette. The tender *entrecôte* served with satiny mashed potatoes was such a filling *plat* that, during dessert, I could only admire the fresh fruit tarte my companions were devouring. If you go for dinner and are not ravenous, the friendly waiters will encourage you to graze through the *entrées*. Depending on the season, you could order the carrot soup accented with *coquilles St-Jacques* and cumin, followed by the all-vegetable *antipasti du si* or *parmentier de canard confit.* For dessert, you will probably have just enough room to succumb to the warm chocolate cake, but if you are feeling virtuous, enjoy the whipped yogurt layered with honey and pistachios. More demanding appetites will be sated by main courses of a lobster-and-mussel ragout or a honey-glazed chicken brochette, served on a bed of rice and fresh vegetables.

TEL 01-42-78-02-31
OPEN Mon–Fri: lunch 12:30–2 P.M., dinner 8–11 P.M.; Sat: dinner 8–11 P.M.
  CLOSED Sat lunch, Sun; holidays, Aug
À LA CARTE Lunch: *entrées* 7€, *plats* 10€, desserts 7€; dinner: *entrées* 8€,
  plats 18€, dessert 8€ **PRIX FIXE** Lunch: 14€, 2 courses, 18€, 3 courses;
  dinner: 24€, 2 courses, 29€, 3 courses; all BNC **CREDIT CARDS** V
RESERVATIONS Essential **ENGLISH SPOKEN** Yes

Fourth Arrondissement

Point zero is a compass rose set in the pavement in front of Notre Dame Cathedral. This is the spot from which all distances are measured in France, but more than that, the cathedral serves as the spiritual and emotional heart of the country.

Île St-Louis was developed by Henri IV in the seventeenth century. It has been home to Voltaire, Baudelaire, Colette, and George Sand. Today it is one of the most expensive plots of real estate in Paris. Full of atmosphere, the narrow streets house beautiful *hôtel particulières* (private mansions) occupied by film stars, authors, the Rothschilds, and six thousand other lucky people. In the Marais, the place des Vosges is the oldest square in Paris, and some consider it the most beautiful and romantic. It dates from 1612 and was built to celebrate the engagement of King Louis XIII. Once a swamp and slum, it was an up-and-coming area some years ago—now it has arrived. Young fashion designers fight for shop space and rents are astronomical. The famous fashion houses on the rue de Faubourg St-Honoré and avenue Montaigne appeal largely to an affluent, international clientele, but truly stylish French men and women know to shop in the Marais for the latest word in affordable clothes. The area is also the center of the Parisian Jewish and gay communities. Take a stroll down rue des Rosiers and discover marvelous kosher delicatessens, bakeries, and restaurants. The gay crowd fills the bars and restaurants on and around rue Vielle du Temple. While you are in the fourth arrondissement, you can visit the museum of modern art, better known as the Centre Georges Pompidou, or the Beaubourg.

RIGHT BANK

Centre Georges Pompidou (Beaubourg)
Hôtel-de-Ville (City Hall)
Île St-Louis
Jewish Quarter
Maison de Victor Hugo
Marais (continuation)
Notre Dame
place des Vosges

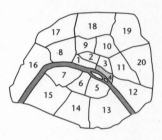

FOURTH ARRONDISSEMENT RESTAURANTS
(see map page 78)

($) indicates a Big Splurge; (¢) indicates a Cheap Eat

AU BISTROT DE LA PLACE (29)
2, place du Marché Ste-Catherine
Métro: St-Paul

On a warm sunny day or summer evening, it would be hard to imagine a more delightful setting for a meal than this popular spot on the quiet place du Marché Ste-Catherine, a few minutes from place des Vosges. The interior is definitely a mishmash of decor: bejeweled lights, Chinese lanterns shining on hanging peppers, a model of Fatima, a seashell collection, copper pots, a wild mosaic-tile mirror reflecting a bubbling waterfall, a painting of the Statue of Liberty, a struggling palm, pictures of American film stars from the forties and fifties, assorted Christmas decorations that tend to stay in place for weeks, and a handful of small tapestry-covered tables, which are served by one or two hard-pressed waiters. But never mind the inside: you want a table outside on the pretty traffic- and fume-free terrace, where you can enjoy a typical bistro meal and delight in watching the passing parade of Parisians.

The menu is the same for lunch and dinner and offers reliable fare with few surprises. Look for standard-bearers of hot goat cheese on toast, snails in a light pastry with garlic butter, chicken liver pâté flavored with Armagnac, and warm lentil salad with gizzards and sausage. Sweet-and-sour duck breast and a hearty Provençale beef stew are both served with sautéed garlic potatoes. The chef's specialty—*confit cassoulet*—comes with white beans, duck, sausage, and thick bacon. Lamb tossed with olives and served on a bed of wild rice, and a veggie lasagna with a green salad wrap up the *plats*. For dessert, the house tiramisu is a good bet, and so is the ever-present chocolate *fondant* floating in a light custard sauce.

If you don't come for lunch or dinner, remember that they are open all day long, and it is a nice place to come for a drink in the afternoon or early evening.

TEL 01-42-78-21-32
OPEN Daily: breakfast (summer only) 8 A.M.–noon, lunch noon–2:30 P.M.,
drinks and afternoon tea 3–7 P.M., dinner 7–11:30 P.M. **CLOSED** Breakfast
in winter, NAC
À LA CARTE 26–33€, BNC **PRIX FIXE** Lunch: 15€, 2 courses; dinner: 24€,
3 courses; both BNC **CREDIT CARDS** MC, V (16€ minimum)
RESERVATIONS Recommended for terrace **ENGLISH SPOKEN** Yes, and English
menu

AU BOURGUIGNON DU MARAIS (27)
52, rue François Miron
Métro: St-Paul

Au Bourguignon is an address cherished by knowledgeable Parisians for its rich, robust Burgundy-style cooking, designed to complement the restaurant's large selection of Burgundy wines. On cold days, patrons jockey for a table in the wood-paneled dining room;

in warm weather, they are all positioned at tables on the large corner terrace. Despite the hearty nature of this type of food, everyone is eager to devour slabs of the house specialty—*jambon persillé*—garlic-infused snails, and poached eggs in wine before tackling plates of steak or tuna tartare, a piece of rare beef, or *andouillette* served with a mound of cheesy mashed potatoes. Desserts don't take a back seat here, especially not the crème brûlée or the bowls of Berthillon ice cream or sorbet (for more on this wonderful ice cream, see page 92). Only wines from Burgundy are available, either by the glass or bottle, or purchased to go.

TEL 01-48-87-15-40

OPEN Mon–Fri: lunch noon–3 P.M., dinner 7:30–11 P.M. **CLOSED** Sat–Sun; holidays, July 15–Aug 15

À LA CARTE 30€, BNC **PRIX FIXE** None **CREDIT CARDS** AE, DC, MC, V

RESERVATIONS Essential **ENGLISH SPOKEN** Yes

AU LYS D'ARGENT (39)
90, rue St-Louis-en-l'Île
Métro: Pont-Marie

Forty varieties of tea, light meals based around quiches, *tartes,* salads, and crêpes, plus homemade pastries keep visitors well fed here when they are on Île St-Louis—an island in the middle of the River Seine that is a picturesque micro-slice of Paris. On weekends and holidays, the waves of tourists, browsers, and occasional natives can be very discouraging. For those looking for a bit of sustenance, Au Lys d'Argent provides something on its menu for just about everyone. They serve a daily brunch, which includes freshly squeezed orange juice, coffee, or tea, *fromage blanc* with dried fruits, pancakes and maple syrup, toast, and a choice of four types of eggs, including a cheese omelette and scrambled eggs with smoked salmon or ham. Not to be forgotten are their rich chocolate drinks made to order from melted bars of pure chocolate, whole milk, and cream (allow ten minutes, please, and don't tell your cardiologist). For a complete chocolate blowout—and why not?—order a slice of their dark chocolate cake to go with your *chocolat à l'ancienne.*

TEL 01-46-33-56-13

OPEN Summer (May 1–Oct 31): Mon, Wed–Sat lunch noon–3:30 P.M., dinner 6:30–10:30 P.M. (Fri–Sat till 11 P.M.), Sun noon–10 P.M.; Winter (Nov 1–April 30): Mon,Wed–Sat noon–10 P.M. (Fri–Sat till 10:30 P.M.), Sun 11:30 A.M.–6:30 P.M., continuous service **CLOSED** Tues, NAC

À LA CARTE 15–20€, BNC **PRIX FIXE** Lunch & dinner: 10.90€, 14€, 17€, all 3 courses and BNC; brunch: 18€, BC **CREDIT CARDS** MC, V (16€ minimum)

RESERVATIONS Not necessary **ENGLISH SPOKEN** Yes, and English menu

AU PETIT FER À CHEVAL (19)
30, rue Vieille du Temple
Métro: Hôtel de Ville, St-Paul

Cheap, cheerful, and truly French—that's Au Petit Fer à Cheval, a popular meeting place for everyone from shopkeepers and stray tourists to New Wave patrons just in from Mars.

This slightly seedy Marais landmark has been in operation since 1903 and consists of sidewalk tables and a marble-top horseshoe *(fer à cheval)* bar in the front room. In back, there is a larger room with booths made from old wooden métro seats. For Flash Gordon and Captain Marvel fans, the stainless-steel WCs are not to be missed. The nice thing about this place is that you can come in anytime for a quick *café* standing at the bar, or you can sit down and consume lunch or dinner. While the food doesn't inspire rave reviews, it is filling and typical native grub consisting of salads, daily *plats,* and the dessert standards of chocolate mousse and fruit tarts.

TEL 01-42-72-47-47
OPEN Daily: 9 A.M.–2 A.M., continuous service **CLOSED** Never
À LA CARTE 15–30€, BNC **PRIX FIXE** None **CREDIT CARDS** MC, V
RESERVATIONS Not necessary **ENGLISH SPOKEN** Yes

BARACANE—BISTROT DE L'OULETTE (30)
38, rue des Tournelles
Métro: Bastille

For one of the best bistro meals going, book a table at Baracane—Bistrot de l'Oulette on the edge of the Marais. Owner and chef Marcel Baudis opened this place many years ago, and his impeccable dishes from Quercy in southwestern France have remained a hit. Baudis has since moved to a larger location in the Bercy area near the Gare de Lyon (see L'Oulette, page 227), but the kitchen continues to maintain his standards of excellence in every dish served.

The real appeal of this narrow bistro lies in its consistently fresh foods complemented by an excellent wine list. The *formule* menus—available for either lunch or dinner—offer a wide selection from the seasonal menu. Some favorites remain at the insistence of loyal patrons. For starters, you can count on *salade de chévre* or the satiny-smooth duck foie gras spread on pieces of chestnutbread. For the main course, the *cassoulet, confit de canard* with parsleyed potatoes, and the grilled *magret de canard* are surefire winners. Seasonal specialties and fresh fish round out the choices. Sweet endings no one wants to miss include a pistachio-flavored chocolate cake, a refreshing prune ice cream with Armagnac, and the satisfying *croustillant aux pommes* (apples in flaky pastry).

TEL 01-42-71-43-33 **INTERNET** www.l-oulette.com
OPEN Mon–Fri: lunch noon–2:30 P.M., dinner 7 P.M.–midnight; Sat: dinner
   7 P.M.–midnight **CLOSED** Sat lunch, Sun; holidays, NAC
À LA CARTE 35–40€, BNC **PRIX FIXE** Lunch: 11€, *plat du jour,* BC (wine
   & coffee); 16€, 2 courses, BC (wine); lunch Mon–Thur: 23€, 2 courses

(choice), BNC; lunch & dinner: 28€, 3 courses, BNC; 38€, 3 courses, BC (wine & coffee) **CREDIT CARDS** MC, V
RESERVATIONS Essential **ENGLISH SPOKEN** Yes

BERTHILLON (43)
31, rue St-Louis-en-l'Île
Métro: Pont-Marie

Ask any Parisian where to find the most famous ice cream in the capital, and the answer is unanimous: Berthillon. You don't need to remember the address. Just look for the long line that inevitably winds down the block, no matter the weather. This isn't the only place to sample Berthillon's addictive ice creams and sorbets, since they are featured in scores of restaurants; however, it is where the multimillion-euro empire began and the most authentic place to scoop up their extravaganza of seventy-five revolving flavors. All are made here with absolutely fresh, preservative-free ingredients and sold in scoops or cups. Enjoy them as you stroll through this picturesque part of Paris, or purchase larger hand-packed containers to eat at home. What are the most popular flavors? Believe it or not, tried and true French vanilla bean, dark chocolate, and summer peach rank as the best-sellers. There is a tearoom in back that serves a few pastries, a light breakfast, and afternoon ice cream delights.

TEL 01-43-54-31-61 **INTERNET** www.berthillon-glacier.fr
OPEN Wed–Sun: 10 A.M.–8 P.M. **CLOSED** Mon–Tues; school holidays (not Christmas), July 14–Sept 1
À LA CARTE 1 scoop 2€, 4 scoops 5€; half-liter 7.50€ **PRIX FIXE** None
   CREDIT CARDS None
RESERVATIONS Not accepted **ENGLISH SPOKEN** Yes

BRASSERIE BOFINGER ($, 33)
5–7, rue de la Bastille
Métro: Bastille

What better way to spend the evening than in the company of friends, enjoying good food and wine in the oldest and most handsome brasserie in Paris, located only a few minutes from the opera house at place de la Bastille? While not the place for a romantic tête-à-tête, you can't help feeling glamorous and festive when dining here. The two floors of magnificent Belle Epoque decor—a maze of mirrors, brass, stained glass, stunning wood carvings depicting five continents, and huge bouquets of fresh flowers—provide the perfect backdrop for the see-and-be-seen crowds of fashionable French who flock here every night. Do not even consider arriving without a reservation, and when booking, if you are a smoker, request a seat under the stained-glass dome, the most beautiful part of the restaurant.

While culinary fireworks are not the order of the day, the food is dependable, and the generous servings cater to healthy, meat-loving appetites. Platters of oysters, traditional *choucroutes,* and grilled meats lead the list of the best dining choices. The house Riesling is a good wine selection. The service by black-tied waiters, who sometimes ferry plates over the heads of diners, is swift and accurate.

NOTE: Le Petit Bofinger (see page 100) is a less lavish spin-off right across the street.

TEL 01-42-72-87-82 **INTERNET** www.bofingerparis.com, www.flobrasseries.com
OPEN Mon–Fri: lunch noon–3 P.M., dinner 6:30 P.M.–1 A.M.; Sat–Sun: noon–
1 A.M., continuous service **CLOSED** Never
À LA CARTE 40–50€, BNC **PRIX FIXE** Lunch (Mon–Fri): 24.50€, 2 courses,
BC; lunch & dinner (daily): 35€, 3 courses, BC; Faim de Nuit (nightly
after 11 P.M.): 25€, BNC **CREDIT CARDS** AE, DC, MC, V
RESERVATIONS Essential **ENGLISH SPOKEN** Yes

BRASSERIE DE L'ÎLE ST-LOUIS (38)
55, quai de Bourbon
Métro: Pont-Marie

A stroll over the pedestrian bridge behind Notre Dame to Île St-Louis brings you right to the doorstep of this picturesque old *auberge,* which is the favorite watering hole and gathering place for many of the writers, entertainers, and expatriates who live on the island. Its outdoor terrace is prime seating for a lazy afternoon spent with friends, admiring the beautiful people passing by or just celebrating your visit to Paris. Inside, the atmosphere is bustling, colorful, and friendly, making it impossible to feel lonely here for long.

The food . . . well, in all honesty, that is not this place's *raison d'etre.* It is the camaraderie that counts; eating is secondary. So, what to expect? The menu features typical brasserie dishes as well as Alsatian specialties of tripe in Riesling wine, pig's knuckles, omelettes, terrines, pâtés, *cassoulet,* and onion *tartes,* served with pitchers of house wine or mugs of frothy beer. Desserts tend to be uninspiring. Instead, walk down the center of the island to the renowned Berthillon (see page 92) and treat yourself to several scoops of their famous ice cream or sorbet, with equally famous prices and long queues.

TEL 01-43-54-02-59
OPEN Mon–Tues, Fri–Sun: 11 A.M.–2 A.M., Thur: 6:30 P.M.–2 A.M., continuous
food service until 11 P.M. **CLOSED** Thur lunch, Wed; 1 week Feb (dates
vary)
À LA CARTE 25–30€, BNC **PRIX FIXE** None **CREDIT CARDS** V
RESERVATIONS Not accepted **ENGLISH SPOKEN** Yes

FINKELSZTAJN: FLORENCE AND SACHA

FLORENCE FINKELSZTAJN (22)
24, rue des Écouffes, at 19, rue des Rosiers,

SACHA FINKELSZTAJN (23)
27, rue des Rosiers
Métro: St-Paul, Hôtel-de-Ville

The two Finkelsztajn bakery/*traiteur* shops sell treats not to be missed. For over five decades, they have been household names in the Jewish Quarter, where they dish out daily supplies of sweet and savory

Russian and Eastern European Jewish foods. At Florence's, nicknamed "The Blue Bakery," prepare yourself for authentic recipes of borscht, blini, Polish almond *babkas,* strudels, and a dozen or more home-style breads, either plain or bursting with seeds and dried fruits. Walk into Sacha's yellow location a few doors away on rue des Rosiers and try the traditional Russian cheesecake, along with *linzertort, pirojkis, tarama,* latkes, cold meats, and herring. It is run by the third family generation (see their family photos on the back wall), but that doesn't stop great-uncle Willy from manning the cash register in the back. At both sites, plan to look, order, pay, and take your food with you because the corner stools in each are almost always full.

TEL Florence: 01-48-87-92-85; Sacha: 01-42-72-78-91 **INTERNET** Florence: florencefinkelsztajn.free.fr; Sacha: www.laboutiquejaune.com
OPEN Florence: Mon–Tues, Thur–Sun 10 A.M.–7 P.M., continuous service; Sacha: Mon 11 A.M.–7 P.M., Wed–Sun 10 A.M.–7 P.M., continuous service
  CLOSED Florence: Wed, also Mon–Tues in July–Aug; Sacha: Tues, NAC
À LA CARTE 3–15€, BNC **PRIX FIXE** None **CREDIT CARDS** None
RESERVATIONS Not accepted **ENGLISH SPOKEN** Yes

LA CASTAFIORE (41)
51, rue St-Louis-en-l'Île
Métro: Pont-Marie

La Castafiore has had many lives. When I lived on Île St-Louis, it was a family-owned bistro and one of my favorite dining destinations. Since then, it has had a series of owners, but none of them seemed to make it until Gerrard and Edward took over fifteen years ago and began serving basic Italian-inspired dishes. There is room for only eleven closely packed small tables, and to make sure you are sitting at one of them, you must make a reservation.

If your budget is tight, order the 12€, two-course lunch menu, which comes with a bowl of onion soup, a green salad, or mozzarella on toast followed by a plate of gnocchi with tuna sauce, turkey Marsala, or pepper steak. Desserts are extra, but frankly, the main-course portions are so big you won't be able to consider anything more. The two-course dinner menu allows you to select from any of the *entrées* and any of the pastas on the menu. This bargain meal, good until 8:30 P.M., draws many of the visitors staying in the several charming hotels on the island (see *Great Sleeps Paris*), creating an unfortunately hot, stuffy, sardinelike atmosphere. Later, around 9 P.M., when the rush is over, the mood is much more peaceful and romantic in the candlelit room. When ordering, think light and order grilled *aubergines* (eggplant), or the traditional tomato and mozzarella di bufala salad drizzled with extra virgin olive oil. You will then have room for one of ten pastas, six meat or seafood dishes, flowing house wine, and a wicked tiramisu. I wish I still lived in the neighborhood.

TEL 01-43-54-78-62
OPEN Daily: lunch noon–2:30 P.M., dinner 6:30–11 P.M. **CLOSED** Dec 24–25

À LA CARTE 32–38€, BNC **PRIX FIXE** Lunch: 12€, 2 courses, BNC; dinner
(until 8:30 P.M.): 18.50€, 2 courses, BNC; dinner (all evening): 28.50€,
3 courses, BNC **CREDIT CARDS** AE, DC, MC, V
RESERVATIONS Essential, especially for dinner **ENGLISH SPOKEN** Yes

LA CHARLOTTE DE L'ÎLE (45)
24, rue St-Louis-en-l'Île
Métro: Pont-Marie, Sully-Morland

Sylvie Langlet is the well-loved owner and mother superior of
this quarter-century-old Paris tearoom, which specializes in her own
rich chocolate pastries and candies, poetry readings, puppet shows,
occasional live music performances, and most important, warm, fuzzy
good cheer. Just being in her cluttered two-room shop—which is
filled with a whimsical collection of baskets, children's drawings,
chocolate sculptures of children and animals, old teapots, and painted
plates—makes you feel like you are having tea with *grand-mère*. For its
regular customers, it obviously is an ideal oasis for meeting friends for
a good dose of gossip, mild flirtation, listening to music, or treating a
child to sweets before a puppet performance (there are two Wednesday
shows only, reservations required). Whenever you go, order a hot chocolate made from melted bars of pure chocolate (thinned with milk,
if you must dilute it) or Sylvie's bittersweet *chocolate tarte de tantie,* a
baked chocolate mousse with a chocolate glaze. Don't overlook her
candied orange peel dipped in chocolate, which I buy by the bagful.
At one time, a small handwritten sign in the window said: "Here we
sell happiness." They still do.

TEL 01-43-54-25-83 **INTERNET** www.la-charlotte.fr
OPEN Thur–Sun: tearoom 2–8 P.M., continuous service; Wed: puppet shows,
by reservation at 2:30 and 4 P.M.; sometimes live music Fri 6–8 P.M.
  CLOSED Mon–Wed; most holidays, July and Aug
À LA CARTE 10–18€, BC **PRIX FIXE** None **CREDIT CARDS** MC, V
RESERVATIONS Required for puppet shows (minimum 12 children)
  ENGLISH SPOKEN Yes

L'AS DU FALLAFEL (¢, 24)
34, rue des Rosiers
Métro: St-Paul

There is no question: Issac and Daisy sell the best falafel in Paris.
Their place is on a food-lined street smack in the heart of the Jewish
Quarter, and you can't miss it—look for the shiny green exterior
and the line snaking up to the takeout window. For years, that's all
there was: you selected your falafel, made to order by a team of swift
fry cooks, and then walked down the street eating it as the sauce
dripped off your chin. Caving in to demands for tables, they have
now added several inside seats as well as a few chairs out front. A
wide audience—including everyone from members of the Rolling
Stones to mink-clad matrons toting little dogs in Louis Vuitton carry-
cases—arrives nonstop every day (but Saturday) to order either the
fallafel normal, with shredded cabbage and sesame sauce, or the *spécial,*

heaped with fried eggplant and hummus. Whichever you order, wash it down with a glass of their homemade lemonade or a bottle of Israeli beer. If dessert is on your mind, go across the street to either of the Finkelsztajn bakeries (see page 93).

TEL 01-48-87-63-60
OPEN Mon–Fri, Sun: 11:30 A.M.–midnight, continuous service **CLOSED** Sat;
Jewish Passover, NAC
À LA CARTE 10–12€, BC **PRIX FIXE** None **CREDIT CARDS** MC, V (10€
minimum)
RESERVATIONS Not accepted **ENGLISH SPOKEN** Enough

LA TABLE DES GOURMETS (15)
14, rue des Lombards
Métro: Châtelet, Hôtel de Ville (exit Centre Pompidou or rue de Renard)

Ray Lampard, co-owner of RothRay apartments (see *Great Sleeps Paris*), once said, "Paris is like a treasure box, and when you open it, there is always something wonderful and interesting inside." Though he meant the entire city, he just as easily could have been describing La Table des Gourmets, a hidden find on one of the most touristy trails in Les Halles. From the outside it looks like nothing, and even when you walk inside, the first level is barren with the exception of a plant or two and an aquarium. The surprise comes when you are ushered past the bubbling fountain and singing birds to the dining room, which is housed in a twelfth-century chapel, complete with stone arches and pillars. Though the setting is matchless—with soft lighting, white linen–covered tables, and solicitous service—the food doesn't quite keep up. Still, it is dependable, there is plenty of it, and most important, it is priced right.

My advice is to keep it simple, ignore the à la carte menu completely and select one of the prix-fixe menus offered for both lunch and dinner. You could start with the *salade gourmande* with *mousse de canard* (duck mouse) and slices of smoked duck, or two pieces of *chèvre chaud* on a bed of lettuce. Skip the fatty lamb chops as a main course and stick with any fresh fish or the *plat du jour*. With the exception of the crème brûlée, desserts are not the kitchen's forte.

TEL 01-40-27-00-87
OPEN Mon–Sat: lunch noon–3 P.M. (last orders 2:15 P.M.), dinner 7–11:30 P.M.
(last orders 10:30 P.M.) **CLOSED** Sun; Aug
À LA CARTE 30–40€, BNC **PRIX FIXE** Lunch & dinner: 16€, 30€, both
3 courses; 30€, 4 courses; all BNC **CREDIT CARDS** MC, V
RESERVATIONS Recommended for 4 or more **ENGLISH SPOKEN** Enough to order

LA TÊTE AILLEURS (36)
20, rue Beautrellis
Métro: St-Paul, Bastille

La Tête Ailleurs joins the latest generation of trendy restaurants catering to a youthful, edgy, urban crowd. Don't even think of dropping in without reservations or you will be relegated to one of the hard banquette seats at the entrance. No, no, no . . . you want to be part of the scene in the large stone-walled room at the back with its dramatic pitched glass roof. Candles and low lighting add a touch of *amour,* but this is mitigated by the blasting music (which I was finally able to get turned down only after three requests). Service is well-meaning, but at times reflects the restaurant's name, La Tête Ailleurs: the head is elsewhere.

The menu is stylishly appealing with a Méditerranean emphasis on fresh vegetables and fish. A nice beginning to share is the plate of grilled vegetables on a bed of roquette, topped with creamy mozzarella di bufala. The vegetable and shrimp tempura is another good beginning. Second courses star tender fillets of lamb and creamy polenta, pasta tossed with fresh truffles, tuna with an unusual mango sauce, and an intriguing fillet of sea bass served with pistou-flavored potatoes. Desserts are a must; try the panna cotta, which is served in two goblets: one topped with caramel, the other with a raspberry sauce.

TEL 01-42-72-47-80
OPEN Mon–Fri: lunch noon–2:30 P.M., dinner 8–11 P.M.; Sat: dinner 8–11 P.M.
   CLOSED Sat lunch, Sun; Aug
À LA CARTE 35€, BNC **PRIX FIXE** Lunch: 13.50€, 2 courses & coffee
   CREDIT CARDS MC, V
RESERVATIONS Essential **ENGLISH SPOKEN** Yes

LE COUDE FOU (20)
12, rue de Bourg-Tibourg
Métro: Hôtel de Ville, St-Paul

To paraphrase an old saying, "Life is too short to drink bad, boring wine." That will never happen at Le Coude Fou, Patric Segall's appealing *bistro à vins,* which is a nice, enjoyable, safe place to try various wines at a reasonable cost. The food is secondary to the wines, but the locals still indulge in lunchtime plates of sturdy hot meals and return in the evening for more of the same, including plates of French country cheeses and *charcuteries.* On the weekends, brunch is the draw, and no wonder when the meal includes a plate of cold cuts, scrambled eggs with caviar, green salad, *fondant au chocolate* (warm chocolate cake), a large glass of wine, and coffee. Everyone stands around the bar or spills into the two rustic rooms, sitting at the bare tables made from wine casks. The lighthearted mood is enhanced by murals depicting party-goers from ancient times and caricatures of Parisian barflies. As for the wines, try the specials of the month.

TEL 01-42-77-15-16
OPEN Daily: lunch noon–3 P.M. (Sun till 4 P.M.), dinner 7:30 P.M.–midnight
   CLOSED Dec 24 & 31, 2 weeks in Aug (dates vary)
À LA CARTE 30–35€, BNC **PRIX FIXE** Lunch (Mon–Fri): 17.50€, 2 courses,
   20.50€, 3 courses, both BC (2 glasses of wine); brunch (Sat–Sun): 24€,
   3 courses, BC; dinner (Mon–Thur): 28€, 3 courses, BNC
   CREDIT CARDS AE, MC, V
RESERVATIONS Recommended on weekends **ENGLISH SPOKEN** Yes

LE DÔME ($, 34)
2, rue de la Bastille
Métro: Bastille

Good tips often come from readers, and this is one of them. However, if you do not like fish, move on . . . because fish is the only thing you can order here. The sunny, yellow interiors by noted restaurant designer Philippe Slavik are casually elegant, creating a sleek and contemporary look that gives diners a feeling of space in the uncluttered two-level surroundings.

As everyone knows, fish is never cheap in Paris, whether you buy it at the market or order it in a restaurant. Here, all the fish is guaranteed fresh—nothing is frozen. Prices here are not for penny pinchers, but they are certainly competitive. Depending on the main course, you may want to vary your starter. The *salade de langoustines* (prawn salad), the *soupe de poissons* (fish soup), or the *moules sautées au thym* (mussels sautéed with shallots and thyme) are hearty and delicious beginnings. Popular early winter *plats* are the *coquilles St-Jacques au pistou* (fresh scallops tossed with basil, garlic, cheese, and olive oil) and *brandade de morue* (creamed salt cod). For something unadorned, try the *bar grillé* (grilled sea bass) or the traditional sole *meunière*. For dessert, you must try to save a little space for the *tarte fine aux pommes chaud* (warm apple tart) and the chestnut mousse with cocoa cream sauce.

NOTE: There is a second location in the fourteenth arrondissement (see page 243).

TEL 01-48-04-88-44
OPEN Daily: lunch 12:30–2:30 P.M., dinner 7:30–11 P.M. **CLOSED** Dinner on Dec 24; first 3 weeks of Aug
À LA CARTE 40–48€, BNC **PRIX FIXE** None **CREDIT CARDS** AE, MC, V
RESERVATIONS Recommended **ENGLISH SPOKEN** Yes

LE DOS DE LA BALEINE (14)
40, rue des Blancs-Manteaux
Métro: Hôtel de Ville, Rambuteau

For pleasing twists on the usual French menu standards for every course, book a table at this late-night Marais dining favorite. The stone-arched back room has plank floors with comfortable banquettes and settees positioned amid changing art exhibits. The tables are set with huge wine glasses that almost require two hands to lift to your mouth. Waiters provide friendly service to the definitely mixed all-French crowd, but sometimes on the weekend as the evening builds, the service can be stretched to its limits and decibel levels rise considerably.

The evening menu changes every two months, the lunch menu every day, with the exception of beef tartare (lunch only) and a steak, which are permanent. Both menus are driven by what is best at the *marché*. For lunch there are three choices for each course, always including a soup and salad to start, fresh fish for the main course, and a fruit tart for dessert. The stakes are higher at dinner, and so is the level of imaginative selections. Sometimes, in fact, the chef's creative juices seem to run into overdrive, resulting in dishes loaded with too many ingredients. My best advice is to think simple, and you will not be disappointed. For example, gnocchi with lobster and coconut sauce didn't need coriander pesto. Better starters include a wild mushroom fricassée or chilled snow pea soup dusted with tomato slivers, crispy bacon bits, and a dollop of whipped cream. Another dish with too much going on is the main course salmon fillet, which is hidden in a filo pastry crust, served with shallot and curry chutney, balsamic vinegar, and crab sauce and then garnished with turnips and spinach. On the other hand, unqualified winners are the spice-infused honey roasted duck served with mashed potatoes perfumed with apples and olive oil, and the simple turbot, which comes with a parsley and pine nut pesto and colorful julienne of vegetables. Nor should you miss the to-die-for chocolate cake with chocolate sauce hidden in a ball of vanilla ice cream—a dessert that is aptly named black chocolate orgasm.

TEL 01-42-72-38-98
OPEN Tues–Fri: lunch noon–2:30 P.M., dinner 8–11 P.M.; Sat: dinner 8 P.M.–midnight **CLOSED** Sat lunch, Mon, Sun; holidays, 1 week between Christmas and at New Year's, Aug (dates vary)
À LA CARTE None **PRIX FIXE** Lunch: 15€, 3 courses; dinner: 30€, 2 courses, 35€, 3 courses; all BNC **CREDIT CARDS** MC, V
RESERVATIONS Essential for dinner **ENGLISH SPOKEN** Yes

LE FIN GOURMET (44)
42, rue St-Louis-en-l'Île
Métro: Pont Marie

L'Île St-Louis is one of the city's most sought-after addresses, catering to the rich and famous. But it is also visited by almost every tourist to Paris, which can make dining out here an expensive, hit-or-miss affair, since it's hard to tell the real deals from the dining-traps geared to one-time diners.

One honest find is the charming Le Fin Gourmet, whose reputation among residents is growing not only for its sophisticated food but the great value for money it offers. Inside, there is an elegant, romantic glow to the stone-walled dining room, which is tastefully decorated with soft lighting, fresh flowers, and well-spaced tables that preserve a sense of intimacy. The main floor is reserved for nonsmoking patrons; smokers sit on the lower ground floor. The two owners, who honed their culinary skills with Guy Savoy and at l'Arpège, are on hand daily: Yohann Gerbout, who is the *chef de cuisine,* and David Magniez, who greets guests and assures that no details go unnoticed or unattended, whether with the food or its gracious presentation.

While you decide what to order, an *amuse bouche* (tiny appetizer) is served to whet your appetite. One excellent lunch choice is the two-course prix-fixe menu made up of the daily specials. This Great Eat value also includes a glass of wine and coffee. For a wider choice in dishes, opt for the two- or three-course menus (which also include a glass of wine and coffee). In early spring, I like to start with the fat white asparagus lightly dressed with a basil and sea salt dressing or little raviolis with mushrooms and garlic sauce. The *plats* are equally tempting, especially the braised lamb garnished with olive and herb mashed potatoes, or the duck served with a red and yellow pepper and honey sauce, then spiked with Szechuan pepper. For dessert, the warm chocolate cake in a pool of chicory custard cream ends the meal on just the right note.

TEL 01-43-26-79-27 **INTERNET** www.lefingourmet.fr
OPEN Tues: dinner 7–10:30 P.M.; Wed–Sun: lunch noon–2:30 P.M., dinner
    7–10:30 P.M. **CLOSED** Tues lunch, Mon, NAC
À LA CARTE *Entrées* 13€, *plats* 24€, cheese or dessert 9€ **PRIX FIXE** Lunch:
    27€, 2 courses, BC (wine & coffee); lunch & dinner: 27€, 2 courses, 35€,
    3 courses, both BC (wine & coffee) **CREDIT CARDS** AE, MC, V
RESERVATIONS Preferred **ENGLISH SPOKEN** Yes, and English menu

L'ENDROIT (31)
24, rue des Tournelles
Métro: Bastille

There is an arty bonhomie at L'Endroit, a Great Eat pick in the Marais. Owners Nicolas and Catherine have kept the spirit of the interior intact, keeping the old mosaic-tiled floor and leaving the bare bistro tables simply adorned with colored napkins and tumblers. Service by the lone waitress, even at the peak of the 9:30 P.M. crunch, is a study in how to keep your cool. Somehow she sees to everyone, keeps the wine glasses filled, and delivers the warm plates with dispatch.

Aside from the food, the wines from small producers throughout France keep the cognoscenti coming back for more. You can order the reasonably priced wine by the glass, but if you order a bottle with your meal, you pay for only what you drink; you can also buy a bottle to go. The prix-fixe menu reflects a repertoire of standards based on the day's *marché* offerings, along with a few tried-and-true staples everyone loves: a carmelized tomato *tarte Tatin,* a crêpe bursting with ham, mushrooms, and cream, or a hearty beef stew, reminiscent of *grand-mère.* Desserts are not to be forgotten, especially the pear wrapped in a light orange-flavored pastry and shrouded in hot chocolate sauce.

TEL 01-42-72-03-07
OPEN Tues–Sat: lunch noon–2 P.M., dinner 7:15 P.M.–midnight **CLOSED** Mon,
    Sun; Sept 1–15
À LA CARTE 38€, BNC **PRIX FIXE** Lunch & dinner: 18€, 2 courses, 30€,
    3 courses, both BNC **CREDIT CARDS** AE, MC, V (20€ minimum)
RESERVATIONS Preferred **ENGLISH SPOKEN** Yes, and English menu

LE PETIT BOFINGER (35)
6, rue de la Bastille
Métro: Bastille

The demands of Parisian life make it both unrealistic and unfashionable to spend huge sums of money dining out on a regular basis. People no longer have the time to spend hours over large lunches or drawn-out dinners accompanied by expensive wines and liquors. The trend is toward lighter food, quickly prepared and consumed, all without sacrificing quality. Many two- and three-star restaurants have jumped on the bistro bandwagon and opened less expensive venues. Not to be left behind in the race to attract diners, Brasserie Bofinger opened a spin-off called Le Petit Bofinger, located right across the street from their beautiful brasserie near the place de la Bastille. The decor is simple by comparison and evokes the old neighborhood of the Bastille with black-and-white photos of the area, an original tile floor, and a mural along one wall. A nonsmoking section demonstrates the management's desire to please the growing number of French who find life more pleasant when not dining in a smoke-induced haze.

The food is not lavish, but it is reasonable and dependable. Pay attention to the daily specials, the seasonal dishes indicated with a star, and the two prix-fixe menus. Other plusses worth remembering: you can order just one dish at a time and not be subjected to icy stares from a frosty waiter, and children are welcomed with their own menu. Two excellent starters are always the *foie gras de canard maison* and half a dozen Brittany oysters. The kitchen has a sure hand with fish and meat, as demonstrated by the *choucroute de poissons* (a brochette of mussels, *coquilles Saint-Jacques,* sea bream, haddock, and salmon), and the steak tartare, served with a side of *pommes frites* and a small salad. Popular desserts are the modish crème brûlée spiked with bourbon or clafoutis made with seasonal fruit.

NOTE: Le Petit Bofinger has another branch in the seventeenth arrondissement (page 270).

TEL 01-42-72-05-23
OPEN Daily: lunch noon–3 P.M., dinner 7 P.M.–midnight **CLOSED** Never
À LA CARTE 33–38€, BNC **PRIX FIXE** Lunch: 21€, 2 courses, BC; dinner:
29€, 3 courses, BC; children (under 12): 8€, 2 courses, BC
CREDIT CARDS AE, MC, V
RESERVATIONS Recommended **ENGLISH SPOKEN** Yes

LE PETIT MARCEL (¢, 12)
65, rue Rambuteau
Métro: Rambuteau

The only imitation in this Les Halles bar about a two-minute stroll from the Centre Georges Pompidou is the telephone. Everything else you see is the real thing: the marble bar, the half-tiled mirrored walls, the banquette seating hiding storage bins for coffee, tea, and sugar, and the brass hat and coat racks. The young and enthusiastic owners, M. and Mme. Renaudin, are on hand daily serving food, drinks, and good cheer to the regulars, who either stand at the bar for their morning coffee and *tartine* (a half baguette split in two and spread with butter and sometimes jam) or sit at the tables inside or at the few tables squeezed along the sidewalk. Given the café atmosphere and fast turnover, you should leave high gourmet expectations at the door. However, it is amazing that the cook can turn out delicious renditions of onion soup, *boudin noir* (black blood pudding), and *farci de veau* (stuffed veal) in addition to salads, omelettes, pâtés, and *pain Poilâne* spread with tomatoes, chèvre, and olive oil. Desserts come up a bit short except for the only one made here: the crème brûlée.

TEL 01-48-87-10-20
OPEN Daily: 8 A.M.–1 A.M., continuous service **CLOSED** Never
À LA CARTE 11–15€, BNC **PRIX FIXE** Breakfast: 4.70€, hot drink, fresh
    orange juice, croissant (plus 0.70€ for jam) **CREDIT CARDS** None
RESERVATIONS Not necessary **ENGLISH SPOKEN** Yes

LE SOLEIL EN CAVE (13)
21, rue Rambuteau
Métro: Rambuteau

Le Soleil en Cave is definitely one to put on your Great Eats map. It's perfect for a light meal with a glass or two of interesting wine after a workout at the nearby Centre Georges Pompidou. The atmosphere is young and casual, and the prices are designed to please. The yellow-splashed walls and matching tile tabletops set the bright, cheerful tone. The food puts a modern spin on hot and cold *tartines* (large open-faced sandwiches), plates of *charcuterie* and cheeses, composed salads, and a hot *plat du jour.* These are designed to complement the selection of little-known wines from around the world, twenty-two of which are available by the glass. The Sunday brunch is filling and a great value: it's made up of assorted cheeses and *charcuterie,* eggs, sautéed potatoes, fresh fruit salad, pastries, bread, and orange juice or coffee. Of course, you don't have to eat here to buy wine from the knowledgeable partners, Dominique Mendez and Pascal Sergent, who will let you taste before you buy.

TEL 01-42-72-26-25
OPEN Wed–Sun: wine cave/bar, 10 A.M.–10 P.M.; restaurant, lunch noon–
    3 P.M., dinner 7:30–10 P.M. **CLOSED** Mon–Tues; Christmas and New Year's
    Day, 2 weeks mid-Feb, 3 weeks from mid-July (dates vary)
À LA CARTE 8–25€, BNC **PRIX FIXE** Lunch (Wed–Fri): 12€, 1 course, green
    salad, BC; lunch & dinner (Wed–Sun): Tasting Menu, 22€, 3 courses,
    BNC; Sun brunch (noon–5 P.M.): 20€, 3 courses, BC
    CREDIT CARDS MC, V
RESERVATIONS Recommended **ENGLISH SPOKEN** Yes

LES VINS DES PYRÉNÉES (32)
25, rue Beautreillis
Métro: Bastille, St-Paul

In the Marais, not far from place des Vosges, Les Vins des Pyrénées specializes in a changing selection of wines bought directly from small producers throughout France. The decor mirrors the crowd—low-key and casual—and has a certain stylized vintage charm that many newer places never achieve: it's ringed with red banquettes, has choir-pew seating in front, and a window crammed with a dusty collection of old wine corks, themed liquor bottles, and old wooden skis and skates.

On one wall is a collection of World War II–era postcards featuring photos of pretty girls. Men would buy these cards, write to the girl, and then hope to meet her. It all seems quite tame now.

The blackboard menu provides a good mix of bourgeois comfort food, including a delicious foie gras *maison,* braised kidneys with mustard sauce, *confit de canard* with parsleyed potatoes, beef tartare with fries or a salad, roast lamb, and chicken fricassée served with puréed potatoes and olive oil. For dessert, chocoholics will lap up the *molleux au chocolat*—a creamy chocolate cake served warm with vanilla ice cream. Otherwise, the choices include apple crumble with raspberry sauce, cinnamon baked apple, or a plate of cheese to enjoy with another glass of interesting wine.

TEL 01-42-72-64-94
OPEN Mon–Fri, Sun: lunch noon–3 P.M., dinner 7:30–11:30 P.M.; Sat: dinner 8–11:30 P.M. **CLOSED** Sat lunch; Sun lunch (summer), lunch on major holidays; Aug 15–31
À LA CARTE 35€, BNC **PRIX FIXE** Lunch: 14€, 2 courses & BNC or *plat du jour* & BC (wine & coffee) **CREDIT CARDS** MC, V
RESERVATIONS Recommended **ENGLISH SPOKEN** Yes

LE TEMPS DES CERISES (37)
31, rue de la Cerisaie
Métro: Sully-Morland, Bastille

Le Temps des Cerises is the place to have a cheap lunch and a beer or two while polishing your fractured French. When you arrive, you won't miss owners Michelle and Yves Boukobza, and their little dog, Batman, greeting their guests, pouring drinks for the regulars, and helping hardworking Sylvie—the waitress who has been serving here for a quarter century. Lunch is the liveliest time (and the only hot meal served), attracting a neighborhood clientele who accept the crowded conditions as the inevitable price for enjoying the kind of honest home cooking that Mother never has time to make anymore. The blackboard menu selections read like a café cookbook and include all the basics, from Auvergne sausage and grilled steak with a pile of sinful *frites* to a plain fruit *tarte* for dessert. If you see fish on the menu, best to forget it because it's usually frozen. Before and after the hectic lunch scene, the café is calm and only cold food is served, with old-timers standing at the bar dusting off memories. Sometimes there are musical concerts in the evenings, when only wine and bar snacks are served. No one, except Michelle, speaks much English, and you might have to share a table or elbow your way to a space at the bar, but go ahead: don't be shy. Everyone is friendly, and new faces are welcome.

TEL 01-42-72-08-63
OPEN Mon–Fri: bar 7:30 A.M.–8 P.M., continuous bar service; lunch 11:30 A.M.–2:30 P.M. **CLOSED** Sat–Sun; holidays, Aug
À LA CARTE 15–20€, BNC **PRIX FIXE** Lunch: 15.50€, 3 courses, BNC
CREDIT CARDS None
RESERVATIONS Not necessary **ENGLISH SPOKEN** Generally

LE TRUMILOU (28)
84, quai de l'Hôtel-de-Ville
Métro: Pont-Marie

It's a bar, a bistro, or a restaurant depending on where you sit in this institution of cheap eating. Located in a sixteenth-century building along the Seine and run by the members of the Charvin family, Le Trumilou has been rewarding artists, writers, students, and many other devotees for years with low tabs, good service, and uninspired but sensible food that has survived the changing times, trends, and food crazes that periodically roll through Paris. The place radiates authenticity. The large main room is crowded with tables for two or four and filled with farm and family memorabilia from the Charvins' grandparents' farm in the Auvergne; the slightly smaller, more intimate dining room has vases of flowers and crystal chandeliers; and then there's the bar (with pinball machine) and the sidewalk terrace. However, it doesn't matter where you eat; the only thing to concern yourself with is the food, which brings diners back time after time. The regulars know enough to go early for both lunch and dinner to avoid the inevitable crowds.

The tried-and-true *plats du jour* change for winter and summer, but the options on the three-course menu change daily. You may start with a cauliflower *tarte* or *poireaux vinaigrette,* then move on to veal kidneys, a bowl of mussels, or steak with blue cheese sauce, and finish with cheese, crème caramel, or a fruit *tarte*. Naturally, choices widen if you go for the à la carte menu. Look for terrines, a *salade de chèvre chaud,* herring with potatoes, or a dozen escargots. Main dishes include the usual lamb, beef, and veal preparations, plus their house specialties: duck with prunes or veal sweetbreads. Desserts usually fail to get my attention, but if you need something sweet, the apple *tarte* is a safe bet.

TEL 01-42-77-63-98
OPEN Daily: bar 8 A.M.–1 A.M., lunch noon–3 P.M., dinner 7–11 P.M. (Sun till 10:30 P.M.) **CLOSED** 10 days at Christmas, Aug 1–15
À LA CARTE 25–30€, BNC **PRIX FIXE** Lunch & dinner: 14.50€, 2 courses, 17.50€, 3 courses, both BNC **CREDIT CARDS** MC, V
RESERVATIONS Recommended for large parties **ENGLISH SPOKEN** Yes

L'OSTERIA VIANELLO ($, 25)
10, rue de Sévigné
Métro: St-Paul, Bastille

No name or menu outside, no atmosphere or cheap eats inside, but no kidding—this is the best Italian food in Paris. When coming from rue de Rivoli, stay on the right side of rue de Sévigné and look for the old-fashioned lace curtains hanging in the window. What about the service? Well, there's not much of that either, as just a single overworked waitress is responsible for all twenty tables, which are squeezed into the noisy room. And English? Are you serious?

So why bother? For the food, of course! It's all made here, including melt-in-your-mouth gnocci sauced with butter and sage, gorgonzola, or *coquilles St-Jacques,* and tagliolini tossed several ways: with black truffles in the winter, white truffles in the summer, and with juicy langoustines or a lusty veal ragout anytime. The menu changes daily, with the specials written in faded pencil . . . no computer-generated menus here! Because the portions are so filling, I suggest starting light with an artichoke and roquette salad with shaved parmesan cheese, or grilled vegetables drizzled with extra virgin olive oil. If you are fond of risotto, it is fabulous here, especially with winter black truffles. Will you find this on the menu? *Mais non.* You must ask for it, even though it is one of the house specialties. Other mouthwatering preparations include ossobuco, veal with lemon, or, really, just about anything else you see on the menu or on your neighbor's plate. No room for dessert? What! You are not going to at least sample the tiramisu, the divine *baba au rhum* soaked in limoncello, or the light ricotta mousse? When it is time to pay the bill . . . remember that hardworking waitress and be patient.

TEL 01-42-71-37-08
OPEN Mon: dinner 8–10:30 P.M.; Tues–Fri: lunch noon–2:30 P.M., dinner
8–10:30 P.M. **CLOSED** Mon lunch, Sat–Sun; holidays, Feb 4–18, Aug
À LA CARTE 40–60€, BNC **PRIX FIXE** None **CREDIT CARDS** MC, V
RESERVATIONS Essential, several days in advance **ENGLISH SPOKEN** Not really

MARIAGE FRÈRES (18)
30–32, rue de Bourg-Tibourg
Métro: Hôtel de Ville, St-Paul

"Un parfum d'adventure et de poésiés évade à l'infin de chaque tasse de thé." (A perfume of adventure and poetry endlessly escapes every cup of tea.)

—Henri Mariage

No serious tea lover can afford to miss the Tiffany of tearooms in Paris: Mariage Frères, which for more than 145 years has been dedicated to the art of tea drinking. Over 500 teas from thirty-five countries are prepared in these world-famous shops by master tea makers who still do everything by hand, including carefully cutting and stitching each tea bag out of tissue or muslin.

As the menu states, "Tea is not all in the pot." The ambience is an important part of the experience of drinking tea in this civilized establishment, which is reminiscent of colonial times. Waiters in white suits present the tea menu, suggesting the appropriate tea to drink with each meal with the seriousness of a sommelier. The tea is prepared with filtered water and served in an insulated pot at the temperature best suited to its taste. Many of the dishes are prepared with tea, from jams and jellies to sauces, ice creams, and sorbets. The food in general is not as remarkable as the teas, but the pastries do keep pace, so plan to go for a lovely pastry and a sublime cup of tea.

However, if you arrive outside of afternoon tea hours, you must order a meal. The prices are slightly high and so are the noses of some of the management, but it's all worth it for the experience.

Adjoining each of the tearooms is a wonderful tea boutique. The one at this location uses the original cash box from the first tea shop and houses a small tea museum. There is also a *comptoir* (tea shop) across the street where you can buy teas and many of the pastries packaged to go (35, rue du Bourg-Tibourg; 01-44-54-18-54; same hours). The other tearoom locations do not quite have the wide range of teas and tea accessories that these two shops do, but the hours, food, and prices are the same.

NOTE: At all the tearooms, patrons are requested not to smoke. For other locations, see the sixth and eighth arrondissements, pages 155 and 194, as well as outlets in Bon Marché and Printemps department stores

TEL 01-42-72-28-11 **INTERNET** www.mariagefreres.com
OPEN Daily: lunch noon–6:30 P.M., afternoon tea 3–6:30 P.M., tea boutique and tea museum 10:30 A.M.–7:30 P.M. **CLOSED** Never
À LA CARTE 25–40€, BC **PRIX FIXE** Lunch (Mon–Fri): 33€, 2 courses, BC; brunch (Sat–Sun): 29€, 35€, 38€, 40€, all 3 courses & BC; afternoon tea: 16–28€, BC **CREDIT CARDS** AE, MC, V
RESERVATIONS Recommended **ENGLISH SPOKEN** Yes

MON VIEIL AMI (40)
69, rue St-Louis-en-L'Île
Métro: Pont Marie

If anyone needs another reason to be on l'Île St-Louis, here is a delicious one: Mon Vieil Ami, where the sophisticated, imaginative cuisine is drawing increasing crowds. The dining room is relatively small, with a dark brown interior, rough beams, a stone wall along the back, and banquettes framing a row of closely placed tables in the center. The restaurant was opened by Antoine Westermann, a well-known chef from Strasbourg, who has since moved on, but he still oversees the menu and the cooking by his talented assistant, Fréderic Crochet.

There are two seatings for dinner, at 7 P.M. and 9:30 P.M. Normally, I do not like the two-seating method, but here it works beautifully and no one is made to feel rushed. Welcoming touches that count include being offered a glass of wine or freshly pressed juice as an apéritif and sweet butter served with the bread. At lunch, I like to order one of the several *plats du jour,* which change weekly. For instance, on Wednesday you might be served braised rabbit with a carrot and celery purée, Thursday a *blanquette de veau* with baby vegetables, and on Sunday, tender lamb shoulder with baby carrots and turnips. Interesting noontime *entrées* include a salad of bitter dandelion greens with a softly cooked egg and a pastry-covered eel on top, which gives it just the right salty kick, or you might have warm asparagus with rabbit liver lightly sautéed with shallots. For dinner, the three-course menu is filled with more creative takes on old favorites. Start with a variety of beets served with carmelized lotte (monkfish), or a warm mix of seasonal vegetables flavored with raisins and almonds and a mushroom tartine on the side. If you like veal kidneys, order them here, garnished with tart red onions cooked in vinegar and tempered by a soft mound of potato purée on the side. The seasonal *coquilles St-Jacques* are accompanied by braised endives, and the roast duck comes with browned turnips and semolina with dried fruits. For dessert, *baba au rhum* lovers will be pleased with this version, which is served with whipped *fromage frais*. The *tarte au chocolate* is dense and divine, and the caramelized apples with green apple sorbet makes a refreshingly light finale to one of the best meals you will have in Paris.

TEL 01-40-46-01-35 **EMAIL** mon.vieil.ami@wanadoo.fr

OPEN Wed–Sun: lunch noon–2:30 P.M., dinner seatings at 7 P.M. and 9:30 P.M. **CLOSED** Mon–Tues; Jan 1–15, Aug 1–15

À LA CARTE Lunch: *plat du jour* 15€, BNC; dinner: *entrées* 10€, *plats* 21€, desserts 10€ **PRIX FIXE** Dinner: 39€, 3 courses, BNC **CREDIT CARDS** AE, DC, MC, V

RESERVATIONS Essential **ENGLISH SPOKEN** Yes

NOS ANCÊTRES LES GAULOIS (42)
39, rue St-Louis-en-l'Île
Métro: Pont-Marie

"Our Ancestors the Gauls" promises raucous fun and all-you-can-eat farm food in beamed and vaulted rooms with trestle tables, which are set for two to twenty revelers. Up to 350 party animals can be served each night by the tireless, rough-hewn waiters, who coerce guests into making gluttons of themselves. You start by munching on loaves of dark country bread and raw vegetables and helping yourself to a buffet of cold meats, pâtés, and prepared salads. In a while, the waiter will bring your ordered main dish, which might be a steak, lamb chops, or beef, lamb, or duck shish kebabs grilled over an open fire and accompanied by potatoes and a vegetable. The main course is followed by great platters of cheese, a basket of fruit, and a choice of six desserts. As much red wine as you can drink, served from a huge cask at the center of the restaurant, is included in the price of this staggering meal. Strolling guitarists and a singer entertain during the 7 P.M. seating. Although gorging yourself and drinking quantities of barrel wine do not an intimate, romantic evening make, this is a great place to unwind with a group and have a Rabelaisian feast you will long remember.

TEL 01-46-33-66-07, 01-46-33-66-12 **EMAIL** nos-ancetres-les-gaulois@wanadoo.fr **INTERNET** www.nosancetreslesgaulois.fr

OPEN Daily: dinner seatings at 7 P.M. and 10:30 P.M.; Sun and holidays: also lunch noon–2 P.M. **CLOSED** Lunch Mon–Sat; NAC

À LA CARTE None **PRIX FIXE** Lunch & dinner: 38€, children 15€, all you can eat, BC **CREDIT CARDS** AE, DC, MC, V

RESERVATIONS Recommended, especially on weekends **ENGLISH SPOKEN** Yes

RESTAURANT L'ALIVI (21)
27, rue du Roi de Sicile
Métro: St-Paul, Hôtel de Ville

The warmth of Corsica is reflected in the abundant cooking and welcome at L'Alivi, which their patrons can rely on 364 days of the year. In a pretty corner setting, the restaurant has outdoor tables on a little terrace and tapestry-covered tables inside the sixteenth-century stone building, which still has its original tile floor. The food remains true to the spirit of its origins, right down to the bread and butter. Indeed: "Everything is Corsican, from the food and digestives to the water, wine, and music. Just the salt and pepper are not from Corsica," our waiter assured us one night.

The menu changes several times a year, but you usually can count on *entrées* such as *pranzettu* (a plate of Corsican *charcuterie* and cheese), vegetable tarts, fresh sardines flavored with fennel, cheese-and-spinach dumplings, and flaky pastry stuffed with fresh basil and fish. Eggplant tapenade served with a pungent tomato sauce and melted sheep cheese; the tender, roasted baby goat perfumed with herbs; and *dorade* (sea bream) stuffed with fresh anchovies and ripe olives are reliable main course stalwarts. For dessert, either order the lemon cheesecake or ask your waiter to recommend one of their Corsican *digestifs*.

TEL 01-48-87-90-20 **INTERNET** www.restaurant-alivi.com
OPEN Daily: lunch noon–2:30 P.M., dinner 7–11:30 P.M. **CLOSED** Christmas, NAC
À LA CARTE 35–40€, BNC **PRIX FIXE** Lunch & dinner: 22€, 2 courses, BNC **CREDIT CARDS** MC, V
RESERVATIONS Recommended on weekends **ENGLISH SPOKEN** Yes

Fifth Arrondissement

The Latin Quarter is named after the Latin-speaking students who came to Paris in the Middle Ages to study at the Sorbonne. Since that time, this area has remained the student quarter of the city. Associated with youth, intellectuals, artists, writers, poets, and a bohemian lifestyle, the area is filled with restaurants, cafés, bars, bookstores, and movie theaters. Many of the eateries are nothing more than greasy spoons, especially on rue de la Harpe and rue de la Huchette. A visit to one of the most colorful outdoor markets in Paris, along rue Mouffetard, is a must. Open Tuesday through Sunday from 8 A.M. to 1 P.M., the *marché* overflows with every kind of food imaginable, plus clothing boutiques, little cafés, and a fascinat-

LEFT BANK
Cluny Museum
Institut du Monde Arabe
Jardin des Plantes
La Mosquée de Paris
Latin Quarter
Muséum National d'Histoire
      Naturelle
Panthéon
place St-Michel
rue Mouffetard
Sorbonne

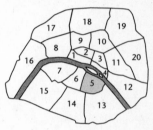

ing parade of people. The nearby Panthéon is where many famous French are buried, including Rousseau, Voltaire, Alexandre Dumas, and Émile Zola. At La Mosquée de Paris, you can take either tea or a Turkish bath, and from the roof of the Institut du Monde Arabe, there is a sensational view of Notre Dame. Of interest to plant enthusiasts is the Jardin des Plantes, a botanical garden with beautiful old trees, masses of flowers, and an educational garden where all plants are labeled.

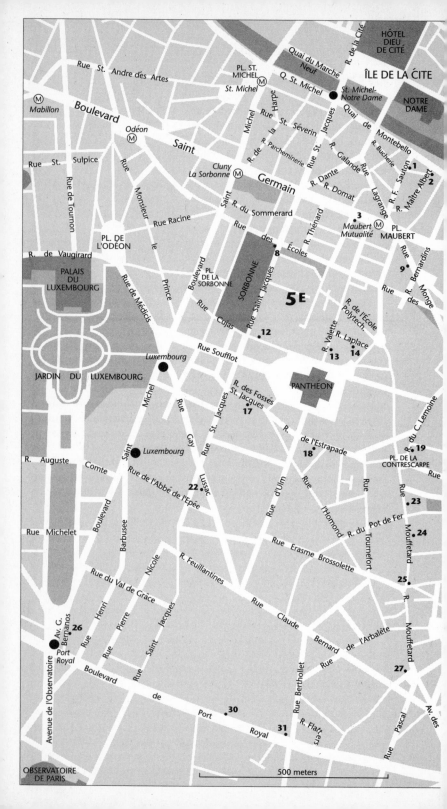

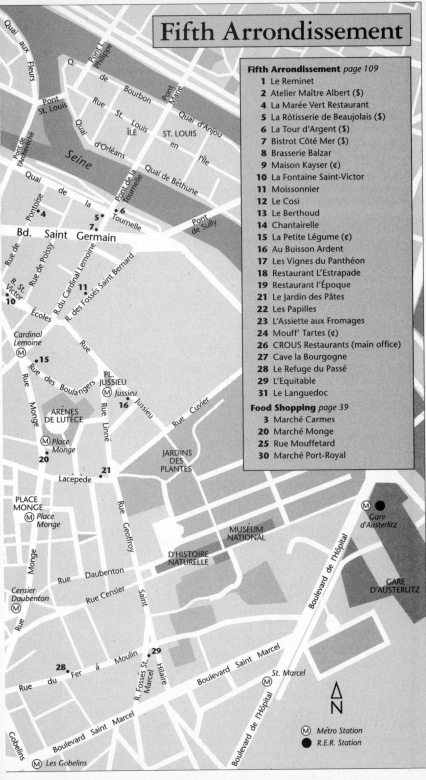

Fifth Arrondissement

Ⓜ *Métro Station*
● *R.E.R. Station*

FIFTH ARRONDISSEMENT RESTAURANTS

($) indicates a Big Splurge; (¢) indicates a Cheap Eat

ATELIER MAÎTRE ALBERT ($, 2)
1, rue Maître-Albert, angle 73, quai de la Tournelle
Métro: Maubert-Mutualité

The prime-time location—just off quai de la Tournelle across the Seine from Notre Dame—couldn't be better. At any time the setting is beautiful, but at night it is without equal: you look across the river and see the majestic cathedral and its stained-glass windows bathed in light.

Famed three-star chef Guy Savoy has lent his *savoir faire* to this venerable restaurant. The stripped-down, sleekly modern, charcoal gray interior boasts a roaring fireplace (in the winter) and a huge rotis-serie along the back wall of the open kitchen. Flanking the entrance is the popular bar, where the perfumed, coiffed, and perma-tanned urbanites come nightly to preen and pose in the cushy leather arm-chairs on one side and at the bar on the other. The best value here is definitely at lunch; for dinner you will pay almost double, but you do have more choices. The cuisine revolves around spit-roasted meat and poultry; try free-range chicken and velvety whipped potatoes, leg of lamb, veal shank garnished with a silky spinach and mushroom gratin, and beef sirloin with béarnaise and scalloped potatoes. Two fish and a vegetarian dish complete the offerings. Because these plates are so generous, the *entrées* should be kept to simple choices of a salad sprinkled with chicken livers, a soup *du jour,* or a fricassée of snails. Desserts seem a heavy afterthought, and the hot chocolate cake with vanilla ice cream certainly tips the scales, but if you love chocolate, you will find room.

TEL 01-56-81-30-01 **INTERNET** www.ateliermaitrealbert.com

OPEN Mon–Fri: lunch noon–2:30 P.M., dinner 6:30–11:30 P.M. (Thur–Fri till 1 A.M.); Sat–Sun: dinner 6:30 P.M.–1 A.M. **CLOSED** Sat–Sun lunch; sometimes part of Aug (call to check)

À LA CARTE 45–55€, BNC **PRIX FIXE** Lunch: 23€, 2 courses, 28€, 3 courses, both BNC **CREDIT CARDS** AE, DC, MC, V

RESERVATIONS Recommended **ENGLISH SPOKEN** Yes

AU BUISSON ARDENT (16)
25, rue Jussieu
Métro: Jussieu

This restaurant once sparked the beginning of a romance of mine. The romance did not last too long, but my affection for this old Left Bank landmark has never wavered. For years, nothing changed: not the drab decor, not the *bourgeoise* menu served in daunting portions, not even the prices enough to speak of, and certainly never the rosy-cheeked, middle-aged waitresses who insisted you clean your plate. Then, several years ago, things did change, dramatically and all for the better. Today, Chef Philippe Duclos's consistently good cooking, the two Great Eat lunch menus, the brightened decor, and the warm welcome keeps the regulars coming back, and word-of-mouth is bringing in many more.

Recent samplings from the changing prix-fixe lunch menu included starters of a tangy watercress salad tossed with feta cheese in a balsamic vinaigrette, an anchovy *tarte,* and fresh herring served with warm potatoes and olive oil. Among the main course selections were tender beef stew with carrots, fresh perch with a fennel and tomato compote, and a lusty dish of sausage and lentils.

The selections on the expanded dinner menu include such seasonal favorites as white asparagus, duck carpaccio served with *cantal* cheese and avocado purée, and a delicate tarragon-flavored crab custard surrounded by a tomato and basil coulis. The long-baked lamb shank literally falls off the bone, the fillet steak served with an aromatic pepper sauce is cooked to pink perfection, and the tender roast quail on a bed of foie gras and lightly sautéed cabbage receives rave reviews. The rum-infused, roasted pineapple served with sorbet is delicious, as is the moist chocolate cake with a scoop of pecan ice cream. Wines are served by the *pichet,* but I definitely recommend upgrading to a bottle.

TEL 01-43-54-93-02
OPEN Mon–Fri: lunch noon–2:30 P.M., dinner 7:30–10 P.M. **CLOSED** Sat–Sun;
holidays (call to check), week between Christmas and New Year's, Aug
À LA CARTE Lunch & dinner: *entrées* 9€, *plats* 17€, desserts 6€
PRIX FIXE Lunch: 13€, 2 courses, BC (coffee); 16€, 2 courses, dessert or
coffee; lunch & dinner: 29€, 3 courses, BNC; dinner: *menu dégustation*
(served to entire table) 35€ (BNC), 45€ (BC), includes *entrée, 2 plats,* and
dessert **CREDIT CARDS** MC, V
RESERVATIONS Recommended **ENGLISH SPOKEN** Yes

BISTROT CÔTÉ MER ($, 7)
16, boulevard St-Germain-des-Prés
Métro: Maubert-Mutualité

Fish is the *raison d'etre* at this bastion of seafood firmly moored on
the Left Bank, only a block from the Seine. The rush of traffic racing by on boulevard St-Germain-des-Prés tells you this is Paris, but
once inside the cheery yellow-and-blue interior you feel you could be
along the coast in Brittany. The menus are written on china plates; the
Breton-inspired food is absolutely fresh, simply executed, and nicely
served, which is the way it should be with fish and seafood. No gloppy
sauces or breaded fish filets emerge from this kitchen. The short,
two-course lunch menu is a Great Eat that includes a glass of wine
and coffee. Depending on the season, look for a zesty soup *de poisson*
to start, then either a seared tuna steak or *filet de dorade* (sea bream)
with baby turnips for the second. Tiramisu comes in a tiny cup, and
it is frankly a better ending than the chocolate banana tart, which
seems just too heavy after the rest of the delightful meal. If you stray
into à la carte territory, your choices expand, and so does the final bill.
However, I think the fried scampi with pesto and parmesan followed
by the scallop and ricotta–filled ravioli and the hot bitter chocolate
soufflé are worth the extra cash. They alone are reasons enough to
come back again and again.

TEL 01-43-54-59-10 **INTERNET** www.bistrotcotemer.com
OPEN Mon–Fri: lunch 12:30–2 P.M., dinner 7:30–10 P.M., Sat dinner
7:30–10 P.M. **CLOSED** Sat lunch, Sun; Aug
À LA CARTE 35–55€, BNC **PRIX FIXE** Lunch: 19€, 2 courses, BC (wine &
coffee) **CREDIT CARDS** MC, V
RESERVATIONS Essential **ENGLISH SPOKEN** Yes

BRASSERIE BALZAR (8)
49, rue des Écoles
Métro: Cluny–La Sorbonne

You will find sawdust on the floor and waiters in white shirts and
black cutaway vests in this genuine old Left Bank brasserie, which
was founded in 1890 by the same family who began Brasserie Lipp.
In its life, Brasserie Balzar has had several owners, but none have been
as controversial as the present ones: Group Flo, an umbrella company
that also runs Brasserie Flo (see page 207), Brasserie Bofinger (see
page 92), and numerous other well-known and respected Parisian

brasseries and restaurants. When Group Flo took over in 1998, Balzar regulars formed the Friends of the Balzar to ensure that nothing would change and that the veteran staff would be treated fairly. To everyone's great relief . . . nothing changed. In fact, I think the food is better. Located close to the Sorbonne's sprawling campus, it still remains a favorite of Left Bank intellectuals and would-be bohemians of all types. Sartre and Camus were customers, and it is said they had their last argument here. During the day you will find it has a faded charm, one you will quickly learn to appreciate and enjoy as a reflection of the literary and political life of the *quartier*. In the evening the pace picks up, and the clientele is a bright mix of pipe-smoking professors, artists, actors, and pretty young singles, making this one of the liveliest places to be in the Latin Quarter. On Sunday nights, it's considered *de rigueur* for the neighborhood regulars to dine here.

When you go, zero in on the succulent *poulet rôti* (roast chicken) and a basket of *pommes frites* made the correct way—with beef suet, not boiling oil. Or try the *gratin dauphinoise* (creamed potatoes) and the *raie au beurre* (skate fish) with a bottle of the house Beaujolais. But please forget the tough beefsteak and the salmon. Top your meal off with a piece of warm *tarte Tatin* or *millefeuille,* and you will have had a truly traditional Parisian meal without straining your pocketbook.

TEL 01-43-54-13-67 **INTERNET** www.brasseriebalzar.com,
www.flobrasseries.com
OPEN Daily: 8 A.M.–midnight, continuous service **CLOSED** Never
À LA CARTE 35–40€, BNC **PRIX FIXE** Breakfast: 7€, *tartine* or croissant,
coffee & juice; dinner (after 10 P.M.): 20.90€, 2 courses, BNC
CREDIT CARDS AE, MC, V
RESERVATIONS Essential **ENGLISH SPOKEN** Yes

CAVE LA BOURGOGNE (27)
144, rue Mouffetard
Métro: Censier-Daubenton

In the fifteenth century, rue Mouffetard was known as hell raisers' hill because of the many taverns and brothels in the area. The long steep street, which begins at place de la Contrescarp and winds down to the St-Mediard church near the Censier-Daubenton métro stop, is still full of greasy spoons and, who knows, probably a brothel or two if you look hard enough. The best reason to go there today is to wander through the colorful open-air morning street *marché* and the inexpensive clothing shops that line both sides of the street.

At the end of the market street, the sprawling Cave la Bourgogne seems to be the rallying point for locals, who gather throughout the day and evening to catch up on the latest news and gossip. Inside, there is the usual zinc bar and worn mosaic-tile floor; the surrounding walls of mirrors reflect a cross-section of Parisians, everyone from workers in overalls quaffing down a few at the bar to millionaires relaxing at a terrace table with cell phones and girlfriends at their side. The surefooted waiters have seen it all, and this is evident in their rather detached manner as they swing through carrying plates piled with fat *andouillettes,* steak tartare, juicy roast chicken, and daily specials, all garnished with sizzling *frites.* Also on board are huge salads, tartines made with *pain Poilâne,* and the usual desserts: crème caramel, *fromage blanc, mousse au chocolat,* and *le tarte de jour.* No one claims this deserves gourmet status, but it is the best watering hole around, and it is an authentic slice of this colorful corner of the fifth arrondissement.

TEL 01-47-07-82-80

OPEN Daily: bar 7:30 A.M.–2 A.M., lunch noon–3 P.M., dinner 7–10:30 P.M., continuous service for cold plates, salads & sandwiches **CLOSED** Never

À LA CARTE 18–30€, BNC **PRIX FIXE** None **CREDIT CARDS** MC, V (15€ minimum)

RESERVATIONS Not necessary **ENGLISH SPOKEN** Sometimes

CHANTAIRELLE (14)
17, rue de Laplace
Métro: Maubert-Mutualité, Cardinal Lemoine

If you cannot get to France's Massif Central and the area of Livradois-Forez located between Clermont-Ferrand and Lyon, then you must promise to treat yourself to a taste of the region by dining at Chantairelle in the heart of Paris. This regionally inspired restaurant offers guests a total experience of the area, one that involves the eyes and ears as well as the palate. Tapes of chirping birds, mooing cows, and ringing church bells from owner/chef Frédéric Bethe's native village of Marsac float through the rustic, beamed dining room, where guests sit on rush-seated, ladder-backed chairs placed around bare wooden tables and admire a back garden filled with native trees and plants. At the entrance, a boutique overflows with products from this little Auvergne village. Even the house mascot, a black cat named Maurice, is an Auvergne native.

The food is as authentic as the surroundings, and the portions are so enormous you might want to share an *entrée* of AOC *lentilles verts de Puy* with *jambon* (ham), the *forest croustade livradois* (deep fried wild mushrooms), or a copious serving of assorted Auvergne *charcuterie. Les plats* feature *truffade* (made with thin slices of potatoes, *cantal* cheese, and ham from Marsac-en-Livradois), stuffed cabbage (layered, *mille-feuille*-style, with beef, mushrooms, sausage, and cabbage), sturdy pork *potées* (stews), and lean duck cooked with mountain honey and thyme. Dessert—if you have room—should be the *millard aux myr-tilles* (blueberry) *tarte* served with cream or the honey-based warm apple *tarte* with prunes in Armagnac ice cream. *Apéritifs,* wines, and even the mineral water all come from the region, guaranteeing a total immersion in this lovely part of France, if only for a few hours.

TEL 01-46-33-18-59

OPEN Mon–Fri: lunch noon–2 P.M., dinner 7–10 P.M.; Sat: dinner 7–10 P.M.

CLOSED Sat lunch, Sun; holidays, 15 days in Aug (dates vary)

À LA CARTE 25–40€, BNC **PRIX FIXE** Lunch: 16€, 2 courses, 21€, 3 courses, both BC (wine); lunch & dinner: 30€, 3 courses, BNC; children's menu (under 10 years): 10.50€, 2 courses, BNC **CREDIT CARDS** MC, V
RESERVATIONS Essential **ENGLISH SPOKEN** Yes

LA FONTAINE SAINT-VICTOR (10)
Maison de la Mutualité, 24, rue St-Victor (off rue des Écoles)
Métro: Cardinal Lemoine, Maubert-Mutualité

Who would ever want to eat here? This is what I thought the first time I arrived at the French Social Security building just off rue des Écoles. Things began to pick up as I ascended the expansive Art Deco staircase to the second-floor dining room. And as I finished the last bite of my *sabayon aux pomme rôtie et Calvados* (apples spiked with Calvados, blanketed with soft custard sauce), I knew why this bargain-priced sleeper is so popular with dignified French pensioners, who have been lunching here for more than half a century.

From the bar you can order a gin and tonic, a dry martini, or a scotch and soda in addition to the usual kir or *coupe de champagne*. To polish off your lunch (the only meal they serve) in grand style, try an Armagnac or cognac, which will set you back less than 7 or 8€. Along with the booze, you will probably want something to eat. The traditional menu is varied, the food good, and above all, it is well priced, especially if you stick to the set menus, which have a variety of choices. I like either of the four-course menus because they include a sampling of cheeses along with everything else. It is a big meal, but you can go easy on dinner. The service by jacketed waiters is flawless, the tables are set with linens and fresh flowers, and during your quiet and proper lunch you will be surrounded by sweet, nicely dressed *grand-mères* and *grand-pères* who haven't forgotten how to dine well.

TEL 01-40-46-12-04
OPEN Daily: lunch 11:45 A.M.–2 P.M. **CLOSED** Holidays, Aug
À LA CARTE *Entrées* 14.50€, *plats* 20.50€, cheese 8.50€, desserts 8€
PRIX FIXE Lunch: 16€, 3 courses, BC; 25€ & 33€, both 4 courses, BNC
CREDIT CARDS V
RESERVATIONS Accepted for groups only **ENGLISH SPOKEN** Yes

LA MARÉE VERT RESTAURANT (4)
9, rue de Pointoise
Métro: Maubert-Mutualité

La Marée Vert's green facade hides a maritime theme carried out by a life raft in front of the tiny bar and pictures of sailing ships hanging on the yellow enamel walls. Regulars are warmly greeted with hugs and shown to small, linen-covered tables that are candlelit at night. The service by the owner and his wife is always accommodating and correct. After you sit down, a dish of salmon butter cream or perhaps olive, anchovy, and garlic tapenade is brought to the table for you to spread on freshly cut bread while deciding what to order. The specialties of the house center around fish and are the most popular. An *entrée* highlight is the filling *soupe de poissons,* which is served in a seemingly endless tureen along with garlicky *aïoli* to spread on croutons you float in the soup and grated cheese to sprinkle on top. Other notable *entrées* include seafood ravioli, deep-fried sardines with a tangy lemon-horseradish *remoulade,* steamed mussels in a creamy curry sauce, and an interesting fricassée of artichoke hearts and *pleurottes,* accompanied by slices of duck confit. Wonderful main course choices include the *poêlée de l'océan aux sucs des tomates et pistou* (a trio of scorpion fish, fresh cod, and salmon sautéed in tomatoes and served with pasta), roasted seabass with fennel, or cod with celery purée. Carnivores are happy with the rosemary-scented rabbit and sautéed mushrooms or the duck served with flavorful Morello cherries. The best dessert is the light *oeufs à la neige*—a mountain of meringue floating in a vanilla custard sauce and streaked with caramel.

TEL 01-43-25-89-41 **INTERNET** www.maree-vert.com
OPEN Mon: dinner 7:30–10:30 P.M.; Tues–Sat: lunch noon–2:30 P.M., dinner
  7:30–10:30 P.M. **CLOSED** Mon lunch, Sun; NAC
À LA CARTE 40–45€, BNC **PRIX FIXE** Lunch: 14€, 2 courses, 16€, 3 courses,
  both BNC; lunch & dinner: 34€, 3 courses, BNC **CREDIT CARDS** MC, V
RESERVATIONS Recommended **ENGLISH SPOKEN** Yes, and English menu

LA PETITE LÉGUME (¢, 15)
36, rue des Boulangers
Métro: Cardinal Lemoine

"Live well, eat sensibly" is the motto at Michel and Patricia's La Petite Légume. And they deliver: a meal here is prepared without refined sugar, salt, added fat, or meat products and is served in a friendly, smoke-free atmosphere. For cash-strapped vegetarians or anyone eager to watch what they eat, this is a bargain spot worth noting. For between 10€ and 16€ you can walk out guilt-free and full of food that's nutritious and satisfying. All types of vegetarians should find something appealing on the menu, which lists everything from whole-cereal dishes with seaweed, miso, and tofu to salads, soups, and an overflowing *plat du jour* of crudités, rice and grains, vegetables, dried fruit, and nuts. Order a nonalcoholic beer, organic wine, or a tumbler of freshly pressed carrot juice, and indulge in a slice of their nonfat cheesecake or chocolate cake to round out the repast. Don't have time to stop for a meal? They will pack everything to go and even charge a bit less to do so. On your way, take a minute or two to glance through the shop, which sells macrobiotic books and natural products.

NOTE: No smoking is allowed.

TEL 01-40-46-06-85
OPEN Mon–Sat: lunch noon–3 P.M., dinner 7–10 P.M.; shop 9:30 A.M.–10 P.M.
  CLOSED Sun; major holidays, NAC
À LA CARTE 12–18€, BNC **PRIX FIXE** Lunch: 10€, 13€, both 3 courses, BNC;
  16€, 3 courses, BC **CREDIT CARDS** MC, V
RESERVATIONS Not taken **ENGLISH SPOKEN** Yes, and English menu

LA RÔTISSERIE DE BEAUJOLAIS ($, 5)
19, quai de la Tournelle
Métro: Maubert-Mutualité, Pont Marie

It is easy to become a regular at the hugely popular Rôtisserie du Beaujolais, situated along the Seine in the shadow of the renowned Claude Terrail's other famed temple of cuisine: La Tour d'Argent. However, the Rôtisserie bears as much resemblance to the formally starched La Tour d'Argent as the bicycle does to the Rolls-Royce. The Rôtisserie is a happening spot: always bustling, noisy, and crowded. Folks arrive in droves for their rations of great grills and roasts served with sides of velvety purées and washed down with bottles of good red wine. Meals kick off with world-class *entrées* of *poireaux tiédes vinaigrette* (warm leeks in vinaigrette), slabs of foie gras, *soupe à l'oignon gratinée,* escargots, or meaty terrines. Next come main courses of roasted chicken, pigeon, or duck, grilled sausages, and blood rare steaks. Grand finales include huge helpings of *île flottante* (floating island), lemon meringue tarts, crème brûlée, bread pudding, chocolate mousse, and slabs of glistening fruit *tartes*. It all takes place in a glass-enclosed street-side terrace and in a bright room where diners sit at closely packed, yellow-and-white clad tables with a full view of the chefs strutting their stuff in the open kitchen along the back.

TEL 01-43-54-17-47
OPEN Tues–Sun: lunch noon–2:15 P.M., dinner 7:30–10:15 P.M.
   CLOSED Mon; NAC
À LA CARTE 45–50€, BNC **PRIX FIXE** None **CREDIT CARDS** MC, V
RESERVATIONS Essential **ENGLISH SPOKEN** Yes

L'ASSIETTE AUX FROMAGES (23)
27, rue Mouffetard
Métro: Place Monge

Smile, say "Cheese," and head for L'Assiette aux Fromages, a bright garden restaurant not far from place de la Contrescarpe on the colorful rue Mouffetard. This is a great place to go for lunch with a small group, quaff a couple bottles of the house red or white wine, and then walk off the consequences in the nearby Jardin des Plantes. At the restaurant, don't look at anything on the menu that doesn't feature cheese, but don't worry, your opportunities for a cheese-inspired Great Eat include salads, tartines, and their two popular specialties: fondue and *racelette*. For the uninitiated, *raclette* is bubbling-hot melted cheese served over boiled new potatoes and sometimes accompanied with air-dried meat or ham, but it's always served with tangy *cornichons* (pickles) and tiny pickled onions. I absolutely guarantee that it is as delectable as it is filling and fattening.

TEL 01-42-36-91-59
OPEN Daily: lunch noon–3 P.M., dinner 6 P.M.–midnight **CLOSED** Dec 24–25, Dec 31–Jan 1
À LA CARTE 15–30€, BNC **PRIX FIXE** Lunch & dinner: 15€, 3 courses (no fondue), BNC; 20€, 2 courses (with fondue), BNC **CREDIT CARDS** MC, V
RESERVATIONS Not necessary **ENGLISH SPOKEN** Yes

LE BERTHOUD (13)
1, rue Valette
Métro: Maubert-Mutualité, Cardinal Lemoine

Comfortable seating in two adjoining tapestry-hung rooms, high-lighted by a stunning collection of hand-painted glass lamps with beaded-fringe shades, creates the romantic atmosphere for dining at Le Berthoud. Owner Nicolas Memin has breathed renewed vigor into the kitchen, and his gastronomic menu now offers a more contemporary slant on seasonal, market-fresh food. His three-course menu is well-priced when you consider it includes five *entrée* choices, including foie gras lightly poached and served with caramalized pears and a *cassolette* of calamari and sweet peppers. Keeping everyone happy are seven *plats,* including slow-cooked lamb, a tender *côte de veau* served with fresh mushrooms, and *bar* (sea bass) accompanied by an eggplant/pistou *fondant.* Finally, four tempting desserts keep dieters promising to "start tomorrow," especially after enjoying the apple-rhubarb crumble with a scoop of *fromage blanc* ice cream melting over the top.

TEL 01-43-54-38-81
OPEN Mon–Fri: lunch noon–2 P.M., dinner 7:30–11 P.M.; Sat: dinner 7:30–
    11:30 P.M. **CLOSED** Sat lunch, Sun; holidays (call to check), last 3 weeks
    of Aug
À LA CARTE 30–38€, BNC **PRIX FIXE** Lunch: 26€, 2 courses, BNC; lunch &
    dinner: 30.50€, 3 courses, BNC **CREDIT CARDS** MC, V
RESERVATIONS Recommended, especially dinner on Fri & Sat
    ENGLISH SPOKEN Yes

LE COSI (12)
9, rue Cujas
Métro: Cluny-La Sorbonne

Everyone loves this popular bistro because it consistently turns out generous portions of food from the L'Île de la Beauté, the French name for Corsica. Corsican food embraces southern French country fare with homey Italian, and it is served up here in a cheerful room with a huge mirror reflecting the russet-red walls, black banquettes, and wraparound picture windows.

    Consider starting with a bowl of *soupe Corse,* served overflowing with white beans, root vegetables, and pieces of tender pork and veal. A lighter beginning is the *Brocciu,* Corsican sheep cheese cannelloni stuffed with vegetables and basil. Another special *entrée* is the tomato tart accompanied by a tangy green salad and an onion compote. Your main course has to be either *Cabri*—Corsican baby goat, tenderly roasted with herbs—veal *stufattu,* or Corsican veal stew liberally infused with wine, and so large it would easily feed two. Dessert may out of the question, but I wouldn't miss the hot chestnut souffle, a made-to-order light ending to this Great Eat from Corsica.

TEL 01-43-29-20-20
OPEN Mon–Sat: lunch noon–2:20 P.M., dinner 7:45–11:30 P.M. **CLOSED** Sun;
    2 weeks mid-Aug (dates vary)

À LA CARTE 35–45€, BNC **PRIX FIXE** Lunch: 15€, 2 courses, 20€, 3 courses,
  both BNC **CREDIT CARDS** MC, V
RESERVATIONS Essential **ENGLISH SPOKEN** Yes, and English menu

LE JARDIN DES PÂTES (21)
4, rue Lacépède
Métro: Jussieu, Place Monge

Le Jardin des Pâtes has two homes, this one near the Jardin des
Plants and another in the thirteenth arrondissement (see page 232).
At both locations, an arty, youthful tone is set by bare tables, spindly
slat chairs, and white surroundings tempered by endless green plants.
Fresh food simply served continues to be the guarantee at both locales.
One taste tells you that you have found something *very* good, and the
crowded tables confirm it.

Everything here is made with products that are free of artificial
additives, pesticides, and synthetic ingredients, and, of course, the
wines and beers are organic. The house specialty is homemade pasta
made from organic rice, corn, wheat, and rye flours ground in their
kitchens and topped with imaginative sauces. Everything is prepared
to order and served à la carte with baskets of whole-meal bread. One
of the most popular pastas is the *pâtes de châtaigne* (a *châtaigne* is a type
of chestnut), a rich mixture of pasta topped with duck fillet, mushrooms, crème frâiche, and just a hint of nutmeg. Another is the rice
pasta served with stir-fried vegetables and chunks of tofu, seasoned
with fresh ginger. Appealing to a distinct few is the filling combination of buckwheat pasta tossed with chicken livers, sesame sauce, and
prunes. Seasonal soups, salads, and some rather heavy desserts fill out
the rest of the menu card. Worthy of serious consideration by all who
count chocolate as a daily necessity is the (calories, who's counting?)
chocolate-marmalade *tarte*. Wrap it all up with a coffee and a glass of
farigoule, a thyme liqueur.

TEL 01-43-31-50-71
OPEN Daily: lunch noon–2:30 P.M., dinner 7–11 P.M. **CLOSED** Several days at
  Christmas (dates vary)
À LA CARTE 20–25€, BNC **PRIX FIXE** None **CREDIT CARDS** MC, V
RESERVATIONS Not necessary **ENGLISH SPOKEN** Yes, and English menu

LE LANGUEDOC (31)
64, boulevard de Port-Royal, at rue Berthollet
Métro: Port Royal, Les Gobelins

Run by the DuBois family, Le Languedoc has the relaxed feel of an
old-fashioned Parisian restaurant, where its contented regulars enjoy
the authentic atmosphere and know to stick to the basics when ordering. Red-checked tie-back curtains, wooden tables covered with yellow
linen and white paper overlays, three coat racks, a grandfather clock,
assorted copper pots—everything has been in the same position for
thirty-four years and . . . there is no hint of change on the horizon.

The purple-and-pink, handwritten, stenciled menu offers plenty
to choose from, and really, there's no reason to delve into anything

but the house wine or to stray from the bargain-priced prix fixe, which allows a wide choice from the à la carte selections. Start with bowls of herring fillets or flavorful terrines brought to the table and left for you to help yourself, or try the artichoke hearts vinaigrette. Follow with a good *cassoulet,* the *confit canard maison,* the *plat du jour,* or the grilled *entrecôte,* which comes with crispy *frites* and a side salad. Seasonal desserts or chocolate mousse are a nice ending to a very well-priced meal.

TEL 01-47-07-24-47

OPEN Mon, Thur–Sun: lunch noon–2 P.M., dinner 7–10 P.M. **CLOSED** Tues–Wed; Dec 21–Jan 5, Aug

À LA CARTE 25–30€, BNC **PRIX FIXE** Lunch (Mon–Fri): 11€, 2 courses, BNC; lunch & dinner (daily): 20€, 3 courses, BC **CREDIT CARDS** MC, V (19€ minimum)

RESERVATIONS Advised on weekends **ENGLISH SPOKEN** Limited, but English menu

L'EQUITABLE (29)
1, rue des Fossés St-Marcel
Métro: Gobelins, Censier-Daubenton

Up-and-coming chefs who have trained under well-known Michelin star chefs, or at the temples of *haute cuisine* in Paris, continue to venture out on their own, opening bistros in parts of Paris that visitors would normally never see. Such is the case with Yves Mutin, who worked at Jules Vern in the Eiffel Tower and Les Bouchons de François Clerc before opening his increasingly popular restaurant in the bottom of the fifth arrondissement.

The exposed stone walls, dark beamed ceiling, and high ladderback chairs give L'Equitable's two rooms the feel of an old country *auberge.* Formally set tables are well spaced. Service by the two waiters is polite and helpful, but in the evening it can be slow between courses. That's okay . . . sip your wine, nibble on the basket of wholegrain sourdough bread (served with tomato chutney and a bowl of crème fraîche and chives), and know that each awaited course will be imaginative in both execution and presentation.

The exceptionally good-value 30.50€ menu allows you to choose from the entire à la carte menu. One of the most popular *entrées* is poached eggs served with a mushroom cream sauce garnished with toast fingers lightly spread with foie gras. Another wonderful beginning is the lightly cooked foie gras presented on a bed of caramelized onions. The duck fillet, garnished with orange-scented couscous and a filo-dough flower, is as delicious as it is artistic. Cod is served with Provençale vegetables, and the steak is gilded with a marrow bone and celery crêpes. Desserts do not fall by the wayside: save room for the slice of dark-chocolate pecan cake topped with coffee sauce or for the *chocolat île flotante* drizzled with kiwi sauce.

The weekday lunch menus change weekly and offer two interesting choices for each course. Starters could include an artichoke risotto topped with fresh Parmesan, or salad *frisée* with a poached egg on top, followed by stewed chicken or dorade fillet accompanied by tiny *ratte* potatoes and anchovies in a shallot vinagrette. Crêpes Suzette or chocolate mouse with rum sauce are only two of the changing desserts. An additional 5€ buys you a *pichet* of red or white wine.

TEL 01-43-31-69-20
OPEN Tues: dinner 7:30–11 P.M.; Wed–Sun: lunch noon–2:30 P.M., dinner 7:30–11 P.M. **CLOSED** Tues lunch, Mon; holidays, first 3 weeks Aug
À LA CARTE *Entrées* 10.70€, *plats* 17.80€, cheese 6.50€, desserts 7.90€
PRIX FIXE Lunch (Wed–Sat): 16€, *plat* & dessert, 18€ *entrée* & *plat,* 22€, 3 courses, all BC (coffee); lunch & dinner (daily): 30.50€, 3 courses, BNC
CREDIT CARDS AE, MC, V
RESERVATIONS Essential **ENGLISH SPOKEN** Yes

LE REFUGE DU PASSÉ (28)
32, rue du Fer à Moulin
Métro: Gobelins

"Le Refuge du Passé offers the savory specialties from the Auvergne and Les Landes regions of France's southwest," said William Dowling, an American expat living nearby and my Great Eat source for this hidden find near the rue Mouffetard. This is the type of restaurant where you can take your spirited in-laws, your kids, your mom, and your spouse, and everyone will love it. The interior, a shrine to kitch and flea market finds, is festooned with old coffee grinders hanging from the ceiling, feathery hats, posters, cowbells, and old Victrola records glued to the walls. It is safe to say that on my first visit, I had my fears that amidst all this gee-gaw, the food might be just as over-done as the decor . . . *mais non!* The food is great and worth the trip to this blue-collar corner of Paris. English-speaking owner Hubert Dupont and his chef, Stephane Durand, are firm believers in hearty, stick-to-your-rib dishes, such as tender leeks under a cover of melted Cantal cheese, a plate of assorted *charcuterie,* pork knuckles and lentils, *cassoulet,* and duck fixed several ways (the best is *à la orange*). Among the seasonal main courses are *civet de biche* (venison stew), *lapin de la moutarde* (rabbit with mustard sauce), and *blanquette de veau.* Save room for the grand finale: a wicked, molten chocolate cake or the carmelized *tarte Tatin* served in an individual sizzling skillet. I agree with my friend William, who theorized that, had Ernest Hemingway dined at this Great Eat, he'd have called it "a small, good place."

TEL 01-47-07-29-91
OPEN Daily: lunch noon–2 P.M., dinner 7–10:30 P.M. **CLOSED** Never
À LA CARTE None **PRIX FIXE** Lunch (Mon–Sat): 18€, *plat* & coffee; lunch & dinner: 26€, 2 courses, 30€, 3 courses, both BNC **CREDIT CARDS** AE, DC, MC, V
RESERVATIONS Preferred **ENGLISH SPOKEN** Yes

LE REMINET (1)
3, rue des Grands-Degrés
Métro: Maubert-Mutualité, St-Michel

Le Reminet is buzzing at most mealtimes, which is not surprising given chef Hugues Gournay's good-value menus, which are based on seasonal fresh market produce. This small stone-walled restaurant seats fewer than forty at white linen–covered tables. Mirrors add depth, crystal chandeliers lend a touch of class, and fresh flowers appear everywhere, including the candlelit loo, all suggesting that management is attentive to detail.

Gournay has an imaginative approach. In the late fall, you can expect such *entrée* delights as creamy pumpkin soup with a dollop of whipped cream and a dusting of nutmeg and chestnuts, warm oysters and celeriac with truffle shavings, or fat mushrooms stuffed with Parma ham and served with crispy duck. The pleasures continue with main courses of pork filet mignon in an onion and parmesan crust, scallops sautéed in olive oil, accompanied by a vegetable risotto, and rabbit, seasoned with fresh sage and served on a bed of artichoke tagliatelli. Crème brûlée is omnipresent on Parisian dessert menus, but here it is way above average. For something more inventive, I like the *pastis mousse* served with an anise-flavored cookie or the armagnac-spiked prunes in a puff pastry, capped with praline cream and crystalized chestnuts. Chocolate lovers will be very happy with the coffee meringue topped with bitter chocolate mousse and drizzled with a light cocoa sauce. The prix-fixe lunch menu, based on blackboard specials, is somewhat limited in scope, but the astounding low price is further proof that Great Eat values are often found at lunchtime. However, the *menu gastronomique* is a real *tour de force.* It includes two *entrées,* two *plats,* a plate of cheese, and the chef's repertoire of desserts. You will diet for days after . . . but it is a small sacrifice.

NOTE: I recommend arriving at the start of the lunch and dinner service because, as often happens, the serving staff (one person and a busboy) get steadily overwhelmed as the hours progress. On a Sunday night, we had to ask for our espressos three times, and the bill was presented before the coffee ever arrived, when it was plunked down with the rude admonition that we "hurry, people are waiting for your table." With luck, the waitress's behavior was an exception, not the rule. I also recommend requesting a table on ground level, not downstairs in the subterranean basement; arriving early will help ensure you get it.

TEL 01-44-07-04-24
OPEN Mon, Thur–Sun: lunch noon–2 P.M., dinner 7:30–11 P.M.
    CLOSED Tues–Wed; holidays, week in Feb, first 3 weeks Aug
À LA CARTE 35–45€, BNC **PRIX FIXE** Lunch (Mon, Thur–Fri): 13€, 3 courses, BNC; lunch & dinner (Mon, Thur–Sun): *menu gastronomique,* 50€, 6 courses, BNC **CREDIT CARDS** MC, V
RESERVATIONS Essential **ENGLISH SPOKEN** Yes, and English menu

LES PAPILLES (22)
30, rue Guy Lussac
Métro: Luxembourg

Normally I don't go to an *épicerie* (a food and wine store) to sit down at a tiny table in a packed atmosphere and be served while shoppers stand next to my table and reach overhead to grab a bottle of wine or a jar of pickles. However, at Papilles (meaning "little tastes") by the Luxembourg Gardens, the *branché* fan base of diners ignores all this because the food is great. In fact, you'll need reservations if you want to join them for the no-choice, four-course meal served for lunch and dinner Monday to Saturday. Papilles is run by two couples; while the men scout the wines, the women hold down the fort in the kitchen. Overseeing everyone is Fifi, the vocal house mascot, who befittingly wears a pink sweater with "woof" stenciled on it.

The copious meal usually starts with a tureen of soup, perhaps creamy artichoke spooned over a mound of foie gras or a velvety lentil enhanced with chunks of smoked duck and a showering of croutons and chopped chives. A *blanquette de veau* with onions, carrots, mushrooms, and fluffy basmati rice might be your lunch *plat,* or maybe slow-cooked lamb with a Provençale ratatouille. Brie de Meaux, or another cheese plus dessert, maybe a *baba au rhum* or a créme brûlée follow. Your wine choices surround you, and you are charged only the shelf cost of the wine and a corkage fee . . . no further mark up.

TEL 01-43-25-20-79
OPEN Mon–Sat: shop 8:30 A.M.–1 A.M.; lunch noon–2 P.M., dinner 7:30–10 P.M. **CLOSED** Sun; first 3 weeks Aug
À LA CARTE None **PRIX FIXE** Lunch & dinner: 28.50€, 4 courses (no choices), BNC **CREDIT CARDS** MC, V
RESERVATIONS Mandatory **ENGLISH SPOKEN** Enough

LES VIGNES DU PANTHÉON (17)
4, rue Fossés St-Jacques
Métro: Luxembourg

The food at Les Vignes du Panthéon draws an appreciative audience who like the rather sedate yet intimate atmosphere and the wholesome food, adeptly prepared by Lionel Maliere, a well-tested, traditional chef. The front room houses bar and banquette seating and a hand-painted ceiling. Farther along past the kitchen is another stone-walled dining room that's large enough to accommodate several changing art exhibitions throughout the year. Small table lamps add just the right air of romance.

The classic Parisian hallmarks of foie gras and *terrine de canard maison,* eggs poached in a bacon and red wine sauce, *chèvre chaud* on a bed of greens, fillet of sole, steak with marrowbone, beef tartare, *rognon de veau à la moutarade* (veal kidneys in a mustard sauce), and *l'île flottante* with bourbon-flavored custard sauce are all here. No, it is not a place club-going cute-young-things would find appealing, but their parents would endorse the reliability of the food and the care with which it is prepared and served.

TEL 01-43-54-80-81
OPEN Mon–Fri: lunch noon–2:30 P.M., dinner 7:30–10:30 P.M.; Sat: dinner
7:30–10:30 P.M. **CLOSED** Sat lunch, Sun; holidays, first 3 weeks Aug
À LA CARTE 40–48€, BNC **PRIX FIXE** None **CREDIT CARDS** MC, V
RESERVATIONS Recommended **ENGLISH SPOKEN** Yes

MAISON KAYSER (¢, 9)
8 & 14, rue Monge
Métro: Maubert-Mutualité

Locals religiously queue three times a day for their bread at these
temples to the art of breadmaking, which is the original location for
the famed baker Eric Kayser. At the 14, rue Monge shopfront, all
the loaves are organic, and there is a small deli counter from which
you can put together a nice *pique-nique* to take with you, though you
can eat here at an inside counter or at sidewalk tables. No matter
which address you frequent, you will be impressed with the sublime
fragrances and quality of everything: flaky croissants, buttery crusted
apple tarts, baguette sandwiches, savory quiches, and *chaussons* or *pain
au chocolate* for after-school snacks. If you are here on Wednesday,
Friday, or Sunday, take a few minutes to stroll through the Marché
Monge at 5, place Monge, one of the nicest morning markets in the
arrondissement.

NOTE: There are several other convenient locations: in the
6th arrondissement at 87, rue d'Assas and 10, rue de l'Ancienne
Comédie; in the 8th arrondissement at 85, bd Malesherbes and
73, bd de Courcelles; and in the 9th at Lafayette Gourmet, 40, bd
Haussmann.

TEL 01-44-07-01-42 (8, rue Monge); 01-44-07-17-71 (14, rue Monge)
OPEN Wed–Sun 8 A.M.–8:15 P.M. **CLOSED** Mon–Tues, NAC
À LA CARTE 1.20–10€ **PRIX FIXE** Breakfast: 7.30€, hot drink, fresh orange
juice, pastry or *tartine* **CREDIT CARDS** None
RESERVATIONS Not accepted **ENGLISH SPOKEN** Not much

MOISSONNIER (11)
28, rue des Fossés St-Bernard
Métro: Cardinal Lemoine, Jussieu

Moissonnier is a forty-five-year-old family-owned Left Bank
landmark that specializes in Lyonnaise cooking. It is run by Philippe
and Valérie Mayet: he cooks and she runs the dining room, making
sure that all of her guests are happy and well-fed. The best seating
in the two-floor restaurant is on the ground floor, with its high ceiling, massive bouquet of fresh flowers, and tiny service bar along one
side. The best time to go is for a weekday lunch, when they offer a
prix-fixe menu.

The well-rounded selection of Lyonnaise dishes makes this an
excellent dining choice and a good culinary value considering the
quality of the food. Look for the regional and house specialties written in red on the menu. A good *entrée* choice is the *saladier,* a large
cart rolled to your table laden with salads, terrines, herring in cream,

marinated vegetables, and many other tempting appetizers. But proceed with caution . . . if you don't go easy on the first course, you may not be able to manage the rib-sticking specialties that follow, such as *quenelles de brochet* (light pike dumplings in a smooth tomato sauce), *tablier de sapeur* (fried tripe), veal kidneys in mustard sauce, or a rack of lamb with potatoes au gratin. Complete the meal with an assortment of fine regional cheeses, ethereal *oeufs à la neige* (puffs of egg whites floating in vanilla custard), or a seasonally perfect *tartlette aux fraises* (strawberry tart). House wines are served in *pots,* heavy, thick glass bottles that keep the wine cool.

NOTE: The *saladier* cannot be rolled upstairs, thus if you sit upstairs and order this as your *entrée,* the salads will be brought to you on a plate, and you won't have the pleasure of looking and deciding for yourself.

TEL 01-43-29-87-65

OPEN Tues–Sat: lunch noon–2 P.M., dinner 7:30–10 P.M. **CLOSED** Mon, Sun; major holidays, Aug

À LA CARTE 35–45€, BC **PRIX FIXE** Lunch (Tues–Fri): 24€, 3 courses, BNC
   CREDIT CARDS MC, V

RESERVATIONS Recommended **ENGLISH SPOKEN** Yes, and English menu

MOUFF' TARTES (¢, 24)
53, rue Mouffetard
Métro: Place Monge

When you first arrive at this Cheap Eat, check out the window display of homemade quiches—both savory and sweet—then go in and sit at one of the green-and-white-covered tables set with bright orange and pink napkins and enjoy a filling, easy-on-the-wallet repast. All the food is made and served by a brother-and-sister team: he makes the sweet tarts, she does the savory; neither are light-weight or delicate, but they are guaranteed to satisfy any appetite. A baker's dozen of savory quiches and as many sweet ones comprise the menu, along with a choice of salads. This is a good pit stop if you have hungry children on your hands or need a filling snack on the run. They will also pack any order to go.

TEL 01-43-37-21-89

OPEN Tues–Sun: noon–midnight, continuous service **CLOSED** Mon; 2 weeks Feb, sometimes in Aug (call to check)

À LA CARTE 4–10€, BNC **PRIX FIXE** Lunch (Tues–Fri noon–2 P.M.): 8.40€,
   2 tarts, BNC, or 1 tart & a nonalcoholic drink **CREDIT CARDS** None

RESERVATIONS Not accepted **ENGLISH SPOKEN** Yes

RESTAURANT L'ÉPOQUE (19)
81, rue du Cardinal Lemoine
Métro: Place Monge

L'Époque is located just beyond the hype along the rue Mouffetard and its endless line of touristy restaurants reaching out for your wallet with loud music, gaudy fake decor, windows full of sizzling meats, and sweaty chefs serving poor fare. This is a utilitarian pick that doesn't put on airs with either the decor or the food, but it is amazingly good quality and value for the price. The small room's wooden bistro tables are topped with straw placemats and paper napkins. The customer profile shifts with the hour: at lunch it is workers and shopkeepers, and at night students, couples, and just plain folks.

All pocketbooks are accommodated with a series of well-constructed prix-fixe menus for both lunch and dinner. À la carte is also available, but frankly, don't bother: it's not the best value meal here. When ordering, remember: the less complicated, the better. Depending on your budget and taste, start with a plate of crudités, a salad with *chèvre chaud,* onion soup, or herring served with warm potatoes. With the exception of an herb omelette, the main courses are meat based, with heaps of potatoes costarring. Desserts are the usuals: chocolate mousse, *tartes,* chocolate cake, or *fromage blanc* with fruit sauce.

TEL 01-46-34-15-84
OPEN Mon–Fri: lunch noon–2:30 P.M., dinner 6–11 P.M.; Sat: dinner
    6–11 P.M. **CLOSED** Sat lunch, Sun; 3–4 days at Christmas, Aug
À LA CARTE 25–30€, BNC **PRIX FIXE** Lunch: 10€, 1 course, 12€, 2 courses,
    23.50€, 3 courses, all BNC; dinner: 15€, 23.50€, 3 courses, both BNC
    CREDIT CARDS MC, V
RESERVATIONS Recommended on Fri & Sat **ENGLISH SPOKEN** Yes

RESTAURANT L'ESTRAPADE (18)
15, rue de l'Estrapade
Métro: Luxembourg

Cozy, cheap, and cheerful: that is the Restaurant l'Estrapade, which is located behind the Panthéon. There is no hard-copy menu, only what is written on the blackboard or on the mirrors around the small room. The traditional choices are delightfully *bourgeoise,* recalling the good old days when heartwarming dishes were enjoyed in the family kitchen. With the exception of the daily specials, most stay the same, but wines change weekly. It is all kept perking along by one calm waiter and his chef, who cooks in a closetlike space and turns out the usual starters of *salade de chèvre chaud,* marinated herrings, and leeks vinaigrette. Diners dig into main courses of *lapin à la moutard* (rabbit in mustard sauce), pork roast with silky mashed potatoes, slow-cooked lamb on the bone, and they usually end with a simple crème caramel.

TEL 01-43-25-72-58
OPEN Mon–Fri: lunch noon–2 P.M., dinner 8–10:30 P.M. **CLOSED** Sat–Sun;
    major holidays, 2–3 weeks Aug (dates vary)
À LA CARTE None **PRIX FIXE** Lunch & dinner: 22€, 2 courses, 28€, 3 courses,
    both BNC **CREDIT CARDS** MC, V
RESERVATIONS Essential, especially for dinner **ENGLISH SPOKEN** Enough

Sixth Arrondissement

The sixth is a continuation of the Latin Quarter, but *plus chic*. Running from the Seine to the busy boulevard du Montparnasse, the sixth is symbolized by the trendy yet scholarly neighborhood around the church of St-Germain-des-Prés, the oldest church in Paris. The emphasis is on art galleries, antiques, fashion boutiques, restaurants, and hotels in all categories. Café society in Paris has always been epitomized by two famous cafés here: Les Deux Magots and Café de Flore. In their glory, they were the prime haunts of the existentialists of the postwar years, notably Sartre, Camus, and Simone de Beauvoir. While their original luster has dimmed, they are still crowded day and night and offer some of the best people-watching in Paris. An hour spent sitting in the Luxembourg Gardens is one of the delights of Paris, especially on a sunny Sunday afternoon when the children are floating their boats on the pond. The Palais du Luxembourg was built for the widow of Henri IV, Marie de' Medici, in the 1620s. The palace now houses the French Senate.

LEFT BANK
École des Beaux-Arts
Luxembourg Gardens
Musée Delacroix
Odéon National Theater
place St-Michel
St-German-des-Prés Church
St-Séverin
St-Sulpice (paintings by Delacroix)

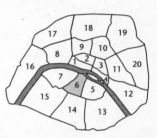

Sixth Arrondissement

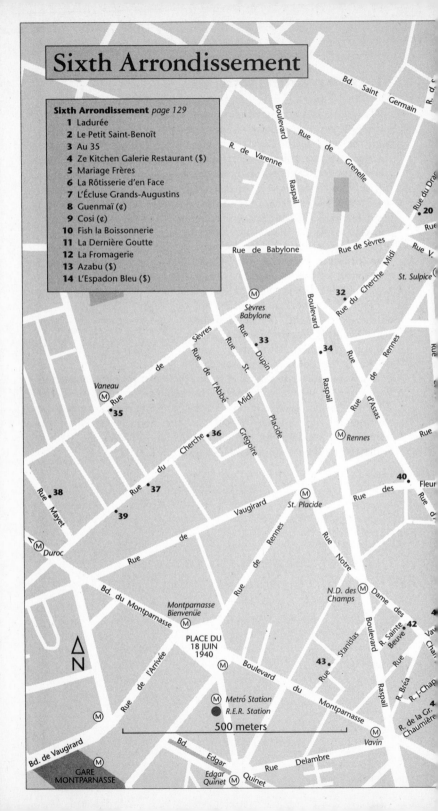

Bd. Saint Germain

R. d s

Boulevard

Rue

de

R. de Varenne

Grenelle

Rue du Drac

Raspail

20

Rue

Rue de Sèvres

Rue V.

Rue de Babylone

St. Sulpice

Sèvres
Babylone

Rue du Cherche Midi

32

Boulevard

Sèvres

Rue

Dupin

33

34

Rue

de

Rennes

Rue

Rue

de

l'Abbé

St.

Midi

Rennes

Vaneau

Rue

Raspail

Rue

d'Assas

35

Cherche

36

Grégoire

Placide

Rennes

du

40

Fleur

38

Rue

37

Vaugirard

St. Placide

Rue

des

Rue

d

39

Mayet

de

Duroc

Rue

Vaugirard

Rue

de

Rennes

Rue

Notre

Bd. du Montparnasse

Montparnasse
Bienvenüe

N.D. des
Champs

Dame

des

42

Stanislas

R. Sainte

Boulevard

Beuve

N

PLACE DU
18 JUIN
1940

Boulevard

43

Rue

Rue

Bréa

R. J-Chap

Raspail

R. de la Gr.
Chaumière

Rue de l'Arrivée

du

Montparnasse

Ⓜ Metró Station
● R.E.R. Station

500 meters

Vavin

Bd. de Vaugirard

Bd.

Edgar

Rue

Delambre

GARE
MONTPARNASSE

Edgar
Quinet

Quinet

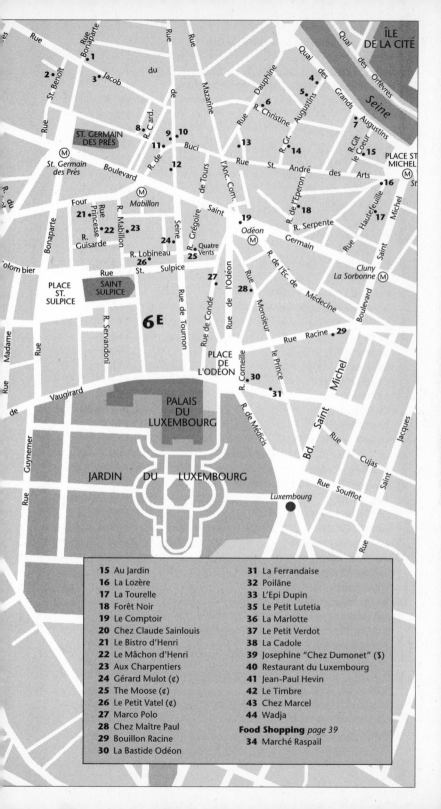

SIXTH ARRONDISSEMENT RESTAURANTS

($) indicates a Big Splurge; (¢) indicates a Cheap Eat

AU 35 (3)
35, rue Jacob
Métro: St. Germain-des-Prés

Au 35 is a long-standing fixture that doesn't try to be fancy or clever in either appearance or food. Instead, it sticks to a basic repertoire for which its devoted patrons return day after day, year after year. Tables and banquettes are sandwiched in a properly set room ringed with a collection of YSL Love posters. Upstairs is another smaller room with two large windows and more YSL Love posters. To keep things interesting for the lunch crowd, the noontime menu changes daily. The dinner *carte* is seasonally based and, of course, more expensive. The chef does a credible job on such straightforward *entrées* as carrot and orange soup, leeks in a beetroot vinaigrette, fois gras *maison,* and snails served with garlicky parsley butter. The chicken and vegetables under a pastry crust with a cinnamon and honey sauce or shepherd's pie and a green salad are only two examples of main-course reliability. For dessert, you need look no further than the poached pear in red wine at lunch or the chocolate soufflé with vanilla ice cream at dinner.

TEL 01-42-60-23-24
OPEN Daily: lunch noon–2:30 P.M., dinner 7 P.M.–midnight
   CLOSED Christmas, New Year's Day, May 1, NAC
À LA CARTE 24–32€, BNC **PRIX FIXE** Lunch: 18€, 2 courses, 22€, 3 courses,
   both BNC **CREDIT CARDS** AE, MC, V
RESERVATIONS Recommended **ENGLISH SPOKEN** Yes, and English menu

AU JARDIN (15)
15, rue Gît-le-Coeur
Métro: St-Michel

Au Jardin has weathered many a storm in ownership and food quality, but under the helm of owner/chef Philippe Gomes, the restaurant has finally come back into its own and can be recommended. The small room has a garden theme, with outdoor wooden furniture, hanging lanterns, and framed floral prints. For the most authentic dinner experience, try to go around 8:30 or 9 P.M. when the locals arrive; the hour before is Tourist Central. However, no matter when you go, or whether you are alone, with children, or with friends, the service will be polite and eager to please.

The reassuringly traditional dishes are on the mark in most instances, especially the snails in garlic and parsley butter, the smoked salmon and potato *tartiflette,* and the pan-fried foie gras topped with tangy cranberries. The salads are fine for their ingredients and presentation, but the dressing (balsamic vinaigrette) is poured on each with abandon and sends them off track. Best bets for the main course are the daily specials, whatever fresh fish is offered, and the pork flambéed with Calvados and garnished with an apple and celery *tarte.* Desserts are a strong suit, especially the hot made-to-order apple tart, which is one of the best you will ever have, or the duo of chocolates melded into the warm chocolate cake.

TEL 01-43-26-29-44
OPEN Mon–Fri: lunch noon–2:30 P.M., dinner 7–10:30 P.M.; Sat: dinner
7–10:30 P.M. **CLOSED** Sat lunch, Sun; last 2 weeks Aug (dates vary)
À LA CARTE 35€, BNC **PRIX FIXE** Lunch: 18€, 2 courses, 23€, 3 courses, both
BNC; lunch & dinner: 30€, 3 courses, BNC; child's menu: 13€,
2 courses, BC **CREDIT CARDS** MC, V
RESERVATIONS Preferred **ENGLISH SPOKEN** Yes, and English menu

AUX CHARPENTIERS (23)
10, rue Mabillon
Métro: Mabillon

Aux Charpentiers—The Carpenters—is the type of Parisian
bistro I hope will never die, with its zinc bar, wooden floors, and
diners straight out of central casting. The name commemorates the
important role of the eighteenth-century journeyman carpenter and
cabinet-maker's guild in the politics and architecture of France. Next
door is a small museum that displays scale models created by guild
members in preparation for the construction of the spires and roofs of
such famous landmarks as Notre Dame and Ste-Chapelle.

The solid, stick-to-your-ribs fare includes platters of roast duck
and olives, beef fillet cooked with bone marrow, pig's feet, veal kidneys, roast Bresse chicken, and blood sausage. If these do not appeal,
take advantage of the Monday through Sunday *plats du jour: veal
Marengo* (breast of veal simmered in an herb, tomato, olive oil, and
white-wine sauce), *boeuf mode* (beef braised in red wine with carrots),
petit salé (salt pork and lentils), *pot-au-feu* (beef and vegetables cooked
in broth), *aïoli de morue* (dried cod with garlic mayonnaise sauce), *chou
farci* (stuffed cabbage), and *gigot d'agneau* (leg of lamb). While you will
not be overwhelmed with delicate or subtle cooking, you will enjoy a
typical French meal at a properly set, linen-clad table.

TEL 01-43-26-30-05
OPEN Daily: lunch noon–3 P.M., dinner 7–11:30 P.M. **CLOSED** Never
À LA CARTE 35–45€, BNC **PRIX FIXE** Lunch (Mon–Fri): 19€, 2 courses, BC;
lunch (Sat–Sun) & dinner (daily): 26€, 3 courses, BNC **CREDIT CARDS** AE,
DC, MC, V
RESERVATIONS Recommended **ENGLISH SPOKEN** Yes, and English menu

AZABU ($, 13)
3, rue André-Muzet
Métro: Odéon, St-Michel

For a delicious change of dining pace in Paris, reserve a place at
Azabu, the Left Bank's premier teppanyaki restaurant. The best seats
are the eight at the U-shaped counter, around the open grill, where
you can watch the ballet of the chef turning out the orders, each one
looking more appealing than the last. These prime seats are so popular that at dinner they must be reserved for either 7 P.M. or 9 P.M. If
the counter is full, request one of the four or five tables nearby, but
try to avoid the downstairs room, which is pretty but windowless and
a bit claustrophobic.

No matter where I sit, I like to start with the black radish salad made with seaweed, or the lotus root, quickly seared and lightly flavored with garlic and cheese. Another winner is the barely sautéed shiitake mushrooms and Japanese beans. The quickly grilled tuna, farm chicken, or duck breast make wonderful main course selections, especially when accompanied by a side of grilled vegetables. There are two dessert choices: green tea ice cream or a Japanese cake. Unless you go with one of the two prix-fixe menus, everything is à la carte and can quickly dip into the Big Splurge category, but if there are two or three of you, it is always fun to order several dishes and share. After a little sake, lively conversation, and a wonderful, healthy meal, you will quickly make Azabu a pleasant dining habit.

NOTE: Film buffs who love vintage movies will want to check out what is playing at the Action Christine theater, located around the corner on rue Christine.

TEL 01-46-33-72-05
OPEN Tues–Sat: lunch noon–2:30 P.M., dinner 7–10:30 P.M.; Sun: dinner
  7–10:30 P.M. **CLOSED** Sun lunch, Mon; 2 weeks mid-June, 2 weeks Aug,
  2 weeks at Christmas (all closings vary)
À LA CARTE 40–50€, BNC **PRIX FIXE** Lunch: 14.50€, 2 courses, BNC;
  18.50€, 2 courses; 33€, 3 courses; dinner: Zen Menu, 33€, 3 courses;
  Azabu Menu, 39€, 3 courses; Menu du Chef, 49€, 3 courses; Menu
  Gourmand, 59€,4 courses; all menus but first come with dessert or coffee
  CREDIT CARDS AE, MC, V
RESERVATIONS Essential **ENGLISH SPOKEN** Enough

BOUILLON RACINE (29)
3, rue Racine
Métro: Odéon

The first Bouillons appeared in 1855, serving a dish of meat and bouillon to the *marché* workers in Les Halles. By 1900 there were 250 Bouillons in Paris, and they have been credited as the first chain restaurant in the city. At the time, the era of Art Nouveau was in full flower, and even though the food in the Bouillons was simple and cheap, luxurious Art Nouveau decoration formed the dining background. Now, only a few authentic Bouillons remain, including Restaurant Chartier (see page 205) and this one on rue Racine. Here, you will find the original bevelled mirrors, stained glass, carved wood, marble mosaics, and gold-leaf lettering, which make for beautiful surroundings in this national historic site.

Fortunately, the food is not forgotten and satisfies by performing the basics with just enough twists to keep everyone interested. Things get off to a filling start with French onion or smoky bean soup, poached eggs in red wine with mushrooms and croutons, duck foie gras with Guérande sea salt and fig compote, and snails by the dozen. Spit-roasted suckling pig, shank of pork cooked in beer with a side of sauerkraut, lamb shanks with glazed carrots, and *Waterzöi* (chicken and vegetables in cream sauce) keep up the pace. Desserts are designed to please all sweet-tooths: they serve chestnut mousse à la Jack Daniels, crème brûlée with maple syrup, and a host of ice creams, including a lemon, mint, and white rum creation splashed with champagne.

TEL 01-44-32-15-60 **INTERNET** www.bouillonracine.com
OPEN Daily: lunch noon–2 P.M., dinner 7–11 P.M. **CLOSED** Dec 24–25; Mon in Aug (can vary)
À LA CARTE 35–42€, BNC **PRIX FIXE** Lunch (Mon–Fri): 14.50€, 1 course, 15.50€, 2 courses, both BNC; lunch & dinner (daily): 27€, 3 courses, BNC **CREDIT CARDS** AE, MC, V
RESERVATIONS Recommended **ENGLISH SPOKEN** Yes, and English menu

CHEZ CLAUDE SAINLOUIS (20)
27, rue du Dragon
Métro: St-Germain-des-Prés, St-Sulpice

Claude Sainlouis promises no surprises, just good food and plenty of it. As a result, it attracts scores of hungry French diners, all eager to enjoy the two-course lunch or dinner *formule* that includes the famous *salade Claude Sainlouis* (made with nuts and apples), followed by blood sausage, warming beef *pot-au-feu* with marrow bone, *tripes maison à la provençal* or *tête de veau* (calf's head). The à la carte main courses are a dozen in number and include fish choices of fat shrimp or salmon along with roast leg of lamb or *côte de boeuf à la moêlle* for two, frog legs, and beef tartare, all garnished with the potatoes of your choice. Desserts are almost impossible to fit in, but some find room for the warm profiteroles dusted with almonds or the prunes soaked in armagnac. That's it: good, dependable, well-cooked food served by career waiters (wearing name tags!) in a congenial room with tufted red banquettes and white linens.

TEL 01-45-48-29-68
OPEN Tues–Sat: lunch noon–3 P.M., dinner 7 P.M.–midnight **CLOSED** Mon, Sun; holidays, week at Christmas, Aug
À LA CARTE *Entrées* 11€, *plats* 20€, desserts 11€ **PRIX FIXE** Lunch: 16€, 1 course, 19.50€, 2 courses, both BC (wine & coffee); lunch & dinner: 30€, 3 courses, BNC **CREDIT CARDS** V
RESERVATIONS Recommended **ENGLISH SPOKEN** Yes

CHEZ MAÎTRE PAUL (28)
12, rue Monsieur-le-Prince
Métro: Odéon

Upscale patrons continue to fill this refined, comfortable restaurant presided over by Jean François Debert. The nicely spaced tables are formally set with starched linens, fresh flowers, and sparkling crystal in a soft gray room with subdued lighting and attractive artwork on the walls.

The decidedly rich, full-flavored cuisine features specialties from the Franche-Comté region in eastern France. Among the *entrées* you will find a *terrine maison* made with chicken livers, a plate of garlicky sausages served warm with tiny potatoes, and in the spring, fat white asparagus in warm vinaigrette. A main course must is the *poulet au vin jaune*—tender chicken in a tomato, mushroom, and wine sauce. Two other award-winning chicken dishes are the *poulet sauté au vin rouge d'Arbois* and the *poulette à la crème gratinée* (chicken in a cream and cheese sauce). Most of the other main course dishes are served with Jura wine sauces that are perfect for mopping up with crusty baguettes. If you can still think about dessert, the crème brûlée or thin, warm cinnamon-apple *tarte* are both definitely worthwhile, and the local cheeses are interesting.

TEL 01-43-54-74-59
OPEN Daily (Sept–June): lunch noon–2:30 P.M., dinner 7–10:30 P.M.;
    Tues–Sat (July–Aug): same hours **CLOSED** Sun–Mon in July–Aug; May 1,
    Christmas, NAC
À LA CARTE 35–45€, BNC **PRIX FIXE** Lunch: 28€, 3 courses BNC; 35€,
    3 courses, BC **CREDIT CARDS** AE, DC, MC, V
RESERVATIONS Recommended **ENGLISH SPOKEN** Yes

CHEZ MARCEL (43)
7, rue Stanislas
Métro: Notre-Dame-des-Champs, Vavin

In this area of Paris, where you are likely to see more baseball caps than berets, it is hard to find an authentic neighborhood restaurant. Chez Marcel is just that—a local pick, nothing elaborate or worth a taxi ride across town, but worthwhile if you are nearby. It is a comforting choice, the sort we all go to when we don't feel like cooking. The place could double as a set on the back lot of a Hollywood film studio: old walls hung with curling posters, two original 1936 chandeliers, an antique buffet displaying desserts, fresh flowers in a pretty vase, a table or two on the sidewalk, and gentle owners, the Daumails, who have been here twenty years . . . plenty of time to know all of their customers by name.

The Lyonnaise food is served à la carte for lunch and dinner, and there is a bargain lunch *formule*. The food choices run from A to almost Z, ranging from artichokes vinaigrette, escargots, and pâtés to Lyonnaise sausages, lamb, beef, and veal. The *tarte au chocolat* or *l'île flottante* are my desserts of choice.

TEL 01-45-48-29-94
OPEN Mon–Fri: lunch noon–2 P.M., dinner 7:30–10 P.M. **CLOSED** Sat–Sun;
    holidays, Aug
À LA CARTE 30–38€, BNC **PRIX FIXE** Lunch: 16€, 2 courses, BNC
    CREDIT CARDS MC, V
RESERVATIONS Recommended **ENGLISH SPOKEN** Yes

COSI (¢, 9)
54, rue de Seine
Métro: Odéon, Mabillon

Cosi is a chichi gourmet sandwich shop just off rue de Buci. A delicious, made-to-order-while-you-watch hot sandwich on warm bread, a glass of good wine, and classical opera music—that's Cosi, a fast-food concept that has caught on big-time, keeping the little spot continually busy and crowded. The idea was developed by a New Zealander who made violins in Italy, learned how to make bread there, and then moved to Paris, adapted the bread recipe, and *voila!* The colorful and tasty sandwiches are made with focaccia-style bread, cooked as you watch in a wood-fired oven and filled while still hot with an ingenious combination of tasty ingredients. You pay according to the ingredients you select, which could be anything from chèvre and cucumbers to roasted eggplant, guacamole, tomatoes, salmon, chili, cole-slaw vinaigrette, tuna, and roast beef. Your order is placed on a tray that you carry to an attractive upstairs dining room, where you eat surrounded by photos of famous opera stars while listening to them sing. In addition to the marvelous sandwiches, there are soups and salads served with bread on the side and desserts made with a thousand calories of butter and sugar . . . especially Marianne's New York cheesecake and the apple crumble.

NOTE: Everything on the menu can be wrapped to go, but you will still pay the menu price.

TEL 01-46-33-35-36

OPEN Daily: noon–11 P.M., continuous service **CLOSED** Christmas, New Year's Day, NAC

À LA CARTE Sandwiches 5.50–9€, soups & salads 5–8€, desserts 4€

PRIX FIXE None **CREDIT CARDS** MC, V

RESERVATIONS Not taken **ENGLISH SPOKEN** Yes

FISH LA BOISSONNERIE (10)
69, rue de Seine
Métro: St-Germain-des-Prés, Odéon

Drew Harré, who owns Cosi across the street (see page 137), and Juan Sanchez, who runs La Dernière Goute, a great wine shop nearby (see page 142), have joined forces and opened Fish la Boissonnerie. You can't miss the building on rue de Seine—it is the one with the colorful mosaic tiles dating from the early twentieth century that cover the entire front. The original lettering said *poissonnerie* because this used to be a fish shop, but Drew wanted it to be a place to eat fish *and* drink, so the *p* was changed to a *b*.

You consult the menu while sipping a glass of wine and munching on black radishes dipped in toasted sesame seeds. Naturally, the best order of the day will be one of the fresh fish catches. I like to start the meal on a light note with the zucchini-mint soup or the crab salad in an orange vinaigrette dressing. If pasta is your preference, consider the linguine with clams. Carnivores aren't left out; they can dig into roasted duck garnished with tart red cabbage and a potato pancake, or a beef fillet capped with poached foie gras and served with potato purée and a broccoli fritter. There are always four or five fresh fish *plats,* and depending on the season you will find sea bass, tuna, cod, and sea bream. For dessert, order the chocolate *tarte* with raspberry ice cream and matching sauce. Wines are all selected by Juan, feature weekly choices available by the glass or *pichet,* and are available for purchase at his nearby shop, La Derniére Goutte.

NOTE: This is a nonsmoking restaurant.

TEL 01-43-54-34-69

OPEN Tues–Sun: lunch 12:30–2:30 P.M., dinner 7–10:45 P.M. **CLOSED** Mon; week between Christmas and New Year's, 1 week Aug (dates vary)

À LA CARTE Lunch only: *entrées* 8€, *plats* 15€, desserts 8€ **PRIX FIXE** Lunch: Flying Fish Menu, 11.50€, 1 course & salad (no fish), BNC; 22.50€, 3 courses, BNC; dinner: 29€, 2 courses, 33.50€, 3 courses, both BNC

CREDIT CARDS "We readily accept Mastercard and Visa, but American Express . . . please leave home without it."

RESERVATIONS Essential **ENGLISH SPOKEN** Yes

FORÊT NOIR (18)
9, rue de l'Éperon
Métro: Odéon

For an intimate téte-à-téte with a loved one, it will be hard to beat a table in this inviting lunch/tearoom, nestled on a side street off the busy boulevard St-Germain-des-Prés. Most of the tables face onto a terrace garden, giving the charming room a country feel. The grandmotherly food is designed to push dieters off the wagon, not only with the *plats,* but with a sideboard covered with tempting sweet decisions. The menu starts with salads, moves on to *croustillants,* baked potatoes with assorting toppings, and highlights one or two hot dishes, including a tender lamb in a honey-and-sesame sauce. On Sunday a copious brunch is served that includes fresh fruit juices, hot drinks, pastries, scrambled eggs with smoked ham or salmon, a green salad tossed with raw vegetables, potatoes with chive cream sauce, and a choice of desserts (a black forest cake with cream or a semisweet cheesecake). For the moment, tea and desserts are served on Saturday and Sunday afternoons only, but plans are to serve it daily, as well as to add dinner service.

TEL 01-44-41-00-09

OPEN Daily: lunch noon–3 P.M.; also Sat–Sun, tea 3–7 P.M. **CLOSED** Major holidays; last 3 weeks Aug (dates vary)

À LA CARTE Lunch: 18–25€, BNC; tea: 10–12€ **PRIX FIXE** Sun brunch: 20€, 3 courses, BC **CREDIT CARDS** MC, V (15€ minimum)

RESERVATIONS Not necessary **ENGLISH SPOKEN** Yes

GÉRARD MULOT (¢, 24)
76, rue de Seine
Métro: Odéon

A passion for French pastries can be satisfied at this beautiful shop, where a full range of traditional and sublime French sweets and baked goods are made each day with the freshest ingredients. The appreciative audience is not too busy to queue ten deep to buy their cloudlike macaroons, chewy *pain aux noix* (walnut bread), and handcrafted chocolates. In addition to the almost museum-quality *pâtisseries,* they have a magnificent selection of hot and cold dishes that can be packaged to go, making it a place to remember for a Parisian fast-food lunch. Why settle for a plebian ham-and-cheese baguette when you can sample fresh salmon or creamy pâté garnished with crudités, a savory herb quiche filled with chèvre and tomatoes, or wild mushroom fricassée and a salad for just a little more money? The only seating is at a window counter, but on a warm day you can put together *le pique-nique* and enjoy it sitting on a park chair in the beautiful Luxembourg Gardens, only a few minutes away on foot.

TEL 01-43-26-85-77
OPEN Mon–Tues, Thur–Sun: 7 A.M.–8 P.M., continuous service **CLOSED** Wed;
   July 15–Aug 15
À LA CARTE 2.50–15€, BNC **PRIX FIXE** None **CREDIT CARDS** None
RESERVATIONS Not taken **ENGLISH SPOKEN** Very little

GUENMAÏ (¢, 8)
6, rue Cardinale
Métro: St-Germain-des-Prés, Mabillon

No one stands on ceremony at this natural foods restaurant and shop, and servers can be distracted during the noon mob scene. Despite these slight flaws, Guenmaï attracts a crowd in an upmarket neighborhood known for having every type of restaurant imaginable and favoring all pocketbooks.

The food leans toward the macrobiotic and uses no meat, butter, sugar, milk, or eggs. Limited amounts of fish are served. The entirely à la carte menu features such creations as vegetable spring rolls and tempura, croquettes, *tartes,* and *plats du jour* based around grains, tofu, and seaweed. The daily *plat* comes with two proteins, two cereals, crudités, and pickles, and on Saturday, the chef turns out a tofu soufflé. There is also a nice array of freshly squeezed juices, *biologique* (organic) wines, and nonalcoholic beers. For the best selection and variety, arrive before the hungry herd, no later than 12:30 P.M.—after that, selections can begin to narrow.

TEL 01-43-26-03-24
OPEN Mon–Sat: lunch noon–3:30 P.M., shop 9 A.M.–8:30 P.M. **CLOSED** Sun;
   holidays, Aug
À LA CARTE 12–16€, BNC **PRIX FIXE** None **CREDIT CARDS** V
RESERVATIONS Not accepted **ENGLISH SPOKEN** Yes

JEAN-PAUL HEVIN (41)
3, rue Vavin
Métro: Vavin

At this location, there is no tea salon. Please see page 53 for complete details about this famous chocolatier.

TEL 01-43-54-09-85

JOSEPHINE "CHEZ DUMONET" ($, 39)
117, rue du Cherche-Midi
Métro: Duroc, Falguière

Josephine "Chez Dumonet" is on everyone's list of favorites, and rightfully so. It is a textbook perfect Parisian restaurant: it has a hearty and appealing classic menu served with old-time flair and

PRICES From 5–8€ and up **CREDIT CARDS** AE, MC, V
ENGLISH SPOKEN Yes

LADURÉE (1)
21, rue Bonaparte, at rue Jacob
Métro: St-Germain-des-Prés

Leave it to Ladurée to continue to outdo themselves in their St-Germain emporium of sweet treats, which is the *pâtisserie* darling of ladies who lunch. Occupying the pivotal Left Bank corner of rue Bonaparte and rue Jacob, this branch opened in July 2002 with a refined theme designed to symbolize *"l'art de vivre à la française."* This atmosphere has been beautifully created in the downstairs veranda, inspired by the Brighton Pavilion in England, and upstairs in the Salon Bleu de Pruss, which reflects nineteenth-century opulence with its heavy, dark taffeta curtains and dainty upholstered chairs. Waitresses in long black skirts with white polka-dot accents serve the beautifully composed salads, sandwiches, fat omelettes, and myriad desserts and ice cream delights that take up eight single-spaced menu pages.

NOTE: Ladurée has several other locations in Paris (including two in the eighth arrondissement, pages 189 and 190), and a tearoom in Printemps department store.

TEL 01-44-07-64-87 **INTERNET** www.laduree.fr
OPEN Mon–Sat: pastry counter 8:30 A.M.–7:30 P.M., breakfast 8:30–11:45 A.M., lunch noon–3 P.M., tea 3–7:30 P.M.; Sun & holidays from 10 A.M. **CLOSED** Christmas, New Year's Day, NAC
À LA CARTE Pastries 6–9€, lunch 25–35€, BNC; afternoon tea 14–20€, BC
PRIX FIXE Lunch: 27€, 1 course, 32€, 2 courses, both BNC
CREDIT CARDS AE, DC, MC, V
RESERVATIONS Recommended for lunch, especially on weekends
ENGLISH SPOKEN Yes

LA FERRANDAISE (31)
8, rue Vaugirard
Métro: Luxembourg, Odéon

Wide cross beams, thick white stucco walls hung with pictures of Ferrandaise cattle, and bare dark wood tables make up the rough-hewn interior in the three connecting rooms of this convivial bistro across from the Luxembourg Gardens. The short menu concentrates on a well-loved battery of classics, with the odds-on favorites of *terrine de chèvre et betterave rouge* (chèvre and red beet terrine), *oeuf cocotte, fricassée de champignons* (soft-boiled egg on a bed of mushrooms), and *crème de topinambour au foie gras* (cream of Jerusalem artichoke soup ladled over foie gras). Heading the list of mains is milk-fed Ferrandais veal served with root vegetables, or herb-crusted milk-fed lamb. There is also guinea hen, risotto with *coquilles St-Jacques* (scallops), and pan-seared *onglet* (flank steak). For dessert, the roasted mango spiked with basil makes an unusual ending to another good value Great Eat in Paris.

TEL 01-43-26-36-36
OPEN Tues–Fri: lunch noon–2:30 P.M., dinner 7–11 P.M. (Fri till midnight); Sat: dinner 7 P.M.–midnight **CLOSED** Sat lunch, Mon, Sun; Aug

À **LA CARTE** Lunch only: *entrées* 7€, *plats* 16€, dessert 7€ **PRIX FIXE** Lunch
& dinner: 30€, 3 courses, BNC; *menu dégustation:* 38€, 6 dishes, BNC
CREDIT CARDS MC, V
RESERVATIONS Recommended **ENGLISH SPOKEN** Yes

LA FROMAGERIE (12)
64, rue de Seine
Métro: Mabillon, St-Germain-des-Prés

France reportedly produces over four hundred varieties of cheese,
a fact that can be overwhelming to anyone used to only Roquefort,
Cheddar, and Swiss. While you won't find all four hundred at La
Fromagerie, you can still sample over a hundred varieties of seasonal
French cheeses, which you can enjoy here or buy to take with you. If
you eat here, seating is at one of the four tables in the glass-enclosed
dining area or, weather permitting, at one of six sidewalk tables.

The owners are passionate about their cheeses and consider it their
mission to help you discover new types. If you order one of the cheese
plates to eat here, you do not get to select the cheeses you want.
Instead, you tell them what you *don't* like, and they choose the varieties of cheese for you, starting clockwise from mildest to strongest.
Your cheese feast will be served with a basket of bread and a green
salad. In addition you can order large composed salads, *l'aligot* (potatoes whipped with cheese and liberal lashings of garlic), and a bowl of
comforting vegetable soup with chèvre and fresh cream (winter only).
It may be impossible, but try to save room for a slice of the homemade
cheesecake or chocolate cake for dessert. Wines by the glass, *pichet,* or
bottle round out this super Great Eat on a colorful shopping street in
St-Germain-des-Prés.

NOTE: Your purchases can be vacuum packed for transport back
to your home.

TEL 01-43-26-50-31
OPEN Tues–Thur: lunch 10 A.M.–3 P.M., dinner 5–8:30 P.M.; Fri–Sat: 10 A.M.–
8 P.M.; Sun: store only 10 A.M.–1:30 P.M. **CLOSED** Sun food service, Mon;
15 days mid-Aug
À **LA CARTE** 18–25€, BNC **PRIX FIXE** Cheese plates: 9.80€, 5 choices,
13.80€, 7 choices, 17.80€, 9 choices, all BNC **CREDIT CARDS** AE,DC,
MC, V
RESERVATIONS Not accepted **ENGLISH SPOKEN** Yes

LA LOZÈRE (16)
4, rue Hautefeuille
Métro: St-Michel, Cluny-La Sorbonne

The menu highlights the cuisine from the rugged Lozère region of
central France. At a wooden table positioned extremely close to your
neighbor, you will sample popular country hams, sausages, cheeses,
and hearty regional specialties. Once you are seated, a huge loaf of dark
country bread is brought to your table for you to slice as much as you
want. Go easy: there is much more to come . . . such as *tripoux Lozère*
(mutton tripe cooked with white wine and tomatoes) or *La Maoucho* (a

soul-food dish of cabbage and sausage baked with potatoes). There is also smoked trout and veal roasted with prunes. On Thursday, a line forms at lunch and dinner for La Lozère's potato specialty: *l'aligot,* a dish of creamy mashed potatoes mixed with melted *cantal* cheese and flavored with garlic. These potatoes make heaven out of any meal they accompany. For Thursday lunch, you must order your *l'aligot* twenty-four hours ahead, and there is a two-person minimum. On Thursday night, only prix-fixe menus are available, and they include *l'aligot.*

NOTE: A few doors down the street is the tourist bureau for the Lozère region.

TEL 01-43-54-26-64 **INTERNET** www.lozere-a-paris.com
OPEN Tues–Sat: lunch noon–2 P.M., dinner 7:30–10 P.M. **CLOSED** Mon, Sun; holidays, Christmas week, Easter week, mid-July to end of Aug (dates vary)
À LA CARTE 30–35€, BNC **PRIX FIXE** Lunch: 14.90€, 2 courses,16€, 3 courses, both BC; lunch & dinner: 22€, 3 courses, 26€, 4 courses, both BNC **CREDIT CARDS** MC, V
RESERVATIONS Essential; required 24 hours ahead for Thur meals
   ENGLISH SPOKEN Some

LA MARLOTTE (36)
55, rue du Cherche-Midi
Métro: St-Placide

Dining at La Marlotte, adeptly run by Eric Roset, the owner, and Patrick Duclos, his chef, is a truly pleasurable experience. The setting—especially at night, with its subdued lighting, pretty provincial paintings, and formally clad, candlelit tables—is elegantly romantic and quietly discreet. The stylish guests have every table filled by 9 P.M., making reservations mandatory as far in advance as possible.

The cooking is the best kind: generous, fresh, and resolutely traditional. Regulars come often for the time-honored renditions of *tarte à l'oignon, escalope de foie gras,* a *salade délicieux* made with green beans and foie gras, and, in spring, white asparagus dressed in a light vinaigrette. *Coq au vin, sole meunière, magret de canard de citron et au miel,* seasonally fresh fish simply grilled or sauced, and an out-of-this-world lemon tart that positively melts in your mouth are other all-time favorites.

TEL 01-45-48-86-79 **INTERNET** www.lamarlotte.com
OPEN Mon–Sat: lunch noon–2:30 P.M., dinner 8–11 P.M. **CLOSED** Sun; lunch on holidays, first 2 weeks Aug
À LA CARTE 38–45€, BNC **PRIX FIXE** Lunch: 21.50€, 2 courses, BC
   CREDIT CARDS AE, DC, MC, V
RESERVATIONS Essential **ENGLISH SPOKEN** Yes

LA RÔTISSERIE D'EN FACE (6)
2, rue Christine, off rue Dauphine
Métro: St-Michel

Spit-roasted meats, imaginative desserts, and good wines add up to the success story of Jacques Cagna's La Rôtisserie d'en Face, located across the street (*en face*) from his very high-priced restaurant known simply as Jacques Cagna. Sometimes you will see him eating lunch at the table by the door, accompanied by his dog, a whippet named Monsieur Patton (after the general). The easy elegance of La Rôtisserie draws a high-octane mix of dark-suited businessmen at lunch and designer-clad couples at night. A word of caution is in order at the start: when ordering, watch out for the supplements, which are added to high-ticket items such as frog's legs, fresh scallops, prime rib, leg of lamb, and wild game in season. At lunch and dinner, the prix-fixe menu includes only one spit-roasted meat: free-range chicken with mashed potatoes. However, there are plenty of other meaty dishes of note, such as pepper steak, *cassoulet* (made with pork, lamb, and duck and big fat white beans), or for a lighter touch, the sole tempura with zucchini pudding. The servings of meat and garnishes are not diet-size, so you may be too full for a dessert, but do consider sharing the *Mont-Blanc,* a chestnut pudding glazed with whipped cream and candied chestnuts, or the *vacherin glacé,* a caramel-and-walnut ice cream cake that is one of the house specialties.

TEL 01-43-26-40-98 **INTERNET** www.jacques-cagna.com
OPEN Mon–Fri: lunch noon–2 P.M., dinner 7–11 P.M.; Sat: dinner 7–11 P.M.
   CLOSED Sat lunch, Sun; Dec 24–25, NAC
À LA CARTE Lunch: 40€; dinner: 45€; both BNC **PRIX FIXE** Lunch: 18€,
   1 course, BC; 25€, 2 courses, BNC; 28€, 3 courses, BNC; dinner: 42€,
   3 courses, BNC **CREDIT CARDS** AE, DC, MC, V
RESERVATIONS Essential **ENGLISH SPOKEN** Yes, and English menu

LA TOURELLE (17)
5, rue Hautefeuille
Métro: St-Michel, Cluny-La Sorbonne

Busy, cost-conscious Parisians have had a long love affair with the prix-fixe menu, especially at lunch. And why not, especially when you can be in and out the door in under an hour and spend around 10€ to 20€ for a decent two- or three-course meal. Nowhere is this better demonstrated than at La Tourelle, an unassuming old bistro, where the prices make up for the lack of culinary imagination. Don't worry—the food is solid, just nothing new. Here you will eat cream of vegetable soup, *oeufs dur mayonnaise,* and grated carrot salad, followed by beef tartare, *confit de canard,* and for dessert, crème caramel, a slice of fruit tart, or a chunk of Brie. Things do pick up slightly at dinner, with the addition of *chèvre chaud* on a bed of greens or a half dozen escargots to start, followed by a cumin-flavored lamb brochette. Or, for a few euros more, order a beef steak with Roquefort or béarnaise sauce, sautéed potatoes, and a green salad. For dessert, the *île flottante* or pear clafoutis are best bets. At lunch, regulars pay their tab at the bar while exchanging a few words with owners Robert and Cecilia.

TEL 01-46-33-12-47
OPEN Mon–Fri: lunch noon–2:30 P.M., dinner 7–10:30 P.M.; Sat: dinner
   7–10:30 P.M. **CLOSED** Sat lunch, Sun; holidays, Aug

À LA CARTE Dinner only: 20€, BNC **PRIX FIXE** Lunch: 11€, 2 courses, 15€,
3 courses, both BNC; dinner: 18€, 3 courses, BNC **CREDIT CARDS** MC, V
RESERVATIONS Not necessary **ENGLISH SPOKEN** Yes

LE BISTRO D'HENRI (21)
16, rue Princesse
Métro: Mabillon

If you like Le Mâchon d'Henri (see page 149), chances are excellent you will like Le Bistro d'Henri, just around the corner and under the same management. The small dining room, with its black-and-white tile floor, offers somewhat comfortable leatherette banquette seating, and the open kitchen gives it a larger feeling. Time-honored bistro fare is featured, with daily changing *entrées* and *plats du jour*. Featured wines of the month are extra, but you will still be able to eat a three-course meal here for a fraction of what it would set you back for three-star splendor elsewhere. While neither of the Henri restaurants is a temple of gastronomic art, both provide a Parisian dining experience that includes friendly waiters and that results in many satisfied guests.

TEL 01-46-33-51-12
OPEN Daily: lunch noon–2:30 P.M., dinner 7–11:30 P.M. **CLOSED** Christmas,
New Year's Day, NAC
À LA CARTE 25–30€, BNC **PRIX FIXE** None **CREDIT CARDS** MC, V
RESERVATIONS Recommended **ENGLISH SPOKEN** Yes

L'ÉCLUSE GRANDS-AUGUSTINS (7)
15, quai des Grands-Augustins
Métro: St-Michel

There are several other locations of this well-known wine bar. For a complete description and full information, see the one in the first (page 59), but I also include locations in the eighth (page 193), eleventh (page 218), and seventeenth (page 269) arrondissements.

TEL 01-46-33-58-74

LE COMPTOIR (19)
9, Carrefour de l'Odéon
Métro: Odéon

Parisian and visiting gourmets alike have found what they are looking for at Yves Camdeborde's Le Comptoir. Several years ago, Camdeborde took a leap of faith and opened La Régalade, a small restaurant in an unimpressive corner of the fourteenth. From the get-go, it was a resounding success; proof of this was the three nightly dinner seatings that still left people clamoring to get in. Then he suddenly sold the restaurant and took some time off. Now he has resurfaced at Le Comptoir, and as then, his cooking has an authority that commands attention, and he has the hottest tables in Paris. The real buzz centers on his Monday-to-Friday, five-course dinner tasting menu, which offers no choices. For this meal, reservations are mandatory as far in advance as possible, and six months is not too far. (Note that the tasting menu is not served in August, but the brasserie is open.) To show you how popular his place has become, when the linen-covered tables inside are full, people are willing to sit at the half dozen or so tables on the sidewalk—even wrapped in blankets (provided by the restaurant) in the middle of January when the temperature drops below five degrees! The menu changes nightly and is printed on a postcard, so you can save it or send it to jealous foodies back home. Is the food worth the scrimmage for reservations and decent seating? Everyone, myself included, answers with a resounding yes. The tasting menu is a tour-de-force: it showcases Camdeborde's skill in preparing dishes from his native Béarn in southwestern France, and it also challenges the notion that good has to be outrageously expensive.

To begin, a bowl of colorful vegetable crisps are brought to the table along with a loaf of Camdeborde's whole-grain bread. The appetizer might be shredded fresh crab surrounded by a spicy tomato sauce, or tender asparagus tips lightly dressed with a creamy herring caviar sauce. Next, there will be a colorful terrine, perhaps of wild mushrooms and foie gras with an artichoke *mousseline*. The main course on my lucky night to be here was fork-tender milk-fed lamb from the Pyrénées, served with baby peas and fava beans along with a thyme-flavored eggplant mousse. Fortunately, portions are small, enabling you to fully enjoy all the flavorful dishes without becoming too full. This course is followed by a magnificent cheese tray, where diners help themselves from at least ten choices of little-known cheeses from La Maison Boursault. Fresh fruit plays a major part in the desserts, and I loved mine, which was a rich combination of strawberries folded into whipped cream, accented by a sesame-orange crisp. Chocolate bonbons are presented with the bill, which includes everything but the beverages.

If the tasting menu and its reservation policy are not for you, then consider Le Comptoir for lunch or for dinner on Saturday and Sunday nights, when the menu reverts to brasserie choices from an entirely à la carte menu, and no reservations are accepted. The dishes served at these times have the creative Camdeborde touch, and they deliciously cover the bases from a simple *oeuf dur mayonnaise* or *croque monsieur* made with smoked salmon to leg of lamb, grilled tuna, and beef stew. Soup, large salads, and plates of cold meat are also served. *Tarte Tatin*, crème brûlée, and *chocolat pot de crème* are just three of the favorite desserts.

NOTE: Camdeborde never seems to rest! His latest venture is Crêperie du Comptoir, which is next door at 3, carrefour de l'Odéon. This takeout boutique serves *gaufres* (waffles), sweet and savory crêpes, assorted pastries, sandwiches, ready-made salads, ice cream, sorbets, and cold drinks. It is open daily and prices range from 3€ to 10€. Also, Camdeborde and his wife, Claudine, own the charming four-star Relais Saint-Germain hotel next door. See *Great Sleeps Paris* for a description.

TEL 01-44-27-07-97
OPEN Mon–Fri: lunch noon–6 P.M., dinner (one seating, tasting menu only)
8:30 P.M.; Sat–Sun noon–11 P.M., continuous service. **CLOSED** Dec 24, 31,
NAC
À LA CARTE 20–40€, BNC; daily specials: *entrées* 9€, *plats* 12€, dessert
7€ **PRIX FIXE** Tasting menu (Mon–Fri dinner only): 42€, 5 courses (no
choices), BNC **CREDIT CARDS** AE, DC, MC, V
RESERVATIONS Required as far in advance as possible for Mon–Fri dinner
(tasting menu); not accepted at other times **ENGLISH SPOKEN** Yes

LE MÂCHON D'HENRI (22)
8, rue Guisarde
Métro: Mabillon

Le Mâchon d'Henri is a pocket-size bistro that seats twenty-six
people sandwiched around twelve tiny marble-top tables. It is the sort
of place where an up-to-date clientele comes for a good, honest meal
carefully prepared with seasonal ingredients.

The menu is written in very tiny lettering on a blackboard. The
main courses are filling, so start with the fresh green beans or beets
tossed in vinaigrette. If you like liver, you must order it here; cooked
to pink perfection, it is served with grilled onions and creamy potatoes. Another good selection is the rich beef stew with carrots. The
lamb chops can be avoided with ease. Chocolate fans will relish every
bite of the chocolate cake, and traditionalists will love the lemon *tarte*
or fruit clafoutis. Good wines of the month are reasonably priced.

NOTE: Le Bistro d'Henri, around the corner at 16, rue Princesse
(see page 147), is under the same management.

TEL 01-43-29-08-70
OPEN Daily: lunch noon–2:30 P.M., dinner 7–11:30 P.M. **CLOSED** Christmas,
New Year's Day, NAC
À LA CARTE *Entrées* 7–9€, *plats* 12–15€, desserts 6–7€, BNC **PRIX FIXE** None
CREDIT CARDS MC, V
RESERVATIONS Essential **ENGLISH SPOKEN** Yes

LE PETIT LUTETIA (35)
107, rue de Sèvres
Métro: Vaneau, Sèvres-Babylone

Given the reasonable price for the three-course menu—which is
served for both lunch and dinner every day they are open—it is no
wonder that the tables in this Art Nouveau–style bistro are always
full. At lunchtime the cast of characters is made up of well-heeled
businesspeople and many art and antiques dealers. Early in the evening,
it favors middle-aged locals and the occasional tourist, while later
on, it is filled with an upmarket, young crowd that considers dining
before 10 P.M. *trés declassée.* The dependable food promises no surprises,
just authentic dishes guaranteed to please. You know the drill almost
before you sit down: herring and potatoes in oil, smoked salmon, *chèvre
chaud* on a mound of designer greens, house terrine, and foie gras to
start. Steak tartare, *confit de canard,* daily blackboard specials, the *plat*

du jour, fresh fish, and rump steak in a peppercorn sauce sum up the main courses. Floating island; gooey, warm chocolate cake; rice pudding spiked with orange peel and raisins, plus an interesting platter of cheese close out this Great Eat in Paris.

TEL 01-45-48-33-53
OPEN Daily: lunch 11:30 A.M.–3 P.M., dinner 7–11 P.M. **CLOSED** Dec 24–25, NAC
À LA CARTE 30–35€, BNC **PRIX FIXE** Lunch & dinner: 30€, 3 courses & coffee
   CREDIT CARDS AE, V
RESERVATIONS Recommended **ENGLISH SPOKEN** Yes, and English menu

LE PETIT SAINT-BENOÎT (2)
4, rue St-Benoît
Métro: St-Germain-des-Prés

Le Petit Saint-Benoît—which celebrated its centennial under the same family ownership in 2001—is a marvelous bistro sitting smack in the heart of St-Germain-des-Prés. The interior is vintage Paris: brown walls aged by years of heavy cigarette smoke, brass hat racks, fresh white paper covering red tablecloths, and at times, a big, lazy dog crowding the busiest aisle. Outside, several hotly contested sidewalk tables offer front-row seating for the passing parade. Motherly waitresses serve meals to a cross section of intellectuals, BCBGs *(bon chic bon genre:* French yuppies), artists, and portly gentlemen with young companions.

The handwritten, mimeographed daily changing menu lists low-priced basics that are cooked to a T and served in portions worthy of lumberjacks. Start with a soothing vegetable soup, a plate of crisp radishes and sweet butter, or an avocado vinaigrette, and go on to a nourishing serving of roast chicken and mashed potatoes, liver with a bacon cream sauce, or *petit salé* (salt pork with cabbage). Top it all off with a pitcher of the house wine and a bowl of chocolate mousse. Lingering over a *café express,* you will no doubt begin to seriously consider moving to Paris.

TEL 01-42-60-27-92
OPEN Mon–Sat; lunch noon–2:30 P.M., dinner 7–10:30 P.M. **CLOSED** Sun; week in Feb, 4 weeks in Aug (dates vary)
À LA CARTE 17–25€, BNC **PRIX FIXE** None **CREDIT CARDS** None
RESERVATIONS Not accepted **ENGLISH SPOKEN** Yes

LE PETIT VATEL (¢, 26)
5, rue Lobineau
Métro: Mabillon, Odéon

Le Petit Vatel continues to be a good choice for hard-core budgeteers, 80 percent of whom are lunchtime regulars, or so states the owner, Catherine, who runs the place with her husband, Sixte. Everyone sits close together on assorted rush-seated chairs or on stools at tables set with colorful plastics (from Ikea). The menu includes seasonal hot and cold soups, a homemade terrine, *plats* that change several times a week, and a vegetarian plate. Always available is the chef's own *pamboli,* which started out as an *entrée* but is now his most popular main course. It is two pieces of toasted whole-grain bread spread with olive oil and then covered with spiced tomatoes, ham, and a slice of mountain cheese—a filling meal in itself that costs around 8€. For dessert there is a choice of chocolate cake, *l'île flottante,* or *tomme crayeuse de Savoie,* a very special chalky cheese sent specially to Le Petit Vatel. Wines are sold by the glass, *pichet,* or bottle, with nothing costing over 25€.

NOTE: There is no smoking allowed.

TEL 01-43-54-28-49

OPEN Mon–Sat: lunch noon–2:30 P.M., dinner 7–10:30 P.M. **CLOSED** Sun; holidays, Feb, week in July or Aug (dates vary)

À LA CARTE *Entrées* 4–5€, *plats* 10€, desserts 4–5€ **PRIX FIXE** Lunch (Tues–Fri): 12€, 2 courses, BNC **CREDIT CARDS** MC, V

RESERVATIONS Not accepted **ENGLISH SPOKEN** Yes, and Spanish

LE PETIT VERDOT (37)
75, rue du Cherche Midi
Métro: Vaneau

There are only twenty-five places in this two-level, napkin-size *bistrot* named after a type of Bordeaux grape. Bare tables set with white napkins, a wall of banquettes opposite spindly hard chairs, and a charming old fireplace mantle sum up the interior. The menu is short and modern, but with traditional overtones and daily changing dishes that keep the local lunch and dinner patrons eager to return. The two-course, 20€ *ardoise* (blackboard) lunch is a Great Eat buy, but since there is no choice, you had better like what will be on your plate. Most likely that won't be hard, with such favorites as *oeufs pochette en meurette* (eggs poached in wine), fresh *raie* (skate fish) seasoned with capers, and a spicy *crème créole* for dessert. Other popular lunch orders are the large salads filled with everything from tomatoes and baby green beans to smoked duck, foie gras, and smoked salmon. The choices expand for dinner, but the unfussy menu always includes some fresh fish, grilled *entrecôte* garnished with *aligot de l'aubrac,* and perhaps a *pot au feu* or an over-the-top calorie-charged *boudin noir* (blood sausage), which is served *mille-feuille*-style, layered with buttery potatoes in a *mousseline* sauce (hollandaise with whipped cream). If your cholesterol level can take it, order the warm, runny chocolate cake or the crispy apple tart with vanilla ice cream.

TEL 01-42-22-38-27 **INTERNET** www.le-petit-verdot.com

OPEN Tues–Sat: lunch noon–2 P.M., dinner 7–10 P.M. **CLOSED** Mon, Sun; Aug

À LA CARTE 40–45€ **PRIX FIXE** Lunch: 20€, 2 courses, BNC; dinner: 30€, 3 courses, BNC; both no choices **CREDIT CARDS** AE, MC, V

RESERVATIONS Recommended **ENGLISH SPOKEN** Yes

L'EPI DUPIN (33)
11, rue Dupin
Métro: Sèvres-Babylone

For over a decade, l'Epi Dupin has been the dining address of choice for legions of contented patrons. It is so popular that sidewalk terrace tables require at least a week's notice, and the dinner services at 7 P.M. and 9 P.M. are routinely sold out. It is easy to see why. The reliably delicious cooking gets it right on all counts: first-rate ingredients, excellent preparation and presentation, good wine, and friendly service . . . not to mention great value.

All the dishes are seasonal and the bread is made here. On my last late-winter visit, the *tatin d'endive et chèvre* was a perfect introduction to *coquilles St-Jacques* served with a Swiss chard fondue, followed by lemon cake with mango sorbet and a warm orange sauce. Another time, I enjoyed fresh cod served with *pistou*-flavored Jerusalem artichokes followed by the thin layers of an apple puff pastry in a buttery caramel sauce for dessert. Similar memories are what drive the popularity of this Great Eat in Paris

TEL 01-42-22-64-56
OPEN Mon: dinner, 2 seatings at 7 P.M. & 9 P.M.; Tues–Fri: lunch noon–
2:30 P.M.; dinner, 2 seatings at 7 P.M. & 9 P.M. **CLOSED** Mon lunch,
Sat–Sun; Aug (dates vary)
À LA CARTE None **PRIX FIXE** Lunch: 22€: 2 courses, BC; lunch & dinner: 31€,
3 courses, BNC **CREDIT CARDS** MC, V
RESERVATIONS Essential for lunch; required for dinner **ENGLISH SPOKEN** Yes

L'ESPADON BLEU ($, 14)
25, rue des Grands Augustins, 75006
Métro: Odéon

Seafood is never a bargain in Paris, and it certainly is not at Jacques Cagna's l'Espadon Bleu, located just down the street from Jacques Cagna, his *haute cuisine* signature restaurant, and around the corner from his other spin-off, La Rôtisserie d'en Face (see page 145). L'Espadon Bleu is all about fish and seafood. Of course, there are a few meat dishes thrown in for hard-core carnivores, but you should come here to concentrate on fish. As is often the case, the Great Eat value is at lunch, which features a short but well-constructed two- or three-course prix fixe menu that reflects the best of what the fresh fish markets have to offer. Well-dressed neighborhood businesspeople come for the pleasing starters, which might include the house-smoked Scottish salmon topping a bed of perfectly arranged designer greens, and the seafaring mains, perhaps steamed cod with vegetables and whelks accented with *aïoli* (garlic) sauce. A nice ending is the refreshing orange and pink grapefruit salad sprinkled with citrus zest.

Stepping up several notches to the à la carte side increases the sophistication of the choices three-fold and doubles the price. No wonder when you can have langostine spring rolls on a bed of mixed salad greens lightly sauced with soy and acacia honey, curried mussel soup flavored with coconut milk, or sautéed frog legs seasoned with garlic, parsley, and herbs. For the main course, who wouldn't relish a dish of wild Canadian lobster roasted in its shell, pan-fried scallops cooked in a butter sauce and served with slowly braised leeks, or fresh pasta tossed with prawns, mussels, and cockles and accented with lemon balm. For dessert, don't resist Jacques Cagna's famous meringue cake with caramel ice cream and a showering of walnuts or the apple and rhubarb compote accented with ginger ice cream.

TEL 01-46-33-00-85 **INTERNET** www.jacques-cagna.com

OPEN Mon: dinner 7–10:30 P.M.; Tues–Fri: lunch noon–2:30 P.M., dinner 7–10:30 P.M.; Sat: dinner 7–10:30 P.M. **CLOSED** Mon & Sat lunch, Sun; Christmas, Aug

À LA CARTE 45–60€, BNC **PRIX FIXE** Lunch: 25€, 2 courses, 32€, 3 courses, both BNC **CREDIT CARDS** AE, DC, MC, V

RESERVATIONS Recommended **ENGLISH SPOKEN** Yes, and English menu

LE TIMBRE (42)
3, rue Sainte Beuve
Métro: Vavin, Notre-Dame-des-Champs

After every new edition of this book, friends always ask me, "So what's still a Great Eat on the Paris dining scene?" This time around, Christopher Wright's Le Timbre placed high on my short list of favorites. The restaurant is aptly named; with only twelve tightly wedged tables in a narrow room and an open kitchen in the back, it is indeed the size of a postage stamp. Seating is along two banquettes with not an inch to spare. Before the night is finished, you will have had pleasant conversations with those sitting on either side, which to me only adds to the charm.

The blackboard menu reflects Wright's daily market choices, which means that he buys only what he can use each day. As he told me, "Please don't come at 10:55 P.M. and expect to find a full menu. When we sell out, that's it." The menu is not large, but the creative dishes are varied and may end up being some of the most memorable you will have. Service sometimes stretches out, but there are only two people working here: Wright in the kitchen and one server for the entire twenty-four patrons, so be patient—wonderful food is just ahead. While you are waiting your turn to peruse the portable menu, you are served a glass of crisp white wine and a plate of *amuse bouche*. On one visit, I loved the *entrées* of lightly sautéed calamari and roasted pepper salad and the lentils with meaty bites of flavorful ham mixed in. The roast pigeon, served on a bed of greens, was plump, juicy, and done to pink perfection. The poached salmon in a light dill sauce, accented with snow peas, was another choice I vow to return for. The *mille-feuille* layered with vanilla cream is a huge hit, just like everything else this talented young chef puts his hand to. There is just one thing you must never forget to do at Le Timbre: make reservations.

Without them, you will be waiting a long time, or worse, will not be seated at all because the kitchen is out of food.

TEL 01-45-49-10-40
OPEN Mon–Sat: lunch noon–2 P.M., dinner 7:30–11 P.M. **CLOSED** Sun; holidays, first 2 weeks Aug
À LA CARTE *Entrées* 8€, *plats* 17€, dessert 7€ **PRIX FIXE** Lunch: 22€, 2 courses, 26€, 3 courses, both BNC **CREDIT CARDS** MC, V
RESERVATIONS Essential **ENGLISH SPOKEN** Yes

MARCO POLO (27)
8, rue de Condé
Métro: Odéon

For a welcome change of pace and a taste of wonderful Italian food, the third-generation family-run Marco Polo is the place to be. Don't even think of arriving without a reservation—you will never be seated. This place is so popular for dinner that even the people with reservations are standing in the aisles or milling around outside under the heat lamps waiting for their tables. In the summer, the terrace tables afford great people-watching, so book a table here, pull up a chair, and take it all in.

The food is as genuine as the friendly Italian atmosphere created by the corps of fast-talking waiters. I like to start with the *mozzarella di bufala et tomates,* which could easily feed two—it includes an entire round of cheese and a whole, perfectly ripe tomato. Another starter to consider sharing is the *piatto freddo marco polo,* which is a plate of finely sliced *jambon de parme,* mozzarella, and tomatoes, or, if it is the right season, slices of juicy melon, fresh figs, and *jambon de parme.* The eight well-executed pastas arrive in large bowls and include all the favs: pasta *al pesto;* gnocchi with Gorgonzola; linguini with roasted eggplant, tomatoes, and fresh basil; and pasta brimming with fresh clams. Meats focus on veal scaloppini fixed four ways: *alla romana* (with ham and sage), *piccata* (with lemon and crème fraîche), *fiorentina* (layered with ham and spinach and topped with melted cheese), Marco Polo (with eggplant, mozzarella, and tomato sauce), and *ai funghi* (with mushrooms and cream). You probably won't have room for dessert, but if you do, they run the gamut from *tartufo al cioccolato* (chocolate ice cream truffle) to tiramisu and *pannacotta della casa,* a light pudding. Wash it all down with a liter of the above-average Sicilian house red or white wine. *Buon appetito!*

TEL 01-43-26-79-63
OPEN Mon–Sat: lunch 12:30–2 P.M., dinner 7:15–11 P.M.; Sun: dinner 7:15–11 P.M. **CLOSED** Sun lunch; holidays, NAC
À LA CARTE 35–40€, BNC **PRIX FIXE** Lunch: 19€, 2 courses, BNC **CREDIT CARDS** MC, V
RESERVATIONS Essential **ENGLISH SPOKEN** Yes, and Italian

MARIAGE FRÈRES (5)
13, rue des Grands-Augustins
Métro: St-Michel

For a complete description, see Mariage Frères, page 105. When reserving at this Mariage Frères, ask for a table upstairs in "the room with the fireplace." All other information is the same.

TEL 01-40-51-82-50

THE MOOSE (¢, 25)
16, rue des Quatre Vents
Métro: Odéon

The restaurant bills itself as a Canadian bar and grill. That doesn't begin to describe the doings at "The Moose," which is ably presided over by Michael Kennedy, whose boyish good looks and easy charm endear him to the regulars who claim this sports bar as their home turf. The rest of the serving team is a jovial lot, well-versed in the art of joking, laughing, flirting, swapping sports statistics, and dispensing pint philosophy. The front section is devoted to two dozen or so stools perched along a bar made out of birch tree trunks. In addition to an oversize TV screen, the house mascot, a big moose head, oversees it all. The back room has tables and another bar and mammoth TV, which is tuned to whatever world sporting event is currently taking place.

The Moose is a place anyone can go and feel welcome; every night is guaranteed fun. Early on, the customer profile is quite diverse: from crusty old booksellers to friends meeting up to the occasional tourist who stumbles in by mistake and ends up spending the evening. Scores of twenty- and thirty-somethings swarm in later on for screenings of American TV sitcoms and every major sporting event broadcast. Tuesday night is always ladies night, and every night happy hour lasts until 8:30 P.M. Beer, wine, and Canada-inspired cocktails flow in increasing quantities as the proceedings become more boisterous and continue until the wee hours.

Amid all of this, food is served, and for a sports bar, it is good. The menu lists all the bar food staples: moose wings, burgers, brochettes, sandwiches, salads, and a Québec specialty known as *poutines*. If you like fries, you are going to love *poutines,* which are fries doused with special sauces such as cheese, chicken, sausage, mushrooms, smoked meats, veggies, and ground round steak. They are gooey, high calorie, filling, and addictive. In addition to the menu items, the chef prides himself on international nightly blackboard specials and brunch on Sunday. It all adds up to a great blend of good cheer and good times that reflects the rallying cry of the regulars: "Meet me at the Moose!"

TEL 01-46-33-77-00 **INTERNET** www.mooseheadparis.com
OPEN Mon–Fri: dinner 4 P.M.–2 A.M.; Sat–Sun: 11 A.M.–2 A.M., continuous
    service; Sun brunch 11 A.M.–3:30 P.M. **CLOSED** Dec 24 & 25, NAC
À LA CARTE 10–20€, BNC **PRIX FIXE** Sun brunch: 11€, steak & eggs, BNC;
    12.50€, eggs Benedict, BNC; 17€, eggs, bacon, hash browns, pancakes,
    toast, BC (juice & coffee) **CREDIT CARDS** MC, V
RESERVATIONS Only for groups **ENGLISH SPOKEN** Yes, and English menu

POILÂNE (32)
8, rue du Cherche-Midi
Métro: Sèvres-Babylone, St-Sulpice

With only slight exaggeration, if any at all, Poilâne says in its brochure, "In the memory of every Parisian diner, there is a slice of *Poilâne* bread. Its dense texture and rich taste make an event out of every meal."

Without question, *pain Poilâne* is synonymous with some of the finest bread Paris has to offer; in fact, it is considered France's most celebrated bread. In addition to this bakery, the famous bread is served in countless restaurants and available in many markets, by the slice and by the quarter, half, and whole loaf. The four-pound, round, thick-crusted sourdough country loaf is handmade from whole grain and stone-milled wheat flour that is seasoned with sea salt and raised without yeast or preservatives. Huge oak-fired ovens in the basement can bake up to forty-five loaves at once. The entire process from start to finish takes five hours, including three steps to raise the bread and one hour to bake it. In addition to the famous sourdough bread, a variety of other whole-grain loaves and melt-in-your-mouth butter cookies, called *punitions,* are sold daily in this bakery, which has a perpetual line winding out the door and down the street.

You do not need to be in Paris to have *pain Poilâne* on your dining table. Thanks to modern computer technology and Federal Express, it can be flown to the United States and delivered directly to your door, but brace yourself for the price . . . over $40 per loaf! But if you slice it thinly, a loaf can last up to ten days, and if you are a *Poilâne* fan, it might be worth it to have it in your own kitchen, whether toasted with peanut butter, spread with pâté, or topped with your favorite ham and melted cheese. For details on shipping, check the Website.

NOTE: There is a second location in the 15th arrondissement (see page 255).

TEL 01-45-48-42-59 **INTERNET** www.poilane.com
OPEN Mon–Sat: 7:15 A.M.–8:15 P.M. **CLOSED** Sun; NAC
À LA CARTE 3.50–16€, BNC **PRIX FIXE** None **CREDIT CARDS** None
RESERVATIONS Not accepted **ENGLISH SPOKEN** Yes

RESTAURANT DU LUXEMBOURG (40)
44, rue d'Assas, at rue de Fleurus
Métro: St-Placide, Notre-Dame-des-Champs

The regulars who live in the neighborhood consider the Luxembourg to be an extension of their own homes, a place where they can always go for a dependable variety of fresh food at affordable prices. The friendly *patron,* Sylvain Pommereau, meets and greets everyone with warmth and good cheer. Unless you arrive right when they open, be prepared to wait up to an hour if you are without reservations, especially at lunch. The service is personable, even when it gets hectic. The decor is classic: walls covered with antique and reproduction posters, ceiling fans, the original tile floors, and a bar to the right of the entrance. For most visitors, it is a window on the day-to-day dining of middle-class Parisians.

The food is just as time-honored as the clientele. Snails, foie gras, terrines, salads, and smoked fish lead the way to prime portions of *confit de canard, bavette aux échalottes* (skirt steak with shallots), and *escalope de veau normande* (veal in cream sauce), all liberally garnished with *pommes frites*. Desserts aimed to expand waistlines are centered around homemade *tartes, poire Belle Hélène* (poached pear, vanilla ice cream, and hot chocolate sauce), *île flottante,* and the usual ice creams and sorbets. The wine list is satisfying, with some pleasant alternatives to the basic house variety.

TEL 01-45-48-90-22
OPEN Mon–Fri: lunch noon–2 P.M., dinner 7–9 P.M.; Sat: lunch noon–2 P.M.
CLOSED Sat dinner, Sun; holidays, Aug
À LA CARTE 22–30€, BNC **PRIX FIXE** None **CREDIT CARDS** MC, V
RESERVATIONS Recommended **ENGLISH SPOKEN** Very little

WADJA (44)
10, rue de la Grande-Chaumière
Métro: Vavin

Wadja has an interesting history. From the thirties, during World War II, and for thirty-plus years afterward, it was called Chez Wadja and was run by two brothers and their sister. Very little ever changed, including the poignant collection of photos of the soldiers who ate here, the beat-up bistro tables in the dingy dining room, and the faded curtains at the window and on the door. The food stayed about the same, and so did the prices, which encouraged a loyal band of cheap-eating followers from all walks of life. Then in the early 1990s, Chez Wadja shut its doors. Several owners tried to make a go of it, including one bizarre attempt at a Mexican restaurant. All failed until Denise Leguay took charge, and now, with her talented chef Didier Panisset, she has turned this into one of the favorite bistros in the area, not only for the food but for the warm and friendly atmosphere.

The interior retains its 1930s look, with closely spaced tables, a photo of the first owner, Mariana, and the original bar and tile floor. The food consists of French specialties prepared with a light, modern touch. A simple green salad, creamy Jerusalem artichoke soup flavored with smoked duck, or the leek pancakes served with a piece of thick grilled bacon are perfect beginnings for the filling plates to come. If you like slow-cooked lamb shanks, order the *gigot de sept heures,* which is served with tasty fried potatoes. Other lusty choices are the *magret de canard,* served with caramelized pears and parsnips, and the liver with a lime and chive sauce. The sesame baked swordfish with cumin-scented carrots or the steamed cod surrounded by seasonal vegetables are delicate main courses. Desserts qualify as works of art, particularly the flaky macaroon and pastry shell filled with chocolate and a nutmeg-flavored mousse, or the wild berry *mille-feuille.* The wine list is excessively long, but each week a special wine is featured at a reasonable price.

TEL 01-46-33-02-02
OPEN Mon: dinner 7:30–11 P.M.; Tues–Sat: lunch noon–2:30 P.M., dinner 7:30–11 P.M. **CLOSED** Mon lunch, Sun; NAC
À LA CARTE 35–45€, BNC **PRIX FIXE** Lunch (Tues–Fri): 11€, 2 courses, 14€, 3 courses, both BNC; dinner (Tues–Fri): 14€, 3 courses, BNC
CREDIT CARDS MC, V
RESERVATIONS Essential **ENGLISH SPOKEN** Yes

ZE KITCHEN GALERIE RESTAURANT ($, 4)
4, rue des Grands Augustins
Métro: St-Michel, Pont Neuf

Fusion food where East meets West is becoming increasingly popular in Paris, and nowhere is it more sought-after than at William Ledeuil's Ze Kitchen Galerie, which is at the leading edge of the fusion food concept. The menu covers are as colorful as the art hanging in the starkly sleek, modern interior, which is filled noon and night with an equally colorful array of trend-setting A-listers.

The menu encourages grazing and leans heavily on Thai spices, lemongrass, and seaweed to flavor the dishes. There are several ways to go here: start with *bouillons* (broth) with pieces of artichoke, chicken, and shrimp and scented with lemongrass and Thai basil, or try ravioli pillows filled with sea bream and watercress. Main courses, called "*à la plancha,*" are meals in themselves, especially the winter vegetables and grilled foie gras with a citrus and lemongrass broth, the grilled lobster macaroni, and the veal flavored with ginger and sesame and served with split peas. Desserts keep pace with an interesting chestnut and candied olive poundcake, with a side of mandarin marmalade and sheep cheese sorbet, or there's coconut ice cream with pumpkin, pear, and date marmalade. Fusion cuisine is not for everyone, but here it has more hits than misses and provides an interesting alternative to traditional dining in Paris.

TEL 01-44-32-00-32
OPEN Mon–Fri: lunch: noon–2 P.M., dinner 7:30–10:45 P.M. **CLOSED** Sat–Sun; NAC
À LA CARTE 50–60€ **PRIX FIXE** Lunch: 24€, 2 courses, 33€, 3 courses, both BC (wine & coffee) **CREDIT CARDS** AE, DC, MC, V
RESERVATIONS Essential **ENGLISH SPOKEN** Yes, and English menu

Seventh Arrondissement

The right Paris zip code is 007, as it has been since the early 1700s when blue-blooded families fled Versailles and settled in this part of the city. A sense of good living and a feeling of luxury pervade the streets of this *beau-quartier,* where fashionable people live and pay high rents and young chic meets old guard. The handsome tree-shaded avenues are lined with government offices, foreign embassies, beautiful shops, and lovely, small hotels. This is where you can walk along the Champ de Mars, which serves as the anchor of the Eiffel Tower, visit Napoleon's Tomb at Les Invalides, enjoy the magnificent Impressionist collection at the Musée d'Orsay, see masterful sculptures at the Rodin Museum and shop at the beautiful Le Bon Marché department store, with balustrades and balconies designed by Gustav Eiffel. How to avoid the lines waiting to scale the different levels of La Tour Eiffel? Make a lunch or dinner reservation at Le Jules Verne, the tower's gourmet restaurant, where if you have a reservation, no standing in line is required (see "Gourmet Lunching for Less," page 37). An interesting footnote about the Eiffel Tower is that no building in Paris is allowed to be taller than the Eiffel Tower, which officially stands at 986 feet. The seventh is also one of the most food-conscious neighborhoods, with outstanding restaurants and some of the city's best bakeries, *charcuteries, traiteurs, fromageries, pâtisseries,* and confectioners.

LEFT BANK
Champ de Mars
École Militaire
Eiffel Tower
Invalides (Napoléon's final resting place)
Le Bon Marché department store
Musée d'Orsay
Palais Bourbon (seat of the Assemblée Nationale)
Rodin Museum
UNESCO

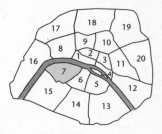

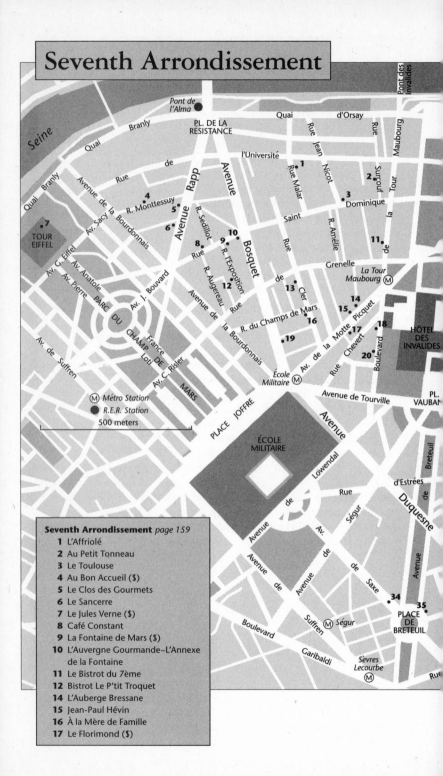

Seventh Arrondissement

Pont des Invalides

Seine

Pont de l'Alma

PL. DE LA RÉSISTANCE

Quai d'Orsay

Branly

Quai

l'Université

Rue Jean Nicot

Rue Maubourg

Rue

de

Avenue Rapp

Avenue

1

Surcouf

Tour

de la

2

3

Dominique

R. Monttessuy **4**

Av. Sacy

Av. de la Bourdonnais

5

6

R. Sédillot

Saint

R. Amélie

Grenelle

11

La Tour Maubourg Ⓜ

TOUR EIFFEL **7**

10

8 **9** R. l'Exposition

R. Augereau

Bosquet

Rue

Rue

de

13 Cler

14

15 **17** Picquet

18

Av. G. Eiffel

Av. Anatole

Av. Pierre

PARC DU

12

Avenue de la Bourdonnais

R. du Champs de Mars

16

Av. de la Motte

Boulevard

HÔTEL DES INVALIDES

Av. J. Bouvard

France

20

Rue Chevert

PL. VAUBAN

Av. de Suffren

CHAMP DE

Loti

Av. C. Risler

19

École Militaire Ⓜ

Avenue de Tourville

MARS

PLACE JOFFRE

Avenue

Ⓜ *Métro Station*
● *R.E.R. Station*
500 meters

ÉCOLE MILITAIRE

Lowendal

Rue

d'Estrées

Breteuil

de

Duquesne

de

Av.

Ségur

Avenue

de

de

Avenue

de Saxe

Avenue

34

35

PLACE DE BRETEUIL

Boulevard

Suffren

Ⓜ Ségur

Garibaldi

Sèvres Lecourbe Ⓜ

Rue

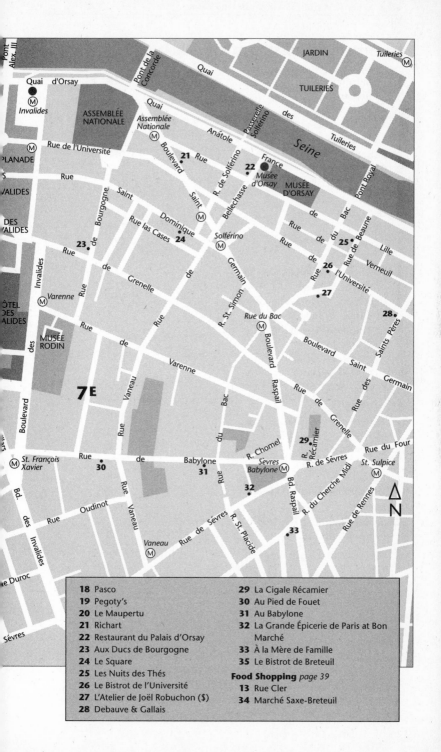

SEVENTH ARRONDISSEMENT RESTAURANTS

Gourmet Lunching for Less

($) indicates a Big Splurge

À LA MÈRE DE FAMILLE
47, rue Cler; Métro: École Militaire (16)
39, rue du Cherche Midi; Métro: Sèvres-Babylone (33)

These are two other convenient locations offering the sames sweets as the original in the ninth arrondissement (see page 199). All other information is the same.

TEL Rue Cler: 01-45-55-29-74; rue du Cherche Midi: 01-42-22-49-99
OPEN Mon: 1:30–7:30 P.M., Tues–Sat: 10 A.M.–7:30 P.M. **CLOSED** Sun

AU BABYLONE (31)
13, rue de Babylone
Métro: Sèvres-Babylone

Time has left its mark on this nostalgic old bistro not far from Le Bon Marché department store. Owner Mme. Garavana has been presiding over her flock for five decades and shows no sign of slowing down or changing anything in her yellow-walled establishment, still hung with the same mirrors, plates, and paintings as the day she opened. Serving only lunch, she sets seventy-six places, and they are always filled with a cross section of Parisians enjoying her *bonne maman* cuisine. These predictable standards are served in amazing portions: pâté and simple salads of grated carrots, cooked beets, or sliced cucumbers paired with dishes of roast veal, lamb, chicken, *andouillettes,* and roast chicken, with potato purée and a vegetable as the garnishes. Fish is served only on Friday. If it is on the menu on Saturday, *île flottante* is the dessert specialty everyone orders. Otherwise, try one of the fruit *tartes.*

TEL 01-45-48-72-13
OPEN Mon–Sat: lunch 11:30 A.M.–2:30 P.M. **CLOSED** Sun; holidays, Aug
À LA CARTE 20–22€, BNC **PRIX FIXE** Lunch: 19.50€, 2 courses, BC
CREDIT CARDS None
RESERVATIONS Recommended **ENGLISH SPOKEN** Yes

AU BON ACCUEIL ($, 4)
14, rue de Monttessuy
Métro: Alma-Marceau

Jacques Lacipière's bistro, in the shade of the Eiffel Tower, retains its well-deserved popularity with natives and visitors alike. Despite the tightly packed tables, the dark wood interior has a clubby feel to it, aided by congenial waiters wearing black Au Bon Accueil aprons and effortlessly serving the happy, sometimes boisterous diners. The three-course prix-fixe menu is a Great Eat sampling of the seasonally based dishes, starting with a vegetable cream soup ladled into a bowl with little vegetable croquettes and slivers of calamari, or a simple salad of herbs and baby greens tossed with truffle oil. The roast pigeon served with a raisin confit and the pink veal kidneys artfully arranged on a ragout of lentils de Puy remind me why I love coming here. Dessert always entails further delicious decisions between the plate of three chocolate desserts or a sangria-infused *baba* decorated with a mango compote and orange-flavored whipped cream.

TEL 01-47-05-46-11
OPEN Mon–Fri: lunch noon–2 P.M., dinner 7:30–10 P.M. **CLOSED** Sat–Sun; major holidays, Aug (dates vary)
À LA CARTE 40–50€, BNC **PRIX FIXE** Lunch: 27€, 3 courses, BNC; dinner: 31€, 3 courses, BNC **CREDIT CARDS** AE, MC, V
RESERVATIONS Essential **ENGLISH SPOKEN** Yes

AU PETIT TONNEAU (2)
20, rue Surcouf
Métro: La Tour-Maubourg

Ginette Boyer's Au Petit Tonneau is a true gem, and it should be a required stop for anyone who wants to scratch the surface of local life. Service is slow-paced, but the regulars don't mind the wait, since the time is well spent enjoying another bottle of their favorite wine while getting caught up on the neighborhood news. The dining room is small and typical, with smoky walls, an old tile floor, mirrored bar, and assorted paintings. Service and linen-covered tables are correct.

Ginette, a natural-born cook, was taught the basics by her grandmother. Her wonderful food is a lesson in superb simplicity, using only the best fresh ingredients, which she personally selects and buys. How do I know? Because I was lucky enough to go with her several times, along with her dog, Wattie, before the crack of dawn to Rungis, the wholesale food market on the edge of Paris. What a trip! It is not for the squeamish or those who blanch at the thought of enormous warehouses filled with row upon row of hanging animal parts, skinned heads, bins of toes, tails, and tongues, icy-cold fowl storage halls, or pungent fish pavilions—all viewed way before breakfast. However, the food enthusiast will be rewarded with a peek at the largest, most all-encompassing food market in Europe. It is a visit you will never forget, if you are lucky enough to have the opportunity to go. Unfortunately, this food mecca is open primarily to people in the trade.

What to order at Au Petit Tonneau? Find out what is fresh from the market and have that. Ginette has a way with fresh fish (especially Scottish salmon and *coquilles St.-Jacques*), cooks only farm-raised poultry, turns out a perfect *blanquette de veau,* prepares the creamiest omelette you will eat in Paris, and creates a chicken liver terrine and velvety foie gras to remember. Seasonal white asparagus is dressed in either vinaigrette or hollandaise sauce, and fresh mushrooms of all types are sautéed in just the right amount of butter and garlic. Her *tarte Tatin* ignores any dietary constraints, especially when you pile on the crème fraîche served on the side. Or, if you prefer a fresh-fruit clafoutis, hers is heavenly.

Eating a meal here makes you feel you have entered a house of plenty, not only for the food we usually only dream of, but for the friendly atmosphere and genuine welcome extended to everyone by Ginette. Before you leave, Ginette, wearing her tall chef's hat and white coat, will come out of her tiny kitchen into the dining room to meet you. She is modest yet generous, with a heart of gold, and she likes nothing better than to share her food with an appreciative audience. When you go, don't forget to say hello for me, and please check on Wattie and Minouche, a black cat with white paws, who is fond of all the guests and seems at home anywhere in the restaurant.

TEL 01-47-05-09-01
OPEN Daily: lunch noon–3 P.M., dinner 7–11:30 P.M. **CLOSED** May 1, Aug 12–22
À LA CARTE 35–45€, BNC **PRIX FIXE** Lunch (Mon–Fri): 20€, *entrée & plat du jour,* BNC **CREDIT CARDS** AE, MC, V
RESERVATIONS Recommended, especially for dinner **ENGLISH SPOKEN** Yes

AU PIED DE FOUET (30)
45, rue de Babylone
Métro: Sèvres-Babylone, Vaneau

This noisy, crowded neighborhood gathering spot draws colorful regulars week in and week out for its belt-popping meals. The restaurant is over two hundred years old, and believe me, not much has been done to it in that time. The walls are artfully hung with curling postcards, the coat hooks could use some polishing, and the seats some new springs. The minuscule kitchen is an original. You definitely want to sit downstairs at one of the tables covered with red-and-white-checked bistro cloths. Upstairs is perilous quarters for anyone over five feet tall.

Lunch and dinner offer routine sustenance: grated carrot or cabbage salad, the time-worn *entrée oeufs dur mayonnaise, confit de canard maison* with mashed spuds, fresh fish, and a daily changing *entrée* and *plat du jour* written on a scrap of notebook paper and stuck on the menu. If you are committed to desserts, pick the *tarte Tatin* as my dining neighbor wisely confided to me. He should know. He owns the film poster shop up the street, across from the famous La Pagode movie theater, and has eaten his lunch here for fifteen years. Coffee is only served standing at the zinc bar, so that they can free the tables faster for the next round of diners.

TEL 01-47-05-12-27
OPEN Mon–Sat: lunch noon–2:30 P.M., dinner 7–11 P.M. **CLOSED** Sun; major holidays; week between Christmas and New Year's, Aug
À LA CARTE 18–20€, BNC **PRIX FIXE** None **CREDIT CARDS** MC, V
RESERVATIONS Not taken **ENGLISH SPOKEN** Yes

AUX DUCS DE BOURGOGNE (23)
30, rue de Bourgogne
Métro: Varenne

The smells are tantalizing and the servings generous at this handkerchief-size *crêperie,* with its cozy kitchen and converted-parlor atmosphere. Open only during the week for lunch, this Cheap Eat fills up quickly with people from the nearby French ministries and the Musée d'Orsay.

The menu lists two things: large salads and mouthwatering plain flour and buckwheat crêpes. Depending on your level of hunger and sense of adventure, you can have everything from the crêpe *Touraine* (filled with salad, warm *chèvre chaud,* and olives) or the *Bourgogne* (loaded with eggs, onions, and tomatoes) to the *Jardin* (leeks, ham, and crème fraîche) or the *Italiene* (with mozzarella, ham, egg, and tomato). If crêpes are not on your radar, go for one of the huge salads; perhaps the *gourmande* featuring chèvre, bacon, and smoked duck, or their salad version of a BLT made with bacon, potatoes, and tomatoes. Saving room for a sweet ending is not difficult when you know the dessert *crêpes gourmandes* include the *Mendiante* (with chocolate, almonds, raisins, and walnuts) and the *Flambée* (with Grand Marnier, rum, or Calvados).

TEL 01-45-51-32-48
OPEN Mon–Fri: lunch 11 A.M.–3 P.M. **CLOSED** Sat–Sun; holidays, Aug
À LA CARTE 16–20€, BNC **PRIX FIXE** Lunch: 10.40€, 2 courses, BC
   CREDIT CARDS MC, V (16€ minimum)
RESERVATIONS Preferred **ENGLISH SPOKEN** Yes, and English menu

BISTROT LE P'TIT TROQUET (12)
28, rue de l'Exposition
Métro: École-Militaire

Bistrot Le P'tit Troquet continually makes my short list of favorite restaurants not to miss whenever I am in Paris. Judging from what many readers have written to me—including such compliments as, "Every course was a treat for the palate and the eyes," and "We should have saved the best for last. Dining here has spoiled us for all that followed"—everyone seems to agree. This is a Paris *must* that continues to please and improve with every visit.

Inside, marble-top bistro tables with linen cloths and vases of dried flowers fill two small rooms imaginatively decorated with assorted paintings, posters, fringed lamps, and flea-market memorabilia from the 1930s. The entire effect is one of comfortable and quiet intimacy. The food is all purchased and prepared by Patrick Vessière and nicely served by his delightful wife, Dominique. Patrick insists on smoking his own duck and salmon, making his own confits, pâtés, and terrines, baking all the breads, and churning his own ice creams. When you consider the fine quality his food represents, the price tags are low.

Depending on the time of year, you might start with some of the best foie gras you will ever be served spread on a toasted brioche, a cold avocado and chicken liver pâté surrounded by fresh tomato sauce, or a colorful summer salad filled with a mélange of fruits and vegetables. Patrick's *côte de veau, lapin à la moutarde, confit de canard, fondant du porc,* and perfectly pink lamb are just a few of the possibilities awaiting you. Of course, no self-respecting diner would forget dessert, and you should not pass up this opportunity to indulge in his expertly prepared crème brûlée, nougat ice cream, or fine pastries filled with the best fruits from the market. As wonderful as the food is the wine list, which features small wineries from throughout France and small *crus* from vintage years. After dinner, coffee arrives with a plate of tiny meringue cookies, winding up a leisurely Parisian meal you will long remember.

NOTE: This is a nonsmoking restaurant.

TEL 01-47-05-80-39

OPEN Mon: dinner 6:30–10:15 P.M.; Tues–Fri: lunch noon–2 P.M., dinner 6:30–10:15 P.M.; Sat: dinner 6:30–10:15 P.M. **CLOSED** Mon & Sat lunch, Sun; holidays, first week of Jan, first 3 weeks of Aug

À LA CARTE *Entrées* 10€, *plats* 17€, desserts 7€ **PRIX FIXE** Lunch: 19.50€, 2 courses, 27.50€, 3 courses, both BNC; dinner: *menu du marché,* 30€, 3 courses, BNC **CREDIT CARDS** MC, V

RESERVATIONS Essential **ENGLISH SPOKEN** Yes, and English menu

CAFÉ CONSTANT (8)
139, rue Saint-Dominique
Métro: École Militaire, Pont d'Alma

Super chef Christian Constant has become a household name epitomizing the best in fine French cuisine. The former chef at Le Crillon has mentored many young cooks whose names now make up a familiar roll-call of successful bistro chefs throughout Paris. After leaving Le Crillon, Constant opened the haute cuisine Le Violin d'Ingres, followed by Les Fables de la Fontaine, a fish restaurant down the street. His latest venture is Café Constant, which has quickly assumed the role of the favorite neighborhood rendezvous serving the staples of French kitchens in unabashed abundance.

In typical café form, it is open in the morning so the business crowd can jump-start the day with coffee and pastries, then later for lunch, in the afternoon for drinks and cold food, and again for dinner. Reservations are not accepted. There is a two-course prix fixe served at lunch, comprising *les plats du jour,* but at dinner, everything is à la carte. The blackboard menu changes daily and is market-based. On a recent lunch visit, I loved the earthy mushroom tart, followed by roast pork with potato purée and a refreshingly light *fromage blanc* mousse. For dinner, the number of home-spun choices increases with such tantalizing *entrées* as *terrine de foie gras de canard* (duck liver terrine) salad with *mâche,* endives, potatoes, and blue cheese, or pumpkin soup with Gruyère cheese. Main courses include a changing *omelette du café,* wild game in season, fresh fish, sausage and mashed potatoes and lentils with pork. Desserts offer homey tributes to rice pudding, *oeufs à la neige* (floating island), and profiteroles swimming in dark chocolate sauce.

TEL 01-47-53-73-34

OPEN Tues–Sat: bar 8:30 A.M.–10:30 P.M., breakfast 8:30–11 A.M., lunch noon–2:30 P.M., dinner 7–10:30 P.M. **CLOSED** Mon, Sun; NAC

À LA CARTE 30€, BNC **PRIX FIXE** Lunch: 16€, 2 courses, BNC **CREDIT CARDS** MC, V

RESERVATIONS Not accepted **ENGLISH SPOKEN** Yes

DEBAUVE & GALLAIS (28)
30, rue des Saints-Pères
Métro: St-Germain-des-Prés

The oldest chocolate maker in Paris, Debauve & Gallais is recognized worldwide as also one of the finest. The company was founded in 1800 by Sulpice Debauve, a former chemist, who was appointed by Louis XVI. For many years, chocolate was considered medicinal; it was thought to "soften the ills better yet than any syrup." Today, those of us who love chocolate agree with Brillat-Savarin's famous quote: *"Qu'est ce que la santé? C'est du chocolat!"*

In Debauve & Gallais' two Parisian shops, chocolate lovers purchase thirty tons of chocolate every year, spending 2.5 million euros. The company uses only the highest quality, pure ingredients, including the best cocoa beans from three continents. Discerning gourmet chocolate lovers owe themselves a visit to this beautiful shop, which is listed as a national public monument. The chocolates are magnificently displayed on a half moon wood-carved counter that has been in place since 1819. If you can't wait until your next trip to Paris for one of their divine chocolates, you can shop online and have yours delivered to your door.

NOTE: Another shop is in the second arrondissement (page 69).

TEL 01-45-48-54-67 **INTERNET** www.debauve-et-gallais.com
OPEN Mon–Sat: 9 A.M.–7 P.M. **CLOSED** Sun; holidays, NAC
PRICES From 4€ up—way up **CREDIT CARDS** AE, MC, V
ENGLISH SPOKEN Yes

JEAN-PAUL HÉVIN (15)
23 bis, avenue de la Motte-Picquet
Métro: École Militaire

This boutique for the famous chocolates does not have a tearoom. For a complete description, please see page 53. All other information is the same.

TEL 01-45-51-77-48

LA CIGALE RÉCAMIER (29)
4, rue Récamier
Métro: Sèvres-Babylone

Arrive early and you will miss the French experience—when the faithful arrive amid a shower of hugs and kisses, even from the chef, Gérard Idoux, who learned his way around the kitchen while working at Ledoyen. The menu lists a balanced selection of daily specials, which, of course, you should pay attention to, but please, not at the cost of missing one of Idoux's wonderful monthly changing savory and sweet soufflés. While you may not want a three-course dinner featuring only soufflés, do consider devoting at least one course to these ethereal clouds. On a recent visit, I enjoyed the leek and chèvre souffle as my main course, with an interesting dish of vegetable ravioli to start. For dessert, I succumbed to the *soufflé vanille, coulis de fruits rouges* (vanilla soufflé with a red fruit sauce), which tasted the way beautiful roses smell. If you are going to be in Paris for a while, be sure to check the back of the menu to see what the special soufflés will be for the following month. The outdoor terrace is one of the best in the area because it is set off from the dust and fumes of the busy street.

TEL 01-45-48-86-58
OPEN Mon–Sat: lunch noon–2:30 P.M., dinner 7:30–11 P.M. **CLOSED** Sun; holidays, NAC
À LA CARTE 35–40€, BNC **PRIX FIXE** None **CREDIT CARDS** MC, V
RESERVATIONS Essential **ENGLISH SPOKEN** Yes

L'AFFRIOLÉ (1)
17, rue Malar
Métro: La Tour-Maubourg

L'Affriolé is a charming restaurant that has become a favorite meeting place for its fashionable patrons, who are attracted as much by its warm Provençal setting as by the imaginative expertise of chef Thierry Verola. The terra-cotta, faux-finished interior is decorated with colorful mosaic-tile tables, hanging lamps, and bountiful dried floral arrangements. The consistently high-quality cuisine is well planned and based on seasonal market produce, which assures freshness at all times. An interesting wine list and capable service complement the fine fare.

The dishes are constantly changing, so I can't predict with certainty what you will find; I can predict, however, that you won't be disappointed, especially for lunch. It is hard to imagine a better value Great Eat than the 19€, three-course lunch, which is composed of the dishes of the day and includes a glass of wine.

On a recent lunch visit, things got off to a wonderful start at our table with a pot of *rillettes* to spread on freshly cut bread, which was brought to the table almost as soon as we were seated. The menu that day began with a lentil salad with smoked duck, followed by sautéed *foie de veau* (liver), fresh carrots and peas, and ended with a rich chocolate *pot de crème*. The two other prix fixe menus allow more choices, but do not include wine. To begin, you might have cream of Jerusalem artichoke soup, spiked with chorizo sausage, or chicken wrapped foie gras . . . both hits. Fish plays a starring role in the five *plat* choices. The best was the *raie* (skate) bathed in lemon butter and garnished with barely cooked green cabbage and coriander. The rich chocolate *ganache* was worth every calorie, and so was the honey-flavored poached pear layered in a praline puff pastry.

At dinner, the choices are the same, but the cost is higher.

TEL 01-44-18-31-33
OPEN Mon–Fri: lunch noon–2:30 P.M., dinner 7:30–10:30 P.M.
   CLOSED Sat–Sun; holidays, last 3 weeks of Aug
À LA CARTE None **PRIX FIXE** Lunch: 19€, 3 courses, BC; 23€, 2 courses, 29€, 3 courses, both BNC; dinner: 35–45€, 3 courses, BNC
   CREDIT CARDS MC, V
RESERVATIONS Essential **ENGLISH SPOKEN** Yes

LA FONTAINE DE MARS ($, 9)
129, rue St-Dominique
Métro: École-Militaire

At La Fontaine de Mars, you can mix with Parisians in one of their favorite eating places. Its two rooms have a cozy, country feel with red-and-white-checked tablecloths on crowded tables; in the summer, there's more seating on the protected terrace. Most of the patrons have been regulars for years, but none moreso than the Army Calvary Club, which has been meeting here for lunch on Thursday for fifty years (the average age of club members falls between seventy-five and eighty-five). To commemorate their long friendship, they put together a book of caricature paintings of each member and presented a copy to the restaurant's owner, Christiane Boudon. She had them framed, and they now hang in the upstairs dining room where the group meets.

The southwestern-inspired food clearly pleases everyone—you'll hear most of them placing orders for house specialties of warm foie gras on a bed of spinach, a dozen snails, *oeufs en meurette* (eggs poached in red wine), blood sausage, roast chicken, *cassoulet, confit de canard,* and plenty of the house red wine from Cahors. Desserts are not forgotten by any means, especially not the illegally rich chocolate fondant or the generous *île flottante.* The lunch menu offers two choices for each course and certainly fits the limits of most pocketbooks. At dinner, everything is à la carte and can dip into the Big Splurge category

NOTE: Upstairs is no smoking. Cigars are sold, so plan accordingly if seated elsewhere.

TEL 01-47-05-46-44
OPEN Daily: lunch noon–3 P.M., dinner 7:30–11 P.M. **CLOSED** Christmas, Dec 31, NAC
À LA CARTE 45–55€, BNC **PRIX FIXE** Lunch (Mon–Sat): 23€, 3 courses, BNC
CREDIT CARDS AE, DC, MC, V
RESERVATIONS Essential **ENGLISH SPOKEN** Yes

LA GRANDE ÉPICERIE DE PARIS AT BON MARCHÉ (32)
38, rue de Sèvres (main floor)
Métro: Sèvres-Babylone

Close your eyes and think of a supermarket in heaven; open them, and you will be in La Grande Épicerie de Paris. Even if you have no intention of buying anything, a visit to this Paris market (across the side street from the main Bon Marché department store) is an interesting break from the usual, almost mandatory, sightseeing and museum-going. Take a few minutes and wander up and down the aisles admiring the magnificent produce, cheeses, and wines, the *pâtisserie, poissonnerie,* and *boucherie* counters, and every kind of canned, bottled, or packaged food on the planet, plus magnificent salads and prepared dishes. There is even an American section if you are suffering withdrawal pangs. If you are planning to put together a picnic, this is the perfect place to create one for the record books.

On the second level is Delicabar, a new restaurant/bar concept that looks as though it just dropped onto the planet from Pluto. Diners poise and perch on red stools around a white wrap-around bar, or squeeze into purple, hot pink, or red plastic–covered banquettes and order soups, sweets, *tartes,* tea, fruit juices, or something much stronger to get them through this one.

TEL 01-44-39-80-00, customer service 01-44-39-82-80
OPEN Mon–Sat: 8:30 A.M.–9 P.M. **CLOSED** Sun; holidays, NAC
PRICES From 10€ and up **CREDIT CARDS** MC, V
ENGLISH SPOKEN Depends on who serves you

L'ATELIER DE JOËL ROBUCHON ($, 27)
5, rue de Montalembert, at rue du Bac
Métro: Rue du Bac

Famed chef Jöel Robuchon has another winner on the Paris dining scene with this casual, yet oh-so-chic and popular dining choice. Would Parisians arriving in Mercedes and Rolls Royces suffer standing in line, or worse yet, risk not even being seated? Or, *quelle horreur* . . . eat dinner at 6:30 P.M.? They do here. For this is one cool canteen, and *tout* Paris is fighting for one of the forty-two bar stools, which are doled out by reservation solely for the 6:30 P.M. dinner seating; after that and otherwise, seats in the two black-and-red minimalistic dining rooms (with open kitchens) are on a first-come, first-serve basis. The chefs wear black, the waitstaff is clad in red. Is it worth all this? Just ask anyone lucky enough to get a seat. The food spins off from tapas and French comfort food, all graced with Robuchon's magic touch. The changing menu is rather long, and portions are small, which allows diners to have a quick bite, a light lunch, or to sample and share three or four dishes. Wines are sold by the bottle or glass. Depending on the time of year, you might start with *mille-feuille* of mozzarella and basil or the gazpacho, followed by an order of quickly seared baby lamb chops, flash-grilled tuna, or Norwegian smoked salmon with a potato waffle. For dessert order the three *pots de créme.* Those with no financial concerns eagerly splash out almost 100€ for the twelve-plate tasting menu. No matter when you go or what you order—provided you are lucky enough to get a seat—you will be rewarded with a stylish and very in Parisian dining experience.

NOTE: This is a nonsmoking restaurant.

TEL 01-42-22-56-56
OPEN Daily: lunch 11:30 A.M.–3:30 P.M., dinner 6:30 P.M.–midnight
CLOSED Christmas, New Year's Day; call to check for other holidays
À LA CARTE 55–65€, BNC **PRIX FIXE** Lunch & dinner: *Menu découverte* (tasting menu): 98€, 12 dishes, BNC **CREDIT CARDS** MC, V
RESERVATIONS Accepted only for the 6:30 P.M. dinner seating
ENGLISH SPOKEN Yes

L'AUBERGE BRESSANE (14)
16, avenue de la Motte-Picquet
Métro: La Tour-Maubourg

If it's a restaurant with a Parisian atmosphere you are after, they don't come any better or more packed than the rustic, wood-paneled L'Auberge Bressane, which a well-turned-out crowd has made their own. At lunchtime, men in suits and women in black skirts predominate. In the evening, the dinner trade attracts a more jovial group, who come for a night of eating and drinking and smoking—not just cigarettes but cigars as well. To avoid the brunt of the haze, request a booth toward the front, or if it is warm enough, on the small protected terrace in front.

The loyalists know to base their meal around at least one of the ethereal soufflés, which literally melt in your mouth, especially the deep dark-chocolate puff that tastes like a bar of Belgian chocolate. Beautifully presented *entrées* of salads are piled high with fresh green beans and mushrooms or Beaufort cheese and ham. Marinated raw salmon is served with herring and warm potatoes and cabbage comes stuffed with fresh crab. Next, the choices include chicken made three ways: in creamy wild mushroom sauce, roasted to a golden brown, or simmered in red wine. For the culinary-curious, there are two good choices: lamb brains bathed in white wine and tripes with truffles. The list goes on with game in season, fresh fish, and the outrageously delicious pan-fried foie gras served with grapes, to mention only a few of the many rich dishes awaiting you at this wonderful dining address near Les Invalides.

TEL 01-47-05-98-37
OPEN Mon–Fri, Sun: lunch noon–2:30 P.M., dinner 8–10:30 P.M.; Sat: dinner
8–10:30 P.M. **CLOSED** Sat lunch; Aug 5–22
À LA CARTE 40–45€, BNC **PRIX FIXE** Lunch (Mon–Fri): 20€, 1 course, 25€,
2 courses, 29€, 3 courses, all BC **CREDIT CARDS** AE, MC, V
RESERVATIONS Essential **ENGLISH SPOKEN** Yes

L'AUVERGNE GOURMANDE–L'ANNEXE DE LA FONTAINE (10)
127, rue St-Dominique
Métro: École-Militaire

This space began as a butcher shop, then it was a cheap-eat pit stop for lunch. Now, it is in its third life as a *table d'hôte,* ably run by Christiane Boudon, who also has La Fontaine de Mars just a few doors away (see page 170). The seating in this slim, pocket-size restaurant is at one long table set for eleven and at a round table for five in back by the kitchen. Everyone sits together on bar stools around the two high tables, and as the meal and the wine continue to flow, so does conversation, making this a great address for solo diners. The copious food is based on old recipes from the mountainous region of the Auvergne, and if you want only one course, or a plate of *charcuterie* or *fromage,* that's fine. Whenever you come, you can also depend on robust lunch and dinner *plats du jour* starring *boudin* (blood sausage), *andouillette* (tripe), seafood lasagne, and roast veal. If these don't appeal, there is always a piece of beef or honey-roasted duck, both garnished with *purée maison* (rich mashed potatoes). The Auvergne wines are sold by the glass and well priced to encourage you to try several.

TEL 01-47-05-60-79
OPEN Mon–Sat: lunch noon–3 P.M., dinner 7:30–11 P.M. **CLOSED** Sun; NAC
À LA CARTE *Entrées* 6.50€, *plats du jour* 12€, cold meat & cheese plates 9€,
   desserts 6.50€ **PRIX FIXE** None **CREDIT CARDS** None
RESERVATIONS Preferred for lunch; essential for dinner **ENGLISH SPOKEN** Yes

LE BISTROT DE BRETEUIL (35)
3, place de Breteuil
Métro: Ségur, Sèvres-Lecourbe

Le Bistrot de Breteuil has what it takes to keep the respect of discriminating Parisian diners: great atmosphere, attentive service, reasonable prices, and food to count on every time. Located not too far away from Les Invalides (the final resting place of Napoléon), the restaurant has one of the most beautiful dining terraces in Paris. Wrapped around an entire corner of the place de Breteuil and in almost full view of the Eiffel Tower, the open and airy glassed-in site hosts a *branché* crowd who make elegance look easy. The tables are beautifully set with heavy white linens and fresh flowers, and patrons are served with precision and aplomb by teams of tradition-ally outfitted waiters.

There is only a prix-fixe menu, which includes a *kir royale* served with a bowl of olives and at least eight seasonal choices for the *entrée, plat,* and dessert. A half bottle of house wine and after-dinner coffee is included for each person. Good *entrée* bets are the dozen Burgundy snails in garlic butter, fresh oysters, duck foie gras, and smoked Norwegian salmon. For the main course, I love the tender rack of lamb, *magret de canard,* or the veal kidneys with morel mushroom sauce. For dessert, who wouldn't relish either the flaming crêpes Grand Marnier, the warm apple tart flambéed with Calvados, or the dark chocolate fondant surrounded by a coffee custard sauce? By Paris standards, Le Bistrot de Breteuil is on the A list, so plan accordingly and don't consider arriving without a reservation.

NOTE: If you go for Thursday or Saturday lunch, allow time before you eat to walk through the street *marché* along avenue de Breteuil. It's one of the best.

TEL 01-45-67-07-27 **INTERNET** www.bistrocie.fr
OPEN Daily: lunch noon–2:30 P.M., dinner 7 P.M.–midnight **CLOSED** Never
À LA CARTE None **PRIX FIXE** Lunch & dinner: 33€, 3 courses, BC (*kir royale,*
   wine & coffee) **CREDIT CARDS** AE, MC, V
RESERVATIONS Advised **ENGLISH SPOKEN** Yes

LE BISTROT DE L'UNIVERSITÉ (26)
40, rue de l'Université
Métro: Rue du Bac

Le Bistro de l'Université promises traditional bistro dishes served by a fast-paced squad of brusque waiters. The neighborhood bespeaks old money and position, and the regulars mirror that image, filling the sixty-five seats to the brim for lunch and dinner from Monday to Friday. Aside from the *entrées* and *plats du jour,* I look forward to the colorful salad of just-cooked vegetables tossed with olive oil and fresh slices of Parmesan. If you are a foie gras or smoked salmon fan, they are both *maison* and exceptional. Fish plays a dominate roll in main-course selections, followed by *magret de canard* and a lusty pork *ragoût de cochon bourguignon* (pork stew) served with potatoes. Nine or ten desserts beckon, but none more than the warm chocolate cake or the house nougat ice cream surrounded by a sauce of fresh fruits.

TEL 01-42-61-26-64
OPEN Mon–Fri: lunch noon–2:30 P.M., dinner 7:30–11 P.M. **CLOSED** Sat–Sun; holidays, 1 week Feb or March, Aug
À LA CARTE 32–38€ **PRIX FIXE** None **CREDIT CARDS** MC, V
RESERVATIONS Preferred **ENGLISH SPOKEN** Yes

LE BISTROT DU 7ÈME (11)
56, boulevard de La Tour-Maubourg
Métro: La Tour-Maubourg

"This meal is worth the price of your book!" exclaimed my dining companions. Indeed, M. and Mme. Beauvallet's restaurant is always consistent, and above all, it offers great value for your money. For a three-course lunch or dinner, your choices include daily specials for each course, plus pâtés, smoked salmon, fish soup in the winter, herring fillets with warm potatoes, and salads topped with chicken livers. Main courses tempt with *confit de canard,* veal in a mushroom cream sauce, grilled sausage, fresh salmon, poached haddock, and the daily special. Ice cream and sorbets dominate the desserts. Reasonable wines allow you to stay happy during the dinner service, which can be somewhat slow when it gets busy.

NOTE: If you like this place, consider trying Le Petit Villiers in the seventeenth arrondissement (see page 270).

TEL 01-45-51-93-08
OPEN Mon–Fri: lunch noon–2:30 P.M., dinner 7–11 P.M.; Sat–Sun: dinner 7–11 P.M. **CLOSED** Sat–Sun lunch; Christmas, NAC
À LA CARTE 25–30€ **PRIX FIXE** Lunch: 11€, 2 courses, 14€, 3 courses, both BNC; dinner: 19€, 3 courses, BNC **CREDIT CARDS** MC, V
RESERVATIONS Essential **ENGLISH SPOKEN** Yes, and English menu

LE CLOS DES GOURMETS (5)
16, avenue Rapp
Métro: Pont d'Alma

Christel and Arnaud Pitrois are warm and friendly hosts in their charming restaurant just minutes from the Eiffel Tower. The room is brightly lit, thus not conducive to intimate dining *à deux,* but the linen-clad tables are correctly set with shining silver and sparkling stemware, the flowers are fresh, and the evening candles add a welcome glow. When the weather permits, the terrace tables are the first to be reserved by the handsome, well-clad regulars, many of whom are diplomats and politicians living in this expensive neighborhood.

The food counterbalances some surprising yet successful ingredients. The sardine fritters, seasoned with fresh mint and sweet pepper sauce, is one good example; another is the tart made with fresh scallops, pieces of Serrano ham, and caramelized chicory. The lush honey and rosemary–scented duck fois gras accompanied by a fricasée of celeriac and dried apricots is a main-course standout, and so are the simple yet perfectly roasted chicken and the sea bream with crisp fennel and star anise. The unusual *mille-feuille* layered with sweet avocado cream and crystallized lemon was a big hit, as was the refreshing mango, pineapple, and grapefruit tartare. Given the setting, the quality of the food, and the prices . . . this is one Great Eat everyone remembers with pleasure.

NOTE: If you would like to extend that pleasure when you return home, you can buy the chef's black olive tapenade (which is served as an *amuse bouche*), duck foie gras, either *au natural* or flavored with vanilla bourbon, and the spicy fennel confit (type of preserve).

TEL 01-45-51-75-61
OPEN Tues–Sat: lunch 12:15–2 P.M., dinner 7:15–10:30 P.M. **CLOSED** Mon, Sun; Aug
À LA CARTE 35–40€, BNC **PRIX FIXE** Lunch (Tues–Fri): 25€, 2 courses, 29€, 3 courses, both BNC; lunch (Sat): 33€, 3 courses, BNC; dinner: 33€, 3 courses, BNC **CREDIT CARDS** MC, V
RESERVATIONS Essential **ENGLISH SPOKEN** Yes, and English menu

LE FLORIMOND ($, 17)
19, avenue de la Motte-Picquet
Métro: École-Militaire

White linens in a burgundy interior set off by lacy window curtains and a small sidewalk terrace form the background for enjoyable dining at Le Florimond, Pascal Guillaumin's twenty-eight-seat restaurant not too far from the Eiffel Tower. People in the neighborhood eat here, and hotels listed in *Great Sleeps Paris* recommend it. After one meal, you, too, are bound to become an enthusiast. It is the perfect choice if you are looking for something geared for a little romance or some serious conversation.

Le Florimond has both seasonal and weekly changing menus derived from creatively updated humble ingredients. In addition, there are some dishes you can always count on, such as the lobster ravioli to start, followed by a fresh fish, a *plat du jour,* or Guillaumin's grandmother's recipe for *chou farci*—slow-cooked cabbage stuffed with pork, onions, and herbs. Desserts will leave you with sweet memories, especially the brown-sugar-crusted crème brûlée or the vanilla *mille-feuille,* followed by a plate of miniature *financiers* and chocolates made by Pascal. Since most of these dishes are available on the lunch and dinner prix-fixe menu, there is no need to stray into the higher priced à la carte territory.

NOTE: This is a nonsmoking restaurant.

TEL 01-45-55-40-38
OPEN Mon–Fri: lunch noon–2:30 P.M., dinner 7–10 P.M.; Sat: dinner 7–10 P.M.
    CLOSED Sat lunch, the first and third Sat of every month, Sun; holidays,
    10 days at Christmas, first week May, Aug
À LA CARTE 45–50€, BNC **PRIX FIXE** Lunch: 20.50€, 3 courses, BNC; dinner:
    35.50€, 3 courses, BNC **CREDIT CARDS** MC, V
RESERVATIONS Recommended **ENGLISH SPOKEN** Yes

LE MAUPERTU (20)
94, boulevard de La Tour-Maubourg
Métro: La Tour-Maubourg, École-Militaire

At another restaurant not too far away, I knew even before the arrival of my main course that it was destined for the rejects pile. Then as I spoke to two diners sitting next to me, they asked if I had been to Le Maupertu, also in the same neighborhood. "Sophie Canton and Alain Deguest know how to keep their customers happily returning on a regular basis. Alain does it with the food, Sophie with her affable, charming attention to each guest," they said. Of course, I had to try it, and I now enthusiastically recommend Le Maupertu to you. I hope you will be as pleased with it as I continue to be.

The two-room setting, especially at night, couldn't be more beautiful, with floor-length windows and a terrace overlooking the beautifully lighted dome of Les Invalides. By all means, try to reserve one of these window tables. The presentation of the remarkable, seasonal, prix-fixe menu and daily chef's suggestions is exceptional, and the portions are balanced to allow you to enjoy three courses without feeling stuffed. Nothing is constant on the seasonal menu: some dishes change daily, others weekly. In the winter, you could find wild mushroom raviolis, zucchini cake with tomato coulis, or warm potatoes with marinated salmon and dill. In the early spring, you may see such starters as a *feuilleté de petits légumes au coriandre* (a flaky pastry layered with coriander-scented vegetables), ratatouille with a poached egg, or scallops baked with tomatoes and herbs. The veal scallops surrounded by pasta lightly dressed with tomatoes and the beef in red wine sauce are even more winning food combinations. At the end, a generous cheese board is brought to your table, or you can order a velvety dark chocolate cake with pistachio sauce, *baba au rhum* with whipped cream, or an assortment of house ice creams or sorbets served with a Florentine cookie. The monthly featured wines are good buys and are available by the glass, pitcher, or bottle.

TEL 01-45-51-37-96 **INTERNET** www.restaurant-maupertu-paris.com
OPEN Mon–Sat: lunch noon–2:15 P.M., dinner 7:30–10 P.M. **CLOSED** Sun;
    Christmas, school holidays in Feb (dates vary), Aug 15–25

À **LA CARTE** *Entrée* 11€, *plat* 20€, dessert 8€ **PRIX FIXE** Lunch: 22€,
2 courses, BNC; lunch & dinner: 29€, 3 courses, BNC
CREDIT CARDS MC, V
RESERVATIONS Recommended **ENGLISH SPOKEN** Yes, and English menu

LE SANCERRE (6)
22, avenue Rapp
Métro: Pont de l'Alma, École-Militaire

The only thing that has changed since the first time I ate here in
1977 is that the back room, with a real fireplace that is lit during
the winter, is now designated for nonsmokers. Other than that, this
venerable Parisian wine bar has remained virtually the same for the
almost fifty years it has been in operation, the last thirty under the
helm of Jean-Louis Guillaume.

The menu is short, but the food and wine always rate an A+ with
the regulars, who flow in nonstop and have made Le Sancerre one of
the most popular lunch spots in this part of the seventh arrondissement. Beyond the somber exterior is a pleasant, rustic interior filled
with the comforting sounds and smells of the busy kitchen. This is the
place for a creamy herb or cheese omelette with a side of golden pan-
fried potatoes and a crisp green salad, or for the more adventurous, a
spicy *andouillette* made with Sancerre wine. For a light choice, order the
crotin de Chavignol, a sharp goat cheese that goes perfectly with a glass
or two of Sancerre. While waiting for your meal, you will be presented
with baskets of Poilâne bread and crocks of sweet butter. Your wine,
of course, will be Sancerre, and your dessert should either be a piece of
the gorgeous house *tarte Tatin* (ask to have it heated), or a plate of the
homemade cookies to dip into the last drops of your Sancerre.

NOTE: If you appreciate Art Nouveau architecture, check out the
facade of the building directly across the street at 29, avenue Rapp,
which was constructed in 1901 by the architect Lavirotle. Then turn
right and walk to the post office at No. 37. At the end of the dead-
end street by the post office you will see more lovely doorways and
latticework.

TEL 01-45-51-75-91
OPEN Mon–Fri: 8:30 A.M.–4 P.M., 6:30–11 P.M.; Sat: 8:30 A.M.–4 P.M.;
continuous service **CLOSED** Sat evening, Sun; holidays, last 3 weeks of Aug
À **LA CARTE** 20–25€, BNC **PRIX FIXE** None **CREDIT CARDS** MC, V
RESERVATIONS Recommended for lunch **ENGLISH SPOKEN** Some

LES NUITS DES THÉS (25)
22, rue de Beaune
Métro: Rue du Bac

Paris tearooms are usually calming places where you can relax for
an hour or so over a light meal, a pastry, and a cup of good tea. Mother
and daughter duo Jacqueline and Florence Cédelle have created just
such a pleasing refuge near the Musée d'Orsay for a quiet break from
the rigors of museum-going or wandering the antique and art galleries
that define this part of Paris. A buffet along one wall is filled with

temptations, all made by Florence. Everything is fresh, including the jam you spread on your scones and buttery croissants. Lunch leans heavily on salads, cold plates, and egg creations. If you are just going for tea, the lemon meringue and chocolate *tartes* are wonderful, and so are the macaroon cake and the chestnut *tarte*.

NOTE: Anything you see can be packaged to go; plus, you can rent the space for your own party or have them cater it in your own home.

TEL 01-47-03-92-07
OPEN Mon–Sat: 11:30 A.M.–7 P.M., continuous service **CLOSED** Sun; Aug
À LA CARTE 20–28€, BC **PRIX FIXE** None **CREDIT CARDS** V
RESERVATIONS Not necessary **ENGLISH SPOKEN** Yes

LE SQUARE (24)
31, rue St-Dominique
Métro: Solférino

The quiet location across from the Square Samuel Rousseau could not be more upmarket Parisian. The square comes alive in the afternoon when children arrive to play on the swings and zoom down the slides. During the rest of the day, retirees pour over their newspapers and neighborhood ladies catch up on all the best gossip. Across the square is the lovely Basilic Sainte Clotide, known for its austere interior and massive organ.

Several seating areas, including banquettes, a contemporary bar with club leather chairs around bare wood-block bistro tables, and a beautiful summer terrace, set the stage for this smart restaurant in the tony seventh. One glance at the menu and it is easy to see why the place is packed solid and rings with the buzz of handsome people eating well. The democratically priced selections leave the competition behind both in variety and quality of products. Of the sixteen *entrées,* great beginnings include the seafood risotto; the *mille-feuille* layered with eggplant, zucchini, peppers, and mozzarella; and the spinach salad piled with raw mushrooms and fresh Parmesan cheese. For the *plat,* keep things simple with braised pork flavored with sage, an entrecôte with béarnaise, or poached sole. Finish with desserts of fresh fruit tarts, warm chocolate cake with caramel sauce, or Berthillon ice cream.

TEL 01-45-51-09-03
OPEN Mon–Fri lunch: noon–2:30 P.M., dinner 8–11 P.M. **CLOSED** Sat–Sun; Dec 24–25 & 31, May 1, 15 days in mid-Aug (dates vary)
À LA CARTE *Entrées* 8–9€, *plats* 13–18€, desserts 8€ **PRIX FIXE** None
CREDIT CARDS AE, MC, V
RESERVATIONS Recommended; essential for the terrace **ENGLISH SPOKEN** Yes

LE TOULOUSE (3)
86, rue St-Dominique
Métro: La Tour-Maubourg

If you love the cuisine from the southwest of France, note this address. Not only can you sample specialties from this popular gastronomic region in this restaurant, but you can purchase them packaged and ready to heat and eat from the boutique and save 10 percent. It is a good idea to arrive with an appetite—this hearty food is far from dainty in portions or structure. Begin with slices of duck or goose foie gras, southwestern-produced cold cuts, or one of the special pâtés, such as wild boar, rabbit, guinea fowl, quail, and *cèpes* (wild mushroom). The riches that follow include servings of *cassoulet* of beef and beans with goose confit, three types of *confit de canard, coq au vin,* wild rabbit, wild pigeon salami, and more duck prepared in stews, served with orange or green pepper sauce, or simmered with lentils, vegetables, and potatoes. Eight salads offer a lighter touch, though even they come laden with a selection of gizzards preserved in fat, Roquefort cheese, dry sausage, slices of game terrines, foie gras, and ham. Desserts? I can't imagine having room, and besides, they don't offer any to speak of. Their wines, however, are worth mentioning, as they all come directly from producers in the region.

TEL 01-45-56-04-31

OPEN Tues–Sat: lunch noon–2 P.M., dinner 7–10 P.M. (Fri–Sat until 11 P.M.); boutique 10 A.M.–10 P.M. **CLOSED** Mon, Sun; holidays, Aug

À LA CARTE 20–25€, BNC **PRIX FIXE** Lunch: 8€, *plat du jour,* BC (wine or coffee); *formule rapid,* 11.50€, 2 courses, BNC; lunch & dinner: *menu du terroir,* 16€, 3 courses, BNC; *menu gourmand,* 22€, 3 courses, BNC

CREDIT CARDS MC, V

RESERVATIONS Recommended **ENGLISH SPOKEN** Yes, and English menu

PASCO (18)
74, boulevard de La Tour-Maubourg
Métro: La Tour-Maubourg

I always try to walk as much as possible in Paris. It is good exercise, certainly, but I also get to know the neighborhoods better and often discover pleasant surprises. Such is the case with Pasco, a smart, open-plan restaurant with a wraparound terrace facing Les Invalides. The sleek interior has an urban, New York look that is confirmed by the BoBo (bohemian *bourgeoise*) crowd eating here. The southwestern-based menu offers good value and just enough imagination to inspire repeat visits. To begin, bowl of olives and a basket of bread arrives with the menu. I like to start with the mesclun salad topped with a poached egg and pieces of bacon or the foie gras lightly cooked in a truffle and vegetable broth. The risotto with Serrano ham and parmesan is heavy on salt; a better *plat* is the grilled steak or the *coquilles St-Jacques,* if they are in season. Desserts are designed to inspire more walking: try the creamy house tiramisu or the baked apple with bourbon-spiked vanilla ice cream.

TEL 01-44-18-33-26 **INTERNET** www.restaurantpasco.com

OPEN Tues–Sun: lunch noon–2:30 P.M., dinner 7:30–10:30 P.M. **CLOSED** Mon, NAC

À LA CARTE 28–40€, BNC **PRIX FIXE** Lunch (Tues–Fri): 15€, 1 course, BC; lunch & dinner (Tues–Sat): 19€, 2 courses, 24€, 3 courses, both BNC; lunch & dinner (Sun): 32€, 3 courses, BC **CREDIT CARDS** AE, MC, V

RESERVATIONS Recommended, especially for the terrace **ENGLISH SPOKEN** Yes

PEGOTY'S (19)
79, avenue Bosquet
Métro: École-Militaire

Every French neighborhood has its share of tearooms, those gentle places that nourish the body and soothe the soul, providing a peaceful place to while away an hour or two over a quiet meal or a pot of tea and dessert. Pegoty's, which is close to the Eiffel Tower, Invalides, and École Militaire, will charm you. The tearoom actually consists of several rooms. The stone-lined front room has a picture window overlooking the street and a sofa-style banquette facing the buffet of sweets. Beyond are a series of comfortable little rooms that are ideal places for an intimate afternoon with someone special or for getting away from it all and catching up on your reading or correspondence.

All the beautiful cakes and *tartes* you see lined up under the three brass lights are made here and served on gold-trimmed white china by the pretty owner and hostess, Veronique. Tea and sweet temptations are not the only delightful possibilities she offers. There are two breakfasts, ranging from a simple continental to the American, which fills you with bacon, sausage, eggs, fried bread (an English breakfast staple), and tomato. Finally, Pegoty's Saturday, Sunday, and holiday brunch includes a glass of champagne or fruit juice, choice of an omelette, scrambled eggs, or ham, and a salad, plus toast and a pastry. All include coffee or tea. Otherwise, choose from several omelettes, a daily *tarte,* salads, a *plat du jour,* and assorted sandwiches and cold meat plates. Your ten choices of tea will be from Mariage Frères (see page 105).

TEL 01-45-55-84-50
OPEN Daily: 9 A.M.–7 P.M. (Sun from 10 A.M.), continuous service
  CLOSED Never
À LA CARTE 22–30€, BC **PRIX FIXE** Breakfast: *petit déjeûner,* 14€; American
  18€; Pegoty's brunch, 33€; all BC (coffee or tea) **CREDIT CARDS** MC, V
RESERVATIONS Not necessary **ENGLISH SPOKEN** Yes

RESTAURANT DU PALAIS D'ORSAY (22)
1, rue de Bellechasse (museum entrance)
Métro: Musée d'Orsay, Solférino

As everyone knows, cuisine and culture are uppermost in life to the French, so it is not surprising that most major museums in Paris have some sort of restaurant. The best of these by far is the Palais d'Orsay in the Musée d'Orsay, which was built for the 1900 World's Fair and served as the city's most ornate train station. Today, diners can sit in wide wicker armchairs in a massive Belle Epoque dining room with magnificent frescoed ceilings by the nineteenth-century painter Gabriel Ferrier. Marble statues, gilt-framed mirrors, sparkling chandeliers, and sprays of fresh flowers complete the spectacular setting, which is on the second level, overlooking the Seine.

Fortunately, the food is almost as impressive as the decor. There is a two-course *menu du jour* plus a host of à la carte *entrées* and main courses from which to choose whatever size meal you want. Tea is served in the afternoon but not on Thursday, which is the only night of the week the restaurant stays open for dinner, since the museum is also open late. Also available is a children's menu. On Friday and Saturday nights when the museum is closed, private parties are held. If you are planning an intimate dinner for a hundred or more of your closest Parisian friends, contact the catering department.

NOTE: You must purchase a museum ticket to eat here.

TEL 01-40-49-48-14
OPEN Tues–Wed, Fri–Sun: lunch 11:45 A.M.–2:30 P.M., tea 4–6:30 P.M.; Thur: lunch 11:45 A.M.–2:30 P.M., dinner 7–9:30 P.M. **CLOSED** Mon; any holiday the museum is closed, NAC
À LA CARTE 25–38€, BNC **PRIX FIXE** Lunch: 14.90€, 2 courses, BNC; children's menu (under 10), 7.10€, 2 courses, BC **CREDIT CARDS** AE, MC, V
RESERVATIONS Not accepted **ENGLISH SPOKEN** Yes, and English menu

RICHART (21)
258, boulevard St-Germain
Métro: Assemblée Nationale, Solférino

Richart is known for pleasing both the palate and the eye, combining the taste and aroma of pure chocolate with visually stunning presentations of magnificent seasonal collections of chocolate. Flavors range from floral and fruity to herbacious and spicy. One of their best-sellers is sack of nine milk or dark chocolate salty butter caramels. To promote the love of chocolate in children, each year the family-owned company asks three thousand children from around the world to "design something delicious in your favorite color." The winners get prize money for their schools, and their designs used in that year's collections. There are outlets worldwide, but this is the only one in Paris.

TEL 01-45-55-66-00 **FAX** 01-47-53-72-72 **EMAIL** paris-stgermain@richart.com
   INTERNET www.richart.com
OPEN Mon–Sat 10 A.M.–7 P.M. **CLOSED** Sun; holidays, NAC
PRICES From 5€ **CREDIT CARDS** MC, V
ENGLISH SPOKEN Yes

Eighth Arrondissement

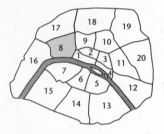

The eighth arrondissement is an area of splendor, elegance, money, and classic Parisian images, especially the sweeping view of the Champs-Élysées from the Arc de Triomphe to the place de la Concorde. The Arc de Triomphe, commemorating Napoléon's reign, is the centerpoint for twelve avenues that radiate in the shape of a star (or *l'Étoile*). The Madeleine Church was built in 1806 by Napoléon and dedicated to his army. The giant colonnades along the front mirror those of the Assemblée Nationale directly across the Seine. Shoppers with impressive bank balances ply the *haute-couture* luxury shops along the avenues Marceau and Montaigne and on the rue de Faubourg St-Honoré. Gourmets and gourmands make pilgrimages to Hediard and Fauchon, the world-famous grocery stores by the Madeleine Church, and tourists dine at Maxim's, the one-time shrine where the beautiful people congregated in Paris. This part of the eighth is alive and bustling during the weekdays, but on holidays and weekends, it is deserted.

The Champs-Élysées is the gathering place of France. It is also the second-most-expensive pavement in the world, exceeded only by New York's Fifth Avenue, and it attracts upwards of 300,000 people per day. On New Year's Eve, July 14 (Bastille Day), and for the final stretch of the Tour de France, the avenue is lined top to bottom with celebrants. At Christmas, the trees are covered in a multitude of white lights, and it resembles a fairyland. However, the lovely Champs-Élysées, with its myriad sidewalk cafés filled with pretty young men and women, is very deceptive. No true Parisian would ever seriously dine here, anymore than a true New Yorker would head to Times Square for a fine meal. Of course, walking along what the French rightfully term "the most beautiful avenue in the world" and stopping at a café for a drink *is* part of being in Paris. But for a real increase in value and quality dining, walk one or two blocks to either side of the avenue. A final word: Watch for pickpockets. This is a fertile picking ground for them, and they can do a number on you faster than you can say, "Stop, thief!"

EIGHTH ARRONDISSEMENT RESTAURANTS

Gourmet Lunching for Less

($) indicates a Big Splurge; (¢) indicates a Cheap Eat

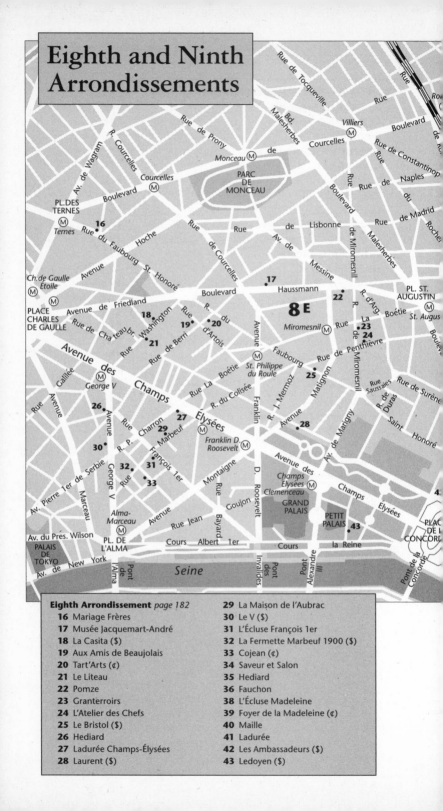

Eighth and Ninth Arrondissements

AUX AMIS DE BEAUJOLAIS (19)
28, rue d'Artois
Métro: St-Philippe-du-Roule

You will know you have found Aux Amis de Beaujolais by the crowds: at lunchtime every bar stool and dining-room table is filled with local businesspeople, and during dinner all the seats are again fully occupied by smart, value-minded Parisians and clued-in visitors. Bernard Picolet's family has been greeting and feeding their devoted regulars since 1921. His son now works with him in the kitchen, and his wife runs the front. Their food is full-bodied and satisfying—and no doubt ruinous for our arteries—but the down-to-earth cooking and generous portions make me a regular whenever I am lucky enough to be in Paris. Here is the place to try homespun dishes of *céleri rémoulade, pâte de campagne,* cucumbers in cream, or *fromage blanc* showered with fresh herbs. The fish changes every day, but in the meat department you can always count on *magret de canard,* beef tartare with *frites* or a salad, and grilled steaks. Beef tongue, sautéed lamb with fat white beans, and an *andouillette* also often make appearances. The suitably soothing desserts are all made here. I love the creamy rice pudding, any of the fruit *tartes,* or the satiny chocolate mousse.

TEL 01-45-63-92-21, 01-45-63-58-64
OPEN Mon–Fri: lunch noon–3 P.M., dinner 6:30–9 P.M.; Sat (Sept–Easter): lunch noon–3 P.M. **CLOSED** Sat from Easter–Sept, Sun; week between Christmas and New Year's, Aug 4–21
À LA CARTE 25–30€, BNC **PRIX FIXE** Dinner: 21€, 3 courses, BNC **CREDIT CARDS** AE, MC, V (15€ minimum)
RESERVATIONS Recommended for lunch **ENGLISH SPOKEN** Yes

COJEAN (¢, 33)
19, rue Clément Marot
Métro: Alma-Marceau, Franklin D. Roosevelt

Fast food that is good for you is served nonstop from breakfast through early evening in a rapidly growing market that targets those who strive to be hip and healthy at the same time. For other locations, please see page 201.

TEL 01-47-20-44-10
OPEN Mon–Sat 8 A.M.–5 P.M., continuous service

FAUCHON (36)
26, place de la Madeleine
Métro: Madeleine

In 1886, August Fauchon opened his *épicerie fine* on place de la Madeleine. The rest was history: a visit to Fauchon, one of the most famous gourmet grocery stores in the world, was long considered one of the must-dos in Paris. It is still worth visiting, but unfortunately, it is no longer quite the same. Fauchon has been sold to Asian investors, and the store is now divided into two buildings on place de la Madeleine: one sells teas, coffees, designer jams, herbs, spices, and other gourmet items, all under the Fauchon name. The other contains a deli and *pâtisserie,* but the magnificent museum-quality window displays have been reduced. For those who considered Fauchon to be the ultimate food shopping mecca, that glory has sadly faded.

TEL 01-47-42-60-11
OPEN Mon–Sat: 9 A.M.–9 P.M. **CLOSED** Sun; major holidays, NAC
CREDIT CARDS AE, DC, MC, V
ENGLISH SPOKEN Yes

FOYER DE LA MADELEINE (¢, 39)
place de la Madeleine, underneath the Madeleine Church on the right
Métro: Madeleine

For the cheapest Cheap Eat lunch in Paris, proceed directly to the basement canteen in the Madeleine Church. Not only is the three-course meal breathtakingly affordable, but it is philanthropic to boot—all proceeds go to the work being done by the church. The massive cafeteria seems to go on forever; it seats 125 people at shared tables. In addition there is a private group room that seats 56 people. Your dining companions will range from pensioners in berets to neighborhood businessmen, workers in dusty overalls, gray-haired couples out for their main meal, and sweet, young girls from the surrounding offices.

The menu changes daily, and fish is often included on Friday. When you sit down, a row of *entrées* is already on the table. When I was there it was a choice between crudités on a bed of *mâche* (lamb's lettuce), pieces of tuna and tomatoes, or a couple of slices of dried sausage. That is followed by a choice of two hot dishes, which are served by a fleet of very gentle, properly attired ladies who volunteer their services. I had the roast lamb rather than the scalloped chicken, and the puréed potatoes instead of the mixed beans. Dessert is fresh fruit, cheese, or ice cream. Wine will set you back another 1.20€; coffee or tea an additional 0.50€. When you arrive, and before you sit down, you will pay the cashier and be asked if you would like to contribute a little bit extra to help cover the people that the church feeds for free. *Mais oui!*

NOTE: Regular diners are asked to pay a 2€ (you read that correctly) yearly membership fee, which entitles them to the subsidized lunch price. No smoking is allowed.

TEL 01-47-42-39-84 **INTERNET** www.eglise-lamadeleine.com
OPEN Mon–Fri: lunch 11:45 A.M.–2 P.M. **CLOSED** Sat–Sun; holidays, July 15–Aug 31, week at Christmas
À LA CARTE None **PRIX FIXE** Regular diners (with yearly 2€ membership card): 7€, 3 courses, BNC; without the card, diners pay 8€ for the same meal. **CREDIT CARDS** None
RESERVATIONS Not taken **ENGLISH SPOKEN** Very little

GRANTERROIRS (23)
30, rue de Miromesnil
Metro: Miromesnil

Granterroirs is the lunchtime embodiment of a food lover's dream in this business neighborhood. The attractive gourmet food shop, deli, and restaurant is open Monday to Friday from morning to evening, but the only meal served is lunch. Everyone sits on chairs at one long communal table in the back or at a few round tables in front. Don't worry if your French is not quite up to par; everyone is friendly, and for the regulars it is their adopted home for lunch, a place they gather on a daily basis for simple food served without fanfare. These are people who know and appreciate the high-quality regional wines and products served and prepared in a straightforward manner by owner Jean-François Gimenez and his staff.

The daily changing selection features soups in the winter, salads in the summer, and *tartines,* a *plat,* organic bread, and always homemade desserts and ice cream. Salads, sandwiches, and desserts can be packed to go. When I was there a variety of organically grown tomatoes were highlighting the menu, along with a chocolate *tarte* that everyone adored. If you like what you're eating, you can buy the products and create the dish yourself. Also for sale are artisanal French olive oils, jams, jellies, candies, sauces, and gourmet gift baskets to warm the heart of any Parisian foodie.

NOTE: No smoking is allowed.

TEL 01-47-42-18-18 **INTERNET** www.granterroirs.com
OPEN Mon–Fri: grocery & deli 9 A.M.–8 P.M.; lunch noon–3 P.M.
   CLOSED Sat–Sun; holidays, 3 weeks in Aug (dates vary)
À LA CARTE 22–28€, BNC **PRIX FIXE** Lunch: 31€, 2 courses, BC (wine & coffee) **CREDIT CARDS** MC, V (15€ minimum)
RESERVATIONS Not accepted **ENGLISH SPOKEN** Yes

HEDIARD (35)
21, place de la Madeleine
Métro: Madeleine

It would be hard to imagine a more regal food shopping experience than at Hediard, which anchors one corner of place de la Madeleine, the gourmet equivalent of Rodeo Drive. Founded in 1854, Hediard was the first retail food purveyor to introduce Parisians to exotic foods from around the world, and today this gourmet fantasyland still carries the best products from far-flung places. Its bright-red branches located throughout Paris are, in a word, fabulous. The stores are beautifully laid out and the staff is exceptionally helpful, even with the most novice gourmand. Just go in to look if all you're hungry for is a delicious feast for the eyes.

NOTE: There is another location in the eighth arrondissement at 118, avenue George V (map key 26; **MÉTRO** Le Peletier; **TEL** 01-47-20-44-44), and another in the sixteenth (see page 260).

TEL 01-43-12-88-88 **INTERNET** www.hediard.fr
OPEN Mon–Sat: 9 A.M.–9 P.M.; Sun (Dec only): 10 A.M.–8 P.M. **CLOSED** Sun;
major holidays
PRICES From 5€ to triple digit figures **CREDIT CARDS** AE, DC, MC, V
ENGLISH SPOKEN Yes

LA CASITA ($, 18)
9, rue Washington
Métro: George V

For years, La Casita has catered to the business trade in this office
district off the Champs-Elysées. Nothing much has been done to the
mid-century decor: the room has elaborate wood paneling, a stained-
glass window, and correctly set tables surrounded by hob-nailed burgandy velvet high-backed chairs. Waiters in black, ferrying plates
heavy on meat and potatoes, complete the vintage theme. The loyalists know to order from the prix-fixe menus, which are available for
both lunch and dinner, and include all their favorites. The predictable
Gallic fare hasn't had a nouvelle cuisine moment ever, and none are
planned. The regulars like this place just as it is, and they routinely
show up for the chef's admirable renditions of foie gras *maison,* avocado
and crab cocktail, creamy soups, beef tartare and *frites, confit de canard,*
cassoulet, grilled beef ribs, and a fried fillet of beef with a variety of rich
sauces, including Roquefort and béarnaise. Also endangering arteries
are the ice creams splashed with liqueur, the chocolate mousse, and
the chocolate cake. There is not an empty seat at 1 P.M., which tells
me that the lusty food at La Casita will continue pleasing its devoted
regulars for years to come.

TEL 01-45-61-00-38
OPEN Mon–Fri: lunch noon–2:30 P.M., dinner 7–10:30 P.M.; Sat: dinner
7–10:30 P.M. **CLOSED** Sat lunch, Sun; major holidays, 2 weeks mid-Aug
À LA CARTE 45–50€, BNC **PRIX FIXE** Lunch & dinner: 27€, 31€, both
3 courses & BNC **CREDIT CARDS** AE, DC, MC, V
RESERVATIONS Preferred **ENGLISH SPOKEN** Yes

LADURÉE (41)
16, rue Royale
Métro: Madeleine, Concorde

It all began in 1862 when Louis Ernest Ladurée, a miller from the
southwest, opened the doors of his bakery at 16, rue Royale. In 1871,
Jules Chéret, a famous *fin-de-siècle* painter, was commissioned to deco-
rate the shop. He drew his inspiration for the painting you see today
from the pictorial techniques used on the Sistine Chapel ceiling and
the Garnier Opera house. As cafés developed during the period of the
Second Empire, Jeanne Souchard, Ladurée's wife, decided to combine
the pastry shop with tea service, and thus began what is still one of the
finest tearooms in Paris. It is also a superb choice for a proper lunch,
Sunday brunch, or a cup of the best *café au lait* or hot chocolate coupled
with one of their famed pastries. Blue ribbons in the dessert category
go to their *royals,* almond-flavored macaroon cookie sandwiches filled

with chocolate, mocha, vanilla, lemon, pistachio, strawberry, or vanilla cream, which are often copied but never equalled. Do not miss treating yourself to one . . . if you can stop at just one. Once sampled, they are habit-forming and unforgettable. Just to show how popular these bites from heaven are, it has been calculated that one is sold every twenty-five seconds throughout the day, which adds up to forty tons per year!

At the rue Royale location, downstairs seating is around postage-stamp-size tables arranged under a pastel ceiling mural of chubby cherubs performing all sorts of heavenly baking duties. Here you can watch the hustle and bustle of the well-dressed crowds standing ten deep at the pastry counter. For lunch or brunch it is much more comfortable to reserve a table upstairs, where the atmosphere is rather solemn and the waitstaff stressed, but the scene less hectic, and no smoking is allowed.

NOTE: There is also a Ladurée tearoom at Printemps department store, 62, boulevard Haussmann (ninth arrondissement; **MÉTRO** Chausée-d'Antin-La Fayette; **TEL** 01-42-82-40-10), but the ambience and spirit are not the same. See also below and page 143 for two other locations.

TEL 01-42-60-21-79 **INTERNET** www.laduree.fr
OPEN Mon–Sat: 8:30 A.M.–7 P.M., lunch noon–3:30 P.M.; Sun & holidays 10 A.M.–7 P.M., **CLOSED** Christmas, New Year's Day
À LA CARTE Pastries and ice cream 6–9€; lunch 25–35€, 2 courses, BNC; afternoon tea 14–20€ **PRIX FIXE** Lunch: 27€, 1 course, 32€, 2 courses, both BNC **CREDIT CARDS** AE, MC, V
RESERVATIONS Recommended for lunch **ENGLISH SPOKEN** Sometimes

LADURÉE CHAMPS-ÉLYSÉES (27)
75, avenue des Champs-Élysées
Métro: Franklin-D-Roosevelt, George V

In September 1997, Ladurée opened this spectacular restaurant, tearoom, and *pâtisserie* on the most beautiful avenue in the world, the Champs-Élysées. The elegant two-level setting looks as though it has been here forever, but that is not so. For a long time, Japanese Air Lines occupied the site; then Ladurée took it over and spent one year creating the magnificent setting you now see, which evokes the refined atmosphere of the Second Empire.

When you go, be sure to sit in one of the five individually decorated adjoining rooms on the first floor. The Salon Mathilde, named after Princess Mathilde, who helped Napoléon III ascend the throne, is furnished in rich wall hangings, wing chairs, and deep sofas. The Salon Castiglione, named after the willful, cunning Countess of Castiglione, who was Napoléon III's mistress, is done in blue and gold with a marble fireplace along one wall. In the center near the wide staircase is the Salon Paeva, named after a famous courtesan. The Chocolaterie, or "chocolate room"—with its wainscoting, antique lamps, ebony marquetry, and gilded mirrors—has the atmosphere of

Vienna's most beautiful cafés. And finally, there is the intimate book-lined Bibliotheque, which is a cozy re-creation of a small library.

Every day forty-five pastry chefs and forty cooks prepare the beautiful food, which is inspired by the regions of France and the cuisines of the world. It is served continuously from breakfast through late supper by a dining-room staff of forty-five and six *maîtres d'hôtel*. With this much staff, you might assume the service would be top-notch. Unfortunately it waivers from barely acceptable to rude and miserably slow.

TEL 01-40-75-08-75 **INTERNET** www.laduree.fr
OPEN Mon–Fri: 7:30 A.M.–11:30 P.M., Sat–Sun & holidays: 8:30 A.M.–
   12:30 A.M., continuous service **CLOSED** Never
À LA CARTE Pastries and ice cream 6–9€, lunch or dinner 25–35€, BNC;
   afternoon tea 14–20€ **PRIX FIXE** Lunch & dinner: 27€, 1 course, 32€,
   2 courses, both BNC **CREDIT CARDS** AE, DC, MC, V
RESERVATIONS Essential for lunch & dinner **ENGLISH SPOKEN** Yes, and English
   menu

LA FERMETTE MARBEUF 1900 ($, 32)
5, rue Marbeuf
Métro: Franklin-D-Roosevelt

Of the many Art Nouveau restaurants flourishing in Paris today, this one is exceptional. For the best experience of it, reserve a table in the *jardin d'hiver*, a spectacular glass-roofed winter garden with Art Nouveau grillwork, five thousand elaborate *faïence* tiles, and beautiful lead-glass windows with intricate floral designs. The room was purchased in total from the Maisons-Lafitte and installed as the *première salle* at La Fermette Marbeuf. The restaurant was declared a national historic monument in 1983.

Fortunately, the breathtaking decor does not overshadow the food, where the culinary cornerstones of beef tartare prepared to order, leg of lamb, and innovative fish preparations, plus a host of artistic desserts, highlight the lengthy menu. The best dining values are the prix-fixe lunch and dinner menus served Monday to Saturday (except holidays). They all have a choice of four starters, including a *terrine des foies de volaille* (chicken-liver terrine) and a choice of four *plats,* followed by either a cheese course or dessert. Of the sweet choices, the *délice chocolat mandarine,* a decadently rich fudge cake flavored with tangerines, is a favorite.

The rooms are too large and brightly lit to be ideal for an intimate dinner, but La Fermette is close to the Champs-Élysées and is a very pleasing formal dining experience, especially on Sunday or holidays when many other restaurants are closed.

TEL 01-53-23-08-00 **INTERNET** www.fermette-marbeuf.com
OPEN Daily: lunch noon–3 P.M., dinner 7–11:30 P.M. **CLOSED** Never
À LA CARTE 55–60€, BNC **PRIX FIXE** Lunch (Mon–Sat): 20€, 2 courses, 25€,
   3 courses, both BNC; dinner (Mon–Sat): 30€, 3 courses, BNC **CREDIT
   CARDS** AE, DC, MC, V
RESERVATIONS Recommended **ENGLISH SPOKEN** Yes

LA MAISON DE L'AUBRAC (29)
37, rue Marbeuf
Métro: Franklin-D-Roosevelt

L'Aubrac is a vast region in the southern section of the Massif Central that is known for its fine beef. It is here that Christian Valette raises the cattle he serves in his restaurant, which he runs with his wife, Élisabeth. Strategically positioned just off the Champs-Élysées, the restaurant dishes up this high-quality Aubrac beef twenty-four hours a day, 365 days a year. Inside the rustic, knotty pine–lined dining room, long-time waiters banter back and forth with their regular diners, who opt for one of the booths or banquette tables rather than sitting in the back room. Solo diners vie for a stool at the bar.

This is not destination dining for anyone who is not a committed carnivore. This is a place for real men to bring real appetites in order to do justice to tripes in a creamy *morille* (wild mushroom) sauce, a choice of five steaks all served with *l'aligot*, or the unbelievable *beef trilogy*, a platter overflowing with beef tartare, grilled sirloin, and beef salad. The choices are the same for lunch and dinner, daily specials run Monday to Friday, and there is no prix-fixe menu. The wine list is as overwhelming as the servings. A veritable dictionary, it covers all regions of France, but since the house specializes in red vintages and offers wines of the week, your search can be narrowed. Try either a Côte du Rhone or one from the Languedoc/Roussillon region. Desserts? After this *grande bouffe*, I can't imagine it, but if you can, order a plate of regional cheeses or a slab of the house specialty, a rich chestnut cake layered with chestnut cream. If your hotel is not too far away, you probably will welcome the walk.

TEL 01-43-59-05-14 **INTERNET** www.maison-aubrac.fr
OPEN 24 hours: bar 8 A.M.–noon, 3:30–8 P.M.; lunch noon–3:30 P.M.; dinner
  7 P.M.–8 A.M., continuous service **CLOSED** Never
À LA CARTE 35–45€, BNC **PRIX FIXE** None **CREDIT CARDS** AE, DC, MC, V
RESERVATIONS Recommended **ENGLISH SPOKEN** Yes

L'ATELIER DES CHEFS (24)
10, rue de Penthième
Métro: St-Philippe-du-Roule

For a memorable Great Eat in Paris that *you* prepare, book a weekday lunch at Atelier des Chefs, where for 20€ you will don an apron and spend thirty minutes in a big, glass-enclosed kitchen, participating in a cooking class with nineteen other wannabe chefs. For children between seven and twelve years old, special classes are held on Wednesday and Saturday afternoons. Everyone gathers around a large work table and follows the tutelage of the professional working chef as you prepare the dish of the day, then you eat the results at one of the tables overlooking the kitchen. The class is conducted in French but is mostly visual, so it is easy for non–French speakers to follow. Wine, cheese, dessert, and coffee are extra. On Saturday, the class curriculum expands to three dishes and lasts an hour and a half or two hours. There are also two-hour cooking classes held in the afternoons with a different theme, where you also get to enjoy eating the fruits of your labor. If you are more into wine than food, sign up for one of the two lunchtime wine tastings (Thursday is wine, Friday is champagne), which includes two wines or two champagnes, lunch, and coffee. For more inspiration, before you leave be sure to browse through the boutique selling books and cooking equipment. To find out what's cooking, and to register, go to their Website.

TEL 01-53-30-05-82 **EMAIL** info@atelierdeschefs.com

OPEN Mon–Fri: 45-minute lunch classes 12:30 & 1:15 P.M.; 2-hour afternoon classes 3:30 & 5:30 P.M.; Thur–Fri: 45-minute wine-tasting lunch 12:45–1:30 P.M.; Sat: 1½-hour lunch class 12:30–2 P.M.; Wed & Sat: 1½-hour children's cooking classes 3:30 & 5:30 P.M. **CLOSED** Sun; major holidays, NAC

PRICES Mon–Fri: 45-minute lunch class 20€, 2-hour lunch class 68€; Thur–Fri: wine-tasting lunch 17€ (champagne), 25€ (wine); Wed & Sat: children's 1½-hour lunch class 51€ **CREDIT CARDS** MC, V

RESERVATIONS Mandatory, make online **ENGLISH SPOKEN** Yes, but classes are in French

L'ÉCLUSE FRANÇOIS 1ER (31)
64, rue François 1er
Métro: Franklin-D-Roosevelt

For a complete description, see L'Écluse, page 59. All other information is the same.

TEL 01-47-20-77-09

L'ÉCLUSE MADELEINE (38)
15, place de la Madeleine
Métro: Madeleine

For a complete description, see L'Écluse, page 59. All other information is the same.

TEL 01-42-65-34-69

LE LITEAU (21)
12–16, rue Washington
Métro: George V

Where do the rank and file find an affordable meal in this strictly business *quartier,* which is not known for economy anything? They go to Le Liteau . . . a big canteen that feeds the hungry hoardes a three-course prix-fixe lunch and dinner meal that has ten choices for each course and rings in for under 20€. And, no, it is not just *oeuf dur mayonnaise,* steak and *frites,* and crème caramel. Try *escargots* or raw salmon with dill to start, *pot au feu,* osso buco, pork with lentils and, okay . . . steak and *frites* for the main course, followed by the fruit *tarte du jour,* chocolate *fondant,* or *poire belle Hélène* (poached pears with vanilla ice cream and hot chocolate) for dessert. For the best French experience, go at lunchtime when it hums with locals who know that eating well is just a block away from the bright lights and restaurant rip-offs along the Champs-Élysées.

TEL 01-42-56-40-15
OPEN Mon–Sat: lunch noon–3 P.M., dinner 7–11 P.M. **CLOSED** Sun; NAC
À LA CARTE None **PRIX FIXE** Lunch: 15.50€, 3 course, BNC; dinner: 19.50€,
   3 courses, BNC **CREDIT CARDS** AE, MC, V
RESERVATIONS Not necessary **ENGLISH SPOKEN** Enough

MAILLE (40)
6, place de la Madeleine
Métro: Madeleine, Concorde

The brochure for Maille, the Rolls-Royce of French Dijon mustard and condiments, accurately states: "Enter the Maille boutique and discover a universe rich in fine savours." Their thirty or more varieties of mustard include balsamic, Calvados, cassis, cognac, honey, pink peppercorn, three herbs, and walnut. But Maille is not only about mustard. For 250 years it has been recognized as a master vinegar maker; try the truffle white wine vinegar, black-current red wine, or champagne. In addition, they are also known for their range of fruity olive oils. Beautiful replicas of antique mustard pots and vinegar and oil cruets are also available, as are recipes using all their products. If you buy one of their small- or medium-size brown mustard pots you can have it refilled with fresh mustard on tap (white wine or fruity chablis) every time you run out, and you pay only for the mustard. They also offer many gift combinations and will ship. And considering the fine quality products, the prices are very reasonable.

TEL 01-40-15-06-00 **FAX** 01-40-15-06-11
   EMAIL am-parisboutique@unilever.com **INTERNET** www.maille.com
OPEN Mon–Sat: 10 A.M.–7 P.M. **CLOSED** Sun; major holidays, NAC
PRICES From 2€ for vinegar, 3.90€ for small gourmet mustard, 11€ for olive
   oil, 2–5€ to refill mustard pot **CREDIT CARDS** MC, V (15€ minimum)
ENGLISH SPOKEN Yes

MARIAGE FRÈRES (16)
260, rue du Faubourg St-Honoré
Métro: Ternes

For a complete description, see Mariage Frères, page 105. All other information is the same.

TEL 01-46-22-18-54
OPEN Daily: tea boutique 10:30 A.M.–7:30 P.M., tearoom noon–7 P.M.
   CLOSED Christmas, New Year's Day, NAC

MUSÉE JACQUEMART-ANDRÉ (17)
158, boulevard Haussmann
Métro: St-Philippe du Roule, Miromesnil

Thanks to Edouard and Nélie Jacquemart-André's passionate and enlightened quest for world-renowned art, Paris enjoys one of the most beautiful private collections in France, comparable to the Wallace Collection in London or the Frick in New York. The Italian

Renaissance, Flemish, and eighteenth-century French masterpieces are shown in their original setting: the couple's fabulous late nineteenth-century mansion. In addition to works of art by Rembrandt, Della Robbia, Botticelli, Bellini, Fragonard, and many more, important pieces of decorative art, priceless tapestries, and one of the finest collections of Italian Renaissance sculpture are displayed throughout fifteen rooms (including the couple's private apartments) that are open to the public. Be sure to get the complimentary audio-guide in English, which has an exceptional narration.

After visiting the collection, please allow time for lunch or tea in the most beautiful tearoom in Paris, with a ceiling fresco by Tiepolo and tapestries from the Vander Borght atelier in Brussels. The nonsmoking restaurant serves a hot *plat du jour* plus an appetizing selection of salads, quiches, pastries, homemade ice cream, and brunch on Sunday. Nearby is an excellent book and gift shop with many items that make ideal, easy-to-pack gifts from this unsung star in the roster of Paris museums.

NOTE: You can go to the restaurant without buying a ticket for the museum. This is a nonsmoking restaurant.

TEL 01-45-62-11-59 **INTERNET** www.musee-jacquemart-andre.com
OPEN Daily: museum 10 A.M.–6 P.M.; tearoom lunch 11:45 A.M.–3 P.M., tea 3–5:30 P.M. **CLOSED** Never
À LA CARTE 18–22€, BNC **PRIX FIXE** Lunch: 15.50€, 2 courses, BNC; afternoon tea: 8.60€, BC; Sun brunch: 25€, 2 courses, BC
   CREDIT CARDS MC, V
RESERVATIONS Not necessary **ENGLISH SPOKEN** Yes, and English menu

POMZE (22)
109, boulevard Haussmann
Métro: St. Augustin, Miromesnil

If you believe the saying, "an apple a day keeps the doctor away," then you have hit the jackpot at Pomze. Apples in every guise imaginable are served with every dish here, and with great success. They are also very well known for their thirty-five to forty French ciders, five or six types of pure apple juice, and twenty or more types of Calvados liqueur. On Saturdays two cider producers are here to offer tastings. I will admit that I thought it was gimmicky, to say the least, but after one wonderful lunch, I changed my tune. For lunch, huge salads are the order of the day, and they are served outside when it is warm or in the lower-level dining room, which is darkly romantic. On the second level is their more formal restaurant, which only serves two- or three-course meals and no salads need apply. On Thursday and Saturday evenings from 8–11 P.M., a live jazz pianist entertains. There is also the apple boutique where you can buy assorted apple jams and jellies, ciders, juices, and yes, even fresh apples.

For under 15€, lunch-goers have a choice of a half-dozen salads, served with a glass of cider or wine, plus tea or coffee. Try the Bombay, with chicken tika, curried rice, and apple chutney. The Casablanca is all about couscous, with cooked apples on the side; the Boston mixes fresh spinach with avocado, Granny Smith apples, and shrimp; and the *Humeur du Jour* is the chef's daily special. At dinner, all the dishes have some sort of apple worked into it, be it a vegetable soup with apple butter escargots (a stretch, if you ask me); Calvados-flavored foie gras; layers of feta cheese, apples, and raisins seared with grilled vegetables; or a cider-basted roast duck. For dessert, what else? Apple tart or *tarte Tatin*.

TEL 01-42-65-65-83 **INTERNET** www.pomze.com
OPEN Mon–Sat: lunch noon–2:30 P.M., dinner 7:30–11 P.M.; boutique: Mon–
    Fri 8 A.M.–11 P.M., Sat 10 A.M.–11 P.M. **CLOSED** Sun; Mon in July & Aug
À LA CARTE 35–40€ **PRIX FIXE** Lunch: 14.50€, large salad, BC (cider or wine
    & coffee); lunch & dinner: 32€, 3 courses, BNC **CREDIT CARDS** AE, MC, V
RESERVATIONS Recommended **ENGLISH SPOKEN** Yes, and English menu

SAVEUR ET SALON (34)
3, rue Castellane
Metro: Madeleine

Follow local Parisians in this neighborhood, and head to Saveur et Salon, where you can rub elbows at noon with a smartly dressed business clientele and in the evening with mellow neighbors of all ages and dress. It is a good idea to reserve, and when you do, avoid the downstairs, which is hot and smoky. The main dining room may be a bit short on French atmosphere, but the food and snappy service more than make up for the sober decor. To keep things interesting at lunch for the regulars, the *formule,* which offers the *entrée* and *plat* of the day and a glass of wine, changes daily. True, dinner will set you back half again as many euros, but the selection is more interesting. I like to start with a salad of pencil-slim green beans, pine nuts, and shavings of Parmesan cheese on a bed of bitter greens. For vegetarians, there is always a pasta and a risotto choice, plus five fish selections. Meat eaters will relish orders of veal with mushrooms, lamb cooked with five spices, or chicken with buttery herb mashed potatoes. The dessert of your chocolate dreams is the warm *moelleux au chocolat glace Grand Marnier.*

TEL 01-40-06-97-97
OPEN Mon–Fri: lunch noon–3 P.M., dinner 7–10:30 P.M.; Sat: dinner 7–11 P.M.
    CLOSED Sat lunch, Sun; lunch on major holidays, NAC
À LA CARTE *Entrées* 14€, *plats* 22€, desserts 9€ **PRIX FIXE** Lunch: 20€,
    2 courses, BC; lunch & dinner: 36€, 3 courses, BNC **CREDIT CARDS** AE,
    MC, V
RESERVATIONS Recommended **ENGLISH SPOKEN** Yes

TART'ARTS (¢, 20)
36, rue de Berri
Métro: St-Philippe-du-Roule, George V

For assured seating, be here at the stroke of noon. After that, a fashionable mix of all ages and types pours in, making it a full house by 12:30 P.M. with no letup in sight. What is the big draw? Artistic hot and cold salads, the *tarte* and winter dish or summer salad of the day, and calories-be-damned desserts. Cold salads include the *Alexandria,* designer greens topped with chèvre, raisins, carrots, and apples. The *Pat'Marine* salad comes with smoked salmon, crab, shrimp, olives, and tomatoes on a bed of greens. If you would like a gratin of chicken, mushrooms, and potatoes on a bed of lettuce, order the *Poulette,* or try the *Seguin,* warm chèvre on toast, surrounded by grated carrots and tomatoes dusted with oregano. The list of daily *tartes* is long—you could probably go every day for three weeks and never have the same one twice. Desserts stay about the same, so I am always assured of the lemon or orange *tartes,* fresh fruit *charlotte* in the summer, and chestnut cake in the winter.

TEL 01-42-25-02-76

OPEN Mon–Fri: lunch 11:30–2:30 P.M. **CLOSED** Sat–Sun; holidays, 1 week at Christmas, NAC

À LA CARTE 14–18€, BNC **PRIX FIXE** Lunch: 15€, 2 courses, BC (coffee) **CREDIT CARDS** MC, V

RESERVATIONS Accepted only until 12:30 P.M. **ENGLISH SPOKEN** Yes

Ninth Arrondissement

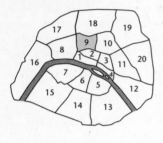

The ninth is predominantly a business area, with many banks, corporate headquarters, law firms, insurance companies, and the Galeries Lafayette and Printemps department stores. The Grands Boulevards, laid out by Baron Haussmann, are those wide thoroughfares that lead from the Opéra Garnier (with a Chagall ceiling) to place de la République. The smart end is at the Opéra, the center of Paris during the Belle Epoque, that period of elegance and gaiety that characterized Parisian life from the mid-nineteenth century to World War I.

À LA MÈRE DE FAMILLE (11)
35, rue du Faubourg Montmartre
Métro: Le Peletier

Even if you don't have a sweet tooth, À la Mère de Famille is worth the trip just to admire the beautiful displays of chocolates and regional candies in this original shop, which dates back to 1761. It is owned by a family as sweet as their wares. They are always helpful and cheerful, whether you are buying an expensive gift box of their own chocolates, a kilo of the special ginger cake, some of the beautiful marzipan creations, or merely an assortment of dried fruits. There are several other locations, but the most convenient are the two in the seventh arrondissement on rue Cler and rue du Cherche Midi (see page 163) and the one in the seventeenth (see page 265). Hours may vary slightly.

TEL 01-47-70-83-69
OPEN Mon–Sat: 9:30 A.M.–8 P.M.; Sun: 10 A.M.–1 P.M. **CLOSED** Aug (dates vary)
PRICES From 5€ (everything sold by weight) **CREDIT CARDS** AE, MC, V
ENGLISH SPOKEN Yes

AUBERGE DU CLOU (1)
30, avenue Trudaine, angle rue des Martyrs
Métro: Anvers, Pigalle

A Parisian friend sent me the following note: "Dear Sandra, Auberge du Clou is one of the few restaurants we have found recently which served good food and wine at a reasonable price, with friendly service and nice atmosphere."

You bet I was there the next day! My dining companion and I were graciously seated at window table upstairs in a timbered room, which is dominated by a wood-burning fireplace and reminiscent of an old country inn. Weather permitting, I also like to sit on the terrace, which provides great people-watching in this rapidly gentrifying neighborhood.

The menu changes with the seasons and uses only fresh products. The Tuesday to Friday *Express Lunch Formule* is a good buy if you only want a main course and glass of wine. However, if you go all the way and order three courses for lunch, you are still getting great value. You can expect such dishes as marinated salmon, *cuise de canard maison,* rabbit served with creamy risotto, and a soul-warming braised beef with carrots, and you should end with a iced Grand Mariner soufflé served with two mini-crêpes.

Thank you Ray, you were right . . . this is another Great Eat in Paris.

TEL 01-48-78-22-48
OPEN Mon: dinner 7:30–10:30 P.M.; Tues–Sun: lunch noon–2 P.M. (Sun till 3 P.M.), dinner 7:30–10:30 P.M. (Fri–Sat till 11:30 P.M.) **CLOSED** Mon lunch, NAC

À LA CARTE *Entrées* 7€, *plats* 12–17€, desserts 7€ **PRIX FIXE** Lunch: Express
   Formule (Tues–Fri), 17–25€, 1 course & wine; 22€, 2 courses, 29€,
   3 courses, both BNC **CREDIT CARDS** MC, V
RESERVATIONS Preferred **ENGLISH SPOKEN** Yes

AU PETIT RICHE (10)
25, rue Le Peletier
Métro: Le Peletier

Au Petit Riche has been on this corner since 1880—well, it's actually been here since 1854, but the original building burned down, and
it reopened as it is now in 1880. The best thing about Au Petit Riche
is that it serves a battery of reliable, classic dishes that are designed to
please every taste and age group. Most Parisian restaurants discourage
children under ten, but they are welcomed warmly at Au Petit Riche,
which has created a three-course menu just for them. Add in the
multiple rooms divided by mirrors and etched glass, and the bevy of
traditionally attired waiters, and this charming restaurant says Paris.

Here is the place to order *gratinée à l'oignon* (onion soup), a chunk
of foie gras *maison,* a lusty lentil salad, or homemade pork *pâté.* The
French love ofal and raw beef, and no restaurant prepares these dishes
any better. Try *andouillette* (roasted tripe sausage), *tête de veau* (calf's
tongue, brains, snout, and cheeks with an herb vinaigrette), fried veal
kidneys, and *boeuf tartare* with fat french fries. Definitely reserve ahead
on Thursday, when their famous roasted country chicken with truffle
sauce is served; otherwise it is standing room only. Other specialties
include sole *belle meunière, magret de canard* with honey and thyme,
lamb with baby turnips, and the usual steaks with rich sauces and
potatoes on the side. The best sweet finale to your meal is a *baba au
rhum* or a flaky, prepared-to-order warm apple tart.

TEL 01-47-70-68-68 **INTERNET** www.aupetitriche.com
OPEN Mon–Sat: lunch noon–2:15 P.M., dinner 7 P.M.–12:15 A.M. **CLOSED** Sun;
   NAC
À LA CARTE 38–42€ **PRIX FIXE** Lunch: 22.50€, 2 courses, BNC; lunch &
   dinner: 25.50€ & 29.50€, both 3 courses & BNC; children's menu: 11€,
   3 courses, BC **CREDIT CARDS** MC, V
RESERVATIONS Essential **ENGLISH SPOKEN** Yes, and English menu

CASA OLYMPE (4)
48, rue Saint-Georges
Métro: Saint-Georges

Several years ago, chef Dominique Versini left her trendy hot spot
in the fifteenth and opened this mellow bistro off the place Saint-
Georges. In another life, the restaurant here had a notoriety of sorts.
It was known as the cheapest restaurant in Paris, charging a mere
five francs (less than one euro) for a three-course meal with wine.
Those days are long gone, and so are the former patrons and down-
and-outers who frequented it. Today, the only thing remaining is the
mosaic-tiled floor. The inside is painted a sunny Provençal yellow
and has a pretty Murano glass chandelier, while the typical crunch

of closely spaced tables is always filled with a tony crowd who know how to dress for success and appreciate creative cooking.

The seasonal menu is based on market availability, and highlights daily blackboard specials. On one visit in the late fall, the specials included escargots in a garlic sauce, rabbit garnished with red and white beans, and a saffron-infused crème caramel. A chestnut crêpe hiding a poached egg was a simple but pleasing beginning, and so was the cream of celery splashed with herring caviar. *Coquilles St-Jacques* sautéed in olive oil, a tender guinea hen served in its own casserole with just-cooked cabbage, and a very filling duck ravioli got us to dessert, which consisted of simple yet very satisfying endings of *fromage blanc* dusted with herbs and a *baba* infused with Calvados.

TEL 01-42-85-26-01
OPEN Mon–Fri: lunch noon–2 P.M., dinner 8–11 P.M. **CLOSED** Sat–Sun; 1 week at Christmas and in May; 3 weeks Aug (dates vary)
À LA CARTE None **PRIX FIXE** Lunch & dinner: 37€, 3 courses, BNC
   CREDIT CARDS MC, V
RESERVATIONS Essential **ENGLISH SPOKEN** Yes

COJEAN (¢, 37)
4-6, rue de Sèze
Métro: Madeleine, Opéra

Healthy fast food *à la française* is yours at Cojean, where the food is both good and good for you. Scores are following the Cojean edict to "experience food, love, equilibrium here and now," and as a result, three more outlets have opened in central Paris.

Owners Alain Cojean and Fred Maquair take their food seriously and turn out daily fare that appeals to both hard-core vegetarians and freewheeling carnivores. It has become a popular lunch destination and may in time help to improve the street, which houses several peep shows and sex shops. It is perfectly safe during the day, and you don't have to worry about the evening because Cojean is closed. Seating is in a large room at chrome-pedestal bar tables. Wheat grass, which ultimately ends up in a drink, thrives in the window. Meat is featured only in the club sandwiches, never in the four daily soups or the two or three *plats du jour*. I like the roasted vegetable sandwich, a winning combination of eggplant, tomato, zucchini, spinach, onion, and the house pesto. Salads and quiches are popular orders, and so are the inspired fruit or veggie drinks. Everything can be eaten here or bagged to go.

NOTE: Cojean has expanded its base of operation. It has two more locations in the ninth arrondissement: at 17, boulevard Haussmann, (map key 15; **TEL** 01-47-70-22-65; **OPEN** Mon–Sat: 8 A.M.–7 P.M.) and at 66, rue de Provence (map key 7; **TEL** 01-45-26-25-85; **OPEN** Mon–Sat: 8 A.M.–4 P.M.). It also has a location in the eighth, at 19, rue Clément Marot (see page 186). All other information is the same.

TEL 01-40-06-08-80 **INTERNET** www.cojean.fr
OPEN Mon–Fri: 8 A.M.–6 P.M., Sat: 9 A.M.-7 P.M., continuous service
   CLOSED Sun; major holidays, NAC

À LA CARTE 7–15€, BNC PRIX FIXE None CREDIT CARDS MC, V
RESERVATIONS Not accepted ENGLISH SPOKEN Yes

FRUCTIDOR (¢, 8)
67, rue de Provence
Métro: Chausée d'Antin La Fayette

Teas from Mariage Frères and some of the best sweet and savory tarts served anywhere are prepared here (and at its sibling restaurant, see below) daily for lunch. The eager crowd knows to arrive when the doors open or else they'll have to spend time standing in line waiting for a place to open. If you are shopping at Galeries Lafayette or Au Printemps, try this little Cheap Eat for a nutritious lunch that will leave plenty of money in your wallet for afternoon purchases. Order a fresh, sugar- and additive-free vegetable cocktail with a tomato, carrot, or apple base by the glass or carafe. Or try a slice of a savory tart, maybe the *alsacienne* (onions and bacon), the *chèvre oseille* (goat cheese and sorrel purée), or the *forestière* (mushrooms and Auvergne blue cheese), all of which come with a green salad. There are also large one-meal salads and hot tofu dishes, and for dessert . . . carrot cake and more tarts. Choose from fresh fruit, cheese, or chocolate.

At both locations, the tarts are available to go, either whole or by the slice. At the rue de Provence location, chicken tandoori is the specialty, prepared by the chef, Roland, from a recipe given to him by the owner, Sathi, who is Indian. The changing art you see hanging on the walls has been done by local artists and is for sale.

NOTE: Both locations are entirely nonsmoking.

TEL 01-48-74-53-46
OPEN Mon–Sat: lunch 11 A.M.–5 P.M.; also Sun in Dec when the stores are open CLOSED Sun (except in Dec); holidays, NAC
À LA CARTE 15–18€, BNC PRIX FIXE None CREDIT CARDS None
RESERVATIONS Not taken ENGLISH SPOKEN Yes

FRUCTIDOR ST-GEORGES (¢, 5)
46, rue St-Georges
Métro: Notre-Dame-de-Lorette

See preceding entry for description. All other information is the same.

TEL 01-49-95-02-10
OPEN Mon–Fri: lunch 11 A.M.–3 P.M. CLOSED Sat–Sun; NAC

GEORGETTE (6)
29, rue Saint-Georges
Métro: Saint-Georges, Notre Dame de Lorette

The restaurant name is adapted from the name of the street and of the nearby métro and square. Staffed by women—none of whom are named Georgette—it reminds me of a sixties-era dining room with plastic-covered chairs and banquettes and a vintage tiled bar. At dinner, the place is jammed with a French crowd made up of neighborhood couples and a stray tourist or two. Once the dinner service hits

its stride (around 9 P.M.), service can become absent-minded; on one visit, our bottle of wine was opened out of our sight and then served. Aside from the *andouillette* and the rumpsteak, the food tends to be on the lighter side with top-quality vegetables starring in many of the *entrées* and the daily pasta. To start off on a simple but delicious note, I recommend the artichoke hearts and grilled fennel sitting on a bed of roquette and drizzled with olive oil. I also loved the baby zucchini flowers stuffed with chèvre and the sautéed *pleurots* (oyster mushrooms) quickly cooked with garlic and olive oil. There are usually two pastas every day, plus three or four meat choices and seven or eight desserts. For dessert, the chocolate cake leads the pack, followed closely by the *financier* (little pound cake served with fig sorbet and a honey custard sauce) and the roasted figs garnished with honey-chestnut ice cream.

TEL 01-42-80-39-13
OPEN Tues–Fri: lunch noon–2:45 P.M., dinner 7:30–11:30 P.M.
  CLOSED Sat–Mon; Aug (dates vary)
À LA CARTE 30–35€, BNC **PRIX FIXE** None **CREDIT CARDS** MC, V
RESERVATIONS Essential **ENGLISH SPOKEN** Enough

LAFAYETTE GOURMET (9)
99, rue de Provence, at rue Charras
Métro: Chausée d'Antin–La Fayette, Auber, Havre-Caumartin

It is Christmas Day and your birthday rolled into one at Lafayette Gourmet, the magnificent food department that is part of (but around the corner from) Galeries Lafayette. Food lovers will feel they have hit the jackpot with the multitude of riches on display. Even if you are not shopping for groceries or other gourmet items to take with you, you can come to eat at one of the food stations, where salads, fruits, cheeses, wines, coffees, pastries, pasta, grills, caviar, and sushi are served nearly all day, every day but Sunday.

TEL 01-48-74-94-71 **INTERNET** www.lafayettegourmet.com
OPEN Mon–Sat: 9:30 A.M.–8 P.M. (Thur till 9:30 P.M.), continuous service
  CLOSED Sun; holidays, NAC
À LA CARTE 5€ and up **CREDIT CARDS** AE, MC, V
ENGLISH SPOKEN Yes

LE BISTRO DES DEUX THÉÂTRES (2)
18, rue Blanche
Métro: Trinité

Le Bistro des Deux Théâtres is a fine *formule* restaurant with a single prix-fixe menu that has preserved its good cooking and authenticity despite its commercial setting near the Gare St. Lazare. This solid bistro manages to fill a variety of needs with its traditional charm, pressed linens, fresh flowers on each table, and quality of preparation, which you would expect to find in a place charging twice as much.

The choices are excellent, at least nine or ten for each course. Consider starters of king prawn ravioli, fresh asparagus in a chervil

sauce, duck foie gras with stewed grapes, a dozen snails in garlic butter, or raw smoked salmon marinated in lemon and dill. Liver cooked
with honey and spices, rack of lamb, or roasted duck served with figs
are just a few of the possible main courses, which change frequently
based on the season.

This is a good place to save room for dessert—indulge in flaming
Grand Marnier crêpes, a hot apple tart with Calvados, dark chocolate
cake, or a dreamy crème brûlée. Both an apéritif and wine are included
in the price, and so is the strong espresso that ends the meal.

TEL 01-45-26-41-43
OPEN Daily: lunch noon–2:30 P.M., dinner 7:15 P.M.–12:30 A.M.
  CLOSED Never
À LA CARTE None **PRIX FIXE** Lunch & dinner: 33€, 3 courses, BC
  CREDIT CARDS AE, MC, V
RESERVATIONS Advised **ENGLISH SPOKEN** Yes

LES DIABLES AU THYM (13)
35, rue Bergère
Métro: Grands Boulevards

If I could, I would return to Serge and Patricia Uriot's Les Diables
au Thym every night. Whenever you are fortunate enough to be in
Paris, you can always come here for an exquisite meal and impeccable
service. Being here makes me feel I am a guest in a good friend's
small, intimate dining room. Fresh flowers and hurricane candles
grace the linen-covered tables, the china is Villeroy and Boch, and
the seating on banquettes and padded chairs is comfortable. Serge is
in the kitchen, working his magic on his seasonally inspired food. I
know he buys only the best high-quality ingredients because when
I am in Paris I see him loading his baskets almost every morning on
my shopping street, which is the famous rue Montorgueil (and all
that remains of the old "belly of Paris"). Patricia and one waiter serve
the entire room, which has tables filled by 8:30 P.M. and people still
arriving at 10:30 P.M., just before the kitchen closes.

The à la carte menu is seasonal, but the prix-fixe selections change
every few weeks. No matter what you order, every beautifully prepared and presented dish is a winner, especially the terrine of foie gras
you liberally spread on toast, and the colorful assortment of fresh vegetables with a soft poached egg on top. Next, consider lamb *tournedos*
flavored with tarragon, pigeon roasted in lavender and honey, lobster
and scallops stewed in a light saffron sauce, a pair of spicy roasted
quail, or the tender rabbit, sometimes roasted with sage, sometimes
served with a broccoli and mustard cream sauce (in spring), and sometimes with wild mushrooms (in winter).

For dessert bliss in the winter, look no further than these two
dishes: the *moelleux au chocolat et sa glace caramel au beurre salée,* a
voluptuous creation that oozes bittersweet chocolate with every bite,
or the *clafoutis minute aux fruits rouges et sa glace à la canelle* (fruits baked
in a light crust with a custardy filling and served with cinnamon ice

cream). Otherwise, coffee comes with a plate of homemade cookies and pieces of white and dark chocolate.

TEL 01-47-70-77-09

OPEN Mon–Fri: lunch noon–2:30 P.M., dinner 7–10:30 P.M.; Sat: dinner 7–10:30 P.M. **CLOSED** Sat lunch, Sun; major holidays, 2nd week Feb, last week July, first 3 weeks Aug

À LA CARTE 40–45€, BNC **PRIX FIXE** Lunch: 19.95€, 2 courses, 25.95€, 3 courses, both BNC **CREDIT CARDS** AE, MC, V

RESERVATIONS Essential **ENGLISH SPOKEN** Yes

RESTAURANT CHARTIER (14)
7, rue du Faubourg Montmartre
Métro: Grands Boulevards

You can trust the French to know a good food bargain when they smell it, and for decades penny-wise Parisians have made Restaurant Chartier a major destination. Not much has changed over the years in this authentic Parisian *bouillon* (soup kitchen) with its fin-de-siècle decor, squads of scowling white-aproned waiters, and basic "no parsley" food. There is no glamour or tinsel here either. Big, noisy, barn-like, and always crowded, it is the blue-collar worker's Maxim's, and they and many others eat here in droves every day of the year.

The menu, which changes daily, is long, but if you select carefully, you will have a satisfying and cheap meal. Choose the dishes that have to be made to order and save the fancier ones for another place. You could start with a beet or tomato salad, hard-boiled egg and mayonnaise, or a plate of ham. Order a jug of the house wine to go with your main course of roast chicken, fish, or grilled beef, along with potatoes that have been boiled. All garnishes cost extra, even the ketchup and mayonnaise, but they are not much. If it is listed, the most reliable dessert is a fruit *tarte*.

TEL 01-47-70-86-29

OPEN Daily: lunch 11 A.M.–3 P.M., dinner 6–10 P.M. **CLOSED** Never

À LA CARTE 15–20, BNC **PRIX FIXE** Lunch & dinner: 16€, 3 courses, BC

CREDIT CARDS V (15€ minimum)

RESERVATIONS Not necessary **ENGLISH SPOKEN** Limited

VERDEAU DROUOT (12)
25, passage Verdeau Drouot (across from 6, rue de la Grange Batelière)
Métro: Richelieu-Drouot

Just because a Frenchperson goes to an office every day does not mean he or she is going to sacrifice having a proper lunch or, worse yet, brown bag it. On the other hand, French office workers, like those around the world, usually have only an hour to eat, and they don't want to spend big money on a wine-infused, expensive meal. Enter Verdeau Drouot, which brings a touch of class to *la cuisine rapide*. The restaurant is in the passage Verdeau Drouot, a nineteenth-century shopping arcade, which houses small shops selling old books, cameras, early rock-and-roll records, and other collectibles. It has a welcoming interior, with assorted art and photos of film stars, including Lana Turner and Lauren Bacall. Along the back, the tempting desserts are attractively arranged on a mirrored buffet.

Verdeau Drouot offers a host of choices that all include a salad and are brought to you on a single plate. Some have been given a catchy name, such as *baïkal* (a piece of grilled salmon with basmati rice), *whitney* (salty dried beef, raclette cheese, a baked potato, and pickles), and the *berrichonne* (goat cheese and tomato topping a baked potato). For gourmets on the run, a variety of toasted sandwiches are offered: tuna, goat cheese, onions and bacon, all served with a side salad. While these meals are well priced, the sage values here are the three prix-fixe menus, again all accompanied by a green salad. For example, the *Rossini* offers a selection of toasted sandwiches or a baked potato topped with curried boneless breast of chicken plus dessert. The *Batèliere* is either sautéed beef with peppers or a main course salad and your choice of desserts. All desserts are made here; the most popular is the Norwegian apple and cinnamon cake adapted from a recipe of the owner's mother. No matter how you order, it will be a filling meal that is much more interesting and French than a burger and fries or a sandwich *mixte* someplace else.

TEL 01-45-23-15-96
OPEN Mon–Fri: lunch noon–3 P.M. **CLOSED** Sat–Sun; holidays, Aug 15–30
À LA CARTE 15–22€, BNC **PRIX FIXE** Lunch: 13€, 15.90€, 16.50€, all
2 courses & BNC **CREDIT CARDS** MC, V (18€ minimum)
RESERVATIONS Not necessary **ENGLISH SPOKEN** Yes, and English menu

Tenth Arrondissement

Although most visitors to Paris only pass through the tenth arrondissement when they take a train from either the Gare du Nord or the Gare de l'Est, there are other good reasons to venture into this *quartier populaire,* or traditional working-class neighborhood: to shop for china and crystal along rue de Paradis and to stroll along the pretty Canal St-Martin, which is rapidly emerging as a hip destination, not only to live but to play.

RIGHT BANK
Canal St-Martin
Gare de l'Est
Gare du Nord
place de la République
rue de Paradis

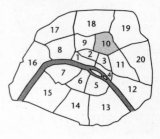

TENTH ARRONDISSEMENT RESTAURANTS

BRASSERIE FLO (2)
7, cour des Petites-Écuries
Métro: Château d'Eau, Strasbourg-St-Denis

Brasserie Flo is another jewel in the crown of Jean-Paul Bucher's resurrected Art Nouveau brasseries, and if you are shopping along rue de Paradis (see *Great Sleeps Paris*), this is a great lunch stop. To say that this one is not easy to find is an understatement. The first time I went, I was sure the taxi driver was taking me on a wild goose chase, and when he left me off at the opening of a dark alley in a questionable neighborhood, I was certain of it. Once inside, however, I completely forgot the approach. Seated at a banquette in one of the two long rooms—with their dark wood walls, zinc bar, and waiters with long aprons serving a dressed-to-the-teeth crowd—you will feel truly Parisian.

Every day of the year Brasserie Flo is a great place to go for platters of oysters, Alsatian *choucroutes* (their specialty), onion soup, foie gras, and grilled meat. Late-nighters and lunch patrons have special menus in addition to the versatile à la carte.

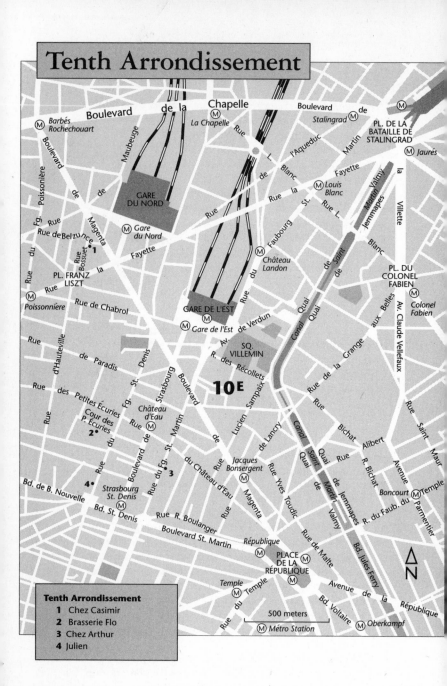

Tenth Arrondissement

Boulevard de la Chapelle

La Chapelle

Barbés Rochechouart

Boulevard de la Chapelle

Boulevard Stalingrad

PL. DE LA BATAILLE DE STALINGRAD

Jaurès

Maubeuge

Rue

l'Aqueduc

Martin

Rue

Fayette

GARE DU NORD

Gare du Nord

Fayette

de

Louis Blanc

St.

Rue L.

de Saint

la Villette

Valmy

Jemmapes

Martin

Boulevard de Poissonnière

Rue du Fg.

Rue de Belzunce

Magenta

la

Rue de la Fayette

Rue du Faubourg

Château Landon

Quai

Quai

de

PL. DU COLONEL FABIEN

Colonel Fabien

Av. Claude Vellefaux

Rue Bossuet

PL. FRANZ LISZT

Poissonnière

Rue de Chabrol

GARE DE L'EST

Gare de l'Est de Verdun

Av.

SQ. VILLEMIN

R. des Récollets

Canal

Rue de la Grange

aux Belles

Rue

Rue

d'Hauteville

de Paradis

St. Denis

Boulevard

10ᴱ

Lucien Sampaix

de Lancry

Rue

Rue

Bichat

Alibert

Saint Maur

Rue des Petites Écuries

Cour des P. Écuries

Château d'Eau

Rue du Fg. St. Martin

du Château d'Eau

Jacques Bonsergent

Rue

Quai de Jemmapes

Rue de Bichat

R. Bichat

Avenue

Boncourt

Temple

Bd. de B. Nouvelle

Strasbourg St. Denis

Bd. St. Denis

Rue R. Boulanger

Magenta

Rue Yves Toudic

Quai

Saint

Quai de Jemmapes

R. du Faub. du Parmentier

Boulevard St. Martin

République

Rue de Malte

Bd. Jules Ferry

N

Temple

PLACE DE LA RÉPUBLIQUE

Temple

Avenue de la République

Bd. Voltaire

Oberkampf

Rue du

500 meters

Métro Station

Tenth Arrondissement
1 Chez Casimir
2 Brasserie Flo
3 Chez Arthur
4 Julien

NOTE: Cour des Petites-Écuries is a small alley between rue de Foubourg-St-Denis and passage des Petites-Écuries. Since the neighborhood is questionable, I would advise taking a taxi at night.

TEL 01-47-70-13-59 **INTERNET** www.brasserieflo.com, www.flobrasseries.com
OPEN Daily: lunch noon–3 P.M., dinner 7 P.M.–midnight **CLOSED** Never
À LA CARTE 35–45€, BNC **PRIX FIXE** Lunch & dinner: 24.50€, 2 courses,
   34.50€, 3 courses, both BC (wine or mineral water); children's menu (age
   4–12): 14€, 3 courses, BC; Faim de Nuit (after 10:30 P.M.): 2 courses,
   BNC **CREDIT CARDS** AE, DC, MC, V
RESERVATIONS Advised, definitely on weekends **ENGLISH SPOKEN** Yes

CHEZ ARTHUR (3)
25, rue Faubourg St-Martin
Métro: Strassbourg-St-Denis, Château d'Eau

The late-night favorite Chez Arthur has been run since 1955 by three generations, starting with the grandfather, Arthur, his son Jackie, and now his grandson Michel. The restaurant is surrounded by five theaters, and its old-fashioned red interior—lined with signed photographs of theater and film stars and lit with bead-fringed lamps—reminds me of Sardi's in New York. The predictable fare offers few surprises, but it is perfectly executed with a certain subtle refinement and is always well-presented. Service is properly old-school. Aside from the daily specials, musts on the short menu include foie gras with a side of onion confit to spread on warm toast, fat shrimp cooked in whiskey and served with ginger-seasoned basmati rice, and a beef fillet, cooked blood rare and served with a side of house *frites*. Pear sorbet splashed with Calvados or the ever-present warm chocolate cake with a scoop of praline ice cream end the meal on a sweet note.

TEL 01-42-08-34-33
OPEN Mon: lunch noon–2:30 P.M.; Tues–Fri: lunch noon–2:30 P.M., dinner
   7–11:30 P.M.; Sat: dinner 7–11:30 P.M. **CLOSED** Mon dinner, Sat lunch,
   Sun; Aug
À LA CARTE None **PRIX FIXE** Lunch: 15€, 1 course, BC (wine & coffee); lunch
   & dinner: 22€, 2 courses, 27€, 3 courses, both BNC **CREDIT CARDS** AE,
   DC, MC, V
RESERVATIONS Recommended **ENGLISH SPOKEN** Yes

CHEZ CASIMIR (1)
6, rue de Belzunce, at rue Bossuet
Métro: Gare du Nord

Chez Casimir is the bare-bones bistro spin-off of Thierry Breton, whose Chez Michel a few doors away has been filled from its first day with Parisian diners eager to encourage talented young chefs to strike out on their own. At lunch, it is a madhouse, with only two waiters working at a semi-trot to keep up, and after one visit it is easy to see the appeal: at Chez Casimir, the prices are reasonable, the mood is simple and relaxed, the atmosphere plain, and the food worth the safari no matter where you are in the city. As with most baby bistros in Paris, the menu is written on a blackboard and reflects the season and the mood of the chef. For either lunch or dinner, you may start with a sardine-and-Parmesan-cheese-filled pastry or perhaps a simple salad of bitter greens. You will be thankful the *entrées* are light when next you are faced with strapping dishes of leg of lamb, roast chicken with mashed potatoes, *boeuf bourguignon* with carrots and garlic confit, rabbit with mushrooms and foie gras, or wild game and venison in season. Desserts, including apple bread pudding (the house specialty) and fruit crumbles, are nostalgic reminders of childhood favorites.

TEL 01-48-78-28-80
OPEN Mon–Fri: lunch noon–2 P.M., dinner 7–11:30 P.M. **CLOSED** Sat–Sun; holidays, one week in Dec or Jan, Aug
À LA CARTE 25–30€, BNC **PRIX FIXE** None **CREDIT CARDS** MC, V
RESERVATIONS Essential **ENGLISH SPOKEN** Limited

JULIEN (4)
16, rue du Faubourg St-Denis
Métro: Strasbourg-St-Denis

Leave the shady red-light neighborhood behind as you pass through velvet curtains into this Art Deco wonderland, which encompasses one of the most beautiful brasserie dining rooms in Paris. The stunning decor is an amazing combination of magnificent stained-glass ceiling panels and Mucha-style molten glass, massive globe lights, huge floral displays, and a collection of vintage *chapeaux* hanging from brass hat racks. Even the tile floor is remarkable. The menu is a standard list of delicious brasserie favorites (without the oyster stand) accompanied by plenty of wine, good cheer, and a formally attired waitstaff serving an audience of fashionable French diners.

NOTE: A taxi is strongly advised at night.

TEL 01-47-70-12-06 **INTERNET** www.julienparis.com, www.flobrasseries.com
OPEN Daily: lunch noon–3 P.M., dinner 7 P.M.–1 A.M. **CLOSED** Never
À LA CARTE 35–45€, BNC **PRIX FIXE** Lunch & dinner: 24.50€, 2 courses, 34.50€, 3 courses, both BC; Faim de Nuit (after 10:30 P.M.): 25€, 2 courses, BNC **CREDIT CARDS** AE, DC, MC, V
RESERVATIONS Essential **ENGLISH SPOKEN** Yes

Eleventh Arrondissement

The Bastille was the site of France's most famous prison, which was over-run on July 14, 1789, marking the birth of the French Revolution. All that remains today of the Bastille is a faint outline traced in cobblestones. The latest revolution is the new Bastille opera house, which, upon completion, instantaneously turned this formerly "off-limits" *quartier* into one of the most trendy, must-go, must-see, and must-try parts of Paris. The area is a mix of back-alley workers and work-shops and hip new designers and their boutiques. Don't be surprised to see overflowing garbage cans, panhan-

RIGHT BANK
Bastille
Colonne de Juillet (July Column)
Opéra Bastille
rue de Lappe and rue Oberkampf (for nightlife)

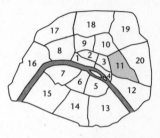

dlers, and some very seedy restaurants and bars mixed in with the hot spots. Action in the eleventh begins around 10 P.M., when it becomes a crowded, boisterous scene, with hipsters cruising the streets, restau-rants, and bars until the first rays of dawn. Unless this jam-packed, pulsating night scene appeals, it's best to avoid this area on Friday and Saturday nights.

ELEVENTH ARRONDISSEMENT RESTAURANTS

($) indicates a Big Splurge; (¢) indicates a Cheap Eat

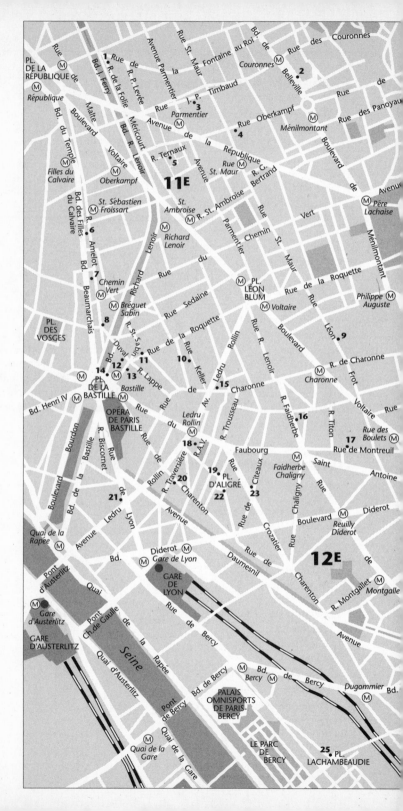

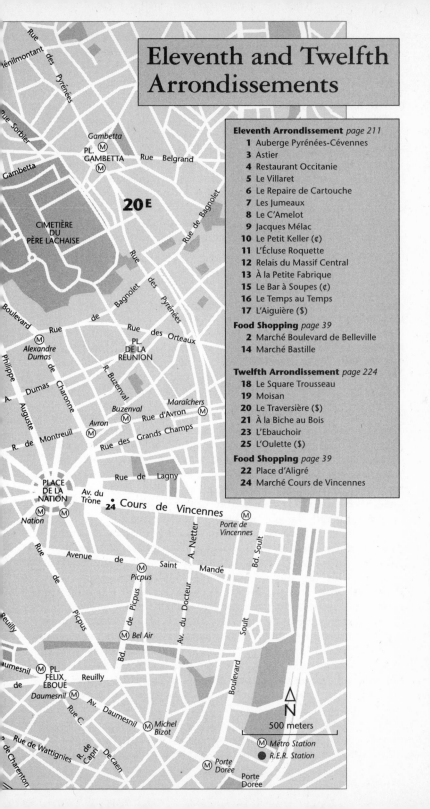

Eleventh and Twelfth Arrondissements

Métro Station
R.E.R. Station

500 meters

À LA PETITE FABRIQUE (13)
12, rue St-Sabin
Métro: Bastille

Fellow chocoholics are invited to join me at Bruno Cagnazzoli's chocolate factory, where artisanal chocolates are made with only pure ingredients: no preservatives, no vegetable fat, and no cream. Notice I did *not* say "no calories." Ranking among the top ten chocolatiers in the city, Corsican-born Cagnazzoli makes run-of-the-mill imitations look and taste like axle grease. Just one bite of his cocoa-dusted truffles, his dark chocolate—dipped orange rinds, or even a simple bar flecked with nuts will spoil you forever for anything but the best. Not only can you buy his chocolates here, but you can watch them being made in the back.

TEL 01-43-14-08-82
OPEN Tues–Sat: 10:30 A.M.–7:30 P.M. **CLOSED** Mon, Sun; 2 weeks in Aug (dates vary)
PRICES 6.10€ per 100 grams, and up **CREDIT CARDS** MC, V
ENGLISH SPOKEN Limited

ASTIER (3)
44, rue Jean-Pierre Timbaud
Métro: Parmentier

If Astier did not exist, it would have to be invented because nowhere is everything you have ever heard about Paris dining more in evidence than in this noisy, sometimes stuffy, always crowded bistro where everyone looks like a regular. The only thing to admire in the plain interior is the graceful staircase, which is almost lost behind the bar. The seating at tightly packed, smaller-than-usual tables puts you practically on your neighbor's lap, and it causes some ducking if the casually clad waiters swing the plates too low. However, if you understand even a little French, your neighbors' conversations might provide some very thought-provoking eavesdropping.

Abundance is the name of the game for the kitchen and a warning is in order: The prix-fixe meal, which is all that's available, includes four *enormous* courses that tend to grow as the meal progresses. The ten-page wine list with over three hundred bottles keeps pace. Be careful when ordering because each course could constitute an entire meal, as my dining companion found out when he ordered the plate of homemade pasta as an *entrée*. When his plate arrived, we both gasped . . . it was enough for both of us, and this was only the beginning. (In this rare case, sharing an *entrée* or a dessert is acceptable, but never a main course.) The handwritten (but legible) menu changes constantly, reflecting the seasonal changes at the market. A safe and sane beginning would be one of the salads, which should leave room to do justice to a *blanquette de porc, lapin à la moutard,* or any of the fresh fish dishes the chef loves to prepare. The cheese platter is magnificent and includes at least twenty choices. You are encouraged to help yourself to as much as you can eat. Desserts do not fall behind.

There is an impressive array of fruit and sugar creations, which are all made here except for the sorbet. Those going for the calorie jackpot will want the chocolate fudge slice floating in a coffee cream sauce. Those hoping to walk out unassisted will probably go for the fresh fruit or the warm apple gratin.

The food at Astier more than makes up for the crowded conditions, scattered service, and uninspired decor. As my friend said, "You can't eat the decor or the service, but you can certainly pay for it." At Astier, you know that all you are paying for is the food, and it is worth every euro—as well as the diet you will swear to start tomorrow.

TEL 01-43-57-16-35
OPEN Mon–Fri: lunch noon–2 P.M., dinner 8–10:15 P.M. **CLOSED** Sat–Sun; holidays, week between Christmas and New Year's, last 2 weeks April, last week July–Aug
À LA CARTE None **PRIX FIXE** Lunch: 23.50€, 3 courses, BNC; dinner: 28€, 3 courses, BNC **CREDIT CARDS** MC, V
RESERVATIONS Essential, as far in advance as possible **ENGLISH SPOKEN** Yes

AUBERGE PYRÉNÉES-CÉVENNES (1)
106, rue de la Folie Méricourt
Métro: République

For a trip to the Pyrénées without leaving the confines of Paris, book a table at this comfortable country auberge in a tourist-free zone just a five-minute walk from the République métro stop. The genuine welcome from Françoise and Danielle Constanten immediately puts you at ease and inspires confidence in the meal ahead.

And indeed, you will eat well, filling up on their generous Lyonnaise specialties, most of which are on a prix-fixe menu, so there is no need to dip into the more expensive à la carte offerings. The main courses and desserts are shamelessly generous and rich, but when tempted by tiny green beans and foie gras served on a bed of greens, *moules marinières,* or the lusty *lentilles vinaigrette,* it is hard to resist, let alone pace yourself for the good things to follow. I loved the fresh salmon and lightly sautéed leeks, which arrived in its own copper pot with a pitcher of béarnaise sauce on the side. Typical regional dishes include *côte de veau à la crème, confit de oie* (goose leg) served with a casserole of buttery *potatoes dauphinoise,* and succulent *pied de porc* with potato purée. For dessert, the best choice is the *île flottante,* which looks like a huge iceberg of meringue floating in a pool of *crème anglaise.* My friend was right when he contentedly said at the end of the meal, "Yes, this is a nice place to be in Paris." I couldn't agree more.

TEL 01-43-57-33-78
OPEN Mon–Fri: lunch noon–2:30 P.M., dinner 7:30–10 P.M.; Sat: dinner 7:30–10 P.M. **CLOSED** Sat lunch, Sun; 10 days at Christmas and New Year's; last week of July to Aug 20
À LA CARTE 38–45€, BNC **PRIX FIXE** Lunch & dinner: 27€, 3 courses, BNC **CREDIT CARDS** AE, MC, V
RESERVATIONS Essential **ENGLISH SPOKEN** Yes, and English menu

JACQUES MÉLAC (9)
42, rue Léon-Frot
Métro: Charonne

The handwritten sign hanging in this wine bar not too far from the Bastille states, *L'eau est ici reservée pour faire çuire les pommes de terre!*— "Water here is reserved for cooking potatoes!" Started by Jacques' father before World War II, Jacques Mélac is extremely popular, 100 percent authentic, and an absolute must for anyone who loves a good time and good wine. Jacques, with his handlebar mustache and infectious enthusiasm, broadcasts a message of welcome loud and clear to everyone who enters. Don't worry if your high school French is a little rusty; after raising a few glasses at the bar with the rambunctious crowd, your communication skills will improve dramatically. Go with a group or alone and you are bound to find good company, sampling wines and munching on platters of *charcuterie* or Auvergne cheeses and loaves of chewy, dark bread. Jacques also serves hot dishes and omelettes for both lunch and dinner.

The wine bar also sells its own wine by the bottle or case. The wine, Domaine des Trois Filles, is a red named for Mélac's three daughters, Marie-Hélène, Laura, and Sara. This is the only wine bar in Paris boasting its own vineyard, with the vines growing on the roof and climbing up the outside walls. In September the grapes are harvested, and usually there is enough for a single barrel of wine, which is always cause for great celebration. Celebration also ensues during the annual arrival of Beaujolais Nouveau, which all but flows in the street in late November, as do the patrons. Don't worry, however, if you miss one of these great parties, since as Jacques says, "Here we celebrate wine every day we're open."

TEL 01-43-70-59-27 **INTERNET** www.melac.fr
OPEN Tues–Sat: lunch noon–3:30 P.M., dinner 7:30 P.M.–12:30 A.M.; bar: noon–4 P.M., 7 P.M.–midnight **CLOSED** Mon, Sun; holidays, 10 days at Christmas, Aug
À LA CARTE 15–25€, BNC **PRIX FIXE** Lunch: 14.50€, 2 courses, BNC
CREDIT CARDS MC, V
RESERVATIONS Not accepted **ENGLISH SPOKEN** Usually

L'AIGUIÈRE ($, 17)
37, bis rue de Montreuil
Métro: Faidherbe-Chaligny

L'Aiguière is the type of place you only hear about from someone who knows the quiet, back residential streets in the eleventh arrondissement. Everyone I have ever taken to L'Aiguière plans to return, even if they are in Paris for only a few days. This is a strong testament to the creative skills of chef Pascal Viallet and Patrick Masbatin, the owner and sommelier, who welcomes guests in their elegant blue-and-yellow Gustavian-style dining room. The crisp linens, tablecloths, candles at night, and fresh flowers are welcoming in the small, formal dining room, which is intimate without being crowded. L'Aiguière is synonymous with fine wines, and the name refers to the vase-shaped decanter used at your table.

The food is as uncluttered and elegant as the surroundings, and the prix-fixe menus offer most of the house specialties, which makes for outstanding value. While you are sipping an apéritif and deciding what to order, a plate of assorted *amuse bouche* and a basket of the homemade bread and butter arrive at you table. The fresh chèvre fritters accompanied by a green salad and a scoop of chèvre ice cream drizzled with honey is always a favorite starter, but it is hard to resist the *escalope de foie gras de canard poêlé* served with an unusual mango chutney to spread on pieces of spiced bread. Whatever fresh fish is offered is worthy of serious consideration, especially the *coquilles St-Jacques* enhanced by a truffle *mousseline*. Beef eaters will relish the house speciality: *tournedos* of beef with a rich spinach and potato *dauphinoise*. The chef also has a magic touch with game in season, as evidenced by the brochette of baby wild boar, flavored with hints of truffle. If it is available for dessert, I would never miss the roasted honey figs circling fragrant lavender ice cream and napped with hot chocolate, but the pear wrapped in warm puff pastry and served with pear sorbet is a close second. Coffee is served with the chef's truffles and miniature *financier* and *baba au rhum,* topping off a memorable Great Eat that epitomizes what fine dining in Paris is all about.

TEL 01-43-72-42-32 **INTERNET** www.l-aiguiere.com
OPEN Mon–Fri lunch: noon–2:30 P.M., dinner 7:30–10:30 P.M.; Sat: dinner 7:30–10:30 P.M. **CLOSED** Sat lunch, Sun; Aug (dates vary)
À LA CARTE 65–75€, BNC **PRIX FIXE** Lunch & dinner: 24€, 3 courses BC (except Fri–Sat night or after 1:30 P.M. or 9:30 P.M.); 29€, 4 courses, BNC; tasting menu (served to entire table), 52€, 4 courses, BC; 62€, 4 courses & cheese, BC **CREDIT CARDS** MC, V
RESERVATIONS Essential **ENGLISH SPOKEN** Yes

LE BAR À SOUPES (¢, 15)
33, rue de Charonne
Métro: Ledru-Rollin

Soups are Anne Catherine's specialty, and she is the proud owner of this sunny yellow soup bar. Every day you can count on at least six soups, four of which change, to be ladled up with chunks of organic dark bread, either to eat here or take away. Side orders are kept to a minimum: a plate of *charcuterie* or cheese and a dessert or two. Forget all the frills: just order soup. The possibilities are mind-boggling. Some examples are *indienne aux lentilles blondes,* flavored with curry, coriander, cumin, tomatoes, onions, and raisins; celery with blue cheese; tomato cream soup topped with pieces of ricotta cheese; *portugaise au haddock,* which blends in cabbage and chorizo sausage; and pea soup flavored with smoky bacon. In the summer, several cold soups join the lineup of one of the best and healthiest Cheap Eats you will have in Paris.

NOTE: There is no smoking allowed. If you would like to make some of her soups yourself, she has written a beautifully illustrated cookbook, which is available for sale.

TEL 01-43-57-53-79 **INTERNET** www.lebarasoupes.com
OPEN Mon–Sat: lunch noon–3 P.M., dinner 6:30–11 P.M. **CLOSED** Sun; NAC
À LA CARTE 6€, soup & bread, BNC **PRIX FIXE** Lunch: 9€, soup, *charcuterie* or
cheese, dessert, BC (wine & coffee) **CREDIT CARDS** None
RESERVATIONS Not accepted **ENGLISH SPOKEN** Yes

LE C'AMELOT (8)
50, rue Amelot
Métro: Chemin Vert

By all appearances, Le C'Amelot is like dozens of other bistros dotted around the eleventh arrondissement: the long room has a bar at the entrance and mirrored banquettes on one side that reflect good, bad, and indifferent artwork hanging opposite. The jeans-clad help is stretched too thin, and the joint is usually jumping at lunch, when the hungry neighborhood packs in for the blue-plate specials. But if Le C'Amelot looks the same, the difference is the homespun philosophy that goes into the food. For lunch, you get two choices for each course, and for dinner, none . . . just like in *maman's* kitchen. What to expect? For a late fall lunch, I selected the vegetable soup (rather than the beef tongue terrine), which was brought to my table in a tureen for me to help myself. I followed with braised beef on a ragout of lentils (instead of the pork sausage with potatoes), and for dessert, pear clafoutis. At dinner, you get four courses, which includes soup *à volunté* (all you can eat) to start, a fish course, a meat course, and dessert. The menus change daily, so if you don't like what's on for today, check out tomorrow's fare.

TEL 01-43-55-54-04
OPEN Mon: dinner 7–10:30 P.M.; Tues–Fri: lunch noon–2 P.M., dinner
7–10:30 P.M.; Sat: dinner 7–10:30 P.M. **CLOSED** Mon & Sat lunch, Sun;
Aug (dates vary)
À LA CARTE None **PRIX FIXE** Lunch: 17€, 2 courses, 24€, 3 courses, both
BNC; dinner: 32€, 4 courses, BNC **CREDIT CARDS** AE, MC, V
RESERVATIONS Recommended **ENGLISH SPOKEN** Usually

L'ÉCLUSE ROQUETTE (11)
13, rue de la Roquette
Métro: Bastille

For a description of this wine bar, see L'Écluse, page 59. All other information is the same.

TEL 01-48-05-19-12

LE PETIT KELLER (¢, 10)
13 bis, rue Keller
Métro: Ledru-Rollin, Bastille

A bar of some sort has been here for at least fifty years—even the pink pig sitting on the counter has been here that long. Today it's a casual establishment, all done up in yellow and red, accented with a mix of wooden or red-and-green plastic-topped bistro tables. No gastronomic fireworks are in store, but the serviceable food is filling sustenance for the struggling artists and financially challenged students who arrive at noon and again after the sun sets. The menu is almost a giveaway, given the number of choices. They kick off with spinach salad tossed with blue cheese, *soupe du jour, terrine de campagne,* and a flan. *Fricassée de boudin noir* (blood sausage), the daily quiche, and roast chicken are just three of the five main-course possibilities. Fruit tart, chocolate cake, and rice pudding with custard sauce or seasonal fruit sum up the endings.

NOTE: While you are in the neighborhood, allow enough time to browse the up-and-coming artist and fashion boutiques that have sprouted up all over this and surrounding streets. If you are young and svelte, pay close attention to designer Anne Willi, whose star keeps rising. She is located next door.

TEL 01-47-00-12-97
OPEN Lunch: Tues–Fri noon–2:15 P.M. dinner 7:30–10:45 P.M.; Sat: dinner
7:30–10:45 P.M. **CLOSED** Sat lunch, Mon, Sun; Aug 1–15
À LA CARTE None **PRIX FIXE** Lunch: 10€, 2 courses, BNC; dinner: 15€,
2 courses, BNC **CREDIT CARDS** MC, V
RESERVATIONS Recommended on weekends **ENGLISH SPOKEN** Yes

LE REPAIRE DE CARTOUCHE (6)
8, boulevard des Filles-du-Calvaire & 99, rue Amelot
Métro: St-Sébastien-Froissart

It is not hard to have a good time dining in this richly wood-paneled, two-room restaurant, which resembles an eighteenth-century inn. The chef, Rodolph Paquin, is known for his modern approach to traditional game, which the portly locals especially enjoy in season. The handwritten menu looks more like heiroglyphics than French, but you will be able to pick out standards of *pot au feu* with foie gras and apples, terrines of *boudin noir* and *sanglier* (wild boar) with chestnuts, roast pigeon and baby turnips, rare roast duck breast with artichokes, and wild hare cooked to tender perfection. For dessert it is easy to spot the *mille-feuille* layered with whiskey-soaked chestnut cream and dark chocolate, or the smooth rice pudding with compote of figs.

NOTE: For some reason, the prix-fixe lunch selected from *l'ardoise* (the blackboard) is only served in the upstairs dining area. Downstairs, the higher prix-fixe fare is more sophisticated. For dinner, it doesn't matter where you sit because there is only à la carte.

TEL 01-47-00-25-86
OPEN Tues–Sat: lunch noon–2 P.M., dinner 7:30–11 P.M. **CLOSED** Mon, Sun;
1 week Feb, 1 week May, Aug (dates vary)

À LA CARTE Lunch & dinner 40–49€, BNC **PRIX FIXE** Lunch upstairs: 13€,
2 courses, BNC; lunch downstairs: 24€, 3 courses, BNC
  CREDIT CARDS MC, V
RESERVATIONS Essential **ENGLISH SPOKEN** Limited

LES JUMEAUX (7)
73, rue Amelot
Métro: Chemin Vert, Bréguet-Sabin

Les Jumeaux means "twins," and in this case it stands for Karl and
Erick Vandevelde, the twin brothers who own and operate this Great
Eat near place des Vosges and the Bastille. It is a good address to
remember if you are looking for an imaginative take on mainstream,
typical French dining. The contemporary room has a simple elegance,
and with the right dinner companion, the mood could be quite
romantic. The prix-fixe menus are market-based, so you never know
for sure what treats await. If you see the foie gras, served with warm
onion *galette* and a citrus confit, you are in luck. The Camembert,
rolled with cumin-seasoned beets, is as lovely to look at as it is to
eat, and the raw, marinated sardines that come with an olive tapenade
are interesting and certainly different. The roast lamb almost melts
in your mouth, as does the tender braised beef served with *gratin
dauphinois* (scalloped potatoes). The fresh *coquilles St-Jacques* (scallops)
served with a purée of peas are cooked to perfection and prove a
memorable dish for those who relish this delicacy. Karl, the chef half
of the duo, spent his formative years in the kitchen at Ledoyen. He
has an equally inspired hand with desserts, turning the most plebeian
ingredients into unexpected taste treats. Try his *financier aux amandes*
(individual rounds of rich, almond pound cake topped with a chunky
prune jam)—or anything with chocolate. While Karl is cooking, his
brother, Erick, is out front taking orders and making sure that all of
their guests are taken care of. They both do a superb job.

TEL 01-43-14-27-00
OPEN Tues–Fri: lunch noon–2:30 P.M., dinner 7:30–10:30 P.M.; Sat: dinner
7:30–10:30 P.M. **CLOSED** Sat lunch, Mon, Sun; major holidays, last 3 weeks
of Aug
À LA CARTE None **PRIX FIXE** Lunch: 20€, 2 courses, BC (coffee); lunch &
dinner: 27€, 2 courses, 33€, 3 courses, both BNC **CREDIT CARDS** MC, V
RESERVATIONS Recommended **ENGLISH SPOKEN** Yes

LE TEMPS AU TEMPS (16)
13, rue Paul Bert
Métro: Feidherbe-Chaligny

Reservations are essential at least a week in advance for one of the
six tables at this napkin-size bistro owned by chef Sylvain Sondra and
his wife, Sarah. In keeping with the name, the tiny room (including
the loo) is decorated with a collection of time pieces all telling a different time. Sylvain's consistent bistro fare reflects high quality at low
prices, and as a result, it is absolutely packed for lunch and dinner.

Upbeat, young crowds have discovered this diamond in the rough and provide a pleasing, buzzy atmosphere.

The blackboard menu in early spring listed asparagus soup spooned over meaty chunks of veal tongue and dotted with fresh green peas or carpaccio of *coquilles St-Jacques* with a ginger-flavored mango sauce, both inventive starters that everyone raved over. One of the best *plats,* anytime, is the mahogany-crusted pork ribs garnished with fresh asparagus and whipped potatoes. Even committed non–pork eaters lapped this one up. For dessert, the strawberry meringue was light and flavorful, and reasonably guilt-free. Not so the chocolate crumble with white chocolate ice cream and dark chocolate foam, whose calorie count could pass for a zip code. For lunch Tuesday through Friday, the prix-fixe menus offer no choices; on Saturday lunch is entirely à la carte. For dinner, there are more selections for the prix-fixe menu as well as à la carte.

TEL 01-43-79-63-40
OPEN Tues–Sat: lunch noon–2 P.M., dinner 8–10:30 P.M. **CLOSED** Mon, Sun; 1 week Christmas, Aug
À LA CARTE 35€, BNC **PRIX FIXE** Lunch: 11€, 1 course, BC (wine or coffee); 13€, 2 courses, 16€, 3 courses, both BNC; dinner: 27€, 3 courses, BNC
    CREDIT CARDS MC, V
RESERVATIONS Essential, at least a week ahead **ENGLISH SPOKEN** Yes

LE VILLARET (5)
13, rue Ternaux
Métro: Parmentier

Le Villaret is another Great Eat that, once found, is never forgotten. The somber inside is dark and plain, but that does not deter the lively French who come often and stay late. The menu is a roll call of dishes that neighborhood Parisian bistros have been serving for years, yet mixed in here and there are contemporary touches that show off the chef's talent. You will start out with an *amuse bouche,* maybe a thimble of mushroom soup with a frothy cappuccino topping or a tidbit of foie gras spread on toast. A memorable starter is sliced house smoked salmon on a bed of tiny new potatoes with a lettuce cream sauce dotted with herring caviar. In season, the white asparagus, perfectly steamed with a sharp vinaigrette drizzled on top, is also a great way to begin the meal. Many times French beef, because it is so lean, is miserably tough. Not here: the beef fillet served with shallots and Jerusalem artichokes *à la dauphinoise* melts in your mouth. If two of you can agree, the rosemary-seasoned leg of lamb, cooked until just pink and served with baby spring vegetables, is a satisfying choice. For those looking to add to their collection of unusual dishes, try *la terrine d'abats de pigeons* (pigeon ofal), which can be tempered by ordering the thyme-roasted pigeon, served with wide green beans and smoked bacon. With the exception of the ginger-scented chocolate fondant slices topped with lime-mango sorbet, desserts do not quite measure up to the first two courses; thus, for some, cheese will make a better last course.

NOTE: If you love truffles, try to come in January or February, when the restaurant serves a five-course truffle menu (80€, BNC).

TEL 01-43-57-75-56
OPEN Mon–Fri: lunch noon–2 P.M., dinner 7:30–11:30 P.M.; Sat: dinner
  7:30–11:30 P.M. **CLOSED** Sat lunch, Sun; 2 weeks at Christmas; Aug
À LA CARTE 45–50€ **PRIX FIXE** Lunch: 21€, 2 courses, 26€, 3 courses, both
  BNC **CREDIT CARDS** AE, MC, V
RESERVATIONS Essential **ENGLISH SPOKEN** Enough

RELAIS DU MASSIF CENTRAL (12)
16, rue Daval
Métro: Bastille

Where do the neighborhood workers and local inhabitants go for a hearty feed and inexpensive wines? They head to Carolina Coutinho's Relais du Massif Central, where the emphasis is on nutritionally incorrect, rib-sticking fare that would make defenders of moderation swoon. Arrive early if you want to nab one of the four best tables (by the window), stick with the handwritten daily specials (rather than plowing through the thick menu), and forget about à la carte.

Typical of the kitchen are such starters as hot smoked sausage with potatoes, onion and bacon *tarte* with a small salad, *chèvre chaud* on toast, or slices of Auvergne ham. Main courses feature steak fixed several ways, all with *frites,* tripes with *aligot,* duck preserved and cooked in its own fat, or *boeuf bourguignon* with noodles. You can be fiscally conservative with the three-course *menu du jour,* add a *pichet* of house wine, and still be out the door for under 20€ and change. Those on even slimmer budgets will appreciate the daily specials, sold at lunch for a mere 10€. Service is honest and kind, and if you need help with the menu, there is usually someone there with enough "menu English" to help.

TEL 01-47-00-46-55
OPEN Mon–Sat: lunch noon–3 P.M., dinner 7:30 P.M.–1 A.M. **CLOSED** Sun; Aug
À LA CARTE 28–35€, BNC **PRIX FIXE** Lunch & dinner (from daily specials):
  9.70€, daily *plat,* 10.20€, 2 courses, 22€, 3 courses, all BNC
  CREDIT CARDS AE, MC, V
RESERVATIONS Not necessary **ENGLISH SPOKEN** Enough to order; also
  Portuguese, Spanish, German

RESTAURANT OCCITANIE (4)
96, rue Oberkampf
Métro: St-Maur, Parmentier

By 12:30 P.M., there is not a vacant chair at Bernard Bouichet's rustic Occitanie. Home cooking without pretense describes the style of the food. Homemade confits, *magrets, cassoulets,* Toulouse sausages, and most of the desserts are created right here in the busy kitchen. The faithful don't worry about consulting the blackboard menu for lunch, scrawled by someone who did not win awards in penmanship—they know to order either of the two stellar bargain lunches, both of which include a salad, main course, and dessert; the lowest priced of the two even tosses in the wine. Try to order this meal in a more tourist-heavy part of Paris and you would pay at least double. Other great deals include huge salads, wooden platters heaped with steak, ground beef, chicken, sausage, or ham and served with a salad, a side of fries, and *fromage blanc*; the go-for-broke 26.50€ meal includes calorie-laden choices of foie gras, *cassoulet, magret de canard,* a cheese, and a choice of dessert to wind it up. There is an à la carte menu, but with the assortment of prix-fixe bargains, who's looking?

TEL 01-48-06-46-98

OPEN Mon–Fri: lunch noon–2 P.M., dinner 7:30–10:30 P.M.; Sat: dinner 7:30–10:30 P.M. **CLOSED** Sat lunch, Sun; holidays, Aug

À LA CARTE 25–35€, BNC **PRIX FIXE** Lunch: 9.50€, 3 courses, BC; 12€, 3 courses, BNC; dinner: 12€, 3 courses, 16.80€ & 26.50€, both 4 courses, all BNC **CREDIT CARDS** MC, V

RESERVATIONS Essential for lunch **ENGLISH SPOKEN** Yes, and à la carte menu in English

Twelfth Arrondissement

RIGHT BANK
Bercy Village
Bois de Vincennes
Le Parc de Bercy
Musée des Arts d'Afrique et
  d'Océanie
place d'Aligré
Viaduc des Arts

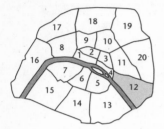

In the past, visitors seldom ventured into the untamed corners of the twelfth, which is situated between the Bastille and Gare de Lyon. A renaissance has taken place, and it is now very *au courant*. The grubby furniture makers have moved on, and people are now discovering its interesting hidden *passages* and courtyards, shopping at the multiethnic street market at place d'Aligré, and filling the new wave of restaurants. The Viaduc des Arts, in a long section of abandoned railway, has had its arched space turned into artist workshops, boutiques, and restaurants. The Promenade Plantée, a walkway with benches, flowers, and a view to the area's characteristic flat-fronted buildings, flows along the top.

TWELFTH ARRONDISSEMENT RESTAURANTS
(see map page 212)

($) indicates a Big Splurge

À LA BICHE AU BOIS (21)
45, avenue Ledru-Rollin, corner rue de Lyon
Métro: Gare de Lyon

À la Biche au Bois remains one of my all-purpose standbys whenever I want to show a first-time visitor what an untouristy meal in Paris is all about. Inside there are about seventy *couverts* (place settings) crowded into a room full of mirrors, starched linens, and contented diners enjoying full-dress fare at medium-range prices. The outdoor terrace is nice if you are here in the evening, when the symphony of squealing tires and screeching brakes calms down.

Go with a big appetite and you will leave with it satisfied. The menu lists a stampede of meats and features fish on Tuesday and Friday, *coq au vin* anytime, and wild game in season. From start to finish everything is good, reliable, well served, and enjoyable. The prix-fixe four-course menu is a virtual steal and includes all the favorite dishes. Wines are well priced.

TEL 01-43-43-34-38
OPEN Mon: dinner 7–11 P.M.; Tues–Fri: lunch noon–2:30 P.M., dinner 7:30–11 P.M. **CLOSED** Mon lunch, Sat–Sun; Dec 23–Jan 2, July 25–Aug 25
À LA CARTE 25–35€, BNC **PRIX FIXE** Lunch & dinner: 23.20€, 4 courses, BNC **CREDIT CARDS** AE, DC, MC, V
RESERVATIONS Essential **ENGLISH SPOKEN** Yes

L'EBAUCHOIR (23)
45, rue de Citeaux
Métro: Faidherbe-Chaligny, Reuilly-Diderot

Lunch is the serious cheap eat at L'Ebauchoir. The cafeteria-like room with wooden tables and chairs is devoid of decor unless you count the messy bookcase by the door or the handful of flowers in a vase on the bar. There are two lunch menus, the cheaper of which is a good deal if you don't mind that your limited selection won't exceed plebian dishes like *oeufs dur mayonnaise, céleri rémoulade,* and two meats, one of which is often offal. For 10€ more, the repertoire expands to one or two terrines, leeks vinaigrette with bacon, *entrecôte,* and fresh fish. The star house dessert, *gâteau de ris* (rice pudding), is part of both packages. At dinner, only à la carte is available, making this a cut-rate eat *only* for lunch—since almost all the same food is served at dinner but at double the lunch prices! The owner's family has a winery in the Loire Valley, so you will have a good choice of these popular wines, which you can buy by the glass, *pichet,* or bottle. Whatever is left in your bottle, you can take with you.

TEL 01-43-42-49-31
OPEN Mon: dinner 8–11 P.M.; Tues–Sat: lunch noon–2:30 P.M., dinner 8–11 P.M. **CLOSED** Mon lunch, Sun; lunch on most holidays, NAC
À LA CARTE 25–35€, BNC **PRIX FIXE** lunch (Tues–Fri): 13.50€, 3 courses, BC; lunch (Tues–Sat): 23€, 3 courses, BNC **CREDIT CARDS** MC, V
RESERVATIONS Not necessary **ENGLISH SPOKEN** Yes

LE SQUARE TROUSSEAU (18)
1, rue Antoine Vollon
Métro: Ledru-Rollin

The appealingly energetic atmosphere surrounding the Bastille carries right to Le Square Trousseau, where the smart ambience possesses all the bustle you expect in a popular Belle Epoque bistro. Overlooking the leafy Square Trousseau, it has become the *rendez-vous-obligé* for a distinctly chic Parisian crowd who want to forget nouvelle cuisine, chichi settings, tiny portions, snooty maître d's, and overbearing waiters. One glance around the two ocher-colored rooms and the attractive sidewalk terrace, both of which are filled night and day, and you know this is a happening place.

The commitment to quality is evident in the well-thought-out menu, which carries the season's freshest offerings. The à la carte menu changes monthly, and the Monday-to-Saturday prix-fixe lunch blackboard menus are new every day. The solid dishes on both are generous yet proportioned sensibly, allowing you to sample a full set of courses. You might start with a springtime *entrée* of asparagus lightly dressed in an olive oil and basil sauce, fresh artichoke hearts and mushrooms with coriander-spiked tomatoes, or the warming cauliflower soup topped with golden croutons and chervil. If you like fish, try any of the daily suggestions and hope one of them is the fresh perch served with fresh spinach. Meat eaters will be happy with the rabbit and black olives on a bed of zucchini and pasta or the thin slices of roasted duck. Equally tempting desserts include lightly cooked, Calvados-infused apples on a crisp crust or an almost fudgelike chocolate *pôt de crème*. If this isn't enough, you will be served sinfully rich bite-size brownies with your strong after-dinner espresso.

NOTE: For a more casual meal, try their *épicerie* next door (**TEL** 01-43-43-65-91; **OPEN** Tues–Sat: 9 A.M.–2:30 P.M., 6–9 P.M.). In addition to selling the house foie gras, smoked salmon, excellent wines, and other quality products from small producers throughout France, there is a *table d'hôte* at lunch (noon–2 P.M.; à la carte 10–17€) and takeout available in the evening. The choices are limited to three hot dishes and plates of cheese or *charcuterie* served with wines from their own *cave*.

TEL 01-43-43-06-00
OPEN Tues–Sat: lunch noon–2:30 P.M., dinner 8–11:30 P.M. **CLOSED** Mon, Sun; Dec 22–Jan 6
À LA CARTE 40–50€, BNC **PRIX FIXE** Lunch (Tues–Sat): 12€, 1 course, 16€, 2 courses, 20€, 3 courses, all BNC **CREDIT CARDS** AE, MC, V
RESERVATIONS Essential **ENGLISH SPOKEN** Yes

LE TRAVERSIÈRE ($, 20)
40, rue Traversière, angle 72, rue de Charenton
Métro: Ledru-Rollin, Bastille

Johny Bénariac is both the owner and the *chef de cuisine* at Le Traversière, which is the kind of place you hope will be a block or two from where you are staying. Unfortunately for most, it is farther than that, but it is absolutely worth the trip. The timbered and stone-walled interior reminds me of a cozy country *auberge* miles from Paris. It is properly arranged with well-spaced linen-covered tables and continually draws a crowd of faithful diners with its emphasis on game in winter, wonderful fresh fish, and a seasonal prix-fixe menu that always maintains its high quality and excellent value.

You might begin with the herb salad mixed with smoked duck and foie gras, wild boar pâté (in season), chestnut or lentil soup with pieces of creamy duck foie gras, or *le feuilleté d'escargot aux pleurottes,* which is an interesting mixture of snails and oyster mushrooms in a very light pastry. The filet mignon with wild mushrooms is a wonderful choice, as is the seasonally available rich venison stew and the *sole meunière. Ris de veau* is not an American favorite, but if you have never had sweetbreads, you can sample this French delicacy here in its best form. Because desserts are as special as you always hope for, you must have one of the artistic creations starring fresh fruit—perhaps a gratin of clementines or a pear poached in red wine—or the foamy white chocolate mousse surrounded by dark chocolate sauce. After sipping a coffee and perhaps a *digestif,* you will agree that this is the perfect place to relax throughout a lovely meal with a bottle of well-priced wine.

TEL 01-43-44-02-10
OPEN Tues–Sat: lunch noon–2:30 P.M., dinner 7:30–10:30 P.M.; Sun: lunch noon–2:30 P.M. **CLOSED** Sun dinner, Mon; holidays, 3 weeks in Aug
À LA CARTE 50–55€, BNC **PRIX FIXE** Lunch: 19€, 2 courses, 22€, 3 courses, both BNC; lunch & dinner: 29€, 39.50€, both 3 courses & BNC
CREDIT CARDS AE, DC, MC, V
RESERVATIONS Recommended **ENGLISH SPOKEN** Yes, and English menu

L'OULETTE ($, 25)
15, place Lachambeaudie
Métro: Cour St-Émilion

"Being here makes you feel you really know something about Paris," mused my friend as we sat on the outside terrace of this superb restaurant on one balmy summer evening.

For a memorable place to celebrate a special occasion or just being with a special person in Paris, L'Oulette is one of my top recommendations. From the standpoint of cuisine, service, and ambience, it is almost unbeatable . . . especially if you choose the exceptionally good-value lunch or dinner *menu de saison,* which must be ordered by the entire table. It not only includes a cheese course but a very good bottle of wine.

A few years ago, Chef Marcel Baudis and his wife, Marie-Noëlle, opened a little bistro near place des Vosges—Baracane–Bistrot de l'Oulette (see page 91) featuring dishes from Baudis's native Montauban in southwestern France. It was soon discovered by *tout le monde* and became the talk of the town. Now they have turned the day-to-day operations of the bistro over to a young and efficient team and have moved to the Bercy district in the twelfth arrondissement. This less-central location has definitely not deterred savvy French diners. Neither has Baudis lost his inspired touch in the kitchen. Reservations as far in advance as possible are absolutely essential for both lunch and dinner.

L'Oulette combines understated elegance in a large room with banquette seating and floor-to-ceiling windows overlooking an umbrella-shaded dining terrace. Pots of jam and preserved fruits are whimsically arranged along with dried flowers, creating a south-western feel that is further enhanced by sunny yellow linens and geometric-patterned fabrics.

While the interior is modern and lean, the dazzling food is any-thing but. Chef Baudis spends hours preparing his seasonally inspired and meticulously arranged dishes, which are politely presented by a staff of knowledgeable, formally clad waiters. Meals like this cannot be rushed, so plan an evening of sitting back, enjoying a good bottle of wine, and savoring the truly outstanding food. Expect delicate per-fection from the chef's talented hands: the innovative dishes include *mousse de crabe, salade aux poivrons confits, feuilleté aux olives* (flaky pastry layered with crab mouse and pepper confit) or a fricassée of escargots made with wild mushrooms. Old favorites have not been cast aside. The *escabèche de calamars*—squid cooked in olive oil and spices and served with warm potatoes—is still one of the most popular spring *entrées*. In the summer, miracles are performed with fresh fish. Making dining decisions even more difficult are the wonderful lamb dishes, such as leg of lamb seasoned with garlic and rosemary, and an inno-vative adaptation of oxtail stew, *queue de boeuf braisée*—slowly cooked beef tail with green cabbage and foie gras. All dishes are served with an assortment of fresh vegetables.

Any dessert is bound to be as impressive as the rest of the meal, especially the *tarte fin aux poires caramélisée, sorbet poire* (a thin, flaky crust with caramelized pears and a scoop of homemade sorbet melting on top) or the *gâteau au chocolat aux noisettes grillées* (a rich chocolate cake with a fudgy interior, dressed with a scattering of toasted nuts). There is really nothing more to say, except that if you love and appre-ciate fine dining, contact L'Oulette for reservations the minute you know when you will be in Paris. This is especially true if you will be celebrating the New Year in Paris. Their special New Year's Eve menu is booked months in advance by regular patrons who close out the year with a fabulous multicourse gourmet meal accompanied by champagne and fine wines (costing around 150€ per person).

NOTE: The newest métro line 14 (stop: Cour St-Émilion) has made getting to L'Oulette much easier. It is also very near Bercy Village, a newly developed shopping and entertainment mall, and Le Parc de Bercy, both cornerstones in the renewal of this area of eastern Paris.

TEL 01-40-02-02-12 **INTERNET** www.l-oulette.com
OPEN Mon–Fri: lunch noon–2:15 P.M., dinner 7:45–10:15 P.M.
    CLOSED Sat–Sun; Christmas Eve & Day, New Year's Day, most other
    holidays (call to check), NAC
À LA CARTE 50–60€, BNC **PRIX FIXE** Lunch: 25€, 2 courses, 32€, 3 courses,
    both BNC; lunch & dinner: *menu de saison,* 47€, 4 courses, BC; *menu des*
    gastronomes, 82€, 5 courses, BC (both menus must be ordered by entire
    table) **CREDIT CARDS** AE, DC, MC, V
RESERVATIONS Absolutely essential, as far in advance as possible
    ENGLISH SPOKEN Yes

MOISAN (19)
5, place d'Aligre
Métro: Ledru-Rollin

    Breads and pastries from Moisan are all made by hand from certified natural ingredients. The bakers can't make the fat loaves fast enough for the lines that perpetually snake out the door and down the street, especially on Sunday morning when the Marché d'Aligré is in full swing. This is a market some people absolutely love because of its raucous ethnic character, its reasonable (and at times questionable) products, and the flea market at one end. Others positively hate it for the same reasons. No one disagrees about Moisan . . . it's fabulous. There is another Moisan bakery in the seventeenth at 74, rue des Lévis; others locations are inconvenient for most visitors.

TEL 01-43-45-46-60
OPEN Tues–Sat: 7 A.M.–8 P.M., Sun: 7 A.M.–2 P.M. **CLOSED** Mon; NAC
PRICES From 1.50€ up **CREDIT CARDS** None
ENGLISH SPOKEN Yes

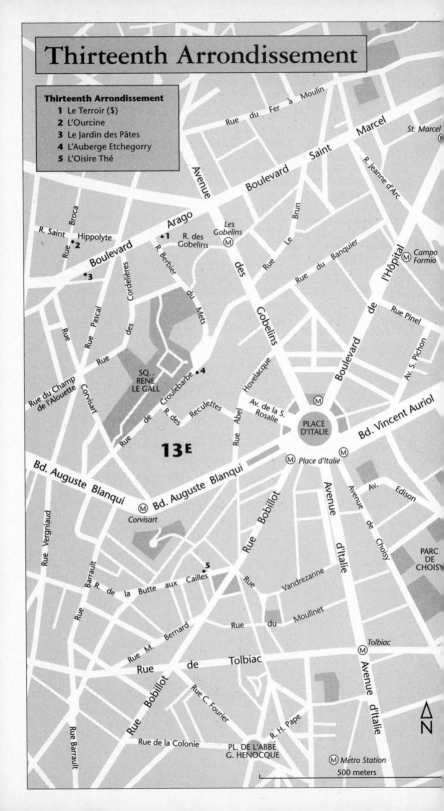

Thirteenth Arrondissement

Thirteenth Arrondissement
1 Le Terroir ($)
2 L'Ourcine
3 Le Jardin des Pâtes
4 L'Auberge Etchegorry
5 L'Oisire Thé

Rue du Fer à Moulin

Boulevard Saint Marcel

St. Marcel

Avenue

Arago

R. Saint

Broca

Hippolyte

Boulevard

Les Gobelins

• 1 R. des Gobelins

R. Jeanne d'Arc

Le Brun

Rue

Campo Formio

• 2

R. Berbier

Rue du Banquier

Rue

des

Cordelieres

du Mets

de

Rue Pinel

• 3

Rue

Pascal

des

Gobelins

l'Hôpital

Rue du Champ de l'Alouette

Corvisart

Rue

SQ. RENE LE GALL

de Croulebarbe

R. des Reculettes

• 4

Hovelacque

Boulevard

Av. S. Pichon

13E

Rue Abel

Av. de la S. Rosalie

PLACE D'ITALIE

Bd. Vincent Auriol

Bd. Auguste Blanqui

Bd. Auguste Blanqui

Place d'Italie

Av.

Edison

Corvisart

Rue Bobillot

Avenue

Avenue de Choisy

PARC DE CHOISY

Rue Vergniaud

R. de la Butte aux Cailles

• 5

Rue

Vandrezanne

d'Italie

Rue Barrault

Rue

du

Moulinet

Rue M. Bernard

Rue

de

Tolbiac

Tolbiac

Rue Bobillot

Rue C. Fourier

R. H. Pape

Rue de la Colonie

PL. DE L'ABBÉ G. HENOCQUE

Avenue d'Italie

Ⓜ Métro Station

500 meters

N

Thirteenth Arrondissement

The thirteenth is slowly becoming more interesting from a visitor's standpoint. One side is still lined with railroad yards and tracks in what seems to be a no-man's-land, and Chinatown occupies the southern part. A perennial bright spot is the area called Butte-aux-Cailles, a pocket of neighborhood charm where the clock stopped ticking fifty years ago. A new star in the arrondissement is the realization of François Mitterand's dream, the Bibliothèque Nationale, which sits proudly along the Quai de la Gare and attracts eight thousand workers and visitors per day.

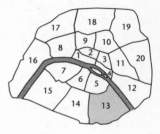

($) indicates a Big Splurge

L'AUBERGE ETCHEGORRY (4)
41, rue Croulebarbe
Métro: Les Gobelins, Corvisart

Remember how we used to eat before we became obsessed with fitness and diet regimes, and before the AMA began publishing their finger-wagging calorie, carb, and cholesterol-reducing food guidelines? Well, the food at this bastion of Basque cuisine turns back the clock to that innocent, long-ago day with its earthy regional dishes all flowing with delicious buttery fat. Despite the fact that it is two blocks past Mars for most Paris visitors, this restaurant is in a pretty neighborhood across the street from a lovely green park where *mamans* take their children to play and sweet old couples walk their dogs.

The restaurant resembles a regional country inn, loaded with charm and filled with a sense of happy camaraderie. It is the type of place where sturdy Frenchpeople go when they want to indulge in soul-warming comfort food. It is clearly a popular destination—every time I have been it has been full, while the dreary place next door stands almost empty. The interior is as robust as the food, with hanging hams and sausages, braids of garlic and onions, and a time-warped collection of knickknacks, indicating that nothing has changed, or will, for decades.

Order from one of the generous prix-fixe menus, and remember to pace yourself—you will need plenty of room to do justice to the meat-inspired *entrées* and main courses, which please carnivores to no end. Accompany your feast with plenty of red wine and finish it all off with a slice of *le gâteau Basque* for a culinary journey back to a time when we ate with abandon.

NOTE: The owners, M. and Mme. Laborde, also run a very nice three-star hotel, Le Vert Galant, next door. For a description, see *Great Sleeps Paris.*

TEL 01-44-08-83-51
OPEN Tues–Sat: lunch noon–2:30 P.M., dinner 7:30–10:30 P.M. **CLOSED** Mon, Sun; Dec 24 dinner, Christmas, 15 days mid-Aug (dates vary)
À LA CARTE 38–45€, BNC **PRIX FIXE** Lunch & dinner: 26€, 4 courses, BNC; 32.50€, 4 courses, BNC; 37.60, 4 courses, BC; *menu dégustation* (entire table must order), 55€, 4 courses, BC (apéritif, wine & coffee)
  CREDIT CARDS AE, DC, MC, V
RESERVATIONS Recommended **ENGLISH SPOKEN** Yes

LE JARDIN DES PÂTES (3)
33, boulevard Arago
Métro: Les Gobelins

For a description of this restaurant specializing in organic pasta, see page 121. All other information is the same.

TEL 01-45-35-93-67
OPEN Daily

LE TERROIR ($, 1)
11, boulevard Arago
Métro: Les Gobelins

If you are looking for a hearty Parisian crowd who value good food—and plenty of it—you will be happy at Le Terroir, where the deliciously meaty food celebrates the time-honored French favorites. For a rousing start to the meal, big bowls of herring or mackerel are brought to the table from which you can help yourself. Foie gras on a mound of crisp green beans and spears of white spring asparagus are just two of the *entrée* possibilities. Then let your belt out a notch or two to get ready for the house *magret de canard* or rich *boeuf bourguignon*. Desserts are not the order of the day here, but you probably won't mind after polishing off the last bite of *tête de veau, saucisse aux lentilles, fricassée de volaille, blanquette de veau,* or *steak au poivre.* However, a bowl of ripe red strawberries or the fruit *tarte* of the day do put a nice ending on this authentic bistro meal. Please remember to book ahead . . . the locals always do.

TEL 01-47-07-36-99
OPEN Mon–Fri: lunch noon–2:15 P.M., dinner 7:45–10:15 P.M.
CLOSED Sat–Sun; holidays, Dec 23–Jan 5, Aug
À LA CARTE 40–55€, BNC **PRIX FIXE** None **CREDIT CARDS** MC, V
RESERVATIONS Recommended **ENGLISH SPOKEN** Some

L'OISIRE THÉ (5)
1, rue Jean-Marie Jego
Métro: Corvisart

La Butte-aux-Cailles is a picturesque dot on the map of Paris where the old and bohemian-funky mix happily alongside the new and fashionably chic—and this applies to the houses, the people who live in them, and the food they eat. One place that stands out from the crowd is this warm and fuzzy little corner tearoom. Nothing matches . . . not the eight tables, the eighteen chairs, or the Thai cloths that cover them. The owners get the award for the most ingenious use of fruit crates, which they have stained brown and made into an *étagère* on which they display their international collection of teapots, all of which are for sale. As eclectic as their surroundings, the patrons range from ladies having a gossipy lunch and couples trading romantic secrets to new *mamans* sharing baby tips. Everyone seems to know each other, but visitors are always made to feel welcome. Thirty-three types of teas are poured, and glorious fruit tarts and pastries inspire a disregard for calorie counting. Soups, savory tarts, and salads dominate the lunch fare. Brunch includes toast with homemade jam, two eggs, puff pastry with either chèvre, salmon, or chicken, plus orange juice, a milk shake (vanilla, chocolate, or banana) and a choice of hot drink, and it is served every day until 6 P.M.

TEL 01-53-80-31-33
OPEN Tues–Sun: noon–8 P.M., continuous service **CLOSED** Mon; holidays, week between Christmas and New Year's, last week March (dates vary), Aug 1–22

À LA CARTE 10–20€, BC **PRIX FIXE** Brunch (noon–6 P.M.): 18€, BC
  CREDIT CARDS MC, V
RESERVATIONS Not necessary **ENGLISH SPOKEN** Yes

L'OURCINE (2)
92, rue Broca
Métro: Gobelins

You must reserve way ahead to sample Sylvain Danière's creative bistro cooking in this off-beat location in the thirteenth. The best way to get to the restaurant is to walk along boulevard Arago to rue Broca. If you take the other way (from boulevard de Port Royal), you will find yourself walking through a pedestrian underpass populated by *clochards* (homeless). Once here, please do not be put off by the nondescript exterior or the unassuming interior. As soon as the tables fill, the place takes on a life of its own, as the wine flows right along with the outstanding food, creating a happy, convivial atmosphere.

The cooking is unbeatable, and everyone who has eaten here agrees. And who wouldn't when you are served generous portions of foie gras, a winter-warming *pot au feu,* and *quenelles de chocolate* for dessert? Interesting wines are sold by the glass, service is friendly, and the bill not a shock, which in my book adds up to a Great Eat in Paris.

TEL 01-47-07-13-65
OPEN Tues–Sat: lunch noon–2 P.M., dinner 7:30–10:30 P.M. **CLOSED** Mon, Sun;
  major holidays, Aug
À LA CARTE None **PRIX FIXE** Lunch (Tues–Fri): 21€, 2 courses, BNC; lunch
  (Sat & holidays) & dinner (Tues–Sat): 29€, 3 courses, BNC
  CREDIT CARDS MC, V
RESERVATIONS Essential **ENGLISH SPOKEN** Yes

Fourteenth Arrondissement

This artistic haven of the 1920s and 1930s is now modernized and for the most part ugly, the unfortunate victim of urban development. The famous cafés—La Coupole, Le Select, Le Dôme, and La Rotunde—were the center of literary and artistic life in Paris between the two World Wars. They are still here, but they lack the soul of their collective past. The area was also home to dancer Isadora Duncan, and singer Edith Piaf performed often at the Bobino Music Hall. Also here are Les Catacombes, displaying the bones of six million Parisians.

LEFT BANK
Les Catacombes
Montparnasse

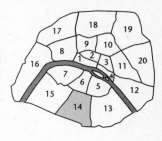

Fourteenth and Fifteenth Arrondissements

Champ de Mars
Tour Eiffel

Rue de la Fédération

Ⓜ Bir Hakeim

Seine

Av. du Président Kennedy

Pont de B. Hakeim

Boulevard

Rue du D. Finlay • 2

1

Charles

Rue du

Quai de Grenelle

Pont de Grenelle

L'Ing. R. K.

Quai André Citroën

Ⓜ Javel-André Citroën

Avenue Émile Zola

Av. de Suffren

Av. de la R. du Laos

ÉCOLE MILITAIRE

Av. de Saxe

Av. de Suffren

PL. VAUBAN

Av. Duquesne

Av. de Villars

Av. de Breteuil

PL. DE BRETEUIL

R. Bouchut

Ⓜ Ségur • 6

Bd. Garibaldi

Sèvres Lecourbe Bd.

de Grenelle

Ⓜ Dupleix

3 G. Larm.

• 4

Ⓜ 5

PL. CAMBRONNE

La Motte Piquet Grenelle

Rue du Théâtre

Rue Saint

R. Letellier

7

R. Frémicourt

Cambronne

Rue Cambronne

Rue de

Avenue Émile

8 •Émile

Zola

Avenue Émile Zola

R. du Commerce

Fondary

Avenue Émile Zola

Charles Michels

Ⓜ

Rue des

Commerce

9

15E

Rue Lecourbe

Rue de Vaugirard

Volontaires Ⓜ Volontaires

Ⓜ Commerce

• 10

11

• 12

Entrepreneurs

PL. PERNET

Félix Faure Ⓜ

R. de l'Église

R. de la Convention

Mademoiselle

R. Blomet

R. Borr.

Rue de

R. P. Barruel

Rue Dutot

Rue Blomet

de G. Beuret

Vaugirard

Ⓜ Vaugirard

PARC ANDRÉ CITROËN

Rue Cauchy

Balard

Rue Saint Charles

Faure

13

R. Lourmel

Ⓜ Boucicaut

14 • Duranton

Rue de la Convention

de l'Abbé

Rue Grout

Rue de la Convention

Ⓜ Convention

Rue de Vouillé

de Félix

15 Ⓜ Lourmel

16

Avenue R.

Vasco

Rue Lecourbe

de Gama

Rue de Vaugirard

Rue de Danzig

17 •

Rue

Bd. du Gal. M. Valin

Ⓜ Balard

Leblanc

Bd.

Victor

PL. DE LA PORTE DE VERSAILLES

PARC GEORGES BRASSENS

Porte de Sèvres

Av. Pt. de Sèvres

R. Pt. d'Issy

Porte de Versailles

Rue E. Renan

N

Ⓜ Métro Station

● R.E.R. Station

500 meters

Bd. Gambetta Ⓜ Corentin Celton

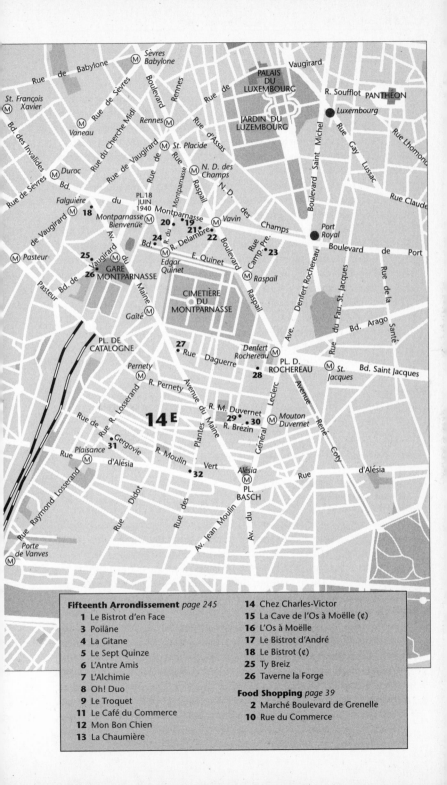

AQUARIUS (31)
40, rue de Gergovie
Métro: Pernety, Plaisance

The politically and nutritionally aware patrons at Aquarius love the all-vegetarian food, which is served on oversize white plates in three small rooms displaying local art work. In one room, there is also a shelf littered with yoga flyers, assorted announcements about New Age meetings and classes, and other notices about alternative lifestyles.

The popular, but rather odd, nut roast is served with sautéed potatoes and vegetables and covered in a mushroom wine sauce flavored with blackcurrant jelly. There is also vegetarian chili, lasagna, and a puff pastry, which is loaded with *pleurottes* (mushrooms), butter, and loads of garlic and comes with a side of two veggies. Other healthy options are the big salads, *tartiflette* (potatoes grilled with soy ham and Reblochon cheese), and the *plat du jour,* all served with homemade bread. Saints can always order the steamed vegetable plate and skip dessert; sinners will enjoy the chocolate cake. Thirst-quenching juices, teas, *biologique* wines, and designer mineral water complete the menu. Admittedly, you must have a certain mind-set to eat here, but if you do, you will be filled with well-executed, wholesome food that won't give you or your budget heartburn.

NOTE: There is no smoking allowed at lunch.

TEL 01-45-41-36-88
OPEN Mon–Sat: lunch noon–2:30 P.M., dinner 7–10:30 P.M. **CLOSED** Sun; Christmas through New Year's, NAC
À LA CARTE 15–20€, BNC **PRIX FIXE** Lunch (Mon–Fri): 11€, 2 courses, BNC; dinner (Mon–Fri): 15€, 2 courses, BNC **CREDIT CARDS** AE, MC, V
RESERVATIONS Not necessary **ENGLISH SPOKEN** Yes

AUBERGE DE VENISE (21)
10, rue Delambre
Métro: Vavin

Buon appetito and welcome to Auberge de Venise, a taste of *bella Italia* in Paris. The restaurant has been in business almost since time began, and it has served such luminaries as Hemingway, Fitzgerald, and Picasso during their heydays in Paris. Today, it continues to fill to capacity with confirmed regulars, who come back not only for the outstanding food but for the comfortable, homey atmosphere and old-fashioned service.

There is a limited-choice prix-fixe menu, but if you love Italian food, treat yourself and order à la carte—some of these wonderful dishes are in many ways better than most you will have in Italy. Any one of the beef carpaccios makes a nice starter, and so does the simply dressed tomato and mozzarella salad. It is easy to get carried away and make a meal of the *entrée,* with several pieces of bread and a good Chianti, but save yourself: there is lots more to come. A rich *tagliatelle al salmone* is a filling main dish, as is the ravioli with either basil or mushrooms. The cream *tortelloni ai 4 fromaggi* won't fit into any diet plan yet devised, but just this once won't kill you. The pastas are not garnished, so if you are feeling really hungry, consider an order of green beans liberally tossed with garlic and sautéed in olive oil. Meat eaters will be pleased with the list of veal dishes; try one prepared with either lemon, Marsala wine, and tomato sauce or the osso buco.

When it comes time for dessert, give yourself a few moments of rest and then order the best tiramisu you will find in Paris. Or, if you love profiteroles, their version of these filled cream puffs, seductively covered with a thick chocolate topping and served cold, is *bellissimo!*

TEL 01-43-35-43-09
OPEN Daily: lunch 11:45 A.M.–3 P.M., dinner 6 P.M.–12:30 A.M. (Fri–Sat till 1 A.M.) **CLOSED** Never
À LA CARTE 35–40€, BNC **PRIX FIXE** Lunch (Mon–Sat): 14€, 2 courses, BNC; lunch & dinner (daily): 19€, 3 courses, BNC **CREDIT CARDS** AE, MC, V
RESERVATIONS Essential, especially for dinner **ENGLISH SPOKEN** Yes, and Italian, with English menu

AU RENDEZ-VOUS DES CAMIONNEURS (32)
34, rue des Plantes
Métro: Alésia

For decades this was a frugal spot tucked away in the bottom of the fourteenth arrondissement near the rue d'Alésia shopping mecca. It was run by Claude and Monique, who fed the fiscally challenged plain food in dull surroundings. Finally the hardworking couple decided to hang up their respective chef's hat and spatulas and retire to the south of France.

The friendly new owners are Anita and Christian; she meets, greets, and serves, and he labors over the hot stove, turning out some of the best food in the *quartier.* When they first arrived, they thankfully junked the haphazard interior, renovated the kitchen, and created a pleasant dining room that includes bare tables set with plain china and colored water glasses and changing artwork on the walls. They reopened with an upmarket menu, too. In addition to the usual bistro fare, there are a few nice *entrée* surprises, such as the curry-flavored *terrine de langoustines* or the creamy *soupe de pétroncle* (scallops). The main courses stick to traditional favorites of beef, fish, and wild game in season. Fruit tarts, the ever-popular warm chocolate cake, and assorted ice creams insure that you will leave very satisfied.

TEL 01-45-40-43-36
OPEN Mon–Sat: lunch noon–2:30 P.M., dinner 7:30–10:30 P.M. **CLOSED** Sun; week between Christmas and New Year's, Aug
À LA CARTE 25–28€, BNC **PRIX FIXE** Lunch & dinner: 14.50€, 3 courses, BNC **CREDIT CARDS** MC, V (20€ minimum)
RESERVATIONS Recommended **ENGLISH SPOKEN** Enough

CHEZ CHARLES-VICTOR (30)
8, rue Brézin
Métro: Mouton-Duvernet

If *Great Eats Paris* gave out "best value" awards, one would go to the two menus offered at this friendly Montparnasse enclave. It is a family affair, with an owner who is on site, speaks English, and loves his work.

The handwritten (and readable) menu on the green chalkboard entices with the house specialties, *canapés de grand-mère* (a slice of toasted *pain Poilâne* spread with liver terrine and served on a green salad), and *coppa maison,* a type of ham. For your *plat,* steak tartare and lamb chops are acceptable but ultimately plebeian choices when compared to the tuna steak, served with the house tapenade, and a pumpkin gratin in winter or ratatouille in the spring and summer. Desserts inspire you to keep going; try the hot chocolate profiteroles, three-chocolate *fondant,* or a fruit crumble, all of which are made here.

NOTE: There is a second location in the fifteenth arrondissement. Please see page 246.

TEL 01-40-44-55-51
OPEN Mon–Fri: lunch noon–2:30 P.M., dinner 7:30–10:30 P.M.; Sat: dinner 7:30–10:30 P.M. **CLOSED** Sat lunch, Sun; Mon if a holiday; few days mid-Aug
À LA CARTE *Entrées* 7€, *plats* 12€, dessert 7€ **PRIX FIXE** Lunch: 14€, 2 courses, BNC; lunch & dinner: 17€, 2 courses, 22€, 3 courses, both BNC
CREDIT CARDS MC, V
RESERVATIONS Recommended for lunch, required for dinner
ENGLISH SPOKEN Yes

CRÊPERIE DE JOSSELIN (20)
67, rue du Montparnasse
Métro: Edgar Quinet, Vavin

Montparnasse is known for its Breton *crêperies,* and nowhere in the *quartier* is this more evident than along rue du Montparnasse, where they line both sides of the street. Let me eliminate the guesswork over which one to try: Crêperie de Josselin is one of the top choices, bringing the best of Brittany to Paris with its spectacular crêpes. Plump Breton ladies make the crêpes as fast as they can in the open kitchen, rosy-cheeked waitresses rush from table to table, and the happy crowd loves every bite, knowing the final tally will be reasonable. Lace-covered hanging lamps cast a romantic glow over the wooden booths and tables. Quimper *faïence* plates line the high plate rail, and an old grandfather clock gently ticks in one corner.

Abundant fillings of egg, ham, cheese, vegetables, fish, meat, and fresh herbs are folded into mammoth whole-wheat crêpes that prove impossible for most to finish. Dessert crêpes are equally overwhelming and heavy, filled with wonderful mixtures of honey, nuts, chocolate, fruits, and ice cream and covered with flaming liqueurs. The most authentic drink to accompany your crêpes is a pitcher of Breton apple cider.

NOTE: Just down the street is Crêperie Le Petit Josselin (59, rue du Montparnasse; **TEL** 01-43-22-91-81), the family's second *crêperie,* which is run by a brother-in-law. The room is smaller, and the hours, crêpes, and à la carte prices are about the same, but they offer a 16€ prix-fixe lunch that includes two courses and a beverage. Other advantages are that it is open Monday (when the first Josselin is closed), and it accepts MC and V credit cards.

TEL 01-43-20-93-50
OPEN Tues–Sun: noon–11:30 P.M., continuous service **CLOSED** Mon; 2–3 days at Christmas; sometimes in Aug (call to check)
À LA CARTE 20–25€, BC **PRIX FIXE** 10€, 2 crêpes, BC **CREDIT CARDS** None
RESERVATIONS Not necessary **ENGLISH SPOKEN** Yes, with English menu

LA CERISAIE (24)
70, boulevard Edgar-Quinet
Métro: Edgar-Quinet

Here it is . . . the little Parisian bistro we all hope to find that serves wonderful food at affordable prices. Yes, La Cerisaie is as good as it gets, and I have yet to meet the person who disagrees with me. The place is tiny: only twenty seats in a narrow room, the linen-covered tables placed with only inches to spare, and one mirrored wall reflecting the always contented diners. The owners are Maryse and Cyril Lalanne, a charming husband-and-wife team who cover all the bases themselves: he's in the kitchen, and she's out front.

Cyril's light southwestern cooking is influenced by the seasons, and he offers a limited but still ambitious blackboard menu. If you love talented cooking, you are sure to find something pleasing. From October to December, game is highlighted, and by all means, do not miss his preparation of wild pigeon surrounded by large foie gras–filled ravioli; it's an inspired dish. In the spring, you'll encounter white asparagus with a tarragon vinaigrette and milk-fed lamb nestled around sweet red peppers that are stuffed with mashed potatoes. If you have not had roast goose in a while, treat yourself to the *magret d'oie,* garnished with spicy roasted pears or peaches. Baskets of Poujauran breads are kept full, and wine from small producers in the southwest are gracefully poured throughout your meal. The only problem with dessert is that you will want one of each . . . especially when the choice includes *baba à l'Armagnac* with whipped cream, hot cherries poured over homemade nougat ice cream, a dense chocolate tart with a scoop of coffee ice cream, or assorted fresh fruit sorbets, also made here. Due to the limited seating, reservations are absolutely essential, and a week ahead would not be too early.

NOTE: This is a nonsmoking restaurant.

TEL 01-43-20-98-98
OPEN Mon–Fri: lunch noon–2 P.M., dinner 7–10 P.M. **CLOSED** Sat–Sun; 10 days at Christmas, Aug
À LA CARTE *Entrées* 8.50€, *plats* 14.50€, desserts 7€ **PRIX FIXE** None
  CREDIT CARDS MC, V
RESERVATIONS Essential **ENGLISH SPOKEN** Yes

LA COUPOLE (19)
102, boulevard du Montparnasse
Métro: Vavin

La Coupole began in 1927 when René Lafon opened this giant Art Deco brasserie and dancehall in the middle of bohemian Montparnasse. Soon it was attracting the movers and shakers of the time: Josephine Baker, Ernest Hemingway, F. Scott Fitzgerald, Isadora Duncan, Colette, Man Ray, Picasso, Chagall . . . the list goes on. This became their canteen, and they became habituées who arrived early in the day and lingered on to drink and dance the night away. After the war, the existentialists took over, headed by Sartre. Art Buchwald held court; James Jones and Françoise Sagan were regulars, as were legions of others who practiced living stylishly, no matter what their circumstances. Over time La Coupole has weathered well and remains every bit as striking as the patrons, who make for first-class people-watching. The service is nonstop, starting with breakfast at 8:30 A.M., lunch at noon, tea in the afternoon, and dinner until the wee hours. The huge menu has something for everyone, excels in beautiful-to-behold fresh seafood platters, offers plate-size mounds of *choucroute,* a famous lamb curry, and doesn't forget desserts. It is all *très* chic, *très* Parisian, and not to be missed.

NOTE: Dinner reservations are not taken later than 8 or 8:30 P.M. After that time, new arrivals are issued a number and seated accordingly; hopefully you won't wait more than an hour.

Shall we dance? If the answer is yes, come by on a Tuesday, Friday, or Saturday night. Tuesday evening begins with salsa lessons (at 7:30 P.M. for beginners, 8:30 P.M. for intermediates), and then from 9:30 P.M. to 4 A.M. everyone dances the night away for the princely sum of 10€, which includes a drink and 20 percent off your dinner tab. On Friday, the theme is Latin, and on Saturday it's rhythm & blues; on these nights, the price doubles to 20€, and lessons are held at 7:45 P.M. and 8:45 P.M. Other dancing events are scheduled throughout the year (check www.coupolelatino.com). Reservations are not necessary.

TEL 01-43-20-14-20 **INTERNET** www.lacoupoleparis.com
OPEN Daily: 8:00 A.M.–11:30 P.M. (Fri–Sat till 1:30 A.M.), continuous service
    CLOSED Never
À LA CARTE Breakfast: 12–20€, BC; lunch & dinner: 35–45€ (no seafood), BNC; seafood platters, from 18€ (six oysters) to 95€ (a feast for two people); tea 10–20€ **PRIX FIXE** Breakfast: 12€, pastries, juice, hot drink; lunch & dinner (Mon–Sat): 22.90€, 2 courses, BNC; lunch & dinner (daily): 24.90€, 2 courses, BC; 34.90€, 3 courses, BC; Faim de Nuit (after 10 P.M.), 24.90€, 2 courses, BNC; Enfant Gourmand (12 and under), 14€, 3 courses, BC **CREDIT CARDS** AE, DC, MC, V
RESERVATIONS Essential for lunch; accepted for dinner only until 8 P.M. (till 8:30 P.M. Fri–Sat) **ENGLISH SPOKEN** Yes

LA MÈRE AGITÉE (23)
21, rue Campagne-Première
Métro: Raspail

La Mère Agitée is about as big as a minute, but the food packs a wallop. Valérie de la Haye and Dominique Decombat are the talented and imaginative cooks, and every day they prepare a different à la carte menu with two choices for each course. There are three things you can count on: there is always a soup (hot in winter, cold in summer); you will always have fish on Friday; and their big dog will bark at you if you are wearing a hat or have a beard.

Other than that, it is potluck, but what good luck you will have. One day you could start with a chilled gazpacho or a cucumber-and-mint soup, then enjoy Lyonnaise sausage, followed by a dish of fresh seasonal berries sprinkled with sugar or a lime mousse. Another day, it could be a slice of pâté, followed by lemon chicken with prunes for the garnish, and for the grand finale, a fruit *tarte*. All the beef and pork comes from Normandy. Before your meal, have the house apéritif, and be sure to order one of the Côte de Rhone wines to accompany the rest of your meal. After you have finished eating and have complimented the cooks on a meal well done, you will be checking to see what they're cooking the rest of the time you are in Paris.

NOTE: If you happen to have a party of ten or more, you can make reservations at La Mère Agitée for Sunday or Monday, when they are otherwise closed.

TEL 01-43-35-56-64
OPEN Tues–Sat: lunch noon–2:30 P.M., dinner 8–11 P.M. **CLOSED** Sun–Mon; holidays, 2 weeks Aug (dates vary)
À LA CARTE *Entrées* 6€, *plats* 11€, cheese or dessert 6€ **PRIX FIXE** None
  CREDIT CARDS MC, V
RESERVATIONS Recommended; required for large groups Sun–Mon
  ENGLISH SPOKEN Yes

LE DÔME ($, 22)
1, rue Delambre
Métro: Vavin, Edgar Quinet

For a full description, see Le Dôme in the fourth arrondissement (page 98). All other information is the same.

TEL 01-43-35-32-00
OPEN Daily: lunch 12:15–2:30 P.M., dinner 7:30–11 P.M. **CLOSED** Mon & Sun for the first 3 weeks of Aug

LE RALLYE PERET (28)
6, rue Daguerre
Métro: Denfert-Rochereau

For a peek into the life of the average Parisian, walk along rue Daguerre in the fourteenth arrondissement. This is a typical *quartier populaire* (middle-class, working area), and rue Daguerre is the principal market street, with shops selling everything the inhabitants need to keep body and soul together. Right in the middle of it all,

Chez Peret has been an important local watering hole since opening in 1910, and it has been run by the same family since 1919. A cross section of regulars comes daily—some for their early morning jolt of espresso or a glass of red, others to trade insults with the bartender later in the day, and most to sit around outdoor café tables into the evening to discuss everything and nothing.

Orders are placed for sandwiches on *pain Poilâne,* plates of warm Lyonnaise sausage and potatoes, daily specials, dishes of Berthillon ice cream, and both of the homemade desserts: apple crumble and fruit *tarte.* Beaujolais and burgundy are the wines of choice, and the tables of choice are on the covered terrace. When the place is full, you may have to resort to pantomime to communicate, but don't be stressed—instead, enjoy the charm and appeal of being part of the real Paris, even if only for an hour or two. If you like the wine you drink here, you can buy it at their wine shop next door.

TEL 01-43-22-57-05
OPEN Daily: 9 A.M.–8 P.M. (Tues–Sat till 11:30 P.M.), continuous service
  CLOSED Never
À LA CARTE 10–30€, BNC **PRIX FIXE** None **CREDIT CARDS** MC, V
RESERVATIONS Suggested in the evening **ENGLISH SPOKEN** Yes

LES FILS DE LA FERME (29)
5, rue Mouton-Duvernet
Métro: Mouton-Duvernet

No matter when you go or what you order, this exemplary neighborhood restaurant is well worth the trip. It is just far enough from the usual tourist haunts around Montparnasse to keep it from being "discovered," and that is just the way local patrons prefer it. By virtue of hard work and talent, brothers Jean-Christophe and Stéphane Dutter have earned a respected place in the hearts and minds of their regulars

In the kitchen, Stéphane employs a light modern touch while adding an inspired spin to his seasonal and weekly menus. He cooks with the freshest possible ingredients and uses only prize-winning cuts of beef, lamb, veal, and game in season. The two- and three-course lunch menus offer superb dining value: you might begin with poached eggs on a bed of polenta with olives, crushed pistachios, and a dash of Szechuan pepper, or chestnut soup with a chiffonade of smoked ham. You may follow with thick venison stew, or rare *faux filet* served with a smooth macaroni gratin, and then end with a barely cooked, flourless chocolate cake with caramel sauce or a mandarin orange *tarte.*

TEL 01-45-39-39-61
OPEN Tues–Sat: lunch noon–2:30 P.M., dinner 7:30–10:30 P.M.; Sun: lunch
  noon–2:30 P.M. **CLOSED** Sun dinner, Mon; Aug
À LA CARTE 30–35€, BNC **PRIX FIXE** Lunch (Tues–Fri): 17€, 2 courses, BNC;
  lunch & dinner: 26€, 3 courses, BNC **CREDIT CARDS** MC, V
RESERVATIONS Recommended **ENGLISH SPOKEN** Yes

Fifteenth Arrondissement

This vast and generally untraveled region for most Paris visitors is exemplified by La Tour Montparnasse, a fifty-nine-story monstrosity that looms from the intersection of the sixth, fourteenth, and fifteenth arrondissements. It is the tallest, and by some standards the ugliest, building in Europe, but on a clear day the view from the top is spectacular. In this basically middle-class residential area, you will find corners of charm, specifically around the Village Suisse, an expensive complex of antique shops selling everything imaginable at prices reserved for international billionaires. Stretching along the River Seine are high-rise apartments and a new park with walking paths and benches for enjoying the views.

LEFT BANK
La Tour Montparnasse
Village Suisse

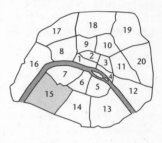

FIFTEENTH ARRONDISSEMENT RESTAURANTS
(see map page 236)

(¢) indicates a Cheap Eat

CHEZ CHARLES-VICTOR (14)
19, rue Duranton
Métro: Boucicaut

For a complete description, please see page 240. All other information is the same.

TEL 01-40-44-55-51

LA CAVE DE L'OS À MOËLLE (¢, 15)
181, rue de Lourmel
Métro: Lourmel

Those yearning for a tourist-free breath of fresh air in a comfortable middle-class area of Paris can put La Cave de l'Os à Moëlle (and its nearby sister location, L'Os à Moëlle; see page 253) on the agenda. The menu and the prices here provide a sophisticated quick fix during the noon rush and a more leisurely one (laced with wines from the *cave*) after the sun sets. The prix-fixe buffet menu is ready at noon and again by 7:30 P.M. Everyone helps themselves and then joins other diners at the communal tables, orders a glass or bottle of one of the excellent wines, and digs in. The robust choices are limited in number but not in flavor. Big tureens of the daily soup and meaty terrines start things off, followed by the daily *plat*—perhaps *boudin blanc aux endives* (white sausage with braised endives)—and then cheese and a trip to the sensuous, all-you-can-eat dessert buffet. Also available à la carte are cheese and cold meat plates and those beckoning desserts. If you are not in the mood for a strapping lunch or dinner, drop in anyway, stand at the bar, and sample a glass or two of wine.

TEL 01-45-57-28-28
OPEN Tues–Sun: lunch noon–3 P.M., dinner 7:30–9:30 P.M. **CLOSED** Mon; holidays, Aug
À LA CARTE None **PRIX FIXE** Lunch & dinner: 20€, 4 courses, BNC
   CREDIT CARDS V
RESERVATIONS Essential **ENGLISH SPOKEN** Yes

LA CHAUMIÈRE (13)
54, avenue Félix Faure
Métro: Boucicant

Talented chef Oliver Amestoy and his delightful Australian wife, Marie-Françoise, consistently give their patrons more than their money's worth, both with Oliver's food and Marie-Françoise's warm welcome. As a result, La Chaumière is filled to overflowing both for lunch and dinner, making reservations absolutely essential. Fellow well-dressed diners will be from the neighborhood—maybe a large family of three generations celebrating a birthday, a young couple all dressed up on their first date, a middle-age couple reliving their first, and you, watching the drama with pleasure.

Amestoy's top-quality, market-fresh fare, served in nourishing, solid portions and artistically presented, could begin with a *gratin de pommes de terre et foie gras crème de morilles* (potato gratin lavishly accented with foie gras and wild mushrooms). His *mille-feuille de crab et artichaut sauce vierge* (light pastry filled with crab and fresh artichoke hearts), *feuille à feuille de thon rouge et tomates confits* (layers of tuna and tomato confit), and smoked Scottish salmon with blini underscore his skill with *entrée* fish preparations. Main courses also lean heavily on fish imaginatively paired with interesting sauces and garnishes, such as fresh perch on a bed of vegetables drizzled with fragrant hazelnut oil or salmon and *langoustines* flavored with a sweet pepper sauce and accented with onion fondue. Besides the fish, one of my favorite dishes here is roasted duck, served with fresh gnocchi.

Desserts are positively heaven-sent, and most must be ordered when you place your main order. From a purely theatrical standpoint, the flaming *crêpes Suzettes* receives top billing from me. The baked Alaska is also very tempting. However, I must be honest: I simply cannot leave without ordering the *soufflé au Grand Marnier,* which looks enormous when served but evaporates with every bite like fluffy clouds.

A meal at La Chaumière will be savored and enjoyed from start to finish, and once tried, this wonderful Great Eat in Paris will surely get placed on or near the top of your list of Parisian dining favorites.

TEL 01-45-54-13-91 **INTERNET** www.restaurant-la-chaumiere.fr
OPEN Tues–Sun: lunch noon–3 P.M., dinner 7–11 P.M. **CLOSED** Mon; Aug
À LA CARTE *Entrées* 9€, *plats* 16€, desserts & cheese 8€ **PRIX FIXE** Lunch &
   dinner: 23€, choice of any *entrée* and *plat*, BNC **CREDIT CARDS** AE, MC, V
RESERVATIONS Essential **ENGLISH SPOKEN** Yes

LA GITANE (4)
53 bis, avenue de La Motte-Picquet-Grenelle
Métro: La Motte-Picquet-Grenelle

Capacity crowds arrive for both lunch and dinner in La Gitane's seventy-plus-seat dining room and secluded, plant-bordered summer terrace. Across from the antique dealers in the Village Suisse and only a métro stop from the Eiffel Tower, it has become an address dear to the hearts of bistro lovers.

When you step inside, you immediately understand what the French mean by a good *quartier* bistro. La Gitane has a warm atmosphere: the tables are placed only millimeters apart, which encourages friendly neighbors to advise visitors on what to order, while offering bites of their food and samples of their wine. The menu, handwritten on hanging blackboards around the room, changes often, reflecting the season and the chef's inspirations. Those with healthy appetites will appreciate the well-constructed list of possibilities, such as *pot-au-feu, cassoulet, boudin noir,* and simply poached fish with light sauces. In the cooler months, look for stuffed cabbage, *petit salé aux lentilles,* and steaming *choucroutes.* Good wines are modestly priced, and the desserts, especially the apples spiked with Armagnac and the *baba au rhum,* are as rewarding as the rest of the meal.

TEL 01-47-34-62-92 **INTERNET** www.la-gitane.com
OPEN Mon–Sat: lunch noon–2:30 P.M., dinner 7–11 P.M. **CLOSED** Sun; few days
   at Christmas, NAC

À **LA CARTE** 30–35€, BNC **PRIX FIXE** Lunch (Mon–Sat): 19€, 2 courses, BNC
 CREDIT CARDS AE, MC, V
RESERVATIONS Essential **ENGLISH SPOKEN** Usually

L'ALCHIMIE (7)
34, rue Letellier
Métro: La Motte-Picquet-Grenelle, Avenue Émile-Zola

Eric Rogoff began two years ago in this outpost far from central
in Paris, and like many of today's young bistro chefs, he's become a
classic example of the truism that, if you have what people want, they
will beat a path to your door—no matter where that door is located.
Rogoff, whose mother is Vietnamese and father is Russian, learned
his even-handed yet imaginative approach to his craft by working at
many of the famed restaurants in Paris. Now on his own, he offers
consistently remarkable value and variety, and he displays not an
ounce of complacency.

A midwinter visit could include such *entrée* choices *salade de Saint-
Jacques poêlées à la vinaigrette de framboise* (warm scallop salad with a
raspberry vinaigrette), wild mushroom risotto, and always his *terrine
de foie gras de canard caramélisé*. There are usually three fish choices
and three meat selections, each one solid in approach and execution,
such as salmon in a caper butter sauce, tuna brochette with cherry
tomatoes and little onions, lavender-scented leg of lamb, and game
in season. To finish, you will usually find three or four desserts plus a
cheese selection. Very drinkable wine is served in carafes.

TEL 01-45-75-55-95 **INTERNET** http//alchimie.lesrestos.com
OPEN Tues–Sat: lunch noon–2 P.M., dinner 7:30–10 P.M. **CLOSED** Mon, Sun;
 week between Christmas and New Year's, first 3 weeks Aug
À **LA CARTE** None **PRIX FIXE** Lunch & dinner: 23€, 2 courses, 28€, 3 courses,
 both BNC **CREDIT CARDS** MC, V
RESERVATIONS Recommended **ENGLISH SPOKEN** Yes

L'ANTRE AMIS (6)
9, rue Bouchut
Métro: Sèvres-Lecoubre

L'Antre Amis is on a pretty square that honors artist Rosa Bonheur,
engineer George Mulot, and Dr. E. Bouchut, a pediatrician for whom
the street is named. It is in the bottom half of the fifteenth arron-
disement, but still within easy striking distance of UNESCO and
the upscale Marché Saxe-Breteuil (held Thur & Sat 8 A.M.–1 P.M.).
Admittedly, it is not a touristy area, but if you do go to the market
or walk along boulevard Garibaldi, you will be rewarded with spectacular views of the Eiffel Tower.

The restaurant has become a very popular *quartier* choice that provides luxury dining for less for its well-to-do clientele. The interior is
brightened by faux-finished orange walls, which set off the changing
art exhibits. The adept kitchen gives distinction to the most ordinary
ingredients. Starters include tuna tartare with avocado, lentil soup

ladled over large pieces of foie gras, and simple poached eggs in red wine. Further proving the kitchen's skills are *ravioles de rouget* (red mullet) in a creamy saffron sauce, medallions of pork sautéed with baby vegetables, and veal picatta on a bed of tagliatelle. Desserts include a particularly good apple crumble and a super-rich warm chocolate cake hiding a pistachio fondant inside.

TEL 01-45-67-15-65
OPEN Mon–Fri: lunch noon–2:30 P.M., dinner 7:30–10:30 P.M.
   CLOSED Sat–Sun; Aug
À LA CARTE *Entrées* 11€, *plats* 20€, desserts 9€ **PRIX FIXE** Lunch & dinner:
   27€, 2 courses, 33€, 3 courses, both BNC **CREDIT CARDS** MC, V
RESERVATIONS Recommended **ENGLISH SPOKEN** Yes

LE BISTROT (¢, 18)
8, avenue du Maine
Métro: Falguière, Montparnasse-Bienvenüe (sortie #2)

Pascal Hardel is a master of the art of reinvention, continually changing his restaurant to suit the demands of the times. When I first met him, he ran a pocket-size spot on L'Île St-Louis. Next time around, he had moved to this bigger corner location in Montparnasse and opened an upscale restaurant. On a subsequent visit, he had revamped the menu and replaced the foie gras and pâté with lots of salads and bouillabaisse. On the last two visits, things remained almost the same: the pretty pastel dining room with the comfortable high-backed chairs was out, replaced by the trappings of a combination bar, bistro, and brasserie that offered continuous food service. Once past all the usual bistro dishes, there are five prix-fixe menus that have wide appeal with the cost-conscious lunch crowd, who appreciates getting in and out for under 12€.

What do you get? First are the *patates farcie:* baked potatoes with various toppings, such as *la parmentière* (filled with ground beef and melted cheese), cod and cheese, and dripping in *raclette* fondue. All combinations are garnished with a generous mixed green salad. Next, for those watching calories, there are six huge salads filled with everything from bacon and chèvre to smoked duck, tuna, shrimp, raw veggies, cheese, ham, and eggs galore. Alternatively, you might have a savory *tarte* with fries and/or salad, or finally, tackle a three-egg omelette, again with fries and/or a salad. Not to be forgotten is the two-course option with five to seven choices, plus the daily specials. All five prix-fixe menus come with a choice of seven desserts, including profiteroles, *poire belle Hèléne,* and an assortment of ice creams and sorbets. No, it isn't gourmet, but it makes for great Cheap Eats if your budget is tight and your appetite considerable.

TEL 01-45-44-39-41 **INTERNET** www.lebistrot-paris.com
OPEN Mon–Sat: 8 A.M.–10:30 P.M. (Sat till 11 P.M.), continuous service
   CLOSED Sun; holidays, Aug
À LA CARTE 15–20€, BNC **PRIX FIXE** Lunch & dinner: 9.50€, *tarte*, fries
   and/or salad & dessert; 11€, large salad & dessert, or filled baked potato,

salad & dessert; 12€, 2 courses; children's menu, 7€, 2 courses; all menus BNC **CREDIT CARDS** MC, V

RESERVATIONS Not necessary **ENGLISH SPOKEN** Yes

LE BISTROT D'ANDRÉ (17)
232, rue St-Charles, at rue Leblanc
Métro: Balard

Hubert Gloaguen purchased this old, tired restaurant and restored it to its original status as a lunchroom for workers from the Citroën factory that once dominated this arid corner of the fifteenth arrondissement. The simple, bright interior now honors automobile pioneer André Citroën and his factory as it was in the old days. True, the bistro is far from the thick of things, but sometimes it is interesting to get away from all the tourist hoopla and see Paris from a Parisian's point of view.

The best time to come is at lunch, when the place is wall to wall with a good-looking crowd, their jackets off and sleeves rolled up. The rushed service is efficient, considering the number of tables each waiter must serve. Other reasons to make this a lunch stop are the Monday to Friday bargain-priced three-course prix-fixe menu, served in addition to an à la carte menu. A nice prix-fixe lunch just after the New Year included pumpkin soup, sliced pork with spicy potatoes, and *fromage blanc* sprinkled with sugar. In the evening, the scene is much calmer, and there is no prix-fixe menu, but the à la carte prices are reasonable. If you are a wine enthusiast, pay special attention to Gloaguen's changing list of little-known French wines at very attractive prices.

NOTE: To avoid a long, dull métro ride, take the No. 42 bus, which will drop you off across the street from the restaurant.

TEL 01-45-57-89-14

OPEN Mon–Sat: lunch noon–2:30 P.M., dinner 8–10:30 P.M. **CLOSED** Sun; holidays, NAC

À LA CARTE 25–30€, BNC **PRIX FIXE** Lunch (Mon–Fri): 13.50€, 3 courses, BNC; children's menu: 8€, 2 courses & a surprise, BC **CREDIT CARDS** V

RESERVATIONS Advised for lunch or for 3 or more **ENGLISH SPOKEN** Yes

LE BISTROT D'EN FACE (1)
24, rue Docteur-Finlay, at rue Sextius-Michel
Métro: Bir-Hakeim

It is a sunny day, you have just finished scaling the Eiffel Tower and dodging the hawkers selling tourist kitch below, and now where to go for a nice lunch? Treat yourself to a pleasing meal at this welcoming bistrot, only a five- or ten-minute walk away. It is a large place, with a wraparound marble-topped bar, big picture windows, and a great outdoor terrace with every table taken during fine weather. The menus change every two or three months and offer the staples of French bistrot cooking: terrines, foie gras to spread on toasted brioche, salad with endives and Roquefort cheese, beef steaks, *coquilles St-Jacques*, and the usual desserts—though the star here is the beautiful made-to-order chocolate soufflé, which you must request when you place your food order.

NOTE: Also under the same family ownership is Le Sept Quinze (see page 252).

TEL 01-45-77-14-59
OPEN Mon–Fri: lunch noon–2:30 P.M., dinner 8–11 P.M.; Sat: dinner 8–11 P.M.
　CLOSED Sat lunch, Sun; 4 days at Christmas, 2–3 weeks Aug
À LA CARTE 32–38€, BNC **PRIX FIXE** Lunch: 15€, *entrée & plat du jour,* BNC;
　lunch & dinner: 28€, 3 courses, BNC **CREDIT CARDS** AE, MC, V
RESERVATIONS Recommended, especially for terrace **ENGLISH SPOKEN** Yes, and
　English menu

LE CAFÉ DU COMMERCE (11)
51, rue du Commerce
Métro: Avenue Émile Zola

The three-story Le Café du Commerce was originally constructed to house a material shop. In 1922, it was converted into a popular restaurant for the workers in nearby automobile factories, and after World War II, it became part of a chain of *bouillons* (soup and beef kitchens). The only one of these famous eateries that remains today is Restaurant Chartier (see page 205). In 1988, Café du Commerce was completely redone and given its present name. Throughout these several reincarnations, it has remained one of the best budget eats in Paris. It certainly is one of the prettiest, though its crew of formally attired waiters display a sometimes limited tolerance for tourists who speak only English. You can only sympathize with the overworked staff, who move at a slow trot while handling more tables than unions in America would allow five waiters to serve. But as long as you don't expect to develop a personal relationship, you will survive.

The restaurant can accommodate three hundred diners at one time on three floors of terrace dining, complete with a skylight that is rolled open on sunny days and lush flowering plants that cascade from each level. As usual, savvy budgeteers don't veer from the prix-fixe menus or the daily specials. What to expect on your plate? All the typical brasserie dishes and drinks, including *tête de veau,* andouillette (certified A.A.A.A.A.), *pied de porc,* and fine *limousine* beef. Everyone leaves pleased—from *les petits enfants* to *grand-mère*—including the person who pays the affordable final tab.

TEL 01-45-75-03-27 **INTERNET** www.lecafeducommerce.com
OPEN Daily: noon–3 P.M., 7 P.M.–midnight **CLOSED** Christmas Day, NAC
À LA CARTE 30–40€, BNC **PRIX FIXE** Lunch (Mon–Fri): 11€, *plat du jour,*
　BNC; lunch (Mon–Sat): 14€, 2 courses, BNC; lunch & dinner: 26.90€,
　3 courses, BNC; children's menu (10 and under): 10€, 2 courses, BC
　CREDIT CARDS AE, MC, V
RESERVATIONS Not necessary except for groups **ENGLISH SPOKEN** Yes

LE SEPT QUINZE (5)
29, avenue de Lowendal, at avenue de Suffren
Métro: Cambronne

Le Sept Quinze is a familiar fixture that attracts a brisk lunch business from officials at nearby UNESCO and a mix of tourists visiting the imposing Musée de l'Armé and Napoléon's tomb at Hôtel des Invalides. Fifty places are set around tables with canvas awning–covered chairs and at a bank of green banquettes. If you are alone or under an acute time crunch, you can be seated and served quickly at the bar. Wherever you sit, you will be served prix-fixe meals for both lunch or dinner, and the final bill will be well within most budgets. For lunch you have a choice of either two or three courses; dinner consists of three courses. The choices range from daily soups and obligatory terrines to a more interesting (for some) polenta mixed with chorizo and dates and a poached egg on top. For *plats,* there are always pasta, fresh fish (perhaps sea bream with sautéed turnips in an orange sauce), and a rotating choice of poultry and red meat. The roster of substantial desserts, such as fruit crumble, bread pudding, or chocolate fondant, guarantees no one leaves Le Sept Quinze feeling even the slightest twinge of hunger for hours to come.

NOTE: Also under the same family ownership is Le Bistrot d'en Face (see page 250).

TEL 01-43-06-23-06
OPEN Mon–Fri: lunch noon–2:30 P.M., dinner 8–11 P.M.; Sat: dinner
8–11 P.M. **CLOSED** Sat lunch, Sun; holidays, Dec 22–Jan 3, Aug (dates vary)
À LA CARTE None **PRIX FIXE** Lunch: 18€, 2 courses, 24€, 3 courses, both
BNC; lunch & dinner: 28€, 3 courses, BNC **CREDIT CARDS** MC, V
RESERVATIONS Recommended **ENGLISH SPOKEN** Yes

LE TROQUET (9)
21, rue François-Bonvin
Métro: Sèves-Lecoubre

It is typical of little hideaways like Le Troquet that the atmosphere consists of the diners, not the decor. In this small chef-owned bistro, the menu changes almost daily and is brought to each table on a blackboard. During a recent dinner, my dining companions and I found most of the dishes hit the mark. Everyone eagerly dug into the plate of *charcuterie* and basket of whole-wheat country bread, and we all happily helped ourselves from the tureen of lentil soup, which warmed us on a very cold Paris night. The tomato and whipped chèvre tart, however, got mixed reviews, from "too bland" to "too salty." For the main course, the roast lamb served with purées of celery and eggplant was a winner, but not the quail, which was dry and chewy. Portions are generous, but the waitress became worried when two of us did not clean our plates. When we told her we were saving room for the feathery light vanilla soufflé served with a cherry confit, she nodded in agreement.

TEL 01-45-66-89-00
OPEN Tues–Sat: lunch noon–2:30 P.M., dinner 7:30–11 P.M. **CLOSED** Mon, Sun;
1 week at Christmas, Aug (dates vary)

À LA CARTE None **PRIX FIXE** Lunch: 24€, 2 courses, 28€, 3 courses, both
  BNC; dinner: 38€, 3 courses, BNC **CREDIT CARDS** MC, V
RESERVATIONS Essential **ENGLISH SPOKEN** Enough

L'OS À MOËLLE (16)
3, rue Vasco de Gama
Métro: Lourmel

Some of the most interesting food served in Paris today often
appears at restaurants in out-of-the-way locations. For proof, consult
the Plan de Paris and place a mark at the corner of Vasco de Gama
and rue Lourmel for Thierry Foucher's L'Os à Moëlle. No two days
are alike, either for lunch or dinner, but in the hands of this talented
chef, one thing is always the same: high quality. Seasonal ingredients
are woven together with skill and imagination to produce many new
takes on old favorites. At lunchtime you can choose from eight or nine
entrées, four or five fish or meat dishes, and at least four desserts. You
might begin with a cream of leek soup flavored with rosemary croutons or scrambled eggs with truffles, crowned with fresh herbs. Main
courses may offer poached *raie* (skate) with spicy sautéed bean sprouts,
red mullet with thick red pepper confit, or tender pieces of pork, slow
cooked and served with a fan of al dente vegetables. The best dessert is
the no-holds-barred *quenelle de chocolate* with saffron cream.

At dinner, *only* a six-course *menu degustation* is served. But don't
worry: the courses are perfectly proportioned, enabling enjoyment of
each one to the fullest. Things always start off with a choice of two
soups, perhaps creamy *langoustine* or meat broth delicately flavored
with coriander. Next, you are served a choice of two *entrées,* two fish
courses, and two meat courses, followed by cheese and salad, and
finally, a plate of four desserts, including the wonderful *quenelle de
chocolate.* As feasts go, it is memorable, luxurious, and definitely worth
the special trip.

NOTE: For lighter fare, try La Cave de l'Os à Moëlle around the
corner (see page 246).

TEL 01-45-57-27-27
OPEN Tues–Sat: lunch noon–2 P.M., dinner 7–11 P.M. (Fri–Sat till 11:30 P.M.)
  CLOSED Mon, Sun; holidays, last 3 weeks Aug
À LA CARTE None **PRIX FIXE** Lunch: 32€, 3 courses, BNC; dinner: *menu
  degustation,* 38€, 6 courses, BNC **CREDIT CARDS** MC, V
RESERVATIONS Essential **ENGLISH SPOKEN** Yes

MON BON CHIEN (12)
12, rue de Mademoiselle
Métro: Commerce

It had to happen. Gourmet fare has finally gone to the dogs in
Paris.

As anyone who has spent even a little time in Paris knows, dogs
are treated royally. They are often far more welcome in public places,
especially restaurants, than children. Now, pampered pooches have
their own *pâtisserie* (the first canine pastry shop in Europe, in fact)

courtesy of Harriet Sternstein, an American entrepreneur from Seattle, who dreamed of living and owning a business in Paris. As she tried to realize her idea, she met with one frustrating experience after another from French authorities, and even more from the workmen she hired to create her boutique. Despite the odds, she and her golden retriever Sophie-Marie never looked back, never gave up, and the result is this great shop, which has substantially upped the poodle-and-limousine traffic in this corner of the fifteenth arrondissement.

Some dogs bring their owners once a day, others twice or three times, for the wholesome sugar-, salt-, and additive-free, slow-baked cookie treats flavored with foie gras, peanut butter, bacon, chicken, garlic and cheese, BBQ beef, banana walnut, and oatmeal cranberry. All in all, there are twelve varieties in three sizes. Older dogs opt for the easier to chew pupcake, with a paw print on top, or the truffles. When it is time to celebrate Fifi's or Jacques' birthday, a large cookie in the shape of a bone, or if it is going to be a big party, a cake, can be personalized for your canine celebrant. The shelf life of the cookies ranges from one month for the hard varieties to two weeks for the truffles and pupcakes. Also available for *les chiens gourmets* is a line of premium dry and moist dog chow.

You dog hasn't a thing to wear? Not if you shop at Mon Bon Chien. Here you will find everything for the well-dressed dog living in Paris: sweatshirts, bathrobes, hats, and custom-made raincoats, beds, and travel bags. Should your canine pal need a shampoo, cut, and blow-dry, book an appointment in the Grooming Salon, which operates in the back of the shop.

Ah, yes . . . it's still a dog's life in Paris.

TEL 01-48-28-40-12 **INTERNET** www.mon-bon-chien.com
OPEN Tues–Sat: 10:30 A.M.–8 P.M. **CLOSED** Mon, Sun; Aug
PRICES Cookies 0.50–2€ each; pupcakes & truffles 2–4€; specialty cookies 3–10€; large birthday cakes 30€ **CREDIT CARDS** MC, V
RESERVATIONS For the Grooming Salon or customized orders
   ENGLISH SPOKEN Yes

OH! DUO (8)
54, avenue Émile-Zola
Métro: Charles-Michels

A reader once wrote: "Dear Sandra: We wanted to write to you about Oh! Duo . . . by far the best meal of the trip. The service was impeccable, the staff constantly smiling. The food was, as I told *la patronne, ne pas de la cuisine, c'est un rêve.* We seriously considered just returning to this one restaurant every night. Please rave about this in your next edition." I did so, and I continue to happily rave about Oh! Duo because there is still so much to rave about.

Judging from other reader letters I've received, numerous *Great Eats Paris* readers have also found this gem and applaud everything about it. The restaurant's name is reflected in the decor, which includes a whimsical collection of photos and posters of Parisian people and animals together in twos. The seating at the correctly set tables allows for pleasant conversation and maybe just a touch of romance, especially the tables upstairs by the window. The service and welcome (for almost two decades) from chef/owner Joel Valéro's wife, Françoise, is always friendly and helpful. To be sure of the quality of everything served, Joel does his own shopping at Rungis.

The four-course prix-fixe menu is definitely the best value. To whet your appetite while contemplating the delicious decisions ahead, you will have a *mise en bouche*—a tiny bite or two of cool cucumbers in cream, a rich pumpkin soup, or pieces of spicy sausage or seafood. The offerings are seasonal, but the popular *foie gras maison* is always available as an *entrée*. In the late spring, a warm leek *tarte* makes a welcome appearance, as does fresh spinach salad with a round of warm *chavignol* cheese, escargots and mushrooms sautéed in garlic butter, and rabbit terrine with a leafy salad. Rabbit is usually a main course possibility as well, as is fresh fish. Also watch for grilled lamb chops, duck served several ways, the *choucroute maison,* and the *plat du jour*. All main courses are liberally garnished with potato gratin or purée, or another vegetable if you wish. Profiteroles with honey and chocolate, sugar-dusted apples fanned into a circle, and oven-grilled pears are only a few of the pleasing finishing touches awaiting you. Finally, wines are fairly priced.

You see, there is always plenty to rave about at Oh! Duo.

TEL 01-45-77-28-82
OPEN Mon: lunch noon–2 P.M.; Tues–Fri: lunch noon–2 P.M., dinner
7–10:30 P.M.; Sat: dinner 7–10 P.M. **CLOSED** Mon dinner, Sat lunch, Sun;
holidays, week between Christmas & New Year's, first week of May (call to
check), Aug
À LA CARTE *Entrée* 10€, *plat* 19€, cheese 6.50€, dessert 8.50€
  PRIX FIXE Lunch & dinner: 25€, 2 courses, 29€, 4 courses, both BNC
  CREDIT CARDS MC, V
RESERVATIONS Recommended **ENGLISH SPOKEN** Yes, and English menu

POILÂNE (3)
49, boulevard de Grenelle
Métro: Dupleix

This is another location of this famous bakery. The main store is in the sixth arrondissement (see page 156).

TEL 01-45-79-11-49
OPEN Tues–Sun: 7:15 A.M.–8:15 P.M. **CLOSED** Mon

TAVERNE LA FORGE (26)
63, boulevard de Vaugirard
Métro: Montparnasse-Bienvenüe, exit Gare Montparnasse

The rough-hewn Taverne la Forge honors German-influenced food from Alsace, while its sister restaurant across the street, Ty Breiz, brings the riches of Breton crêpes to Paris (see next page). Everything about the country chalet is authentic: the wood paneling, the beams, the food, the wines and beers . . . even the radiators have all been imported. What to order? The answer is *flammenküeche* (fondly referred to as Alsatian pizza), which is a thin slice of heavy, peasant-style bread spread with a thin layer of pâté and a voluptuous mixture of crème fraîche and *fromage blanc*, then cooked in a wood-fired oven. Now comes the good part: add combinations of bacon and onions, mushrooms, potatoes, salmon, tomatoes, or chicken, all piled under that robe of cheese. This is not dainty food, so go easy; add a salad and a glass or two of refreshing Alsatian wine, and you will have a completely filling meal. If dessert is on your mind, and you have the appetite to withstand another *flammenküeche*, try one loaded with pears or apples. Otherwise, Berthillon ice cream is served in scoops or hidden under hot chocolate and whipped cream.

TEL 01-43-20-87-10
OPEN Mon–Sat: lunch noon–2:45 P.M., dinner 7–11 P.M. **CLOSED** Sun; major holidays, Aug (call to check)
À LA CARTE 15–25€, BNC **PRIX FIXE** None **CREDIT CARDS** MC, V
RESERVATIONS Not accepted **ENGLISH SPOKEN** Limited

TY BREIZ (25)
52, boulevard de Vaugirard
Métro: Montparnasse-Bienvenüe

The owners of this wonderful spot rightfully boast that *les délices de la Bretagne peuvent également s'apprécier à Paris* (the delicacies of Brittany can also be enjoyed in Paris), and they mean right at Ty Breiz, which was once voted the top *crêperie* in Paris. Inside it is as cute and cozy as a Breton *crêperie* can be. The beamed blue-and-white dining room is decorated with Quimper pottery and old farm implements. There is also a carved wooden bar and an open kitchen, where you can watch the chefs adeptly turning out at least thirty variations of this popular comfort food. Savory buckwheat crêpes *(galettes)* are filled with mouthwatering combinations of eggs, meat, fish, cheese, and sauces. The servings look huge, but they are surprisingly light, and believe it or not, you will find yourself ordering a dessert crêpe—maybe a flambéed *crêpe Suzette* or rum-raisin Berthillon ice cream and rum sauce under a mountain of whipped cream. To keep the experience authentic, order a pitcher of cider to accompany your meal, but be careful: if you are not used to this strong apple drink, a little can go a long way. If not everyone wants crêpes, there are several salads, which overflow with vegetables, cold meats, potatoes, cheese, and smoked fish.

TEL 01-43-20-83-72
OPEN Tues–Sat: lunch 11:45 A.M.–2:45 P.M., dinner 7–11 P.M. **CLOSED** Mon, Sun; major holidays, 3 weeks in Aug, occasionally 1 week in December
À LA CARTE 15–28€, BC **PRIX FIXE** None **CREDIT CARDS** MC, V
RESERVATIONS Not accepted **ENGLISH SPOKEN** Yes, and English menu

Sixteenth Arrondissement

The sixteenth arrondissement, along with the seventh, is one of Paris's best addresses, especially around avenue Foch, where real estate prices are geared to oil moguls and multimillionaires. Elegant shopping can be found along avenue Victor Hugo and rue de Passy. The Trocadéro area, with its gardens, views of the Seine and Eiffel Tower, and complex of museums in the two wings of the Palais de Chaillot (built for the 1889 World Exhibition), forms the nucleus of tourist interest. At night the lighted fountains bring back the glamour of Art Deco Paris. Not to be overlooked is the Musée Marmottan, one of the hidden treasures of Paris museums. Bequests and gifts have enriched the collection so much that it rivals that of the Musée d'Orsay in Impressionist art, especially its collection of works by Monet.

RIGHT BANK
Avenue Foch
Bois de Boulogne
Jardin d'Acclimitation
Musée d'Art Moderne de la
   Ville de Paris
Musée de l'Homme
Musée Marmottan
Palais de Chaillot
Passy
Trocadéro

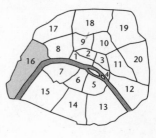

SIXTEENTH ARRONDISSEMENT RESTAURANTS

Au Clocher du Village	**260**
Hediard	**260**
L'Auberge Dab ($)	**260**
Le Bistrot des Vignes	**261**
Le Petit Rétro	**262**
Le Scheffer	**262**
Gourmet Lunching for Less	
Jamin ($)	**37**
Le Prè Catelan ($)	**38**

($) indicates a Big Splurge

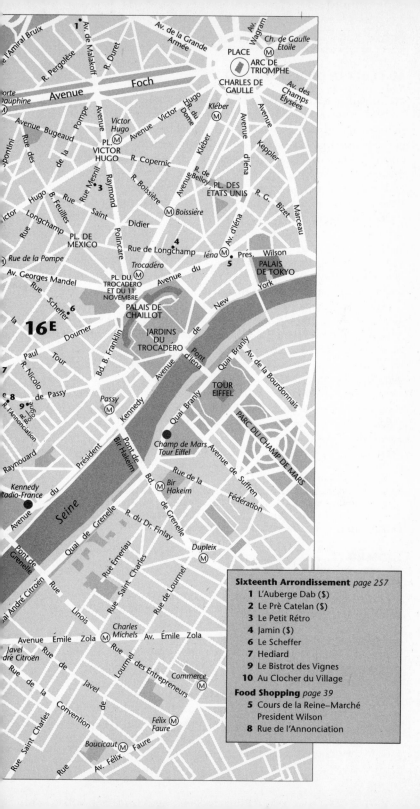

AU CLOCHER DU VILLAGE (10)
8 bis, rue Verderet
Métro: Église d'Auteuil (exit Chardon Lagache)

Wine presses and old baskets hang from beams, posters plaster the ceiling and walls, a massive brass coffee machine sits behind the bar, a huge wooden four-door icebox hovers in the corner of the small room off the kitchen, and enough trinkets and treasure to open a shop fill the rest of the empty spaces in the restaurant. True, it is cluttered, but it all works to create a homey setting for provincial country dining. Reserve a table for a 1 P.M. lunch or a 9 P.M. dinner and you may be the only foreigner there, either in the main room or on the beautiful summer terrace. Admittedly, it is not close, the métro ride is long, and no one admits to speaking much English, but for some it is worth the extra effort and time it takes to get there. I like to combine a stop here with a visit to the Marmottan Museum, especially on a warm day when you can sit outside and enjoy a leisurely lunch.

The food is prepared in the traditional fashion and served by a staff who banter back and forth with longtime customers. When ordering, stick with the traditional *blanquette de veau* or the grilled meats and avoid the *haricots verts* (green beans). For starters, the avocado stuffed with crab and shrimp or the half dozen escargot are good dishes. If you like apple tart, theirs is served warm with a tub of crème fraîche on the side to ladle over it or a scoop of rum raisin ice cream. Or, if chocolate mousse is your downfall, here it is served in a big bowl *à volanté*, which means you can have seconds.

TEL 01-42-88-35-87
OPEN Daily in summer: lunch noon–3 P.M., dinner 7:30–11 P.M.; in winter: Mon–Fri lunch & dinner, Sat dinner only (same hours) **CLOSED** In winter, Sat lunch, Sun; NAC
À LA CARTE Winter: *entrée* 7€, *plat* 14€, dessert 7€; summer add 2€ to all courses **PRIX FIXE** Lunch in winter: 18€, 2 courses, BC; lunch in summer: 25€ (inside) or 30€ (outside), 2 courses, BNC **CREDIT CARDS** MC, V
RESERVATIONS Essential for outside table **ENGLISH SPOKEN** Very limited

HEDIARD (7)
70, avenue Paul Doumer
Métro: La Muette

This is another branch of one of the city's best purveyors of exotic foodstuffs. For a description, see Hediard in the eighth arrondissement (page 188). All other information is the same.

TEL 01-45-04-51-92

L'AUBERGE DAB ($, 1)
161, avenue Malakoff
Métro: Porte Maillot, or Bus #82 stops at the door

The beautiful wood-paneled interior and the secluded outdoor dining terrace have become well-known among businesspeople who like to deal and dine at lunch. In the evenings the restaurant is a stronghold for neighborhood regulars and conference attendees at the Palais de Congrès at Porte Maillot. I like being here because no matter where I am seated, every table feels intimate and private. In the evening, the beautifully set, lamp-lit window tables create a romantically formal atmosphere without being stuffy. A massive curved staircase leads to a second-floor, book-lined library room with a few tables and more wraparound booths. Service by a black uniformed squad of waiters is friendly without being intrusive.

The four-course menu is an outstanding value; it includes a kir to start, wine throughout your meal, and an espresso to finish. The classic fare includes everything from seasonal seafood, escargots, salads sprinkled with foie gras or duck, smoked salmon, beautiful preparations of *belle sole meunière,* bite-size pink lamb chops, a *choucroute royale,* and thick steaks. Don't leave without at least sharing profiteroles filled with vanilla ice cream and served with a pitcher of thick, dark hot chocolate or the *baba au rhum,* with a bottle of rum left for you to decide how doused you want it to be.

TEL 01-45-00-32-22
OPEN Mon–Fri: lunch noon–3 P.M., dinner 7 P.M.–2 A.M.; Sat–Sun: noon–
2 A.M., continuous service **CLOSED** Never
À LA CARTE 45–50€, BNC **PRIX FIXE** Lunch & dinner: 38€, 4 courses, BC
(kir, wine, coffee); Menu Petits Gastronomes (10 & under): 9.50€,
2 courses, BC **CREDIT CARDS** AE, DC, MC, V
RESERVATIONS Essential **ENGLISH SPOKEN** Yes

LE BISTROT DES VIGNES (9)
1, rue Jean Bologne
Métro: Passy

At Le Bistrot des Vignes, stylish Passy inhabitants appreciate the contemporary bistro cooking as well as the excellent-value two-course lunch menu (pairing an *entrée* and *plat* or a *plat* and dessert). The tony mood is set by the bright hot-mustard-yellow dining room punctuated by multicolor chairs. The blackboard menu changes often, but always promises good things ahead, with colorful salads of fresh vegetables, creamy mushroom soup dotted with toasted pine nuts, tuna steak served with a spicy tomato sauce, honey roasted duck with olive oil mashed potatoes, lusty *plats du jour,* and always fresh fish. Reassuring desserts that ignore all calorie considerations include a pear tart served with crème fraîche and a chocolate brownie for those wanting more of a sugar fix to end their meal. Special monthly wines are listed on the blackboard, and they offer a good opportunity to taste something new and different.

TEL 01-45-27-76-64
OPEN Daily: lunch noon–2:30 P.M., dinner 7–10:30 P.M. **CLOSED** 2 weeks Aug
(dates vary)
À LA CARTE *Entrée* 6€, *plat* 14€ (lunch) & 16€ (dinner), dessert 6€
PRIX FIXE Lunch: 20€, 2 courses, 22€, 3 courses, both BNC; dinner: 22€,
2 courses, 28€, 3 courses, both BNC **CREDIT CARDS** AE, MC, V
RESERVATIONS Recommended **ENGLISH SPOKEN** Yes

LE PETIT RÉTRO (3)
5, rue Mesnil
Métro: Victor Hugo

The sixteenth arrondissement has some of the most expensive real estate in Paris. Here a million-dollar apartment is almost a curiosity, and if you did find such a "bargain," you would think nothing of spending two million more to bring it up to speed. As you can imagine, this is not the *quartier* of bargain anything, let alone food. While Le Petit Rétro is not for dining economists, it does fit a majority of pocketbooks, especially at lunch, and offers a visitor a firsthand look at the *quartier*'s inhabitants, from smartly tailored professionals and embassy VIPs to clusters of ladies in Chanel suits carrying miniature Yorkshire terriers in designer tote bags. In addition, the first room of this charming bistro has been classified as a historical monument, and there's no doubting why when you see the colorful hand-painted wall tiles, magnificent solid brass espresso machine, and long zinc bar, all of which date from 1904. The back room is new, but you would never know it; it blends in with the front room perfectly, right down to the tiles.

The honest bistro food prepared and served by members of the congenial Godfroi family aims to please—and it succeeds—with a full list of time-honored dishes that Parisians would never dream of living without. Here you will dine on serious servings of house foie gras and *cassoulet,* smoked salmon, roast lamb served with mashed potatoes, *blanquette de veau,* oxtail in a rich red wine sauce, sturdy *plats du jour,* and fresh fish, all followed by *crêpes Suzette,* glistening fruit tarts, and melt-in-your mouth crème brûlée. The wine list highlights small producers and fair prices.

TEL 01-44-05-06-05
OPEN Mon–Fri: lunch noon–2:30 P.M., dinner 7–10:30 P.M. **CLOSED** Sat–Sun; holidays, Aug (dates vary)
À LA CARTE 35–45€, BNC **PRIX FIXE** Lunch: 19.50€, 2 courses, 24.50€, 3 courses, both BNC; dinner: 27€, 2 courses, 33€, 3 courses, both BNC
CREDIT CARDS AE, MC, V
RESERVATIONS Recommended **ENGLISH SPOKEN** Yes, and English menu

LE SCHEFFER (6)
22, rue Scheffer
Métro: Trocadéro

This is the part of Paris where the scarf is Hermés, the watch Cartier, the little outfit Lagerfeld or Gaultier, and everyone has had a busy day at the boutique. That is why it is a bit of a surprise to discover Le Scheffer, a typical Left Bank bistro—right down to the big dog napping behind the bar, turn-of-the-twentieth-century posters, and original tile floors—where the kitchen dishes out generous and authentic food. A meal with a glass of the house vintage will ring in for around 30€, which is reasonable considering this blue-blooded corner of Paris.

The well-heeled crowd—foreign as well as French—plan repeat visits for the familiar dishes supplemented with daily specials. The encyclopedia of bistro eats includes lentil salad topped with slices of rare duck, cold green beans quickly tossed with a vinaigrette, slabs of pâté and terrine, grilled beef, the usual organ meats, a spicy *andouillette,* fresh fish, and conventional desserts featuring seasonal fruits, chocolate, whipped cream, and anything else to bend a diner's willpower.

TEL 01-47-27-81-11
OPEN Mon–Fri: lunch noon–2:30 P.M., dinner 7:30–10:30 P.M.
  CLOSED Sat–Sun; major holidays, week between Christmas and New
  Year's, 2 weeks Aug (dates vary)
À LA CARTE 30–35€, BC **PRIX FIXE** None **CREDIT CARDS** AE, MC, V
RESERVATIONS Recommended **ENGLISH SPOKEN** Yes, and English menu

Seventeenth Arrondissement

RIGHT BANK
Musée Cernuschi
Musée Nissim de Camondo
Palais des Congrès
Parc Monceau

The seventeenth is a sprawling area that includes leafy boulevards and upscale residences if you stay southwest of rue de Rome. The Palais des Congrès is here, a vast complex comprised of a convention center, a shopping mall, restaurants, movie theaters, and the first stop in Paris for the Charles de Gaulle airport bus. The northeastern part of the arrondissement becomes scruffy as it merges with the eighteenth.

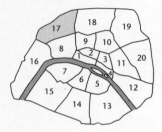

($) indicates a Big Splurge; (¢) indicates a Cheap Eat

À LA MÈRE DE FAMILLE (3)
107, rue Jouffroy d'Abbans
Métro: Wagram

This location offers the same sweets as the main one in the ninth arrondissement (see page 199) and the two in the seventh arrondissement (see page 163). All other information is the same.

TEL 01-47-63-15-15
OPEN Mon 1:30–7:30 P.M.,Tues–Sat 10 A.M.–7:30 P.M.

CHEZ FRED (11)
190 bis, boulevard Péreire at rue Guersant
Métro: Péreire (exit boulevard Péreire Nord), Porte Maillot

All the familiar bistro elements are going full-tilt at Chez Fred, including a crew of career waiters who never fail to remind you just who is boss. Their sometimes gruff service shouldn't deter you from coming, however, because when the food awards are handed out, Chez Fred continually finds itself in the winner's circle. It is a colorful spot, known for its bistro-style cooking, which is meant to be eaten, not admired. The inside is 1930s *grand-mère,* with beveled mirrors, old pieces of china displayed here and there, tightly packed tables, and a collection of hats, Parisian street signs, and a stuffed boar, with a picture of the real one hanging below. At 4 P.M., regulars are still hanging out over the last few sips of their wine.

At the entrance, a big table overflows with first-course temptations: marinated mushrooms, herring, *céleri rémoulade, museau de boeuf,* pâtés, terrines, and assorted salads. The *plat du jour* promises a reliable week's worth of dishes: lamb on Monday and Tuesday, *tête de veau* on Wednesday, *pot-au-feu* on Thursday, *boeuf Lyonnaise* on Friday, and lamb curry on Saturday. In addition, there is a full range of Lyonnaise offerings, truly wonderful if you love *saucisson* or *andouillette.* This is the place to indulge in dessert because the chocolate cake with rich dark chocolate frosting and the fruit *tartes maison* are by themselves worth dieting for a week once you get back home.

TEL 01-45-74-20-48
OPEN Mon–Sat: lunch noon–2:30 P.M., dinner 7–11 P.M. **CLOSED** Sun; holidays, NAC
À LA CARTE 35–40€, BNC **PRIX FIXE** Lunch (until 2 P.M.) & dinner (until 10 P.M.): 28€, 3 courses, BNC **CREDIT CARDS** AE, MC, V
RESERVATIONS Recommended **ENGLISH SPOKEN** Yes

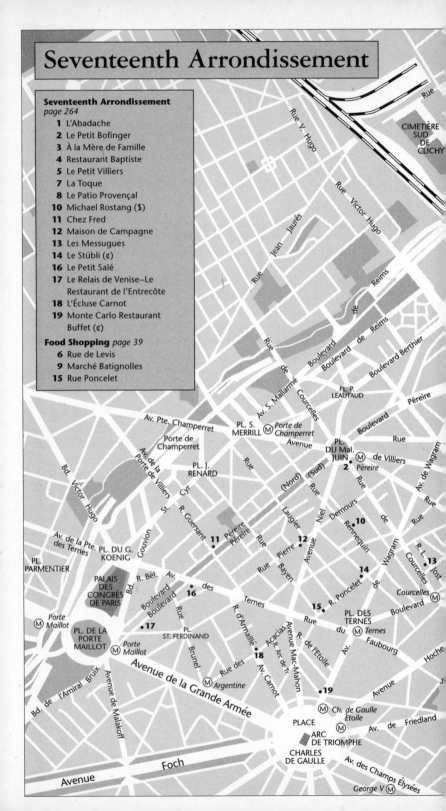

Seventeenth Arrondissement

L'ABADACHE (1)
89, rue Lemercier
Métro: La Fourche

Yann Piton has had a varied background, including time spent as a comedian, but I can assure you there is nothing funny about this young chef's cooking, which represents excellent value in the up-and-coming Batignolles neighborhood. Inside it is nothing . . . bare tables crowded as closely as possible in a brightly lit room with an open kitchen. However, if you haven't reserved at least a day or two ahead, don't plan on eating here. The food comes fresh from the market, not via a freezer or microwave, and the blackboard menu changes often, so you never know what delicious decisions will be ahead. By 9 P.M. the tiny room is filled with assorted locals, dogs in tow, enjoying Yann's changing renditions of baby spinach salad tossed with sweet winter pears, lamb *pot-au-feu,* a flavorful roast pigeon, stuffed with apricots and served on a bed of roquette, or a rare *côte de boeuf.* The crisp apple tart with a scoop of Yann's homemade Calvados ice cream and the warm chocolate cake, both ordered at the beginning of your meal, are superb versions and worth the wait.

TEL 01-42-26-37-33
OPEN Mon–Fri: lunch noon–2 P.M., dinner 7:30–10:30 P.M.; Sat: dinner
    7:30–10:30 P.M. **CLOSED** Sat lunch, Sun; 1 week at Christmas, 2 weeks
    Aug (dates vary)
À LA CARTE None **PRIX FIXE** Lunch: 7.50€, soup, salad & cheese tartine, BNC;
    15€, 2 courses, 19€, 3 courses, both BNC; dinner: 26€, 3 courses, BNC
    CREDIT CARDS MC, V
RESERVATIONS Essential **ENGLISH SPOKEN** Yes

LA TOQUE (7)
16, rue de Toqueville
Métro: Villiers

For a quarter of a century, Chef Jacky Joubert and his family have been welcoming loyal patrons to their restaurant. Normally visitors to Paris would not be drawn to this tourist-free location, but I think that is the perfect reason to go. Wouldn't you rather be the only foreigner in a setting dominated by attractive Parisian couples than join the maddening tourist crowd in some indifferent restaurant that only survives because its "convenient" location guarantees a steady stream of one-time-only customers? At La Toque, the welcome mat is always out. The minute you walk in the door and are greeted by Mme. Joubert or her daughter, you will be glad you came. La Toque's ceiling is painted with fluffy clouds, and the small dining room has red banquettes and tables draped in light-pink linen, set with Mme. Joubert's plates depicting ladies of the 1920s. Fresh flowers add color and candles a touch of *amour.*

M. Joubert knows his way around the kitchen; his seasonal menus are packed with pleasing dishes that let the ingredients speak for themselves. He is not one to mask with sauces and has no use for fusion fads. With few exceptions, almost everything he cooks works well and is artistically presented. The pumpkin soup with chestnuts had appeal on a cold December night but decidedly lacked zip. Not so the smoked salmon ravioli enlivened by an eggplant cream sauce or the rich potato gratin filled with foie gras and wild mushrooms. You can almost close your eyes, point to any of the fish selections, and be satisfied, but if they are listed, try the buttery risotto plumped with sea bass and *coquille St-Jacques* or the fresh cod served with potato purée. Other cold-weather delights are the almost fork-tender veal steak, shrouded in fresh mushrooms, and the wild duck, boned and stuffed with plums and grapes. If you know and love chocolate, and it is making one of its infrequent menu appearances, you must order *eventail de dessert tout chocolat,* a plate with just the right size bites of everything chocolate: mousse, tart, ice cream, cake, and buttery cookies. If you aren't ending with this massive chocolate fix, consider the other worthy contenders: a warm cinnamon apple–flavored terrine with vanilla ice cream or glazed chestnut cream resting between layers of flaky filo pastry. After dinner, coffee is served with a plate of homemade cookies.

TEL 01-42-27-97-75
OPEN Mon–Fri: lunch noon–2:30 P.M., dinner 8–9:30 P.M. (9:30 P.M. is the last reservation); plus Sat dinner Oct–Feb **CLOSED** Sat March–Sept, Sun; holidays, 10 days end of Dec, Aug
À LA CARTE *Entrée* 12€, *plat* 20€, dessert 8€ **PRIX FIXE** Lunch & dinner: 20€, 1 course, 28€, 2 courses, 32€, 3 courses, all BNC **CREDIT CARDS** AE
RESERVATIONS Recommended **ENGLISH SPOKEN** Yes, and English menu

L'ÉCLUSE CARNOT (18)
1, rue d'Armaillé
Métro: Argentine, Charles-de-Gaulle-Etoile

At this l'Écluse location, you can eat, drink, or surf the net in full view of the Arc de Triomphe. It is also the only location that has a wine boutique, Ma Maison, which is next door. For more information, see L'Écluse in the first arrondissement (page 59). All other information is the same.

TEL 01-47-63-88-29

LE PATIO PROVENÇAL (8)
116, rue des Dames
Métro: Villiers, Rome

The Patio Provençal, owned by Frederic Poiri, is a charming slice of Provence deep in Paris. Bright yellow and greens mix with earth tones, lavenders, and oranges to create the feeling you are dining in the sunny south of France. The first room is appealing, with arbors over the tables and tiled and mirrored booths, but it gets noisy and congested, so you are better off asking for a table in the skylighted garden next to the real Provençal fountain. The food is, of course, all about the south, featuring eggplant, squash, fish, lots of garlic and onions, hearty soups, and seasonal fruit-based desserts. For another taste of Provence, try one of Poiri's special apéritifs or liqueurs. All in all, this is a delightful respite for a light lunch or dinner in a part of Paris few visitors ever see.

NOTE: This is a nonsmoking restaurant. Also, Poiri's brother Stephan owns Maison de Campagne (see page 273).

TEL 01-42-93-73-73
OPEN Mon–Sat: lunch noon–2:30 P.M., dinner 7–11 P.M. **CLOSED** Sun; major holidays, NAC
À LA CARTE 30€, BNC **PRIX FIXE** Lunch: 16€, 2 courses, BNC; lunch & dinner: 24€, 3 courses, BNC **CREDIT CARDS** MC, V (15€ minimum)
RESERVATIONS Recommended for lunch **ENGLISH SPOKEN** Yes

LE PETIT BOFINGER (2)
10, place du Maréchal Juin
Métro: Péreire

For a complete description, see Le Petit Bofinger (page 100). All other information is the same.

TEL 01-56-79-56-20

LE PETIT SALÉ (16)
99, avenue des Ternes
Métro: Porte Maillot

Warning: Le Petit Salé is not for the timid eater!

At this little hole-in-the-wall, where heaping plates, good fellowship, and crowded tables are the rule, the substantial specialty is *petit salé:* salt pork cooked with vegetables and lentils and served with a big basket of crusty bread to mop up all the wonderful juices. If salt pork isn't your passion, there are other choices: house terrines, *cassoule maison,* and A.A.A.A.-rated *andouillettes.* In the summer, cold meats, big salads, and light desserts are on the menu. Le Petit Salé has a good cheese selection, and the *tarte Tatin* is worth every filling bite. Order a bottle of Côtes de Rhone to go with your *petit salé* or any other meat-inspired main course. Do note that lunchtime can be very busy, so schedule your arrival accordingly.

TEL 01-45-74-10-57
OPEN Daily: lunch 11:30 A.M.–3 P.M., dinner 6:30 P.M.–11:30 P.M.
CLOSED Christmas Day
À LA CARTE 30–35€, BNC **PRIX FIXE** None **CREDIT CARDS** AE, DC, MC, V (16€ minimum for MC, V; 23€ minimum for AE)
RESERVATIONS Recommended **ENGLISH SPOKEN** Yes, and English menu

LE PETIT VILLIERS (5)
75, avenue de Villiers
Métro: Wagram

Consider stopping at Le Petit Villiers for lunch or an early dinner if you find yourself near the elegant Parc de Monceau; the Musée Nissim de Camondo; or the Musée Cernuschi, filled with East Asian art and artifacts. This excellent *rapport qualité-prix* restaurant is under the competent hands of chef Laurent Beauvallet, whose family owns Le Bistrot du 7ème (see page 174). Both restaurants have built reputations for serving some of the best high-quality bargain bites in Paris. As a result, they are perpetually packed at lunch with a smart business clientele. In the evening, you will mix with attractive neighborhood patrons who don't feel like cooking at home or want some camaraderie. Here the setting is informal Paris: red-and-white checked tablecloths, rush-seated ladder-back chairs, candles at night, and an old tile floor. Best seats are the window tables or anywhere on the terrace.

There are two menus at lunch and one for dinner. There is also à la carte, but what for? Unless you want just one course, all the bistro favs, including daily specials, appear on the prix fixe. For lunch, the two-course menu lets you select from six appetizers, three mains, six desserts, and your choice of wine, mineral water, or beer. Spring for the three-course lunch and you will have to pay extra for your beverage, but you will have an expanded repertoire from which to choose: Greek mushrooms, pâté, and four salads; grilled lamb chops, sausage, steak, and fresh fish; and for dessert, chocolate mousse and several ice cream creations. Dinner is more of the same, with the addition of house foie gras, veal, two duck choices, and fifteen sweets.

TEL 01-48-88-96-59
OPEN Daily: lunch noon–2:30 P.M., dinner 7–11 P.M. **CLOSED** Dec 24 dinner, Christmas Day, NAC
À LA CARTE 25–30€, BNC **PRIX FIXE** Lunch: 11€, 2 courses, BNC, or 1 course, BC; 14€, 3 courses, BNC; dinner: 19€, 3 courses, BNC
    CREDIT CARDS AE, MC, V
RESERVATIONS Recommended **ENGLISH SPOKEN** Yes, and English menu

LE RELAIS DE VENISE–LE RESTAURANT DE L'ENTRECÔTE (17)
271, boulevard Péreire
Métro: Porte Maillot

Le Relais de Venise, better known as L'Entrecôte, is on every Parisian's Great Eats map, and it should be on yours. You cannot call for reservations because they do not take them. As a result, you must go early or very late because there is almost always a line out the door. The waitresses are something else: direct from hell, but they don't seem to deter the meat-loving flock from coming back time and time again. The long-standing formula for success has been widely imitated but never bettered. They offer just a single meal: for 23€, you are served a salad and an *entrecôte* steak with *pommes frites*. Desserts designed to make the finals at a Betty Crocker bake-off are extra and so is the wine. All this is served to an appreciative audience in a cheerful room with a mural of the Grand Canal in Venice along one side. In warm weather, tables set on the sidewalk are hotly contested.

TEL 01-45-74-27-97
OPEN Daily: lunch noon–2:30 P.M.; dinner 7–11:45 P.M. **CLOSED** Some holidays, July
À LA CARTE None **PRIX FIXE** Lunch & dinner: 23€, 2 courses, BNC (desserts add 7.50–8.50€) **CREDIT CARDS** MC, V
RESERVATIONS Not accepted **ENGLISH SPOKEN** Sometimes, depends on the mood of your waitress

LES MESSUGUES (13)
8, rue Léon Jost
Métro: Courcelles

Les Messugues is a prized jewel well worth searching out, because once you've discovered it, you will have found one of the best-value meals of your trip to Paris. The setting is beautiful and so nicely arranged and appointed that I feel as though I am dining in someone's lovely home. The two rooms are small and intensely romantic, with hurricane candles, soft music, and masses of fresh flowers. It is the perfect place to dress for dinner and spend a marvelous evening enjoying a fine French meal with someone special. My friend's comment during our meal really sums up everyone's feelings about Les Messugues: "Anyone cooking and running a restaurant with this much feeling and attention to detail deserves to be a great success."

The service by owner Alain Laforêt is flawless, while the cooking by Gérard Fontaine is nothing short of remarkable for its quality, variety, and presentation. Two excellent prix-fixe menus are served, both of which have a choice of five or six *entrées* and *plats,* assorted cheeses, and dessert. In the evening, however, you start with the house apéritif, which is served with a bite-size appetizer, and in addition, you are offered a half bottle of wine and coffee. As with the rest of the menu, the dishes change to reflect the seasons and inspiration of the chef. While fresh fish is the mainstay of the menu, it by no means overshadows the rest of the offerings. In the evening, you might start with a salad of lightly poached vegetables, topped with a block of house foie gras or a beautiful shrimp salad centered around hearts of artichoke. If it's the early spring, for your *plat* you could have a choice of fillets of red mullet resting on a fondue of vegetables, *filet de plie* (similar to sole) steamed and served with fresh asparagus, or grilled Scottish salmon on a bed of tangy cabbage dressed in a butter sauce. The honey brushed duck with grapes is a rich choice, and so is the liver served with reduced balsamic vinegar.

The desserts are works of art, especially the *fondant au chocolat sauce café* (dense chocolate cake with a coffee sauce), the pear dressed in warm chocolate sauce, and the *gratin de fruits chaud,* which makes a light, refined ending. The abundance of sweet temptations can overwhelm some (myself among them). If this happens, consider a simple solution: *Le Grand Dessert,* which allows you to sample nearly everything on the entire dessert card. Coffee arrives with a plate of Fontaine's truffles and candied citrus, ending a wonderful meal you will want to repeat as often as you are fortunate enough to visit Paris.

TEL 01-47-63-26-65
OPEN Mon–Fri: lunch noon–2:30 P.M., dinner 8–10:30 P.M. **CLOSED** Sat–Sun; holidays, Dec 24–25 & 31, New Year's Day, May 1–10, Aug
À LA CARTE 40–45€, BNC **PRIX FIXE** Lunch: 25€, 4 courses, BNC; dinner: 33€, 4 courses, BC (wine, kir & coffee) **CREDIT CARDS** AE, DC, MC, V
RESERVATIONS Recommended **ENGLISH SPOKEN** Yes

LE STÜBLI (¢, 14)
11, rue Poncelet
Métro: Ternes

Everyone who knows me well knows how much I like going to street markets, even in my own hometown. When I am traveling, a stroll through any local *marché* is the best way I know to see how people live day to day, not to mention the best way to discover first-hand what I can expect to be served wherever I am dining that evening. One of my favorite permanent street markets in Paris is along rue Poncelet. I like to arrive when it opens and then go to Le Stübli, the best German/Austrian bakery this side of the Rhine, and order a steaming coffee or hot chocolate and a slice of apple strudel. If I go later, I never miss a piece of their *schwarzwälderkirschtorte,* known as *la véritable forêt-noire,* a black forest cake that is so rich it is positively illegal.

A nice thing about Le Stübli is that you are not limited to pastries. Upstairs, above the pastry shop and counter, they serve a full breakfast, a delightful lunch and brunch, afternoon tea, and Austrian and German wine and beer. If I am here for lunch on the run, I stop by the painted cart in front and have the French equivalent of *le hot dog,* a white sausage on a warm sesame or poppy-seed roll, slathered in cooked onions. Be careful, the juice could drip to your elbows.

TEL Pâtisserie & tearoom 01-42-27-81-86 **INTERNET** www.stubli.com
OPEN Tues–Sat: breakfast 9–11:30 A.M., lunch noon–3 P.M., tea 3–6:30 P.M.;
Sun: breakfast 9 A.M.–12:30 P.M. **CLOSED** Mon; first 3 weeks in Aug
À LA CARTE 5–18€, BNC **PRIX FIXE** Breakfast: 12€, 15€, 27€, all BC; lunch:
16€, 2 courses, BNC **CREDIT CARDS** MC, V
RESERVATIONS Not necessary **ENGLISH SPOKEN** Yes

MAISON DE CAMPAGNE (12)
18 bis, rue Pierre Demours
Métro: Ternes

Whenever I yearn for a taste of Provence in Paris, I think of Stephan Poiri's charming Maison de Campagne, where the atmosphere is delightful, the food delicious, and prices won't break the bank. Book a table in the back room, and you will feel as though you are dining on the lush terrace of a villa in Provence. The countryside ambience continues throughout the remainder of the restaurant with bouquets of fresh flowers, a bubbling fountain, and a beautiful old fireplace. There is a succinct wine list, but the better choice is to visit the wine *cave,* where Stephan has gathered a selection of wines from small vintners and sells them below retail. He is very knowledgeable about his wines and encourages you to taste before you make your selection.

The wholesome cooking is based on regional foods, with the lunch menu changing daily, and the à la carte with the seasons. If the *crumble aux épinards, foie gras et petits lardons, salade verte* is an *entrée* selection, order it; it's a type of tart that's enriched with foie gras and bacon and surrounded by assorted greens. Another favorite is the pan-fried scallops with chestnuts and bacon. Goose is prepared here roasted in honey and pineapple confit and served with a mountain of mashed potatoes to embrace the sauce. The lamb stew cooked with potatoes, eggplant, and a handful of fresh basil and topped with melted chèvre has precisely the right Mediterranean twist. Lavender is one of the staples used a multitude of ways in the south of France. Here the chef has used it to softly perfume a vanilla *pot de crème* dessert, which is a perfect way to cap this culinary trip to the south.

NOTE: Le Patio Provençal (see page 269) is under the same family ownership.

TEL 01-45-72-28-51
OPEN Mon–Fri: lunch noon–2:30 P.M., dinner 7:30–10:30 P.M.; Sat: dinner 7:30–10:30 P.M. **CLOSED** Sat lunch, Sun; holidays, NAC
À LA CARTE Lunch: *entrées* 8€, *plats* 15€, desserts 7€ **PRIX FIXE** Lunch: 19€, 2 courses, BNC; dinner: 25€, 2 courses, 30€, 3 courses, both BNC
CREDIT CARDS MC, V
RESERVATIONS Recommended **ENGLISH SPOKEN** Yes, and dinner menu in English

MONTE CARLO RESTAURANT BUFFET (¢, 19)
9, avenue de Wagram
Métro: Charles-de-Gaulle-Étoile, Ternes

What! Nine euros for a two-course lunch that includes wine? In Paris? Only two blocks from the Arc de Triomphe and the Champs-Élysées? Impossible—there must be a catch.

No, there's no catch. Just beat your feet to the two-level Monte Carlo Restaurant Buffet, which is on your left as you head away from L'Étoile, down avenue de Wagram. The restaurant opens onto the street and has a glassed-in terrace, so you can't miss it. Who eats here? You might think down-at-the-heel pensioners and old ladies with snapping dogs, certainly no one with a shred of sophistication or dining moxie. Well, *quelle surprise!* I found secretaries, middle-management types, and other savvy diners enjoying a wide array of self-service food, all brightly displayed along a cafeteria line like something you would expect to see in an airport. Seating downstairs is reserved for individuals. Upstairs, it is admittedly groups, but they are served pre-ordered meals, so you won't be mixing with them on the buffet line. There is even a nonsmoking section. It is all quite nice and pleasant.

The Monte Carlo has the benefit of being open 363 days a year from 11 A.M. until 11 P.M. with continuous food service. The give-away 9€ lunch consists of a hot dish, dessert, and a choice of wine, mineral water, beer, cola, or coffee. At dinner, it is all à la carte. If you are a big spender and are prepared to splash out a few extra euros for more variety, a tray piled high from the buffet would come in around 15€. If you don't want a large meal, you can select from one-dish salads, garnished main courses, and good-looking desserts, and be out the door for 10–12€ and change. If you just want to graze through the desserts, you have a wide choice, all coming in under 4€.

You are in Paris, where even the cheapest meal is usually prepared well, but here you cannot expect delicate soufflés or subtle seasonings on wild game. What you see is what you get, and for the best choice and freshest food, get here early. Aside from the prix-fixe lunch, everything you put on your plate is priced individually, from the rolls and butter to the apple tart (whipped cream extra). Salt, pepper, and *l'eau ordinaire* (tap water) are free.

TEL 01-43-80-02-20/21
OPEN Daily: 11 A.M.–11 P.M., continuous service **CLOSED** Dec 24–25
À LA CARTE 10–15€, BNC **PRIX FIXE** Lunch: 8€, 2 courses, BC; no prix-fixe menu served on Dec 31 or Jan 1 **CREDIT CARDS** MC, V
RESERVATIONS Only for large groups **ENGLISH SPOKEN** Not much, but all you have to do is point

RESTAURANT BAPTISTE (4)
51, rue Jouffroy d'Abbans
Métro: Wagram

When evaluating a restaurant, two of the questions I always ask myself are "Would I come back? And, would I recommend it to my friends?" On both counts, the answer for Restaurant Baptiste is a resounding yes! The cooking is as deft and modern as the high-back rose-colored chairs and miniature flowers that grace each white-tablecloth-draped table. The past is also treated with respect, as evidenced by the original multicolored 1930s tile floor . . . and by the sensible selection of honest bistro fare. Start with a salad of mixed greens, liberally tossed with fresh herbs and a lemon vinaigrette. This leaves plenty of room for the tender roast pheasant with a rosemary cream sauce (served on a bed of lentils), the *coquilles St-Jacques* risotto flavored with pumpkin, the wild duck accented with cranberries and celery purée, or any of the fresh fish offerings, all of which are garnished with a pastiche of vegetables. Desserts are excellent, including barely poached strawberries ladled over vanilla ice cream, and the delicate apple tart served with caramel sauce, both of which must be ordered at the beginning of the meal. The short, well-conceived wine list can be expensive, but not if you order by the glass or half bottle.

TEL 01-42-27-20-18
OPEN Tues–Sat: lunch noon–2:30 P.M., dinner 7:30–10:30 P.M. **CLOSED** Mon, Sun; major holidays, Aug
À LA CARTE None **PRIX FIXE** Lunch: 24€, 2 courses, 30€, 3 courses, both BNC; dinner: 32€, 3 courses, BNC **CREDIT CARDS** AE, MC, V
RESERVATIONS Recommended **ENGLISH SPOKEN** Yes

Eighteenth Arrondissement

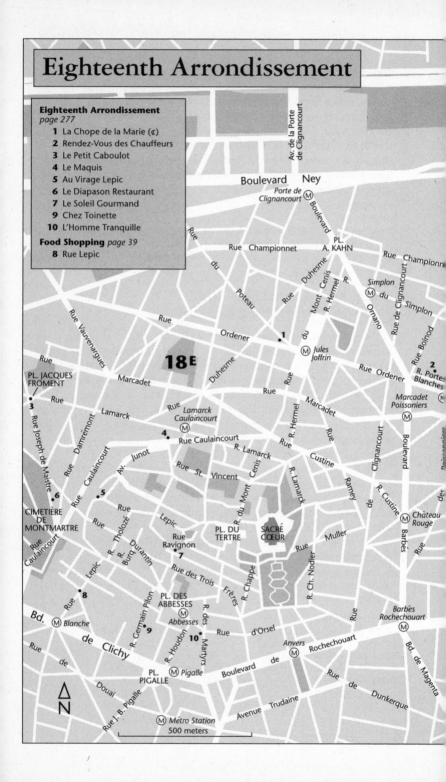

Av. de la Porte de Clignancourt

Boulevard Ney

Porte de Clignancourt

PL. A. KAHN

Rue Championnet

Rue Champion[n]

Rue du Poteau

Rue Duhesme

R. Hermel

Simplon

R. du Ornano

Rue de Clignancourt

Simplon

Rue Boinod

Rue Vauvenargues

Rue Ordener

Mont Cenis

1

du

Jules Joffrin

Rue Ordener

2 R. Portes Blanches

Rue

PL. JACQUES FROMENT

Marcadet

Rue Duhesme

Rue

Rue

Marcadet

Marcadet Poissoniers

3

Rue Joseph de Maistre

Rue

Lamarck

Rue Damrémont

Rue Lamarck Caulaincourt

4 Rue Caulaincourt

R. Hermel

Rue

R. Lamarck

Custine

Clignancourt

Boulevard

Av. Junot

Rue St. Vincent

R. du Mont Cenis

R. Lamarck

R. Custine

Château Rouge

CIMETIÈRE DE MONTMARTRE

6

Rue Caulaincourt

5

Rue

Lepic

PL. DU TERTRE

SACRÉ CŒUR

Ramey

Barbès

Rue

R. Tholozé

Durantin

Rue Ravignon

Muller

R. Ch. Nodier

Rue Caulaincourt

R. R. Burq

7

Rue des Trois Frères

R. Chappe

Lepic

8

PL. DES ABBESSES

Rue

Barbès Rochechouart

Bd.

Blanche

R. Germain Pilon

9

Abbesses

R. des Martyrs

10

Rue

d'Orsel

Anvers

Rochechouart

Bd. de Magenta

de Clichy

R. Houdon

Pigalle

PL. PIGALLE

Boulevard

de

Rue

de Dunkerque

Rue

de

Douai

Rue I. B. Pigalle

Avenue Trudaine

△ N

Ⓜ Métro Station
500 meters

Eighteenth Arrondissement

I'm not from Paris. I'm from Montmartre.
—Longtime Montmartre resident

RIGHT BANK
Marché aux Puces St-Ouen
(Paris's largest flea
market)
Montmartre
Sacré Coeur

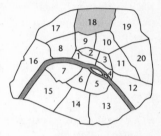

Montmartre captivates visitors with its picturesque winding streets, magnificent view of Paris from the steps and dome of the Sacré Coeur, and its history as the heart and soul of artistic Paris at the turn of the twentieth century, when the Moulin Rouge, its can-can dancers, and Toulouse-Lautrec were at their peak. It was also here at the site of the Bateau Lavoir that Picasso and Braque developed Cubism, and modern art was born. Today, Montmartre is more like a village: a jumble of secret squares and narrow alleyways make up the "Butte," or hill, where the white-domed Sacré Coeur Basilica sits majestically. At 15, rue Lepic, is the brasserie made famous by the film *Le Fabuleux Destin d'Amélie Poulain.* Montmartre is also a study in contrasts, as nostalgia mixes with the crass commercialism of Pigalle and its tawdry fleshpots, and the place du Tertre, a mecca for tourists and third-rate artists hawking their dubious wares.

EIGHTEENTH ARRONDISSEMENT RESTAURANTS

Au Virage Lepic	**278**
Chez Toinette	**278**
La Chope de la Marie (¢)	**279**
Le Diapason Restaurant ($)	**279**
Le Maquis	**280**
Le Petit Caboulot	**281**
Le Soleil Gourmand	**281**
L'Homme Tranquille	**282**
Rendez-Vous des Chauffeurs	**283**

($) Indicates a Big Splurge; (¢) indicates a Cheap Eat

AU VIRAGE LEPIC (5)
61, rue Lepic
Métro: Abbesses, Blanche

The walls are papered with posters and photos of old-time film stars; the tables are covered in red-and-white-check cloths; and the owner puts on a gruff facade, but under it he is a real cupcake. The surroundings and ambience level might lack elegance, but this Montmartre dining favorite is always packed with a young crowd enjoying the plentiful, filling meat-based fare. A meal here may start with traditional onion soup, slices from the homemade duck terrine, or foie gras *maison,* and then move on to *cassoulet, pot-au-feu,* and crispy roast duck and chicken. The veggie of choice is always the same: fried potatoes. Don't look for much in the way of green when dining here. Cheese, *tarte Tatin, oeufs à la neige,* or a seasonal fruit clafoutis wrap it all up. It is simple and successful because it never tries to be more than it is: a decent neighborhood eat that is priced to please.

TEL 01-42-52-46-79
OPEN Tues–Sat: dinner 7–11:30 P.M. **CLOSED** Mon, Sun; 1 week Christmas,
    1 week Aug (dates vary)
À LA CARTE 25€, BNC **PRIX FIXE** dinner: 19€, 2 courses, BNC
    CREDIT CARDS MC, V
RESERVATIONS Recommended **ENGLISH SPOKEN** Yes, and English menu

CHEZ TOINETTE (9)
20, rue Germain Pilon
Métro: Abbesses

Chez Toinette has the cheerful Montmartre bistro spirit down pat; it is a fun and casual place where the prices won't break the bank. The food service begins at 8 P.M., but for the best experience, plan to arrive around 9 P.M., when candlelit tables surrounded by chipped red chairs are filled to capacity with an arty crowd. The food concentrates on the down-home flavors of French *bourgeoise* cooking. The menu changes with the seasons, so in April you are likely to see an asparagus tart or a big, ripe tomato stuffed with chèvre as starters. *Le poulet* (chicken) is a simple dish, yet it always makes a good test of a restaurant: Can it roast the chicken just to the point where the skin is crispy and the meat tender and moist with juices still flowing? The kitchen achieves this, with a half-chicken roasted to a golden brown and flavored with garlic and herbs. More complicated but as well executed is the rabbit, cooked with onions, carrots, and red wine. For dessert, the crème brûlée is a sure thing, and so are fruit tarts, bursting with whatever fruit is at its peak.

TEL 01-42-54-44-36
OPEN Tues–Sat: dinner 8–11 P.M. **CLOSED** Mon, Sun; holidays, Aug
À LA CARTE 25–30€, BNC **PRIX FIXE** None **CREDIT CARDS** MC, V
RESERVATIONS Recommended **ENGLISH SPOKEN** Yes

LA CHOPE DE LA MARIE (¢, 1)
88, rue Ordener
Métro: Jules Joffrin

At first glance, there doesn't seem to be anything special about La Chope de la Marie. It looks like hundreds of others . . . with long lines of paper-covered tables in a brightly lit room and a bar on one side. However, the consistently good food and the weekend entertainment put it in a class by itself. On Friday and Saturday nights from 8 P.M. to 11 P.M., you can come for dinner and listen to live Montmartre music, performed by two accordionists and one guitarist—for no additional cover charge and no increase in regular menu prices. Reservations are required.

Even if you don't come for the music, La Chope de la Marie is a convenient choice on the back side of the Butte de Montmartre for an abundant lunch or dinner. The prix-fixe menus, which offer old-fashioned surprise-free eating, start off with plates of smoked salmon, *chèvre chaud,* crudités, escargots, and savory tarts. Then you can try roast veal with braised endive, roast chicken, trout with steamed potatoes, or one of the house specialties: *filet de canard sauce miel* (tender duck in a honey sauce) or *confit de canard pommes à l'ail* (preserved duck with garlic potatoes). Finish with the house *mousse au chocolat* or *feuilleté aux fraises.*

TEL 01-46-06-46-14
OPEN Mon–Sat: lunch noon–2:30 P.M., dinner 7–11 P.M.; music Fri–Sat: 8–11 P.M. **CLOSED** Sun; NAC
À LA CARTE None **PRIX FIXE** Lunch (Mon–Fri): 9€, *plat du jour,* 13€, 2 courses, 16€, 3 courses, all BNC; lunch & dinner (Mon–Sat): 17€, 2 courses, 20€, 3 courses, both BNC **CREDIT CARDS** MC, V
RESERVATIONS Required for Fri & Sat night; not necessary otherwise
ENGLISH SPOKEN Yes

LE DIAPASON RESTAURANT ($, 6)
12–14, rue Joseph-de-Maistre
Métro: Place Clichy, Blanche

The Terrass Hôtel on the Butte Montmartre has some of the most spectacular views of Paris. In the summer months, the roof garden on the seventh floor with its panoramic view of the City of Light is the perfect place for a casual romantic lunch or dinner *à deux.* More formal meals are served in Le Diapason Restaurant, an understated, contemporary dining room with large windows onto the street. The food is as stylish as the surroundings, and certainly in the Big Splurge category for dinner. Still, you can lunch for less in great style by ordering the seasonal, prix-fixe menu, which is half the price of dinner. There are four choices for each course, and in late fall they include such delights as a pumpkin-chestnut risotto, tuna tartare with lemon confit or vegetable, and fruit stew served in its own copper pot. Main courses might be spicy roast duck garnished with sweet-and-sour endives, loin of lamb artistically dressed with fava beans and sprigs of baby green onions, or roast chicken with polenta gratin. Don't rule out the possibility of dessert. If you think you are too full to manage a chocolate *baba* liberally splashed with Grand Marnier, then share an order of the *trilogy,* which is three choices from among the full dessert repertoire, which includes orange and red currant fruit compote, chocolate mousse with a frothy vanilla cream, panna cotta, pistachio rice pudding, floating island, and crème brûlée. After a morning touring Sacré Coeur and climbing up and down the hilly streets of Montmartre, a beautiful and affordable lunch at Le Diapason underscores why dining in Paris is always a joy.

TEL 01-44-92-34-00 **INTERNET** www.terrass-hotel.com
OPEN Mon–Sat: lunch noon–2:30 P.M., dinner 7:30–10 P.M.; Sun: lunch noon–2:30 P.M. **CLOSED** Sun dinner; NAC
À LA CARTE 45–50€, BNC **PRIX FIXE** Lunch: 22€, 2 courses, 28€, 3 courses, both BNC **CREDIT CARDS** AE, DC, MC, V
RESERVATIONS Recommended **ENGLISH SPOKEN** Yes, and English menu

LE MAQUIS (4)
69, rue Caulaincourt
Métro: Lamarck-Caulaincourt

Montmartre is full of greasy spoons dedicated to scooping in the tourists and, in the process, turning off the locals. Well protected from this dining circus is Le Maquis, one of the increasingly hard-to-find *quartier* restaurants that inspires a loyal following who value sound food at consistently fair prices. The fifty-five-seat, comfortable dining room has pretty table settings, white linen napkins, and the requisite vase of fresh flowers. In the summer, the tiny terrace along the front is a good vantage point for the Parisian hobby of people-watching.

Owner Claude Lesage, who has been here for more than twenty years, does all the baking, including the breads. His *cuisine du marché* menus are dedicated to traditional dishes, which are beautifully prepared from the best ingredients. The *carte* changes twice yearly, and the prix-fixe lunch and dinner menus are different each day, so it is virtually impossible to describe all the possibilities. In the winter, I love the lentil soup with foie gras, the toast spread with brown marrow and sprinkled with sea salt, and the veal kidneys with mustard sauce. If I am here in the late spring, I look for fresh asparagus vinaigrette, the house foie gras on a bed of chilled greens, roast veal with just-cooked zucchini, *lotte* (monkfish) with pesto, fresh sautéed scallops, or the leg of lamb with a trio of fresh vegetables. I never miss one of Claude's tempting desserts, which I always hope will include raspberries on a cinnamon crust, chocolate fondant with Cointreau, or *tarte Tatin* with crème fraîche.

Children are welcomed and have their own menu. Where else but in France would this menu include foie gras, pasta tossed with fresh fish, a *petite salade de chèvre chaud,* and the house fruit tart?

TEL 01-42-59-76-07
OPEN Mon–Sat: lunch noon–2 P.M., dinner 7:30–10 P.M. **CLOSED** Sun; NAC

À LA CARTE *Entrées* 10€, *plats* 16€, cheese & salad 5€, desserts 7€
  PRIX FIXE Lunch: 14€, 2 courses, BC; lunch & dinner: 19€, 29€, both
  3 courses & BC; children's menu: 9€, 3 courses, BNC
  CREDIT CARDS MC, V
RESERVATIONS Recommended ENGLISH SPOKEN Yes, and English menu

LE PETIT CABOULOT (3)
6, place Jacques-Froment
**Métro: Guy-Môquet, Lamarck-Caulaincourt; the No. 95 bus stops
at the door**

Le Petit Caboulot is a spirited neighborhood gathering place that
smacks of old-fashioned Paris: a bustling, crowded dining room with
smoke-darkened walls, varnished paint, worn mirrors, and interesting
habitués sitting at their favorite tables. Early 1900s metal advertising
signs hang randomly around the room, among them a prominent one
stating *Defense de Fumer et de Cracher* (no smoking and no spitting).
Outside there is a terrace, which is filled to capacity the minute the
sun comes out and the temperature creeps into the fifties.

The play-it-safe cooking is from the old school, and to fully enjoy
the experience, your operative mindset should be enjoy today, diet
tomorrow. What else can you do when faced with starters ranging
from double rounds of chèvre placed on a bed of sliced potatoes to
mushrooms au gratin or eggs cooked in wine sauce? *Rognons de veau,
confit de canard,* chicken with mashed potatoes, beef sautéed with buttery shallots, sausage and lentils, steak with béarnaise . . . you get the
picture, and dessert is still to come. And does it ever, with substantial
servings of chocolate fudge cake with a trio of sauces, a huge crème
brûlée, and a wonderful *tarte Tatin* with plenty of crème fraîche. In an
attempt to turn tables at least once a night, the service is swift, and
lingering is not readily encouraged.

TEL 01-46-27-19-00
OPEN Mon–Fri: lunch noon–2:30P.M., dinner 8–11 P.M., bar: 11:30 A.M.–
  3 P.M., 6 P.M.–midnight CLOSED Sat–Sun; holidays, 10 days around
  Christmas & New Year's, Aug (dates vary)
À LA CARTE *Entrées* 6.50€, *plats* 13.50€, desserts 6.50€ PRIX FIXE Lunch:
  10€, 2 courses, BNC CREDIT CARDS MC, V
RESERVATIONS Not necessary ENGLISH SPOKEN Limited, but English menu

LE SOLEIL GOURMAND (7)
10, rue Ravignan
Métro: Abbesses

Many Montmartre restaurants are closed for lunch, so it is always
nice to find one that caters to the lunch crowd and also offers a large
selection of tarts and salads. Le Soleil Gourmand is such a place, and
as such it's filled to capacity noon and night by an artistic, *branché*
Montmartre crowd who between bites and sips engages in lots of
schmoozing, kissing, and laughing. The hip yet homey interior is
done in the warm, sunny tones that speak of the south of France.
Almost everything you see is for sale, including the artwork and

table settings. The food isn't fancy, but it has a certain panache and definitely appeals to those looking for a change of pace from the usual two- or three-course formal French meal. Lots of herbs and spices are used to highlight the light but very satisfying tarts and main-course salads. There are also plates of cheese, smoked fish, and marinated grilled vegetables in addition to the usual diet-defying desserts. Le Soleil Gourmand is run by twin sisters, Elisabeth and Christine, who do it all: meet, greet, banter, joke, flirt, cook, serve, and have just as good a time as their happy guests.

TEL 01-42-51-00-50
OPEN Daily: lunch 12:30–2:30 P.M., dinner 7:30–11 P.M. **CLOSED** Dec 24–25 & 31, Jan 1, June 21, NAC
À LA CARTE 18–20€, BNC **PRIX FIXE** None **CREDIT CARDS** None
RESERVATIONS Recommended for dinner **ENGLISH SPOKEN** Yes

L'HOMME TRANQUILLE (10)
81, rue des Martyrs
Métro: Abbesses, Pigalle

For more than twenty years, Catherine Le Squer has been cooking here—with the help of her mother, who makes all the terrines, and her son Antoine, who acts as host and waits on tables as needed. Casual observers might think this is just another Montmartre-Pigalle eatery dedicated to luring in tourists, plying them with cheap food and drink and then gouging their wallets. Not so. This family-owned restaurant, open for dinner only, is out of the mainstream of Pigalle grunge and just far enough from the tourist traps in Montmartre to maintain its character and staying power. The funky interior has a design-by-garage-sale aesthetic. Collections of flea market finds sit in clusters around the room. Aging posters are taped to equally aging yellow walls, candles are lit at night, and there is the usual bouquet of fresh flowers and assorted green plants. Tables are set with paper mats and chunky wineglasses.

Start with a pitcher of the drinkable house wine and order one of the terrines to spread on chunks of fresh bread. Vegetarians are catered to with the *assiette végétarienne,* which pairs a vegetable terrine (spinach, celery, and carrots) with an assortment of the evening's veggies. Carnivores shouldn't hesitate to order the healthy portions of grilled lamb chops; the honey-glazed chicken flavored with lemon and coriander; or the pork cooked with mangos and red fruits. Dessert specialties include fruit crumble and a slice of chocolate fondant that is so popular with the regulars they have threatened not to come if it is ever taken off the menu. From start to finish, L'Homme Tranquille provides a basic, fairly priced meal in a section of Paris where this is not easy to find.

TEL 01-42-54-56-28
OPEN Tues–Sat: dinner 7:30–11:30 P.M. **CLOSED** Mon, Sun; several days between Christmas and New Year's, Aug 15–31

À LA CARTE 28–32€, BNC PRIX FIXE Dinner: 24€, 3 courses, BNC
   CREDIT CARDS None
RESERVATIONS Recommended ENGLISH SPOKEN Yes

RENDEZ-VOUS DES CHAUFFEURS (2)
11, rue des Portes Blanches
Métro: Marcadet-Poissonniers (exit rue des Poissonniers)

If you are willing to go where most mortal tourists fear to tread, and if what you want is a square meal for a song, go to Rendez-Vous des Chauffeurs. This nostalgic throwback is an honest-to-goodness neighborhood hangout where the decor has been given a minimum of attention and importance.

Nouvelle cuisine never caught on here, and neither will any other passing food fad, but the restaurant is always packed with an older, pennywise clientele eager to lap up the adored cornerstones of French home cooking. There is an à la carte menu, but don't go there. The bargain *du jour* is definitely the 14€ three-course meal, which includes wine. It is served for lunch and dinner, but never on Sunday or holidays or after 8:30 P.M. Starting with a plate of crudités, *saucisson sec, terrine de canard,* or vegetable soup, continuing on to a garnished *plat* of roast pork, kidneys, steak (cooked or tartare), and down to the last bite of *pâtisserie,* diners find a meal here a very filling and satisfying experience, one the economy-minded will especially appreciate.

TEL 01-42-64-04-17
OPEN Tues–Sat: lunch noon–2:30 P.M., dinner 7:30–11 P.M. CLOSED Mon, Sun; NAC
À LA CARTE 25€, BNC PRIX FIXE Lunch: 10€, 2 courses, BNC; lunch & dinner (until 8:30 P.M.): 14€, 3 courses, BC CREDIT CARDS MC, V
RESERVATIONS Not necessary ENGLISH SPOKEN Yes

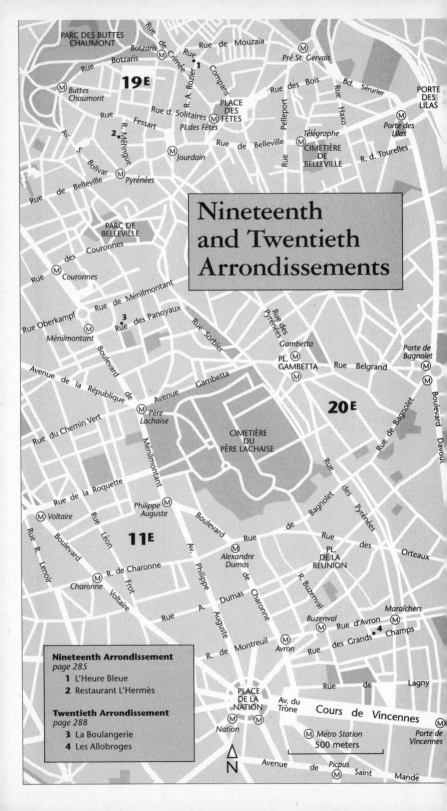

Nineteenth and Twentieth Arrondissements

PARC DES BUTTES CHAUMONT

Botzaris

Rue de Mouzaia

Pré St. Gervais

Rue de Crimée

Rue

Rue Botzaris

Rue R. A. Rozier

Compans

PORTE DES LILAS

Bd. Sérurier

Rue des Bois

Ⓜ Buttes Chaumont

19E

Rue des Solitaires

PLACE DES FÊTES

Pelleport

Rue Haxo

Ⓜ Porte des Lilas

Av. S. Bolivar

Rue Fessart

R. Méhingue

Pl. des Fêtes

Rue de Belleville

Télégraphe

Rue de Belleville

Ⓜ Pyrénées

Ⓜ Jourdain

Rue

CIMETIÈRE DE BELLEVILLE

R. d. Tourelles

PARC DE BELLEVILLE

Rue de Belleville

Couronnes

Ⓜ des Couronnes

Rue Couronnes

Rue de Ménilmontant

Rue des Pyrénées

Rue Oberkampf

Rue des Panoyaux

Gambetta

Porte de Bagnolet Ⓜ

Ⓜ Ménilmontant

Rue Sorbier

PL. GAMBETTA Ⓜ

Rue Belgrand

20E

Avenue de la République

Boulevard de

Avenue Gambetta

Rue de Bagnolet

Boulevard Davout

Rue du Chemin Vert

Ⓜ Père Lachaise

CIMETIÈRE DU PÈRE LACHAISE

Ménilmontant

Rue de

Rue des Pyrénées

Rue de la Roquette

Bagnolet

Rue

Ⓜ Voltaire

Rue Léon

Philippe Auguste Ⓜ

Boulevard

Rue

des

Orteaux

11E

Av. Philippe

Alexandre Dumas Ⓜ

PL. DE LA RÉUNION

R. de Charonne

Frot

de Charonne

R. Buzenval

Maraîchers

Ⓜ Charonne

Voltaire

Rue

A. Dumas

Auguste

Buzenval

Rue d'Avron

Champs

Rue R. Lenoir

Boulevard

R. de Montreuil

Ⓜ Avron

Rue des Grands

Rue

de

Lagny

PLACE DE LA NATION

Av. du Trône

Cours de Vincennes

Ⓜ Porte de Vincennes

Ⓜ Nation

Ⓜ Métro Station
500 meters

Avenue de Picpus Ⓜ Saint Mandé

△ N

Nineteenth Arrondissement
page 285

    1 L'Heure Bleue
    2 Restaurant L'Hermès

Twentieth Arrondissement
page 288

    3 La Boulangerie
    4 Les Allobroges

Nineteenth Arrondissement

The nineteenth is neighborhood *populaire,* a culturally mixed area filled with a mixture of postwar highrise apartments and pockets of winding streets with individual houses and gardens. The biggest reason for a visitor to venture here is to walk in the beautiful Parc des Buttes Chaumont, which was created by Baron Haussmann. In the center is an island with lovely views of Montmartre and St-Denis.

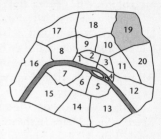

Nineteenth Arrondissement Restaurants

L'HEURE BLEUE (1)
57, rue Arthur Rozier
Métro: Place des Fêtes, Botzaris

When a Parisian friend insisted I try one of her favorite neighborhood restaurants in this out-of-the way, tourist wasteland, I always found some reason not to go because I thought it too far and couldn't imagine the food would be anything other than filling. But it finally got to the point where I knew I had to either stop making excuses or stop the friendship.

A date was selected, and she said she would make reservations. Reservations! Here? In the middle of the week?! Oh, please, give me a break, I thought. As I began the safari, I thought the trip would take forever, but when looking at the métro map, I saw it is only eight stops (or about 10 to 15 minutes) from Châtelet, the same as it is from there to Charles-de Gaulle-Étoile and the Arc de Triomphe. When I arrived at my stop, it was only a five-minute walk, in a post–World War II neighborhood dominated by highrises, to get to L'Heure Bleue. At 8:30 P.M. on this Wednesday night, every stool at the bar was filled, and so were most of the tables, with a local crowd composed of the young, the old, and the in-between. As you can imagine, this is a laid-back, casual place where decor is never a topic of discussion.

I didn't expect the food to be a topic of conversation either, but guess what. . . . It turned out to be well-prepared using only market-fresh ingredients, all nicely presented, and very good. In addition to the standard starters of *chèvre chaud, oeufs cocotte,* and foie gras, there were a few more unusual dishes listed on the blackboard daily specials. We both ordered the cumin-flavored mixed baby veggies wrapped in a tent of puff pastry, and gave it a gold star. The L'Heure Bleue—a large salad consisting of house foie gras, smoked duck and gizzards, crudités, and warm onion confit on a bed of mixed greens—won another gold star. Two pleasing mains were the lamb chops grilled with herbes de Provence and the savory tomato tart garnished with a crisp salad. We finished with fresh pears poached in red wine and dusted with cinnamon and an apple-and-raspberry crumble, served warm with a pot of crème frâiche to spoon over it. The drinkable house wine was good enough to inspire a second carafe.

"What did I tell you?" enthused my friend as we paid the modest bill.

Reservations . . . a good idea after all.

TEL 01-42-39-18-07
OPEN Mon–Fri: lunch noon–2 P.M., dinner 7:30–11 P.M. **CLOSED** Sat–Sun;
2 weeks at Christmas, Aug
À LA CARTE 25–28€ **PRIX FIXE** Lunch: 11€, 3 courses, BNC; children's menu:
8.50€, 2 courses, BC **CREDIT CARDS** MC, V
RESERVATIONS A good idea **ENGLISH SPOKEN** Some

RESTAURANT L'HERMÈS (2)
23, rue Melingue
Métro: Pyrenées

For a memorable dining experience a bit off action central, Restaurant l'Hermès fits the bill to a T. As my dining companion raved on one visit: "This is a find. I feel as though I am really having an honest French dining experience, enjoying exceptional food, and better yet, getting superb value for money." I could not agree more.

The restaurant has been run by Anne Escoffier and Olivier Laterrot for ten years, and it draws a very local crowd of families, couples, and savvy visitors. Anne is a delightful hostess, speaks English, and goes out of her way to explain the menu and to make sure everyone is happy with their meal. The light, southwestern food provides diners with an evocative trip to the sunny south of France, as do the two bright dining rooms done in Provençal yellow and burnt orange. The blackboard lunch menu changes every day, and it is an absolute steal when you consider the quality and the complexity of the ingredients. You might start with a vegetable flan or a fat, red tomato stuffed with chèvre or a salad of designer greens topped with a confit of chicken livers and pieces of dried duck. Follow this with a brochette of *saucisse au boudin noire* and parsnip purée or roast guinea fowl surrounded by spring vegetables. Dessert can be hit or miss: profiteroles or soufflé . . . given the choice, pick the first and avoid the latter.

Dinner is a more drawn-out affair and includes baskets of Olivier's homemade bread. On a recent visit I enjoyed a *tartelette* with langoustines and oyster mushrooms, tender tarragon-flavored lamb, and a flavorful strawberry gratin with a champagne sabayon sauce. Coffee came with chocolate-covered cherries and an assortment of butter cookies.

TEL 01-42-39-94-70
OPEN Tues: lunch noon–2 P.M., dinner: 7:30–10 P.M.; Wed: dinner: 7:30–10 P.M.; Thur–Sat: lunch noon–2 P.M., dinner: 7:30–10 P.M. **CLOSED** Wed lunch, Sun, Mon; major holidays, 1 week Feb and Easter, Aug
À LA CARTE 40–45€ **PRIX FIXE** Lunch: 14.50€, 3 courses, BNC; lunch & dinner: 28€, 3 courses, BNC **CREDIT CARDS** MC, V
RESERVATIONS Recommended **ENGLISH SPOKEN** Yes

Twentieth Arrondissement

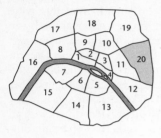

The twentieth arrondissement is proletarian, intensely ethnic, and at times, radical. The northern section, Belleville, is a cultural melting pot. Ménilmontant, in the southern part, is where you will find the Cimetière Père Lachaise. Within its winding maze of paths, you can visit the graves of Balzac, Colette, Molière, Jim Morrison, Gertrude Stein, Edith Piaf, and Oscar Wilde, to name only a few of the famous—and infamous—people who rest here.

LA BOULANGERIE (3)
15, rue des Panoyaux
Métro: Ménilmontant, Père Lachaise

"Here we have good bread, good food, good wine . . . and we are always happy," state owners Hassan and Nordine, two half-German, half-Moroccan brothers who were born in Burgandy. Until a year or so ago they operated Les Bombis Bistrot in the twelfth arrondissement, but they quickly outgrew that location and have since moved here. Hassan still reigns supreme in the kitchen, and Nordine keeps things humming in front. The consistent quality of the food, good lunch prices, and the genuinely friendly owners are the ingredients that pack the place wall-to-wall everyday. If you are visiting the Cimetière Père Lachaise, the famed final resting place of many Parisians, keep this spot in mind, as it is a textbook example of a busy Parisian canteen. In a working-class neighborhood that is generally considered a culinary-free zone, this outpost is a safe, pleasing choice for lunch. But for dinner? I don't think so. The neighborhood tone and the métro after dark might be questionable for the casual visitor.

The thirties-style restaurant, which has been on the corner for decades, draws a midday mix of businesspeople, relieved tourists, and lively locals who value the reliable, wholesome food served at reasonable prices. Parsimonious patrons order the tried-and-true two- or three-course *formules du midi,* which are more filling than inspiring. Splash out a bit more for an expanded three-course *formule* and your choices widen, but play it safe and stick to the standards of foie gras, pork terrines, and escargots, along with rosemary roasted pork and *magret de canard.* You may also see roast quail, grilled shrimp, and for a final sweet treat a macaroon filled with lemon ice cream or a white chocolate mousse.

TEL 01-43-58-45-45
OPEN Mon–Fri: lunch noon–2 P.M., dinner 8–11 P.M.; Sat: dinner 8–11 P.M.
    CLOSED Sat lunch, Sun; major holidays, lunch in Aug
À LA CARTE Lunch: *entrée* 8€, *plat* 18€, dessert 8€ **PRIX FIXE** Lunch: 13€,
    2 courses, 16€, 3 courses, both BNC **CREDIT CARDS** MC, V
RESERVATIONS Not necessary **ENGLISH SPOKEN** Yes

LES ALLOBROGES (4)
71, rue des Grands-Champs
Métro: Maraîchers (see Note)

If you didn't know about Les Allobroges, you wouldn't come here, let alone be able to find it. However, Paris's smart set has definitely got it mapped, and they have been happily traveling to this neighborhood outpost ever since chef Olivier Pateyron and his wife, Annette, opened the doors. The two small dining rooms display pictures and posters of farm animals on the walls, and there are big pots of daisies in the windows. Seating is at comfortably spaced, properly set, linen-covered tables.

With a cooking style that respects the classics, Pateyron creates dishes that represent all that is modern and refreshing about Paris dining. Everything he prepares tastes clean, unmasked, and satisfying. The two sensational value-priced menus are definitely appealing. The cheaper one allows a choice of *entrées,* only the *plat du jour* for the main course, plus cheese and dessert. The more expensive option offers six or seven choices for every course. For many visitors, the addition of the *tous légumes* (all vegetable) menu appeals and makes another reason to include this among the top dining selections in Paris.

The house foie gras plays a starring role in several of the starters. One classic is the *gallete de pommes de terre au lard et foie gras,* a crisp potato pancake holding a generous amount of foie gras. Another is the foie gras terrine in a thyme *gelée.* The hearts of artichokes baked with mushrooms and crowned with a poached egg is almost a meal in itself. The salad with herbs and a showering of Parmesan is a lighter, springtime palate-pleaser that allows enough room to give the second courses plenty of serious consideration. If you love duck, definitely order the *canette longuement cuit aux épices et banyuls,* a melt-in-your-mouth long-cooked duck, flavored with spices and red wine. Otherwise, have the succulent fricassée of squid and sea bass served with baked celery. The inspired dessert list will beguile you with a bread pudding accented with a *fromage blanc* sorbet, a buttery almond cake with coconut and passionfruit sorbet on the side, and a lovely strawberry soup.

Not only are vegetarians not ignored at Les Allobroges, they are attended to in gourmet style with the small vegetable-and-fruit menu. It changes often, but usually includes a mixed salad with tomato confit and an eggplant caviar to start, and then perhaps an asparagus risotto or vegetable ragout with a potato pancake and light chervil cream sauce. Dessert might be Pateyron's famous *feuilleté de rhubarbe*—sweet rhubarb encased in a buttery, flaky pastry—or *marquise au chocolat,* a warm and wonderful hot chocolate cake with a fudgy interior.

NOTE: Admittedly, Les Allobroges is off—way off—the beaten track. You might be tempted to take a taxi, but the ride could cost more than dinner. The best way to go is the métro. Get off at the Maraîchers stop, walk down rue des Pyrénées to rue des Grands-Champs, and turn right. Then walk about a block until you come to the restaurant at No. 71.

TEL 01-43-73-40-00

OPEN Tues–Sat: lunch noon–2 P.M., dinner 8–10 P.M. **CLOSED** Mon, Sun; major holidays, Dec 25–Jan 2, week at Easter, Aug (dates vary)

À LA CARTE *Entrée* 12€, *plat* 16€, dessert 11€ **PRIX FIXE** Lunch & dinner: 20€, 33€, both 4 courses & BNC; *menu tous légumes:* 29€, 4 courses, BNC **CREDIT CARDS** AE, MC, V

RESERVATIONS Essential; don't risk coming this far and not be seated! **ENGLISH SPOKEN** Limited

University Restaurants

Institutional food, even in Paris, is nothing to write home about, but it *is* cheap. CROUS (Centre Regional des Oeuvres Universitaires et Scolaires) runs university restaurants known as Restos-U that offer so-so food at unbeatable prices. These restaurants serve meals that include both cheese and dessert but not drinks. Anyone with an international student ID can buy meal tickets (cash only) either at the main office or during mealtimes at the sites listed below. Accompanying nonstudent guests pay half again as much, but it is still a Cheap Eat. The following list of CROUS Restos-U includes some that are most convenient, but it is by no means exhaustive. All are open for lunch, but only a handful serve dinner. For a complete list and hours, consult the main office.

It is important to know that a visit to the CROUS main office will get you more than a cut-rate meal in Paris. The office is also a place to book a bed in a student residence, arrange a cheap trip, or buy a discounted ticket for sports or cultural events. Of course, you must be a student and present your international ID card to qualify for any of the bargains.

CROUS RESTAURANTS IN PARIS
MAIN OFFICE: 39, avenue Georges Bernanos (see map of fifth arrondissement, page 110)
MÉTRO: Port Royal
TEL 01-40-51-36-00, 37-10, or 37-14 **INTERNET** www.crous-paris.fr
OPEN Mon–Fri 9 A.M.–5 P.M. **CLOSED** Sat–Sun; holidays, Aug

The following information is good for all the CROUS Restos-U listed:

OPEN Mon–Fri: lunch 11:30 A.M.–2 P.M. Those marked with an asterisk also serve dinner.
SINGLE-MEAL TICKETS 4.70€, upon presentation of student card; 6.20€, for a nonstudent guest accompanying a student
CREDIT CARDS None, cash only
ENGLISH SPOKEN Usually

Assas, 92, rue d'Assas (6th), Tel 01-44-41-58-01; Métro: Notre-Dame-des-Champs

*Bullier, 39, avenue Georges Bernanos (5th); Tel 01-40-51-37-85; Métro: Porte Royal. This is the only site open on weekends and school vacations.

Censier, 3, rue Censier (5th), Tel 01-45-35-41-24; Métro: Censier-Daubenton

Châtelet, 10, rue Jean Calvin (5th), Tel 01-43-31-51-66; Métro: Censier-Daubenton

Citeaux, 45, boulevard Diderot (12th), Tel 01-49-28-59-40; Métro: Gare de Lyon, Reuilly-Diderot

Cuvier-Jussieu, 8 bis, rue Cuvier (5th), Tel 01-43-25-46-65; Métro: Jussieu

I.U.T., 143, avenue de Versailles (16th), Tel 01-42-88-85-59; Métro: Exelmans

Mabillon, 3, rue Mabillon (6th), Tel 01-43-25-66-23; Métro: Mabillon

Necker, 156, rue de Vaugirard (15th), Tel 01-40-61-54-50; Métro: Pasteur

Panthéon, 12, place du Panthéon (5th), Tel 01-43-29-56-84, Métro: RER Luxembourg

Pharmacie, 4, avenue de l'Observatoire (6th), Tel 01-46-43-15-98, Métro: RER Luxembourg

Saints-Pères, 45, rue des Saints-Péres (6th), Tel 01-40-20-04-66, Métro: St-Germain-des-Prés

Santeuil, 17, rue Santeuil (5th), Tel 01-45-35-52-25, Métro: Censier-Daubenton

Glossary of French Words and Phrases

Eating out should be pleasurable, but negotiating an incomprehensible menu can ruin a meal. This glossary of French menu terms and phrases—all those used in *Great Eats Paris* as well as many others you may need or encounter—is designed to help make sure there will not be a difference between what you want to eat and what you actually order.

General Phrases

good day, hello	*bonjour*
good evening	*bonsoir*
good-bye	*au revoir*
Excuse me.	*Excusez-moi.*
Do you speak English?	*Parlez-vous anglais?*
I do not speak French.	*Je ne parle pas français.*
I do not understand.	*Je ne comprend pas.*
please	*s'il vous plaît*
Thank you.	*Merci.*
You are welcome.	*De rien; je vous en prie.*
no	*non*
yes	*oui*
Where is the bathroom?	*Ou est la toilette?*
Do you have . . .?	*Avez-vous . . .?*
open	*ouvert*
closed	*fermé*
annual closure (for vacation)	*fermeture annuelle*
on vacation	*en vacances*
holiday	*jour férié*

Days of the Week

Monday	*lundi*
Tuesday	*mardi*
Wednesday	*mercredi*
Thursday	*jeudi*
Friday	*vendredi*
Saturday	*samedi*
Sunday	*dimanche*

Numbers

one	*un (une)*
two	*deux*
three	*trois*
four	*quatre*
five	*cinq*

six	*six*
seven	*sept*
eight	*huit*
nine	*neuf*
ten	*dix*
eleven	*onze*
twelve	*douze*
thirteen	*treize*
fourteen	*quatorze*
fifteen	*quinze*
sixteen	*seize*
seventeen	*dix-sept*
eighteen	*dix-huit*
nineteen	*dix-neuf*
twenty	*vingt*
twenty-one	*vingt-et-un*
twenty-two	*vingt-deux*
thirty	*trente*
forty	*quarante*
fifty	*cinquante*
sixty	*soixante*
seventy	*soixante-dix*
eighty	*quatre-vingt*
ninety	*quatre-vingt-dix*
one hundred	*cent*
one thousand	*mille*

Time

What time is it?	*Quelle heure est-il?*
At what time?	*A quelle heure?*
today	*aujourd'hui*
yesterday	*hier*
tomorrow	*demain*
this morning	*ce matin*
this afternoon	*cette après midi*
tonight	*ce soir*

Eating Out

I am hungry.	*J'ai faim.*
I am not hungry.	*Je n'ai pas faim.*
I would like . . .	*Je voudrais . . .*
I cannot eat . . .	*Je ne peux pas manger de . . .*
I am a vegetarian.	*Je suis végétarien(ne).*
I would like to reserve a table . . .	*Je voudrais réserver une table . . .*
for___people.	*pour ___personnes.*
for this evening.	*pour ce soir.*
tomorrow at___o'clock.	*demain à ___ heures.*
We have a reservation.	*Nous avons réservé*
a nonsmoking area	*une zone non-fumer*

May I have . . .	*Puis-j'avoir . . .*
a glass of	*un verre de*
a bottle/a carafe	*une bouteille/une carafe*
a plate	*une assiette*
silverware	*couvert*
a fork	*une fourchette*
a knife	*un couteau*
a spoon	*une cruillère*
a napkin	*une serviette*
rare	*saignant (almost raw)*
pink	*rosé*
medium	*à point*
well-done	*bien cuit*
to take out	*à emporter*
There must be some mistake.	*Il doit avoir une erreur.*
That is not what I ordered.	*Ce n'est pas ce que j'ai commandé.*
This isn't fresh.	*Ça n'est pas frais.*
I would like to speak to the headwaiter/manager	*Je voudrais parler au maître d'hôtel/patron.*
The bill, please.	*L'addition, s'il vous plaît.*
I think there is a mistake in the bill.	*Je crois qu'il y a une erreur sur l'addition.*
Thank you, that was a good meal.	*Merci, c'etait un trés bon repas.*
headwaiter	*maître d'hôtel, maître d'*
manager/owner	*patron*

French Menu Terms

addition	restaurant bill
à la carte	from the menu (not part of prix-fixe menu)
amér	bitter
amuse-bouche	small nibbles eaten before food is ordered (or *amuse-gueule*)
apéritif	before-meal drink
assiette (de)	plate (of)
biologique (bio)	organic (foods and wines)
boissons (compris ou non-compris)	drinks (included or not included)
bouteille de	bottle of
campagne/campagnard	country style
carafe d'eau ordinaire	pitcher of tap water
carte	menu
carte des vins	wine list
chaud	hot
choix	choice
commande(er)	order (to order)
compris	included

comptoir	counter
couvert	cutlery; also the number of table settings
dégustation	taste or sample
déjeuner	lunch
digestif	after-dinner drink (liqueur)
dîner	dinner
entrée	first course
espace non-fumer	nonsmoking area
fait maison	homemade
ferme	farm fresh
fermé	closed
formule	set-price menu, also known as *prix fixe* or *menu*
goût(er)	taste (to taste or snack)
gratuit	free
gros(se)	large
hors-d'oeuvre	appetizer
jardinière	garnish of fresh or cooked vegetables
jeune	young
léger	light
maigre	thin, no fat
maison (de la)	house (in the style of, or made in house)
marché	market
mélange	mixture
menu	set-price menu, also called *prix fixe* or *formule*
menu dégustation	tasting menu
menu du marché	a menu using fresh products from the market
mets selon de la saison	according to the season
mi-cuit	partially cooked
mollet	soft boiled
monnaie	change
offert	free
ouvert	open
petit déjeuner	breakfast
pièce	a piece of something
plat	main course
plat du jour	dish of the day
prix fixe	set-price menu
repas	meal
saison (suivant la)	season (according to)
salle	inside eating area
sans alcool	without alcohol
selon le marché	according to market availability
serveur/serveuse	waiter/waitress
service compris	service charge included
souper	supper
supplement, en sus	extra charge

verre	glass
sur commande	made to order
volonté (à)	at the customer's discretion
zinc	bar counter

French Food Terms

A

à point	medium rare
abats	offal
abricot	apricot
agneau	lamb
aiguillettes	thin slices, usually of duck breast
ail	garlic
aile	wing
aïoli	garlicky blend of eggs and oil
airelle	cranberry
alcools	spirits
algues	seaweed
aligot	puréed potatoes with melted *cantal* cheese and garlic
allummettes	fried matchstick potatoes
aloyau	beef loin
alsacienne, à la	Alsatian-style, with *choucroute* (sauerkraut) and pork
amandes	almonds
amer, amère	bitter
ananas	pineapple
anchoïade	puree of anchovies, olive oil, and vinegar
anchois	anchovy
andouille, andouillette	chitterlings (chitlins or tripe) sausage (see page 31 for a description of the A.A.A.A.A. designation)
aneth	dill
anguille	eel
anis	aniseed
arachide	peanut
artichaut	artichoke
asperge	asparagus
au four	baked
aubergine	eggplant
avocat	avocado

B

baba (au rhum)	yeast cake (with rum sauce)
baguette	long thin loaf of bread
baies roses	pink peppercorns
ballotine	small bundle, usually meat or fish, boned, stuffed, and rolled
banane	banana

bar	sea bass
barbue	brill
basilic	basil
basquaise	Basque style, with ham, sausage, tomatoes, and red pepper
batard	similar to a baguette, but with a softer crust
bavarois	custard made with cream and gelatin
bavette	skirt or flank steak
béarnaise	hollandaise sauce with tarragon and shallots
béchamel	white sauce with milk, onion, nutmeg
beignet	fritter, usually batter-fried fruit
belon	flat-shelled oyster
betterave	beet
beurre (blanc) (rouge)	butter (sauce with white wine and shallots) (with red wine)
biche	venison
bien cuit	well done
bière/demi/ordinaire	beer/draught beer/cheapest beer
biologique	organic
bifteck	steak (can be tough)
biscuits	cookies
bisque	shellfish soup
blanc (de volaille, de poulet)	breast (of chicken)
blanquette	stewed meat in rich white sauce
blanquette de veau	veal stew with onions, mushrooms, and cream
blette	Swiss chard
bleu	blood-rare or almost raw (for meat)
boeuf à la mode	beef marinated and braised in red wine
boeuf au gros sel	boiled beef with vegetables and coarse salt
boeuf bourguignon	beef cooked with red wine, onions, and mushrooms
boeuf de charolais/de salers	breeds of beef
boeuf en daube	beef cooked with red wine and vegetables
boeuf mode	beef stew with carrots, onions, and red wine
boire	to drink
boisson	a drink
bombe	molded, layered ice cream dessert
bordelaise (à la)	sauce with red wine, shallots, and beef marrow
bouchûe à la reine	sweetbreads in pastry, with cream sauce
boudin blanc	white sausage made with chicken, pork, or veal
boudin noir	pork sausage made with blood
bouillabaisse	Mediterranean fish and shellfish soup

bouilli	boiled
bourgeoise, à la	braised meat or chicken with bacon, carrots, and onions
bourride	a fish stew like bouillabaisse, but without shellfish
braisé	braised
brandade de morue	creamed salt cod
brebis	sheep's milk cheese
brioche	bun, usually made with eggs and sugar
brochette	meat on a skewer
brouillé	scrambled
brûlé	dark caramelization
bulot	whelk, a type of marine snail

C

cabillaud	fresh cod
cacahouètes	peanuts
café	espresso
café allongé	weaker espresso, more water
café crème/au lait	with steamed/warmed milk
café décaféiné/déca	decaffeinated coffee
café double	double espresso
caille	quail
calamar	squid
Calvados	apple brandy
canard	duck
caneton	young male duck
canette	young female duck
cannelle	cinnamon
carbonnade (flambade)	charcoal-grilled meat/beef stew with onions and beer
carotte	carrot
carré d'agneau	rack of lamb
carvi	caraway seeds
cassis	black currants
cassolette	casserole
cassonade	brown sugar
cassoulet	casserole of white beans with combinations of pork, duck, lamb, goose, and sausage
céleri	celery
céleri rave	celeriac
céleri rémoulade	shredded celery root salad with herbs and mayonnaise
cèpe	dark brown mushroom
cerfeuil	chervil
cerise	cherry
cervelas	pork sausage with garlic; can also be fish or seafood sausage
cervelles	brains
champignons (de Paris)	mushrooms (button mushrooms)

chanterelle	trumpet-shaped wild mushroom
chantilly	sweetened whipped cream
charcuterie	cold cuts; terrines, pâtés, sausages; also a shop selling these and other deli items
charlotte	molded dessert, usually lined with ladyfingers
chasseur	sauce cooked with mushrooms, shallots, white wine, and tomatoes
châtaigne	chestnut
chausson	filled pastry turnover
châvignin	sharp goat cheese
cheval (à cheval)	horse (with a fried egg on top—of the food, not the horse)
chèvre	goat cheese
chevreuil	young deer
chicorée	curly endive
chiffonnade	thin strips, usually vegetables
chiperon	Basque word for squid
chocolat (chaud)	chocolate (hot)
chou (rouge)	cabbage (red)
chou de Bruxelles	Brussels sprout
chou farci	stuffed cabbage
chou frisée	kale
chou-fleur	cauliflower
choucroute	sauerkraut, served with assorted meats
choux	cream puff
choux de Bruxelles	Brussels sprouts
ciboulette	chive
cidre	apple cider
citron	lemon
citronelle	lemongrass
citron vert	lime
citron/orange pressée	freshly squeezed lemon/orange juice
citrouille	pumpkin
civet	game stew, with wine, onion, and blood
civet de lièvre	stewed wild hare, thickened with blood
clafoutis	thick batter filled with fruit and baked; served warm
claires	oysters
clementine	small Spanish tangerine
cochon (de lait)	pig (suckling pig)
cochonnailles	assortment of pork parts (ears, tails, feet)
coco	large, white bean
coeur	heart
coeur de filet	best part of beef fillet; chateaubriand
colin	hake
coing	quince
compote	stewed fruit
concombre	cucumber

confit (de canard)	duck leg coooked and preserved in its own fat
confit confit d'oie	preserved goose
confiture	jam
contre-filet	cut of sirloin steak
coq	rooster
coq-au-vin	mature chicken stewed in red wine
coquelet	young male chicken
coquillages	shellfish
coquilles St-Jacques	sea scallops
cornichon	tart pickle
côte	rib, chop
côte d'agneau	lamb chop
côte de boeuf	beef rib
côte de veau	veal chop
coulis	purée of raw or cooked vegetables or fruit
courge	squash
courgette	zucchini
couscous	granules of semolina; a spicy North African dish with semolina, various meats, and vegetables
crème anglaise	custard sauce
crème brûlée	custard with a brown-sugar glaze
crème caramel	custard with caramel flavoring
crème chantilly	sweetened whipped cream
crème fraîche	fresh thick cream with the consistency of yogurt
crêpe	thin pancake
crêpe Suzette	thin pancake flambéed with Grand Marnier liqueur
crêpinette	small, flat, grilled sausage
cresson	watercress
crevette rose	prawn
crevettes	shrimp
croissant au beurre	croissant made with butter
croissant ordinaire	croissant made with margarine
croque-madame	toasted ham and cheese sandwich with an egg on top
croque-monsieur	toasted ham and cheese sandwich, no egg
crottin de Chavignol	small, round piece of goat cheese
croustade	bread or pastry case, deep fried
(en) croûte	in a pastry case
cru	raw
crudités	raw vegetables
crustacés	shellfish
cuisses de grenouilles	frogs legs
cuisse de poulet	chicken leg
cuit (au four)	cooked (in the oven)

D

dauphinois	scalloped potatoes
darne (de saumon)	fish steak (salmon steak)
datte	date
daube	meat stew with red wine
daurade	sea bream (or whitefish)
demi-glace	brown stock with meat jelly
demi-boutille	half bottle
demi-litre	half liter
désossé	boned
diable	reduced sauce with cayenne pepper, shallots, and white wine
dinde	turkey
dorade	red sea bream (not as good as *daurade*)
duxelles	chopped mushrooms and shallots sautéed in butter and mixed with cream

E

eau (minérale)	water (mineral)
eau gazeuse/minérale/ordinaire	carbonated/mineral/tap water
eaux-de-vie	fruit brandies
échalote	shallot
ecrémé	skim milk
ecrevisse	crayfish
émincé	thin slice (of meat)
encornet	squid
endive	chicory
entrecôte	beef rib steak
épaule	shoulder of lamb, pork, etc.
éperlans	smelts
épices	spices
épinard	spinach
escabèche	fried fish, marinated and served cold
escalope	thinly sliced meat or fish
escargot	snail
escarole	slightly bitter salad leaves
espadon	swordfish
estouffade	slowly stewed meat dish
estragon	tarragon
etrille	small crab

F

façon	way of preparing a dish
faisan	pheasant
farci	stuffed
faux-filet	sirloin steak
fenouil	fennel
feuille de chêne	oak leaf lettuce
(en) feuilleté	(in) thin layers of puff pastry

fèves	broad beans
ficelle	a very thin, crusty baguette
figue	fig
filet mignon	tenderloin
financier	small rectangular cake, similar to pound cake
fines de claire	crinkle-shelled oysters
fines herbes	mixture of parsley, chives, and tarragon
flageolet	small, pale-green kidney bean
flambé	flamed
flamiche	cheese pie with leeks or onions
flan	custard tart
flet	flounder
flétan	halibut
florentine	with spinach
flute	thin baguette
foie	liver
foie de veau	calf's liver
foie de volaille	chicken liver
foie gras	duck or goose liver
foie gras cru	raw foie gras
foie gras d'oie (canard)	fattened goose liver (duck)
foie gras mi-cuit (frais)	foie gras barely cooked
fond d'artichaut	heart and base of artichoke
fondant	chocolate dessert
fondue (du fromage) (savoyarde)	melted (cheese) (bread dipped into melted cheese)
fondue bourguignonne	pieces of beef dipped and cooked in hot oil
forestière	garnish of wild mushrooms, bacon, and potatoes
forêt-noire	a rich fudge cake with a cherry topping
fougasse	flat bread made with olive oil and flavored with herbs, olives, or onions
(au) four	baked
fourré	stuffed
fraîche, frais	fresh or chilled
fraise	strawberry
fraise de bois	wild strawberry
fraise de veau	part of a calf's intestine
framboise	raspberry
frappé	chilled
fricassée	stewed or sautéed fish or meat
frisée	curly endive
frit	fried
frites (pommes)	french fries
friture de mer	small fried fish
froide	cold
fromage	cheese
fromage blanc	creamy cheese served for dessert with sugar

fromage de chèvre	goat cheese
fruits confits/frais/secs	candied/fresh/dried fruit
fruits de mer (plateau de)	shellfish (variety of seafood served on ice)
feuillantine	puff pastry cake
fumé	smoked

G

galantine	boned meat, stuffed and glazed
galette	pancake, cake, buckwheat crêpe, flat pastry
gambas	large prawns
garni	garnished
gâteau	cake
gâteau de riz	rice pudding
gaufre	waffle
gazeuse	fizzy, carbonated
gelée	aspic, jellied
genièvre	juniper berry
génoise	sponge cake
gésiers	gizzards
gibier	game
gigembre	ginger
gigot (d'agneau)	leg (of lamb)
gigue	haunch of wild game
girofle	clove
girolles	wild mushrooms
glace	ice cream
glacé	frozen, ice-cold cake icing
glaçons/avec des glaçons	ice/on the rocks
goujons	small catfish, breaded and fried
graine de moutard	mustard seed
grand cru	best-quality wine
graisse	fat, grease
gras(se)	fatty
grasse double	ox tripe
gratin dauphinois	scalloped potatoes
gratin savoyard	potatoes baked with cheese
gratiné	browned with bread crumbs or cheese
grecque, à la	cold vegetables cooked in a seasoned mixture of olive oil and lemon juice
grenade	pomegranate
grenoblois	cream sauce with lemon and capers
gribiche	sauce with vinegar, capers, eggs, and pickles
grillade/grillé	grilled
griotte	Morello cherry
grisons (viande des)	thinly sliced dried meats
gros	large
gros sel	rock salt

groseille	red currant
gruyère	hard Swiss cheese

H

haché	ground or chopped
hachis (parmentier)	minced or chopped meat or fish (shepherd's pie: minced beef covered with mashed potatoes)
hareng	herring
haricot vert	green bean
haricot de mouton	mutton stew with white beans
haricots blancs	white beans
homard	lobster
huile (d'olive)	oil (olive oil)
huîtres	oysters

I

île flottante	floating island, poached meringue in custard sauce topped with caramel; used interchangeably with *oeufs à la neige*
infusion	herbal tea

J

jambon	ham
jambon cru	salt-cured or smoked ham, aged but not cooked
jambon de Paris	cooked ham
jambon persillé	chunks of ham in a molded parsley aspic
jambonneau	ham hock
jambonneau de canard	stuffed duck leg
jarret	shin
joue (de boeuf)	cheek or jowl (beef)
julienne	slivered vegetables
jus de fruits	fruit juice

K

kir	apéritif made with crème de cassis and white wine
kir royale	kir made from champagne instead of wine

L

lait (agneau, cochon de lait)	milk (milk-fed lamb or suckling pig)
laitier	made with milk
laitue	lettuce
landaise	cooked in goose fat with garlic, onion, ham
langouste	small freshwater lobster (sometimes called crayfish)
langoustine	smaller than *langoust,* scampi
langue (de boeuf/de angeau)	tongue (beef/lamb)

lapereau	young rabbit
lapin (à la moutarde)	rabbit (cooked with mustard, crème fraîche)
lard	bacon
lardon	cured, thick bacon
laurier	bay leaf
légumes	vegetables
lentilles	lentils
liégois	with juniper berries or gin
liégoise	sundae made with coffee or chocolate ice cream
lièvre	wild hare
lotte	monkfish
loup de mer	sea bass
lyonnaise, à la	Lyon-style, usually with onions and/or sautéed potatoes

M

mâche	lamb's lettuce
madeleine	small tea cake
magret de canard (oie)	breast of fattened duck (goose)
maïs	corn
maison	homemade, house special
mandarine	tangerine
mange-tout	snow pea
mangue	mango
maquereau	mackerel
marcassin	young wild boar
marchand de vin	sauce with red wine, stock, and shallots
mariné(e)	marinated
marjolaine	marjoram
marmite	stew served in a small pot
marquise au chocolat	rich chocolate mousse cake
marron	chestnut
médaillon	round piece or slice
mélange	mixture
méli-mélo	assortment of fish served in a salad
menthe	mint
merguez	very spicy sausage
merlan	whiting fish
mesclun	mixture of baby salad greens
meunière	rolled in flour and cooked in butter, parsley, and lemon
meurette	red wine sauce made with mushrooms, onions, bacon, and carrots
mi-cuit	semi-cooked
miel	honey
mignonette	small cubes of beef; coarsely ground white or black peppercorns

mille-feuille	puff pastry with many layers, usually filled with pastry cream
mimosa	garnish of chopped hard-boiled egg
mirabelle	yellow plum
moelle	beef bone marrow
mont blanc	chestnut dessert with whipped cream
morceau	piece
morille	wild mushroom
mornay	béchamel sauce with cheese
morue	salted or dried codfish
moule	mussel
moules marinères	mussels cooked in white wine with shallots
mousse	light whipped mixture containing eggs and cream
mousseline	hollandaise with whipped cream
moutard	mustard
mouton	mutton
mûres	blackberries
muscade	nutmeg
museau de boeuf (de porc)	vinegared beef (or pork) muzzle
myrtille	European blueberry
mystère	ice cream dessert; also meringue filled with ice cream and covered in chocolate sauce

N

nappé	covered with a sauce
nature	simple, plain, no sauce
navarin	lamb or mutton stew with root vegetables
navet	turnip
niçoise, à la	in the style of Nice; made with tomatoes, onions, anchovies, olives, and garlic
nid	nest
noisette	center out of lamb chop; small rounds of potato; hazelnut
noix (de coco)	nuts (coconut)
normande, à la	Normandy style, with cream and mushrooms or cooked in cider or Calvados
nouilles	noodles

O

oeuf a la coque	soft boiled egg
oeuf brouillé	scrambled egg
oeuf cocotte	soft boiled
oeuf dur	hard-boiled egg
oeuf en meurette	egg poached in red wine sauce
oeuf poché	poached egg
oeufs	eggs

oeufs à la neige	whipped egg whites poached in milk; served in a custard sauce (used interchangeably with *île flottante*)
oeufs au jambon/lard	ham/bacon and eggs
oeufs au plat	fried eggs
oie	goose
oignon	onion
omelette nature	plain omelet
onglet	beef cut similar to flank steak; can be strong tasting and tough
opéra	chocolate and nut layer cake
oreille	ear
orge	barley
os	bone
oseille	sorrel
oursin	sea urchin

P

pain	bread
pain au noix	rye or wheat bread with nuts
pain complet	whole-grain bread
pain de seigle	rye bread
pain d'épices	honey gingerbread
pain grillé	toasted bread
pain perdu	French toast
pain Poilâne	round loaves of dark bread baked in wood-fired ovens
palombe	wood pigeon
palourde	type of clam
pamplemousse	grapefruit
panaché	denotes any mixture
panais	parsnip
pané	breaded
papillote	cooked in parchment paper
parisian, à la	with mushrooms in white wine sauce
parmentier	dish with potatoes, usually mashed
pastèque	watermelon
pastis	anise liqueur
pâte	pastry
pâté	finely minced and seasoned meat, baked and served cold as a rich spread
pâté en croute	pâté in a pastry case
pâté à choux	cream puff
pâtes (fraîche)	pasta (fresh)
pâtisserie	pastry
paupiette	slice of meat or fish rolled up and tied, usually stuffed
pavé	thick slice of meat
paysan, à la	country style, with vegetables and bacon

pêche	peach
pêche Melba	peach with vanilla ice cream and raspberries
pêcheur	refers to fish preparations
perche	perch
perdreau	young partridge
perdrix	partridge
persil	parsley
petit gris	small snails
petit pain (au cumin/pavots)	roll (with caraway or poppy seeds)
petit salé (aux lentilles)	salted pork/pork sausage (with lentils)
petits-pois	peas
pétoncle	scallop
pichet	carafe, usually of house wine
pied (du porc)	foot (of pork)
pigeonneau	young pigeon, squab
pignon	pine nut
piment(é)	red pepper (spicy)
pintade/pinteadeau	guinea fowl
pipérade	Basque dish of scrambled eggs, pepper, ham, tomatoes, and onions
pissaladière	anchovy, tomato, and onion tart
pissenlits	dandelion greens
pistache	pistachio
pistou	sauce of basil, garlic, cheese, olive oil; sometimes stirred into fish soups
plat	still, uncarbonated
pleurotte	oyster mushroom
poché	poached
poêlé	pan-fried
poire	pear
poire belle Hélène	poached pears with vanilla ice cream and hot chocolate sauce
poireau	leek
poisson	fish
poitrine	breast of meat or poultry
poivrade	brown sauce served with meat
poivre	pepper
poivron (rouge, vert)	sweet pepper (red, green)
pomme	apple
pomme au four/en robe des champs	baked potato in its skin
pomme de terre	potato
pommes â l'huile	cold boiled potato salad with oil dressing
pommes dauphines	mashed potatoes, shaped into balls and fried
pommes dauphinois	scalloped potatoes
pommes frites	french fries
pommes lyonnaises	fried slices of potatoes with onions

pommes mousselines	mashed potatoes
pommes nature	boiled or steamed potatoes
pommes parisienne	fried potatoes tossed in meat glaze
porc (carré de, côte de)	pork (loin, chop)
potage	soups
pot-au-feu	boiled beef with vegetables
pot-de-crème	individual custard dessert
potée	rich soup or stew with cabbage and pork
potiron	winter squash, often called pumpkin
poularde	fatted hen
poule au pot	chicken hen stewed with vegetables
poulet (rôti)	chicken (roasted)
poulet de Bresse	finest chickens from Bresse
poulpe	octopus
poussin	small chicken
prairie	small clam
pressé	squeezed
pression	draught beer
printanière	springtime array of vegetables
profiterole	pastry puff filled with ice cream and covered with chocolate sauce
provençal(e)	cooked and served with tomatoes, garlic, and onion and often with the addition of eggplant, anchovies, or olives
prune	plum
pruneaux	prunes
purée	mashed

Q

quenelle	dumpling, usually fish, veal, or poultry
quetsche	purple plum
queue (de boeuf)	tail (of beef)
quiche Lorraine	*tarte* made with eggs, cream, and ham or bacon

R

raclette	melted cheese, scraped from a special heated cheese wheel onto boiled potatoes, served with *cornichons* (pickles) and pickled onions, and raw or dried ham or beef
radis	radish
ragoût	stew
raie	skate fish (stingray)
raifort	horseradish
raisins (secs)	grapes (raisins)
râpé	grated or shredded
rascasse	scorpion fish
ratatouille	eggplant, zucchini, onions, tomatoes, and peppers, cooked with garlic and olive oil

ratte	small potato
ravigote	thick vinaigrette
ravioles de Royans	small cheese ravioli
reine, à la	with chicken
rémoulade	sauce of mayonnaise, capers, mustard, herbs, and pickles
rillettes (porc)	coarsely minced spread of duck or pork, served in earthenware pot
rillons	pieces of crisp pork belly
ris (d'agneau, de veau)	sweetbreads (of lamb, veal)
riz (sauvage)	rice (wild)
rognon	kidney
romarin	rosemary
roquette	rocket or arugula
rosbif	roast beef
rosé	pink; meat cooked rare, but no longer bleeding
rosette	dry pork sausage from Lyon
rôti	roast
rouget	red mullet
rouille	cayenne and garlic-seasoned mayonnaise served with fish soups
roulade	rolled and stuffed meat or fish
roux	flour and butter sauce
rumpsteak	usually tough cut of beef

S

sabayon	a thick, sweet, wine-based dessert sauce
sablé (au beurre)	shortbread-type cookie
safran	saffron
saignant	rare, still bleeding
St-Pierre	John Dory fish
saisonnier	seasonal
salade	salad
salade chiffonnade	shredded lettuce and sorrel in melted butter
salade mixte/des foies de volaille	mixed salad/with chicken livers
salade verte	green salad
salé	salted
sandre	pike or perch, a freshwater fish
sanglier	wild boar
sarrasin	buckwheat
saucisse	small fresh sausage
saucisson (sec)	small sausage (hard, dry sausage eaten cold)
sauge	sage
saumon (fumé)	salmon (smoked)
saumonette	sea eel, dogfish

sauté	browned in fat
sauvage	wild
savoyarde	flavored with Gruyère cheese
sec, sèche	dry
seîche	squid
sel	salt
selle	saddle of meat
sirop	syrup
soja	soy
sorbet	sherbet
soufflé/Grand Marnier	light, fluffy egg dish/with Grand Marnier
souris d'agneau	slow-cooked lamb knuckle
spec	Italian smoked ham
steak au poivre	fillet steak with green or black peppercorns
sucre	sugar
sucré	sweet
suprême de volaille	chicken breast fillet

T

tapenade	purée of black olives, anchovies, capers, olive oil, and lemon juice
tarama	mullet roe made into a spread
tartare	chopped raw beef, sometimes served with raw egg
tarte	open-faced pie
tarte Tatin	caramelized upside-down apple pie; served warm
tartine	buttered baguette often served with pâté or cheese, open-face sandwich
tendron de veau	veal rib
terrine	baked minced meat or fish; molded into a crock and served cold
tête, tête de veau	head, calf's head
thé	tea
thon	tuna
tian	Provençal gratin, cooked in an earthenware pot
tiède	warm
tilleuil	linden flower tea
timbale	cooked in a pastry case or mold
tisane	herbal tea
topinambour	Jerusalem artichoke
tortue	turtle
toulouse	a large sausage
tournedos	slices of beef fillet
tourte	covered savory tart
torteau	large crab
tranche	slice

travers de porc	spare ribs
tripes à la mode de Caen	beef tripe, carrots, and onions cooked in cider and Calvados (apple brandy)
tripoux	Auvergne dish of sheep's tripe and feet
truffaude	fried mashed-potato cake with cheese, bacon, and garlic
truffe (blanche, noire)	underground fungus (white or black), very expensive delicacy
truite	trout

U–V

vacherin	dessert of baked meringue with ice cream and fresh cream
vapeur, à la	steamed
veau	veal
velouté	cream soup; or sauce made with roux and bouillon
velouté	veal or chicken cream sauce
verdure	salad greens, green vegetables, or herbs
viande	meat
vichyssoise	cold leek and potato soup
vieille prune	plum brandy
viennoiserie	catchall term for croissants and various other pastries
vigneron, á la	wine sauce with grapes
vin blanc/rouge/rosé	white/red/rose wine
vol au vent	flaky pastry shell
volaille	poultry

W–Z

xérès	sherry
yaourt	yogurt
zabaglione	light, foamy custard made of egg yolks, wine, and sugar

Chez L'ami Louis.
Expensive Chicken

Index of Restaurants

Chez L'ami Jean
(Rice Pudding

BOULANGERIES AND PÂTISSERIES

CHEAP EATS

CONTINUOUS FOOD SERVICE

Readers' Comments

The listings in *Great Eats Paris* are described as they were when the book went to press, and as I hope they will stay, but as seasoned travelers know, there are no guarantees. With the passage of time, things change: prices may increase, special menu deals may no longer be offered, chefs and owners may move on. While every effort has been made to assure the accuracy of the information in this book, neither the author nor the publisher can accept responsibility for any changes that occur.

Great Eats Paris is revised on a regular basis. If you find a change before I do, or make an important food discovery you want to pass along, please send me a note stating the name and address of the restaurant, the date of your visit, and a description of your findings. Or, if you prefer, you can visit my Website and leave a message for me there. As the many readers who have written to me know, your comments are *very* important to me, and I respond to as many as possible. Thank you, in advance, for taking the time to write.

Please send your information to Sandra A. Gustafson, *Great Eats Paris,* c/o Chronicle Books, 680 Second Street, San Francisco, CA 94107, or visit www.greateatsandsleeps.com.

De Chez Aux

Pur